CLINICAL PSYCHOLOGY WITH THE ELDERLY

Robert T. Woods, MA, MSc, ABPsS,
Lecturer in Clinical Psychology, Institute of Psychiatry,
University of London, and Honorary Principal Psychologist,
Bethlem Royal and Maudsley Hospitals, London

and

Peter G. Britton, BSc, PhD, ABPsS,
Senior Lecturer in Applied Psychology, Department of
Psychiatry, University of Newcastle upon Tyne, and
Honorary Clinical Psychologist, Newcastle Health Authority

AN ASPEN PUBLICATION
Aspen Systems Corporation
Rockville, Maryland
1985

RC
451.4
.A5
W62
1985

Library of Congress Cataloging in Publication Data

Woods, Robert T.
  Clinical psychology with the elderly.
  "An Aspen Publication."
  Bibliography: p.
  Includes index.
  1. Geriatric psychiatry. 2. Aged—Psychology. 3. Aged—Mental health services.
I. Britton, Peter G. II. Title: [DNLM: 1. Mental Disorders—in old age. 2.
Mental Health Services—in old age. 3. Psychology, Clinical—in old age.
WT 150 W896c] RC451.4.A5W62   1985   618.97'689   84-24323
ISBN 0-87189-090-9

Library of Congress Catalog Card Number: 84-24323
ISBN: 0-87189-090-9

To
Joan, James and Rachel
Ann, Philip and Iain

Printed and bound in Great Britain

CONTENTS

Preface

1. Introduction   1

2. Cognitive Loss in Old Age — Myth or Fact?   25

3. A Happier Old Age — Changes in Personality and Adjustment   59

4. Abnormal Ageing   80

5. Cognitive Assessment of the Elderly Person   129

6. The Assessment of Adaptation   159

7. Treatment Approaches for Affective Disorders   189

8. Treatment and Management Approaches for Organic Disorders   215

9. Intervention in Institutions   250

10. Intervention in the Community   285

11. Conclusions   314

References   326

Index   356

PREFACE

When we were approached about writing this book we were delighted to have the opportunity to draw together the many facets that make up clinical psychology with the elderly. In teaching clinical psychology students on several courses we had become aware of the need for a reference work reviewing and integrating the widespread, and sometimes inaccessible, literature on work with the elderly. This book is intended then, firstly, for clinical psychology trainees as a basic guide to the area, covering both theoretical and practical aspects. Trainees wishing to undertake a research project in this field should find the research reviewed here a useful starting-point for their own work.

The second group that we hope will find the book useful are qualified clinical psychologists. Many such are beginning to work with the elderly, perhaps as part of their other duties, or because they have been appointed to a post specifically with the elderly, having had little or no preparation during their training for work with this client group. This book aims to help fill this gap — which will continue to arise until working with the elderly becomes an essential component of clinical psychology training.

Other clinical psychologists are involved in managing and planning psychology services to the whole range of client groups. They may find themselves in the position of making a case for a psychologist to work with the elderly, without having a clear view themselves of the potential contribution that can be made. We hope this book will enable stronger arguments to be put forward for the expansion of clinical psychology services to the elderly.

Whilst covering the broad range of work with the elderly, we have not given detailed descriptions of methods used throughout clinical psychology, but have concentrated on their application to the elderly, and any modifications or cautions this requires.

Many other professionals working with the elderly are keen to discover what clinical psychology has to offer. By dipping into the parts of the book most relevant to their concerns we trust that senior nurses, social workers, occupational therapists, psychiatrists and physicians in geriatric medicine will find much to consider with regard to their own assessment, treatment, practice and research.

Psychologists have no monopoly on psychological approaches, so other disciplines need not despair if they have no psychologist working with them. There is much they can do to put psychological principles into practice, until they are fortunate enough to have a psychologist working with them on this task!

The chapters of the book fall into several sections. An introductory chapter outlines some demographic features of the elderly, and provides a very brief overview of biological aspects of ageing and of the major physical and psychiatric disorders of old age. Two chapters follow that focus on 'normal' ageing from a psychological perspective, providing an important background for later chapters. Chapter 4 discusses the psychological manifestations of dementia, depression and other disorders that might be considered 'abnormal ageing'. Psychological models of dementia and depression are examined here also. Chapters 5 and 6 cover psychological assessment strategies as well as specific techniques for assessing a wide range of psychological functions. This more practical theme continues in the subsequent four chapters, where intervention methods are discussed in detail. Particular emphasis has been given to the application of these methods in the real world, in institutions and in community settings. Illustrations of the principles and practice of community psychology with the elderly are provided in this section. The final concluding chapter considers the role of a clinical psychologist with the elderly, mentions some of the personal and ethical issues involved, and looks forward to further developments in this field.

We are deeply grateful to many colleagues and students who over the years have stimulated our thinking and improved our ideas, and who have encouraged and supported us in many ways. Many of these are psychologists working with the elderly — too numerous to single out by name — but we have also received a great deal of help from colleagues in the various multi-disciplinary teams in which we have worked: occupational therapists, nurses, social workers and psychiatrists. In particular we count ourselves as fortunate to have worked with some of the world's leading psychogeriatricians — David Kay, Klaus Bergmann, Garry Blessed and Raymond Levy. We thank them and all our colleagues.

We also wish to thank the typists who have helped us to prepare the book, and who have been kind enough not to complain about our handwriting too often! Thanks to Gerry Hendriks, Nora Savage, Geraldine Davis, Maria Priestley and Joan Woods for this help. Thanks also are due to our families for their patience — they will be relieved that it is finally finished!

We have found working with the elderly stimulating, enjoyable and rewarding. We hope that many others will have the same experience in meeting the needs of elderly people and their carers for psychological help.

RTW
PGB

1 INTRODUCTION

The impact of the rapid increase of elderly people amongst the populations of most developed nations is often viewed as a major problem of the late twentieth century. It certainly presents a major challenge. Recent years have seen a slow but significant response. At an international level the World Health Organization and United Nations have taken initiatives. In most nations Governments have started to face up to some of the issues. At ground level voluntary and self-help agencies have seen an increase in demand for their services, and, interestingly, in the supply of resources and volunteers to enable them to respond.

Any attempt to meet the increasing needs of the elderly must be based on a firm foundation of knowledge of elderly people and their resources and abilities as well as their difficulties. The past twenty years has seen a substantial increase in such knowledge. Medical, social and psychological studies have loosened the grip of some of the mythology surrounding the 'ageing process'. Together with improved demographic statistics this knowledge enables us to identify and define more clearly the problem areas and the priorities for intervention.

The primary problems of medical and social support (Arie, 1981; Hobman, 1981) have provided an initial focus for care provision. Growing alongside these has been a rapid increase in awareness of the importance of the psychological aspects of ageing. This is an area where negative mythology has been most deeply rooted in approaches to the individual and where there is much potential for positive change.

In recent years practical and research work with the elderly has attracted an increasing number of psychologists. Understanding of the basic psychological processes of *normal* ageing has been greatly facilitated by efforts to build on the small number of pioneering studies of the 1950s and 1960s. In a parallel development there have been many attempts to understand some of the abnormalities which can arise. Emerging from this basic knowledge has been a slow but steady growth in the application of these findings to improve the quality of life for the individual elderly person. In common with other potentially disadvantaged client groups such as the mentally

1

handicapped, the emphasis has changed from care and containment to optimal development of the individual's potential. In this book we will show how psychological knowledge can be, and in fact already is, applied to understanding the problems of the elderly and to improving their quality of life.

Who Are the 'Elderly'?

There are inevitable problems in even defining the elderly. Who are they? At what age is one old? elderly? aged? There are subjective aspects; 'you're only as old as you feel'; 'old' is my age plus 5, 10 or 20 years! Much depends on the demographic context in which the individual lives. As an extreme example in some less developed regions of the world a 45-year-old may be among the very old, whereas in a developed country many may have a reasonable expectancy of life to an age of 80 or more.

The lower age limit — conventionally retirement age — is becoming vaguer. Only a few years ago, in 1977, the Council of Europe was concerned at the rigidity of retirement age in its member countries. It then seemed that an expectancy of retirement at the age of 60 for females and 65 for males was a barrier to flexible models encouraging optimal adjustment (Palmore, 1972). Changing economic conditions throughout the world mean retirement age is becoming less fixed. It is conceivable that the majority of working people will not find employment beyond age 55 or 60 in the late 1980s. On the other hand some services for the elderly only consider those above the age of 75 to be 'old'.

For the purposes of this book we will arbitrarily restrict ourselves to consideration of the group who, in the developed nations, live beyond the age of 65.

When we consider this age-group and its characteristics, many interesting features emerge. Firstly, and most importantly, the proportion of the population represented by this group is growing rapidly. Many authorities quote a proportion of the UK population of 15–20 per cent over 65 before the end of the century, compared with roughly 5 per cent at the beginning. In a similar way the number of the very old, aged 80 +, is also increasing (UN, 1979). Currently the proportion of people over 65 is stabilising, but within this group the age distribution continues to change, with increasing numbers of 'old old' people (see Figures 1.1 and 1.2). It is felt,

Figure 1.1: Actual and Projected Elderly Population, England and Wales, 1960–2001

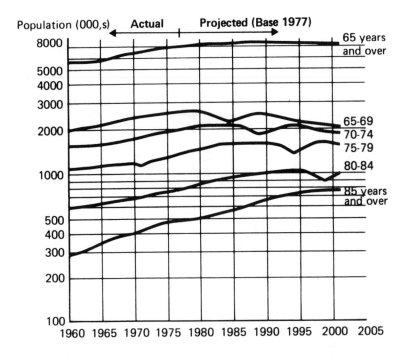

Source: Office of Population Censuses and Surveys (OPCS).

however, that there are unlikely to be further · dramatic developments in these proportions since there appear to be biological barriers to massive extension of the life span. There is also little possibility that the major illnesses of the aged, cancer and cardiovascular problems, are likely to be eradicated in the immediate future. Reports of supposed longevity in particular villages in Asia and South America are seldom supported by careful enquiry — Busse and Blazer (1980) consider them distortions.

The sex composition of the aged group is also of interest (see Figure 1.3). In all societies there appears to be a trend for women to live longer than men. Currently, in both developed and undeveloped countries, a five-year advantage in longevity is claimed

Figure 1.2 Changes in the Elderly Population of Great Britain —
Percentage Change in Each Age-group

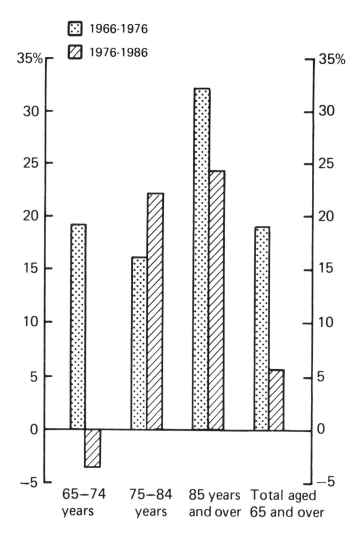

Source: OPCS.

Figure 1.3: Population structure of the Elderly by Age, Sex and Marital Status, Great Britain, 1976

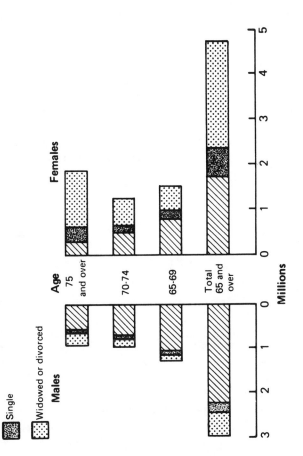

Source: OPCS.

for women. This results in specific problems for the elderly woman often left on her own, in accommodation which had previously contained a family.

The aged, then, are an increasing population. Any problems common in elderly people e.g. health, finance etc., will be more prevalent. The increased number of very old people is becoming a feature of the latter years of the century, and will further increase the likelihood of the many problems that are most frequent in the very old. Women currently live longer than men and, in the foreseeable future, form the majority of elderly people.

Where Are the Elderly?

As Figure 1.4 shows, the vast majority (94 per cent) of elderly people are not living in hospital or in residential care. About an eighth live with their children, but the biggest proportion — two-fifths — live with their spouse only. Just over a quarter live alone — but the proportion rises sharply with age (see Table 1.1), so that half of all women over 85 years old live alone.

Table 1.1 Percentage of Elderly People Living Alone in England, 1976

	65-74	75-84	85+
Male	13.6	19.8	27.3
Female	33.6	47.1	50.0
Total	25.0	37.4	44.0

Source: Derived from Hunt (1978).

Figure 1.5 shows that in 1976 only 5 per cent of elderly households were in sheltered housing complexes with a warden on call, although this is currently a major building priority for local authorities and housing associations. Many elderly people live in inadequate housing — over 10 per cent have only an external toilet, and, in all, a quarter of households headed by a person over the age of 65 are accommodated in a property lacking at least one of the basic amenities of hot water supply, a bath or an inside toilet. Elderly people are much more likely than younger people to live in inadequate housing (Fox 1981).

In these days of greater mobility in search of employment, to

Figure 1.4: Living Arrangements of Elderly People, England, 1976

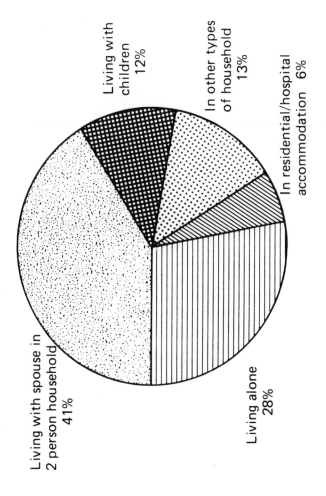

Living with children 12%

In other types of household 13%

In residential/hospital accommodation 6%

Living with spouse in 2 person household 41%

Living alone 28%

Source: OPCS.

Figure 1.5: Type of Accommodation lived in by Elderly Households, England, 1976

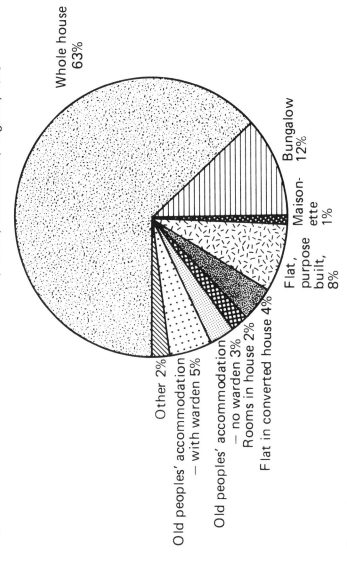

Whole house 63%

Bungalow 12%

Maison-ette 1%

Flat, purpose built, 8%

Flat in converted house 4%

Rooms in house 2%

Old peoples' accommodation — no warden 3%

Old peoples' accommodation — with warden 5%

Other 2%

Source: OPCS.

what extent are elderly people left living in a different part of the country from their children? A survey reported by Abrams (1978) shows that about 60 per cent of elderly people with at least one surviving child have a child living within 6 miles of them — a third live in the same street or neighbourhood, and 15 per cent actually live with a child. In addition, three-quarters of elderly people with a surviving child saw one of them at least once a week during the four weeks preceding the survey — and most old people (60 per cent) were satisfied with this frequency of visiting. Isolation from children is not then a problem affecting the majority of older people with surviving children. It should be borne in mind, however, that 30 per cent of older people never had any children at all, and as we consider an 'old old' population the children will themselves be elderly and perhaps less fit and mobile; already about 8 per cent have no surviving children. As Stevenson (1981) points out, family support cannot be the answer to all the problems of ageing.

Many 'old old' people are bedfast, housebound or need help to go out (Hunt 1979), as Table 1.2 shows. Over a quarter of bedfast

Table 1.2: Percentage of Elderly People Living at Home with Difficulties in Going Out

| | 65–74 | | 75–84 | | 85+ | |
	Male	Female	Male	Female	Male	Female
Bedfast	—	—	—	1	2	2
Housebound	2	2	7	7	15	19
Need help to go out	2	7	4	14	16	31

Source: Derived from Hunt (1979).

and housebound people were living alone. It should be remembered that even in the oldest age-group the majority of old people are able to go out without help, although some of these will not be able to walk as far or as fast as previously, making the proximity of local shops and other amenities even more crucial.

Sheltered housing — small flatlets, with a warden on call — are popular with housing authorities and elderly people. Abrams (1978) reports that 28 per cent of over 75-year-olds would like to live in such a complex and 43 per cent of old people could see no disadvantages to such schemes. A big question mark remains over their ability to cope with increasing levels of dependency among the residents, and over the adequacy of the training and support of the wardens (Fox, 1981). The move to such a place can certainly be disastrous for an elderly person with any degree of memory disorder, who effectively has the props of familiarity removed overnight.

Mechanisms of Ageing

Many factors are involved in what is called 'ageing'. As psychosocial influences will be considered in depth later, here biological aspects and their interaction with environmental forces will be briefly considered. Many attempts have been made to define 'ageing'. One definition describes ageing as a progressive loss of adaptive ability. In the extreme, a total loss of ability to adapt to external change will lead to death. Under the conditions now seen in developed countries, mortality rate decreases until about age twelve and then rises as an exponential function of age throughout life. These curves are not specific to culture or time and might be thought to reflect underlying characteristics of the ageing process.

The similarity of these curves masks considerable variation both in individual ageing patterns and in the ageing of various systems within the body. Any composite age curve must inevitably be an average. An apparent overall decline can result from a group of individuals with functions which change little, if at all, combined with another group who display considerable change.

It is equally inadvisable to assume that all biological functions decline at the same rate within the individual. Studies of physiological ageing have shown much variation in rates of decline with age. Thus, functions requiring only one system (e.g. neuronal transmission) show much less decline with age than those requiring a complex interaction of several systems. A good example of the latter is temperature control, a complex homeostatic mechanism, which can be highly susceptible to ageing effects. These effects may take several forms. The system may react by a reduced ability to adapt; a slowing of reaction to heat or cold. However, it is also possible that the ageing effect is shown by increased instability when reacting. Change in external temperature may result in over-compensation, and an equally violent swing back, with unstable cyclical effects.

We can see from these examples that, whilst ageing curves may seem to be a reflection of commonly held expectations, they can conceal significant variation. A number of attempts have been made to look for models of ageing which seek to identify the source of such variation. Of some value are attempts to separate *real* from *spurious* ageing effects.

Spurious age differences may arise from a variety of influences. These are discussed in more detail in Chapter 2 where we examine their effect on cognitive functions. However, they have a similar effect in studies of other aspects of the ageing process. Amongst the most important of spurious age effects is the *cohort* effect. This is caused by the uneven influence of external factors on different age bands. If we take the current elderly in the United States and Western Europe each early decade of the twentieth Century saw some problem. The First World War was followed by the Depression and the Second World War and a relative period of affluence. Those now aged 40, 60 and 80 have had quite different life experiences and so there are differences between them (cohort differences) over and above any age differences.

A second spurious age effect is the possibility that what appears to be a loss of adaptive ability is not a real difference but is caused by some other external factor particularly affecting older people. We have already referred to the problems of control of body temperature faced by the aged. It can be only too easy to ascribe this effect to the individual's biological ageing process. Problems such as this could, in fact, be artificially exaggerated by social factors such as poor housing, inadequate heating and similar problems more commonly faced by the elderly. Again a spurious ageing effect could operate.

Examination of real ageing effects requires evidence of the separate *and* combined effects of intrinsic, biological or genetic influences *and* extrinsic or environmental influences. Attempts which seek explanations for ageing implicating solely either intrinsic or extrinsic influences as the *cause* of ageing are doomed to failure, as are most genetics vs. environment arguments. The overwhelming evidence from current research is that both factors contribute, but possibly in different ways in different cohorts and cultures.

Intrinsic ageing is the biological or genetic basis for the ageing effect. It should be non-culture or cohort specific and thus show no variability over races, time or environments. Two types of theories relating to intrinsic ageing have been proposed. The first type poses the question '*why* does intrinsic ageing occur?' (ergological theories), whilst the second type asks '*how* does intrinsic ageing occur?' (pathogenic theories). The ergological theories lie more in the realms of scientific philosophy and speculate on reasons why genetic factors should lead to optimal adaptation in *earlier* life. Perhaps some genes which assist in viability during the reproductive phase may be maladaptive later in life.

Pathogenic theories have a more concrete base in research and more overall support. Stochastic pathogenic theories relate ageing to cumulative damage to vital cell structures, perhaps mutations caused by temperature or radiation effects. There is supportive evidence that cumulative error in DNA or RNA sequence may result in a build up of an error catastrophe and cell death (see Strehler, 1982). However, simple experiments involving bacteria do not readily transfer to the complex human with well-established systems to identify and destroy abnormal cells.

Programmed pathogenic ageing is another possible explanation. It does not assume error build up but rather assumes some in-built expectancy of decline and death. Burnet and others have implicated the immunological system as an example of programmed ageing. It may well be that the immune system decreases in its efficiency both to detect and destroy abnormal cells, perhaps eventually becoming self-destructive (Busse and Blazer, 1980).

The work of Hayflick (1965, 1982) gives some support to these effects. In an attempt to produce disease-free human cell cultures he took cells from embryonic tissue. Whilst these cell populations grew and divided normally at first, they eventually slowed, stopped dividing and died. Further research showed that this happened in roughly 50 population doublings in normal embryonic cells. Hayflick went on to show a more interesting phenomenon, cells from young adults survived some 30 doublings and from older adults only 20 or so. He concluded that there could well be evidence that these cells incorporated some 'biological clock' which related to functional loss and probably ageing effects.

These various theories suggest that intrinsic factors are involved in the ageing process, but in a complex way. As yet there is no clear-cut biological or genetic basis to ageing. It is likely that extrinsic, environmental factors modify intrinsic factors to a significant extent.

Extrinsic factors may be identified when differences in ageing occur between cultures and environments. Such phenomena as heart disease, blood pressure problems or the incidence of certain malignancies are related — at least in part — to extrinsic factors. Cultural differences may be seen in the preservation or loss of muscle tissue in middle age and beyond. Whilst genetic influences may have some effect on these phenomena, research suggests that environmental influences such as diet and exercise expectancies are the overwhelming factors.

Obviously a combination of genetic and biological factors interact with environmental influences to produce the varied pattern of human ageing. How do these effects relate to the psychological consequences of ageing? Although some attempts to relate biological and psychological processes have been made (e.g. Strehler, 1982, pp. 15, 43–8, etc.), relationships are unlikely to be clear-cut. Indeed the main feature that each sphere has in common may well be variability.

Physical Health

Elderly people more frequently suffer a variety of illnesses than younger people. A study of elderly people living at home (Hunt, 1979) showed that they most often reported arthritic and rheumatic conditions as handicapping. Pulmonary conditions, strokes, failing sight and circulatory, blood pressure and cardiac ailments also contributed to some respondents not being able to go out from home. The major physical illnesses seen in geriatric medicine are thought to be heart disease, cancer, strokes, bronchitis and diabetes. In old age it seems relatively common for the patient to suffer from several diseases simultaneously. Some diseases, e.g. cancer, seem to be more slowly progressive in older people.

At any one time nearly half the hospital in-patient population in the UK is aged 65 or over, and about a fifth of all patients who consult their family doctor are elderly. For older people these consultations are more likely to be at home than at the doctor's surgery (Age Concern, 1977). Perhaps inevitably resulting from these figures, the amount of medication prescribed to elderly people is high — about a quarter of all prescriptions. In addition, older people have high rates of self-medication, particularly for painkillers and cough mixtures. Death by accidental poisoning from drugs — of which about a fifth occur in older people — represent only the tip of the iceberg in relation to toxic mixtures of drugs, over-high dosage, irregular review of medications, etc. (Age Concern, 1977).

Sensory Loss

Sensory losses are also common in older people (see Marsh, 1980 for a review). The majority of people registered as blind, partially sighted or hard of hearing are elderly. Visual processes are certainly affected by ageing. Simple acuity of vision seems to change little up to late middle age; the vision of most people remains stable between 20 and 40. However, after 60 acuity can noticeably decline and by the time the seventies are reached it is likely that a substantial change will have occurred. This normal process must be identified and corrected.

Whilst the decline in acuity is more obvious in later life, changes in the ability to accommodate, to focus on near objects, occur in middle age. Studies such as that of Bruckner (1967) have shown stability up to roughly the age of 40 with a decline in the 40–50 age-group and surprisingly little change thereafter, unless accommodation to a moving target is tested.

These basic visual processes involving the lens are paralleled by similar changes which affect other mechanisms. The ability of the pupil to respond to intensity of illumination is reduced in the aged both in range and speed of response. So, too, are aspects of colour vision. The ability to discriminate between colours has been shown to deteriorate and the elderly person is also less acute in reaction to level of brightness. Cataracts are more common in older people.

Hearing ability is similarly affected by ageing, although great problems exist in interpretation of findings caused by the difficulties in obtaining valid reports, particularly in old age. It would appear that high-frequency loss tends to be noticeable, particularly at ages over 50, although low-frequency acuity is relatively preserved. Discrimination between tones tends to deteriorate and does so more rapidly for higher frequencies. Sound localization also becomes less accurate. Studies on hearing change are notoriously difficult to relate to ageing *per se*, since so much hearing loss may be due to damage from environmental features. Occupational deafness is a well-established phenomenon, but the long-term effects of the high-powered hi-fi set or the Disco are hard to define! Tinnitus — ringing in the ears — increases in incidence with age, often accompanied by deafness.

Other senses, for example, touch, taste and smell, are similarly found to have a substantial change with age, particularly in the sixties and beyond. These areas are far less well documented than vision and hearing but no less important for their contribution to adjustment and the quality of life.

This brief overview will make it clear that any consideration of, for example, cognitive change in the elderly must identify and control for the sensory abilities of the individuals concerned. Test material which discriminates well with normal adults may become inappropriate for the elderly if simple visual acuity rather than some assumed cognitive process is an important component of what is being assessed. The instructions in an experiment may be heard clearly in a noisy environment by the 30-year-old but not by someone aged 60. A review of the experimental method in studies of cognitive processes in ageing will quickly suggest that simple checks of adequate vision and hearing have often not been made adequately, if at all! The potential effects on results and inference may be substantial.

Mental Health

The Scope of the Problem

The problems of mental health in the elderly have only been seriously considered comparatively recently. The overwhelming impact of physical decline seemed to lead to an acceptance of an inevitable parallel mental decline. Until the 1950s little was done to define the nature and extent of mental illness in the elderly in hospitals or in the community.

The surveys of the 1950s and 1960s proved that the nature of mental illness in the aged was not significantly different from that of younger adults but that its extent may differ. Pioneering epidemiological work in the UK was initiated by Martin Roth firstly in a hospital setting (Roth, 1955) and then in community studies involving extensive surveys of elderly people in Newcastle upon Tyne (Kay, Beamish and Roth, 1964). These community studies still form the basis of our knowledge of the extent of mental illness in the elderly.

Over the age of 65, roughly 70 per cent of the population have no notable psychiatric disorder (see Table 1.3). Some 15 per cent will

Table 1.3: Prevalence of Psychiatric Disorders in Elderly People Over Age 65

	%
Senile and arteriosclerotic psychoses (i.e. dementia)	4.6
Other organic syndromes	1.0
'Mild mental deterioration'	5.7
Major functional disorders	2.4
Neuroses and allied disorders (moderate/severe forms)	8 9
Character disorders	3.6

Source: Kay *et al.* (1964).

Table 1.4: Prevalence of Moderate/Severe Dementia in Elderly People Living at Home

65–9	70–4	75–9	80+
%	%	%	%
2.4	2.9	5.6	22

Source: Kay and Bergmann (1980), p. 43.

have functional mental illnesses (neuroses, anxiety states, depression, etc.) which are usually similar to those in adulthood in presentation and treatment. About 10 per cent will have some form of organic brain disease (dementias, etc.), if the milder forms are included.

Over the age of 75 the incidence of mental-health problems tends to increase to perhaps 20 per cent (or even 30 per cent in some studies) for dementia in the over-eighties (see Table 1.4 and Kay and Bergmann, 1980). The increase in prevalence of dementia with age, from only 2 per cent at age 65–75, may not continue into the nineties and beyond, where the prevalence is thought to decline again. However, studies have included too few 90-year-olds for this to be certain. An increase in the proportion with functional illness is also noted — perhaps some 25–30 per cent of the over-75 age-group.

Awareness of these mental-health problems is important for everyone concerned with care of the elderly. First and foremost it must be recognised that mental illness can both reappear or arise for the first time in late life, and that it must not be viewed as a normal consequence of the ageing process. We have seen many times referrals from general practitioners saying 'this old lady has poor memory and seems senile'. The previous interpretation of this difficulty as part of the normal ageing process had led to inaction and acceptance. However, on several occasions the problem was caused by a depressive illness. Appropriate diagnosis and treatment dramatically wiped away a seemingly overwhelming and inevitable decline, sometimes in extreme old age.

Classification

For a detailed description of the psychiatric disorders of old age a number of texts are available (e.g. Birren and Sloane, 1980; Levy and Post, 1982; Pitt, 1982). In general, psychiatric disorders in adults and in the elderly have much in common both in their features and in their treatment.

Here we will give a brief overview of the major psychiatric syndromes encountered in the elderly.

The basic classification of mental illness in old age of Roth (1955) suggested five major categories, namely:

1. Affective disorder
2. Late paraphrenia
3. Acute — or subacute — delirious state
4. Senile dementia
5. Arteriosclerotic psychosis.

Twenty-five years on the major changes that can be discerned from recent reviews (Levy and Post, 1982; Post, 1982) are, firstly, that arteriosclerotic psychosis has been re-named multi-infarct dementia (to reflect more accurately the pathological changes found in the brain after death, of a number of small infarcts — stroke-damaged brain matter); secondly, affective disorders are now expanded to include the whole range of neurotic dysfunctions in the elderly (see Bergmann, 1971) as well as depressive and manic psychoses; thirdly, senile dementia is now generally recognised as identical pathologically to Alzheimer's disease, leading to terms such as Senile Dementia, Alzheimer Type (SDAT).

Dementia or ?

It should be noted that pre-senile dementias and senile dementias of Alzheimer type differ primarily through an arbitrary age cut-off point; younger patients may deteriorate more rapidly, but there is little evidence to support the continued use of this age distinction. Terms such as chronic brain syndrome, chronic brain failure, etc., are also occasionally used to avoid the term 'dementia'. Levy and Post (1982) recommend that they not be used. However the Royal College of Physicians in London (1981) drew attention to the problems of passive acceptance and apathy which the label 'dementia' may produce in care agencies. This committee preferred to refer to 'organic mental impairment'. We are not convinced that any of the diagnostic labels have yet tackled the crux of the problem — that dementia (or whatever!) happens to *people*; it happens that these people can rarely speak for themselves, and until someone starts speaking on their behalf changes of label will have little effect.

The Royal College of Physicians' definition of dementia is worth repeating here:

> the global impairment of higher cortical functions including memory, the capacity to solve the problems of day-to-day living, the performance of learned perceptuo-motor skills, the correct use of social skills and the control of emotional reactions, in the absence of gross clouding of consciousness. The condition is often irreversible and progressive.

The Nature of Dementia — Clinical Features

A typical senile dementia has an insidious onset which may not be easy to recognise. The major diagnostic indications usually include a disturbance of memory or other cognitive functioning. As we shall see in the next chapter, some changes in these functions are expected to occur in the normal processes of ageing, and similar changes may occur in such disorders as depression. Levy and Post (1982) draw attention to the need for accurate and adequate definition of the whole range of psychological changes associated with the dementias. Particular emphasis is now given to a thorough cognitive examination which defines the developmental history of the problems presented by the client and provides an accurate baseline to use in gauging future development.

Such approaches to the definition of dementia avoid some of the pitfalls of earlier, more dogmatic criteria. For example, Levy and Post point out the dangers of excessive over-diagnosis and the splitting up of dementia into inappropriate or unjustifiable categories. For example, neurohistology has shown that up to 25 per cent of Alzheimer patients may show clear evidence of cerebral infarct in addition to the Alzheimer changes. As with physical disorders, older people may well be unfortunate enough to have two conditions simultaneously.

Multi-infarct dementia is related to raised systemic blood pressure, and is often characterised as consisting of a series of small strokes or 'strokelets'. Its progress is often said to occur in a series of steps, in contrast with the Alzheimer gradual deterioration. Each step downwards reflects a further stroke; often there will be some improvement as recovery occurs following the infarct, before the next step downwards. The pattern of impairment may show more variation across different areas of function than the typical Alzheimer patient, depending on the sites and extent of the infarcts.

Diagnosis of dementia is relatively straightforward when the process is well established, but less easy with a one-off evaluation when impairment is milder. Thus Ron, Toone, Garralda and Lishman (1979) judged the diagnosis of pre-senile dementia not to be supported in 31 per cent of cases that they followed up for 5–15 years. Bergmann, Kay, Foster, McKechnie and Roth (1971) followed up 20 patients who were suspected of having early dementia; only six were confirmed to be dementing, the remainder were normal at follow-up or unchanged. Less intelligent and articulate elderly people are more likely to be misdiagnosed as dementing.

The Nature of Dementia — Neuropathology and Neurochemistry

An introduction to this topic may be found in the chapter by Perry and Perry (1982). This chapter draws together the burgeoning research into the neuropathology of ageing reported over the past 20 years commencing with the work of Professor Bernard Tomlinson, Sir Martin Roth and their colleagues (e.g. Tomlinson, Blessed and Roth, 1968).

This group was among the pioneers in attempts to relate clinical symptomatology, psychological change and neuropathological changes (Roth, Tomlinson and Blessed, 1967). They found that a simple test of cognitive ability (orientation and memory) could be related to quantitative neuropathological changes — the number of 'senile plaques' present in various parts of the cortex. Similar findings have been confirmed in many studies since that time, although from a psychological point of view the sophistication of the design and methodology may leave much to be desired. In many studies the tests of memory and orientation are not sophisticated and much would have been gained from using available psychometric, or better still, experimental tests of the relevant cognitive functions.

The characteristic Alzheimer changes — 'plaques' and neurofibrillary tangles — are still little understood, but are known to occur in many normal elderly people in far fewer numbers. The changes which occur in the brains of those diagnosed as having dementia show some interesting patterns. Some authors have suggested that the posterior frontal and temporal lobes show the most noticeable changes. There are reports that neuronal loss is greater in the hippocampus of Alzheimer's disease patients than normal elderly. The 'neurofibrillary tangles' associated with dementia seem to occur with greater frequency in the hippocampus. However, the 'senile plaques' which were first reported as associated with cognitive change seem not to follow the same pattern of localisation as other neuropathological markers (Crapper, Karlik and De Boni, 1978).

Recent neurochemical findings (Perry and Perry, 1982), showing a deficit in the neurotransmitter acetylcholine system in dementia, have excited hopes of a pharmacological breakthrough in the treatment of Alzheimer's disease, through straightforward replacement therapy (Levy, Little, Chuaqui and Reith, 1983).

Certainly the implication of acetylcholine in memory processes relates these findings to the clinical features of the disorder, and also there is evidence that the extent of the cholinergic abnormality relates to the severity of the disease.

Depression

The nature and extent of depression in the elderly has received much study in the past two decades. Current awareness of the extent of the problem which depression presents has been a major spur to increasing knowledge, and to attempts to explore the area between the dementias and depression. It is important that those conditions which are already treatable from a medical and psychological point of view are clearly defined and isolated from those with poorer prognosis. Too often depression in older people is seen as inevitable rather than as a potentially treatable condition.

As with most mental illness, depression is difficult to define with precision and this confuses attempts to establish incidence in the elderly with any degree of reliability. A range of estimates are reported in the literature from 34 per cent in an American community sample to the figure of 2.4 per cent quoted for the Newcastle community by Kay *et al.* (1964). Many other publications have varied between such figures. An important conclusion is that those working in this area need to be aware of the vast range of potential symptomatology ranging from transient mood swings to the florid psychotic disorder with massive mood disturbance. However difficult it may be to define incidence, it is appropriate to quote Post (1982) who states 'up to the age of 75, depression is the most frequent condition seen in psychogeriatric practice'. Its definition and treatment must then be of concern to the psychologist.

Depression is *not* more common in older people, despite the myths to the contrary. Gurland (1976) points out that milder, 'neurotic' depressions arise most often between the ages of 35 and 45, whilst psychotic depressions occur most often between 55 and 65 years. Suicides are disproportionately common in the elderly — over a quarter of all suicides involve an elderly person. Attempted suicide is *less* common. An older person with suicidal ideas is much more likely to carry out the act successfully than a younger person — perhaps partly because depression is often not recognised or acted on in older people.

Murphy (1982) outlines some of the social factors involved in depression in the elderly. Severe life-events, major social difficulties and poor physical health were associated with the onset of depression. Elderly people lacking a confiding relationship were more vulnerable to depression; often such people had never had a confidant, so this seemed to be related to a lifelong personality vulnerability rather than to the loss of a partner or friend. Outcome of depression (Murphy 1983) was influenced by physical health problems and severe life-events in the follow-up period of a year, but an intimate relationship did *not* protect against relapse if life stresses continued. In this sample of depressed patients only one-third had a good outcome; another fifth had recovered and then subsequently relapsed. These figures illustrate the potential for innovative psychological approaches to treatment even in psychiatric disorders of the elderly where apparently effective pharmacological agents are available.

Other Disorders

Acute confusional states and delirium are reviewed by Evans (1982); a number of causes are possible — infections, neoplasms, drugs, cerebrovascular problems, etc. Treatment consists primarily of treatment of the underlying cause.

Paraphrenia (Post, 1982) is a schizophrenic-like illness occurring first in late life. Delusional ideas of a persecutory nature are usually a feature, and are usually circumscribed, confined to one or two major themes. Deafness and social isolation are commonly associated with paraphrenia.

Why Work with the Elderly?

Most of the caring professions have difficulty in recruitment to posts related to care of the elderly. Twenty years ago it was considered professional suicide to embark on research on old age. That attitudes have changed little may be seen in the results of a survey of intending clinical psychologists applying for training courses (Liddell and Boyle, 1980). Work with the elderly was clearly seen by this group as of low priority, being amongst the least preferred areas for their future activities. In this respect it was viewed similarly to another area of current high priority — mental handicap. This shows a depressing similarity to Wilensky and Barmack's (1966) survey of clinical psychology trainees in New York. There the elderly were the least preferred age-group, geriatric problems the least popular diagnostic category (out of 24) and institutions for the aged seventeenth (out of 18) most popular work setting.

In the medical sphere Gale and Livesley (1974) showed that attitudes towards the elderly become *more* negative during the course of medical training.

These are aspects of a wider prejudice in society against the elderly and work with older people. Perhaps, as Busse and Blazer (1980) suggest, we are dealing with 'gerontophobia', with elderly people being disliked because they remind us of our own ageing and mortality, or work with the aged being devalued because the conditions seen are often chronic and not susceptible to glamorous, high technology treatments. In many respects elderly people are the victims of discrimination based simply on the accumulation of birthdays and not on any rational basis. 'Ageism' is prevalent in our society and in our media. Young is beautiful, old is ugly; young is fast, old is slow; young is strong, old is decrepit. Seldom do we hear that young is inexperienced, old is wise! Elderly people themselves become so enmeshed in these ideas that they themselves *expect* to do badly on new things — because old people can't learn. They blame any everyday lapse of memory on their age; they may even accept the doctor's reassurance that the physical complaints are to be expected — at your age! Increasingly elderly people are resisting the negative attitudes, and realising that — as a substantial minority group — they may have considerable political influence. There is a long way to go, however, before people who are, say, 80 are viewed as individuals who happen to have a certain chronological age rather than having society's expectation of 80-year-olds thrust upon them.

The present emphasis on increasing resources for work with the elderly could help, if the resources actually keep pace with the rising numbers of older people mentioned above, if the resources actually *reach* old age services and if a collaboration is achieved between the professionals, elderly people and the already existing support networks. The aim should be to work *with* the elderly people and their supporters — not to do things for or to the elderly.

In the final chapter we will say much more of the potential role of the clinical psychologist with the elderly. Suffice to say here that work with the elderly has great benefits and spin-offs for the rest of society. Currently many younger people are in poor physical or mental health because of the burden of caring for a dependent elderly person without adequate support. Many health service resources are currently being used inappropriately for the medium-term care of elderly people because alternative forms of care are not available. For instance, many hospital beds designated as being for surgical or acute medical cases are occupied by old people with chronic conditions. Last but not least, adequate care for the elderly *now* gives the whole of society something, if not to look forward to, at least not to fear for their, and our, futures.

Summary

1. Demographic data emphasise the growth of the 'old old' population.

2. Most old people live in the community; a substantial proportion is in inadequate housing. A considerable number have at least one child living nearby, but about a third have no children at all.

3. Biological theories of ageing have been proposed, including the build up of cellular errors and the notion of programmed ageing, a biological 'clock', ticking out the ageing process.
4. Poor physical health and sensory problems are more common in older people.
5. Mental health problems increase in prevalence among 'old old' people. Depression and dementia are the major problems encountered, although neurotic disorders are now being more frequently recognised. Neuropathological research on dementia has made considerable progress. Suicide is more commonly actually achieved by older people compared with younger age-groups.
6. The elderly are a minority group devalued and discriminated against by society and by the caring professions. Work with the elderly has benefits for all sections of society.

2 COGNITIVE LOSS IN OLD AGE — MYTH OR FACT?

Introduction

Cognitive change with age concerned society before psychology was identifiable as a subject or tests of cognitive abilities were developed. The evident link between decline in intellectual powers and inability to cope with environmental change is well reflected in the literature of most civilisations. The coming of more objective means of intellectual assessment in the late nineteenth century enabled the first hesitant studies of intellectual change in later life (e.g. Quetelet, 1842).

The development of intelligence tests and their widespread use during the First World War led to an accumulation of data, exploited in later years, and to many studies of intellectual change. Wechsler (1958), in *The Measurement and Appraisal of Adult Intelligence*, provides an overview and summary of the research in the first half of this century. A view of intellectual change emerged which seemed to emphasise a decline in abilities from a peak in the 20–30 age-group (see Figure 2.1). It is suggested this decline may be up to a third of peak capacity by the age of 75 (Matarazzo, 1972).

This model of inevitable decline seems to accord with the expectancies of the Western 'man in the street'. Perhaps because of strong negative perceptions of the elderly, intellectual decline with age is anticipated. Similarly, many texts for professions such as medicine, nursing and social work display an expectancy of decline in intellect with age.

More recently these views have been increasingly challenged. Age changes are in fact surprisingly difficult to define from a methodological point of view. Results obtained from aggregated groups may confound or obstruct trends within the groups. Within one individual, patterns of intellectual change in specific abilities may be crucial to adaptation but obscured by methodology. We shall see that general intellectual decline is *not* to be expected as a matter of course from early adulthood into old age.

It is important for the reader to be aware of the methodological

Figure 2.1: Decline in Intellectual Test Performance with Age — Cross-sectional Data

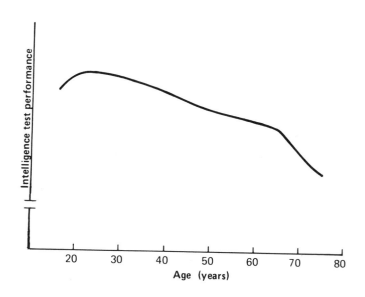

Source: Derived from Wechsler (1955); reproduced from Woods (1982, p. 69), with permission of Blackwell Scientific Publications, Oxford.

difficulties of work in this area in order to allow an effective appraisal of current findings. After overviewing studies which have attempted to look at global changes in intellectual ability, we will consider some specific factors which may influence such changes and models which have been proposed to account for them. Finally, changes in more specific aspects of cognitive function in old age will be discussed.

Methodological Issues

For a fuller account of these complex issues the reader is referred to the extensive account in Chapters 19 and 20 of Botwinick (1978) or

Chapter 11 in Bromley (1974).

The main problem is to distinguish between changes which reflect the ageing process, as a *maturational process*, and those which can be attributed to underlying changes in the culture and environment of the individual, or *cohort influences*. In the studies of Savage, Britton, Bolton and Hall (1973), for example, the population of elderly people assessed had been subjected to a wide variety of influences in early childhood. Some had their education cut significantly by war or economic depression. Indeed, length of education often bore little relationship to the official school-leaving age. Individuals born as little as ten years apart or in urban as against rural environments could have very different early experiences relevant to intellectual development.

As well as education, there might be differences in nutrition, early medical care, occupational opportunities and so on. Thus, someone reaching the age of 70 in 1960 might have had quite a different set of influences than someone in the cohort of people reaching the age of 70 in 1980 (the 1910 cohort). Furthermore, *at the time of assessment* different cultural influences may be operating. For example, conceivably our 70-year-old assessed in 1960 may have had more negative expectations regarding his performance than his counterpart 20 years later, who will have been exposed to numerous TV programmes extolling what can be achieved in later life!

Cross-sectional Studies

In this method groups of individuals aged say 20, 40 and 60 are compared on the basis of data obtained at a single point in time. As far as possible the groups involved are matched on the obvious socio-economic, demographic or other non-experimental variables involved. Conclusions are then drawn from comparison of each age-group's results.

This methodology is tempting to the research worker. The time-scale involved in the study is as short as it can possibly be, and so is more appealing to funding agencies! This procedure can, however, only show age *differences* not age *changes*.

Cultural effects are very strong and evident between cohorts in this type of study. However well-matched the samples there is no way that the 20-year-old group will have comparable early life experiences to the 60-year-old group. So many changes have occurred between 1920 and 1960! How then can one separate the effects of age and cohort differences? In cross-sectional studies it is almost impossible.

Longitudinal Studies

These studies follow a group of individuals over a series of assessments. Thus age-related changes in an individual or group can be followed in that individual or group. To follow individuals needs a number of reassessments over a considerable time span. Follow-up over the individual's life span is beyond the stamina of most researchers! Extensive research backup and, usually, the resources of a large and well-funded institution are needed for a longitudinal study over even a small part of the life span. The relative scarcity of good longitudinal studies reflects these difficulties. A further problem may be changes in the research climate during the period of the study. Ten years later a group of tests which seemed highly justified and relevant at the commencement of a study may have become theoretically and practically overtaken by more appropriate developments which cannot then be easily incorporated into the study.

Longitudinal studies reduce the cohort effects which confuse the interpretation of cross-sectional studies but they do not eliminate them. It is quite possible that changes can occur in a lifetime or in the span of the study due to environmental effects which obscure and confound actual age changes. This problem is particularly acute at times of considerable change in cultural or environmental factors. Thus longitudinal methodologies, whilst providing a model far less prone to unwanted effects than the cross-sectional, still require skill and care in their use and interpretation.

Other factors can influence such studies. The environment of assessment can change. A subject assessed in the relatively non-threatening but 'noisy' environment of their home may later be assessed in a laboratory, much more controlled between subjects but potentially more threatening. Experimenter effects may occur. Tests administered by a non-favoured experimenter may be subject to biases not seen with a more acceptable individual. The subject too may change in motivation and interest in the study over the years, test material may become less personally relevant. Thus, age-related changes due to maturation may become confused with age differences reflecting artifacts of measurement.

Practice effects, arising from familiarity both with the specific test items and with the testing situation, could potentially mask an age-related decline. The severity of these effects will relate to the number of reassessments required, and the interval between them. Certain types of test items may be particularly susceptible to practice, further confusing the findings.

The most serious fault of longitudinal studies is that inevitably some subjects are not available to be reassessed. Some have moved away, others are too busy, some are too ill or have died, others feel once was enough! Whatever the reasons, especially in an elderly population it seems to be impossible to follow a complete group over an extended period. This would not be so damaging if drop-out was a random process, if any subject were as likely as any other to be unavailable. Siegler and Botwinick (1979) point out that it is 'mainly the intellectually, and perhaps physically superior' who persevere and are available to be tested on each occasion. The more demanding the study, in terms of number of re-tests and their frequency, the more marked is this selective attrition. Figure 2.2 illustrates Siegler and Botwinick's findings. Only subjects who were tested on all test sessions up to and including the abscissa test number are represented here. For example, subjects represented at test session 11 comprise only those who had been tested on 10 previous occasions. The trend is clear. At each reassessment those still available have on average a higher *initial* test score than those available at the previous assessment point.

It is clear that longitudinal studies do *not* lead directly to indications of age-related changes.

Sequential Designs

The problems outlined above led in the late 1960s and early 1970s to serious thinking about appropriate new methodologies. The most notable work was by Schaie (1967) and Baltes (1968) which produced designs said to be capable of clarifying the distinction between age effects, cohort effects and time of measurement effects. In essence they carried out a series of cross-sectional studies at different points in time. For example, Schaie, Labouvie-Vief and Buech (1973) and Schaie and Labouvie-Vief (1974) report data from their extensive study of cognitive ability. A cross-sectional study was initially carried out in 1956, with subjects aged from 21 to 70 years. In 1963, a further cross-sectional study was undertaken, using fresh subjects drawn from the same pool (members of a medical insurance plan) over the whole age-range. Similarly in 1970, a third cross-sectional study with a new batch of subjects

Figure 2.2: Mean Intelligence Test Score *at the Time of First Testing* as a Function of the Number of Longitudinal Test Sessions

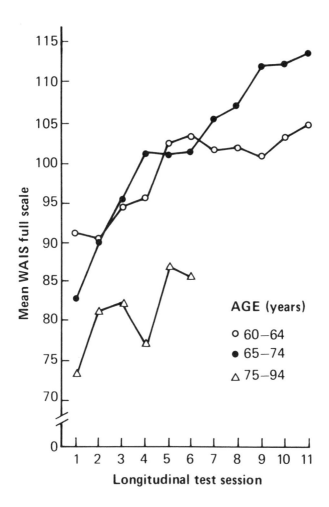

Source: Siegler and Botwinick (1979), reprinted by permission of the *Journal of Gerontology*, **34**, 242–5 and the authors.

aged from 21 to 84 took place. In addition, in 1963 as many as possible of the subjects first tested in 1956 were re-tested, and similarly in 1970 subjects first tested in 1956 or 1963 were re-tested where possible. The cross-sequential design has two major components, then. First, a series of cross-sectional studies on independent random samples; second, a series of cross-sectional studies involving repeated measures on the same subjects. The former method apparently solves the problem of selective subject attrition that, as mentioned above, inevitably affects longitudinal data.

The cross-sequential studies reported by Schaie and his colleagues have demonstrated the extent of cohort effects. Figure 2.3 presents repeated measurement results for one of the tests used, as an example. The upper graph shows the three cross-sectional gradients, reflecting the anticipated 'age-related' decline. The lower half show the longitudinal data; generally the longitudinal gradients are much less marked (except in the oldest age-group). For a number of age points (39–67 in this example), three data points from three different cohorts are available. Comparison of these (e.g. A, B and C) reflects the size of cohort effects for this measure. Figure 2.4 shows Schaie and Labouvie-Vief's (1974) extrapolation of cohort scores on this test predicting an increase in score in spatial ability with succeeding cohorts from 1896. Cohort effects, it is argued, can be as large as age differences for most of the life span.

Unfortunately, not even this most complex methodology can provide all the solutions and satisfy all the critics! A basic criticism is that, whatever comparison is made, another variable is always confounded. For example, when scores at a particular age are examined, from different cohorts, as described above, not only cohort effects but also time-of-measurement effects are in fact operating. The statistical treatment of the results has been the subject of some controversy (see for example, Horn and Donaldson, 1976, 1977; and replies by Baltes and Schaie, 1976; Schaie and Baltes, 1977). Botwinick (1978, p. 372) provides a useful discussion of the limitations of this methodology.

There is then no easy answer in the study of age-related changes; it is important to be aware of the limitations of each and the potential confounding that may occur. The cross-sequential method is attractive, with its combination of the other methods allowing comparisons to be made in several ways, but it can be difficult to implement in practical situations. Certainly increased

Figure 2.3: Cross-sectional and Longitudinal Age Gradients for Space subtest of Primary Mental Abilities Test

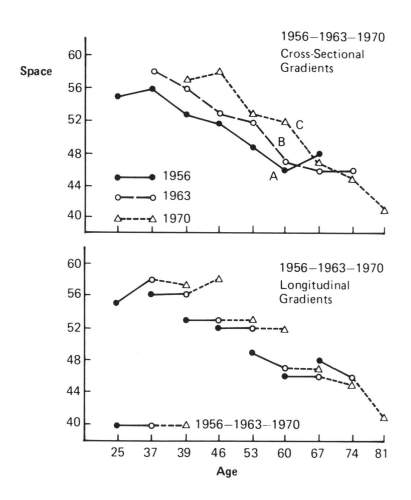

Source: Derived from Schaie and Labouvie-Vief (1974).

knowledge of cohort and time-of-measurement effects may prevent us from being drawn into the mythology of inevitable age-related decline, and help us face a real world where a number of complex, dynamic, interweaving factors interact to produce age differences.

Figure 2.4: Cohort Gradients for Space subtest of Primary Mental Abilities Test

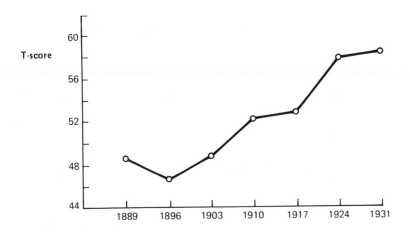

Source: Derived from Schaie and Labouvie-Vief (1974).

Intellectual Change

Earlier in this chapter we drew attention to the traditional model of age-related decline in intellectual abilities. The previous discussion on methodology will have suggested that reinterpretation of such findings is required. However, it is fair to say that some aspects of intellectual performance do show decline on average in older age-groups. The point where this decline becomes evident has been grossly under estimated. It is likely to be at the age of 60 or 70 rather than at 25! The problem is to find out just what is happening; to define the nature of the changes precisely, within groups and individuals, and to identify factors related to the decline.

Psychologists have approached this problem in two ways. The global intelligence test has been a favourite psychometric measure in the past. It has the advantage of sampling a range of intellectual functions using well-defined subtests, in a standardised manner. This should reduce experimenter, subject and environment bias, and to an extent this is so. However, there are many difficulties with these tests and we will mention a few below (see also Chapter 5). The second approach has been to use tasks from experimental psychology; a later section of this chapter examines these studies in detail.

Much controversy has surrounded the relative merits and demerits of these approaches. A review of the contrasting approaches of psychometrician and experimental psychologist is given in the papers by Kendrick (1982a, 1982b) and Rabbitt (1982b).

There can be little doubt that current psychometric tests of cognitive function lead to a blunderbuss approach with little finesse. Tests developed primarily for the assessment of children and young people, to predict educational attainment and work performance, may produce effective discrimination and reliability with a younger adult population but be very poor measures of the extent and subtlety of cognitive change in the elderly. Subtests may contain few items which effectively discriminate at appropriate ability levels. The quest for test reliability may have excluded just those very items or subtests which may have proved to be sensitive indicators of cognitive change in the elderly. Any changes found in the elderly may merely reflect cultural or educational biases in the application of the tests across age-groups.

With these cautions in mind we can examine some of the findings from studies using global intellectual measures. The previously quoted trends in ability summarised by Wechsler (1955) and reflected in Figure 2.1 are typical of those obtained from a wealth of cross-sectional studies. If one looks beyond full-scale IQ to the verbal and performance components of the Wechsler Adult Intelligence Scale (WAIS) it becomes evident that different patterns of age differences are found for different aspects of intellectual ability (see Figure 2.5). Performance IQ is found to decline faster than verbal ability in middle age although in the elderly the declines are roughly parallel.

Explanations for these effects have varied from a consideration of the psychological function involved to methodology. Speed of processing information, involving input systems, central processor time and motor output, has been thought to effect performance tests more acutely, especially the timed tests. However, studies summarised by Botwinick (1977) suggest that the elderly cannot

Figure 2.5: Differential Decline in Verbal and Performance Abilities with Age

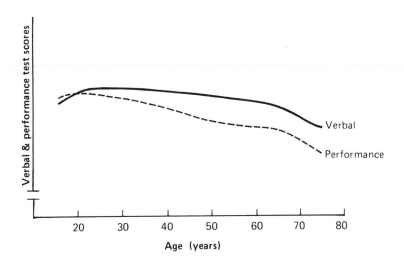

Source: Derived from Wechsler (1955), WAIS data, reproduced from Woods (1982, p. 70), with permission of Blackwell Scientific Publications, Oxford.

improve to the level of younger subjects even if given unlimited time. The cross-sectional methodology used brings in all of the cohort, environmental and other problems seen earlier, which could in theory differentially influence verbal and performance abilities.

In one of the few studies covering a large part of the life span, Owens (1966) reported longitudinal findings (on the Army Alpha Test, a general cognitive measure) on a group of subjects followed up from the age of 19 to the age of 61, with an intermediate assessment at about the age of 49. Subjects showed a general *improvement* in the first 30 years, with hardly any loss evident as the subjects entered their sixties.

Longitudinal studies following intellectual change in elderly people have reported some inconsistent findings. Eisdorfer and Wilkie (1973) assessed subjects initially aged 60–9 on four occasions over ten years, finding a decrement in performance ability (on the WAIS) but no substantial overall decline. Jarvik, Kallman and Falek (1962), following a group with an initial average age of 67.5 years over an eight-year period, similarly reported a decline on the performance tasks. Blum, Fosshage and Jarvik (1972) carried out a 20-year follow-up on these same subjects, when an overall decline was evident. In contrast, Savage *et al.* (1973) found an *increase* in performance ability in their sample (mean initial age 71), who were assessed four times in seven years. A slight decline in verbal level also emerged.

The effects of selective subject attrition (only one-sixth of Savage *et al.*'s sample were re-tested at seven years), different frequencies of reassessment (and so different practice effects) and different ages at the commencement of the studies probably account for these differences between studies. The overall trend seems to be of stability to the age of 60 or so, then a decline in performance level to about the age of 70, when verbal abilities show some decline.

Cross-sequential data (Schaie *et al.*, 1973; Schaie and Labouvie-Vief, 1974) on the Primary Mental Abilities Test suggest that age-related decline is minimal until at least the age of 60 or so. Verbal abilities show decline later than performance, speeded measures. Longitudinal analyses show least decline, cross-sectional most, with the independent measures analysis showing an intermediate level of decline. Age-related decline, if it occurs, is a feature of old age (not middle age as was once thought) and varies greatly for different aspects of intellectual function. For most of the life span, cohort differences are probably of greater significance. The extent of age-related decline in old age does not in general appear to be dramatic enough seriously to affect the adaptive ability of the majority of the elderly.

Individual Differences and Patterns of Intellectual Change

The use of global composite intelligence tests in studies such as those quoted above has led to many attempts to examine the *pattern* of intellectual change in ageing. We have already referred to broad differences in age-related decline seen in verbal and performance components of tests such as the WAIS. More specific cognitive functions reflected in individual subtests have also been related to the ageing process.

This led to a great deal of interest in the construction of

Deterioration and Ageing Indices related to tests such as the WAIS. These were based on an approach by Wechsler who developed a Deterioration Index for the Wechsler–Bellevue Scale. This attempted to assess abnormality of deterioration based on differential combinations of subtests described as 'hold' and 'don't hold' respectively according to whether they were thought to remain stable in ageing or to show a marked decline.

Similar indices were developed by many others perhaps reaching their climax in the work of Hewson (1949) who produced a multi-component index of bewildering complexity. These endeavours continued well into the WAIS era and even to the present day, e.g. Savage (1981). In 1966, Bolton, Britton and Savage concluded that many of the indices developed at that time were dubious in origin, and suspect in practice, with respect to practical validity and reliability. Miller (1977a) compared the search for the right Wechsler subtest combinations to the medieval alchemist's quest for the philosopher's stone!

One of the problems with the indices has been confusion as to whether they are intended to reflect a pattern of deterioration related to ageing or to dementia; the evidence for their utility in the diagnosis of dementia will be reviewed in Chapter 4.

Whilst this pursuit of patterns of decline has proved to be rather futile to date, it is based on the clear awareness that individual changes do exist. All types of study, cross-sectional, longitudinal or cross-sequential, reveal that within the patterns of general stability or gradual change in overall ability there may be significant changes in specific facets of cognition in individuals. This is an area where it is likely that large sample studies may tend to obscure important individual variability. The results observed could be explained in part by the combination of data from individuals who retain to a great extent their capacities together with data from those more severely declining. Siegler and Botwinick (1979), summarising longitudinal data over a 20-year period from the Duke University ageing projects, concluded that 'there is a sizeable proportion of old people who decline very little as old age advances, or decline not at all, except perhaps in extreme old age'. Average findings tell us about the average elderly person, but obscure important individual differences, that may be of great practical importance.

The concept of 'plasticity' has been introduced by Baltes and Willis (1979) who suggest that cognitive functioning in individuals is not a fixed feature but a growing and developing function. To those involved in the area of child development, this is not a novel concept. Children are known to differ considerably in the pace and nature of their intellectual development, in response to genetic and environmental stimuli. Baltes and Willis argue that it is reasonable to expect an equivalent range of rate and type of change in the elderly, subject as they are to a number of powerful environmental and intrinsic influences. This long-term plasticity may well be a reason why generalisations about the intellectual changes in ageing (such as Deterioration Indices) may be very poor predictors in the individual case.

Most middle-aged psychologists have been brought up accepting some model of stability of IQ, and this is reflected in a reluctance to accept easily the concept of long-term plasticity. Even more problems arise when the concept is extended to short-term changes in intellectual ability. The man in the street will tell you that some mornings, some days he is not 'with it'. Arithmetical ability is impaired, memory 'goes', car driving, musical instrument playing and similar overlearned activities are performed very badly. Psychologists have been slow to look for correlates of these every-day feelings. However, the intellectual performance of old people can be improved by various interventions (Baltes and Barton, 1977; Patterson and Jackson, 1980) and a number of factors have been identified that have a specific, adverse effect on elderly people's performance. These include tiredness (Furry and Baltes, 1973), cautiousness (Birkhill and Schaie, 1975) and the effects of elderly people evaluating their own performance negatively. For a variety of reasons elderly people may not be performing at their optimal level when tested cognitively. Intellectual ability, as assessed, is not then a fixed attribute of the elderly person. It may fluctuate in the short term, and show idiosyncratic changes in the long term.

Some apparent under-functioning has been attributed to the nature of the tests and tasks used. The concept of ecological validity of tests has been discussed by Kendrick (1982a). He suggests that tests which do not relate to the day-to-day life of the subject are perceived as (at best) irrelevant. He refers to the phenomenon familiar to most psychologists who have used the WAIS with the elderly of the individual faced with the Block Design subtest who says 'I've never done this since I was a child'. Such tests are held to be prone to exacerbate motivational and attitudinal problems and so reduce their validity as an accurate guide to cognitive performance. Volans and Woods (1983) refer to the need for a fuller consideration of exactly what factors are involved in 'ecological validity' and point out that in some circumstances task difficulty may be just as important in influencing the subject's attitude and motivation.

A more extreme position is taken by Labouvie-Vief, Hoyer, Baltes and Baltes (1974) who state that deficits seen in the intellectual abilities of the elderly reflect *only* a lack of practice and familiarity with the tasks used. The intervention studies mentioned above, showing elderly people to improve with practice on intellectual tests, are often taken as support for this position. Few have included a younger control group; one study that did (Hoyer, Hoyer, Treat and Baltes, 1978) showed that younger subjects actually improved *more* with the same amount of practice.

Current intellectual tests are far from ideal and probably do lack relevance for older people. Often quoted is a study by Demming and Pressey (1957) who developed a test of practical information that seemed more relevant to the culture and life-style of the elderly. Scores *increased* with age on this test!

Not all the apparent age-related changes can be blamed on IQ tests. They almost certainly do produce underestimates of functioning in some older people, which hampers the accurate identification of individual differences in patterns of change as the person ages.

Intellectual Change, Health and Survival

The findings discussed in the previous sections relate to studies of the general population of elderly people. Chapter 4 will review intellectual and other changes associated with overt mental-health abnormalities, such as dementia or depression. We will now look at some interesting findings from research on 'normal' community samples which can shed some light on the relationship of intellectual change to health and survival.

A group emerges of elderly people who are exceptionally well preserved in physical health, adjustment and other factors. Savage *et al.* (1973) report on community samples which were assessed using the WAIS over a seven-year period. The subjects in this study were also given thorough medical, psychiatric and social examinations. From the latter assessments a group of 'supernormals' was identified. They seemed to be free from noticeable physical and mental-health problems, adjustment and social difficulties. The members of this group obtained significantly higher WAIS IQs than their peers. They showed less evidence of intellectual deterioration as measured by verbal–performance IQ discrepancy or subtest scatter. Their involvement in activities within and outside the home was greater and they survived longer than would have been expected.

A similar finding is reported by Botwinick and Birren (1963). Within their samples they differentiated between those with optimal physical health and those with some problems, although the latter group may not have experienced any significant symptoms. The WAIS scores of the healthy group were higher than the others. Turning to specific systems, those with cardiovascular system defects were found by Wilkie and Eisdorfer (1971) to have a greater WAIS decline than their peers.

They followed a group of elderly people over a ten-year period. Those initially in their sixties with raised diastolic blood pressure deteriorated more on the WAIS than those with normal blood pressure. The survival rate for those initially in their seventies with elevated blood pressure was very low. Those of the older group who had slightly raised blood pressure fared a little better intellectually than those whose blood pressure was normal.

Sensory deficits have also been related to impaired performance (e.g. O'Neill and Calhoun, 1975). Granick, Kleben and Weiss (1976) reported poor WAIS performance, particularly on verbal abilities, in elderly people with hearing loss.

An investigation by Bergmann, Britton, Hall and Blessed (1981) of admissions to a screening centre for the elderly looked at relationships between physical and intellectual factors. Overall ratings of increased physical illness related to reductions in scores on a variety of intellectual measures. Of the specific features reported, cardiovascular system defects were found to be more closely related to patchy areas of cognitive impairment than to an overall deficit. An interesting finding was an association between clouding of consciousness, intellectual deficit particularly on motor-perceptual tests and certain biochemical indices notably sodium and potassium levels, often variable in the elderly.

An area of considerable interest over the past 20 years has been the relationship between intellectual change and survival. One of the methodological possibilities for unravelling the complexities of changes observed in the elderly is to shift the age time base. Traditionally one uses chronological age, but in the elderly, particularly with longitudinal studies, there is the possibility of following the subject through to death and then using time of death as the time base. Results of assessment are then analysed in relation to time pre-death.

Kleemeier (1961, 1962) suggested an 'imminence of death' or 'terminal decline' hypothesis, arguing that factors associated with the imminence of death may affect intellectual performance and be detected quite some time before death. Such a decline could, perhaps, account for the results of cross-sectional and longitudinal studies reviewed earlier. At any age there would be a proportion of relatively well-preserved individuals and a proportion approaching death. An increasing number of the latter would lead to an apparent increasing decline in overall population results.

As Siegler's (1980) review indicates, most longitudinal studies have shown clearly that higher intellectual performance at the commencement of the study is significantly related to survival. Savage *et al.* (1973) reanalysed their data arranged with time of death as a base line. A clear picture emerged. A decline in abilities was evident some three years or so before death. In the two years immediately before death a rather interesting pattern emerges (see Figure 2.6). The drop in performance abilities seen in the previous years accelerates, but in the immediate pre-death phase there is a sudden loss of verbal abilities, which have previously held up. These psychometric findings are consistent with the picture seen in life. The normal elderly approaching death often show subtle, then significant, loss in those tasks such as memory and perceptual-motor co-ordination measured by performance subtests whilst retaining verbal abilities, long-term memory and fluency. When these functions also deteriorate, death is often close. One of us (PGB) has observed a similar pattern of pre-death decline in a group of younger patients suffering from renal encephalopathy.

The terminal decline hypothesis requires an accelerated rate of change in cognitive function in the years before death, and is not confirmed simply by associations between intellectual level and survival or even time of death. Some controversy remains as to whether it can be considered more than a hypothesis. While some studies have demonstrated an increased rate of decline, others have failed to do so, and others have reported quite different periods before death during which the decline occurs (3 months to 7−10

Figure 2.6: Pre-death Decline in Intellect; Short WAIS Scores Expressed as a Percentage of Initial Test Scores, Plotted in Relation to Time of Assessment Before Death

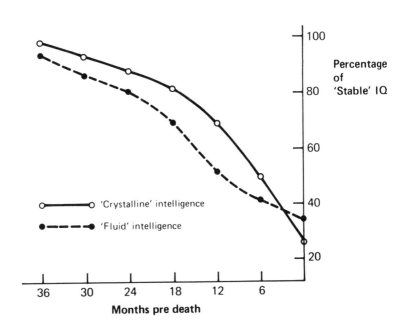

Source: Previously unpublished data from Newcastle studies, Savage *et al.* (1973).

years). Siegler (1980) reports that in one study at least, when initial age and age at death were controlled for, the characteristic terminal drop was no longer apparent. She comments that some of the mis-predictions, i.e. a subject with a terminal drop pattern who survives, are related to an intercurrent illness, with cognitive performance improving when the illness improves. This whole concept of terminal drop is obviously linked to considerations of physical health. Siegler concludes that 'any large change in the cognitive capacity of an older person should be treated with suspicion — it may be a terminal sign, or it may indicate a potentially treatable illness'.

Finally, it is worth noting that some attempts have been made to specify more precisely which cognitive tasks are sensitive to this probable health-related deterioration. For example, Botwinick, West and Storandt (1978) list 13 measures which seem to be predictive, with some indications present up to five years before death.

Models of Intellectual Change

A number of models have been suggested to explain and integrate these findings on changes in intellectual ability. Early, often fortuitous, combinations of subtests from global intellectual measures provided some ideas, such as the verbal/performance groupings. Later workers added to these patterns with factor analyses of bewildering scope, complexity and often contradictory findings. There are behavioural theories, and those involving almost purely biological explanation. Eventually, some integrative models have emerged with increasing maturity of thought.

Wechsler (1955) suggested that the elderly's differential decline in verbal and performance abilities provided a useful model to explain age-related change. As mentioned in a previous section, this model extended to an examination of those subtests which tended to remain stable with advancing age — 'hold' subtests — and those which did not, the 'don't hold' subtests. The 'hold' tests reflected largely the stored or aggregated experience of individuals. Vocabulary level is a good example. The 'don't hold' tests emphasise new learning or problem-solving abilities. Block Design is a good example.

These early models were largely inferential, the techniques of factor analysis not having evolved enough to be easily applied to such data. When the advent of the computer turned factor analysis from an esoteric statistician's toy into a readily available technique, it was soon applied to the problems posed by the structure of intellect in the aged. We have already seen that the changes observed in intellect as age advances can be crucially affected by methodology. The same is true of factor analysis. Theoretical models of factor analysis have been many and varied ranging from relatively pure component analysis through the range to models involving complex rotations. The cynic appraising the results obtained might conclude that the technique may possibly have been adapted to suit the results expected!

Leaving aside such lack of charity, factor analysis has produced consistent findings, e.g. on the WAIS. Most analyses have produced clear-cut factors reflecting the verbal and performance groupings of subtests (Savage *et al.*, 1973). Aged groups may differ from younger by an increasing tendency for the 'memory' factor often identified as separate in younger groups to lose its distinct identity and to load instead on the first two factors. This is held by Radcliffe (1966) to reflect 'an increasing emphasis on the role of experience in the measurement of adult intelligence'.

Savage and his colleagues (1973) reported a variety of analyses. In the normal elderly they confirmed the earlier findings; two factors emerged consisting largely of verbal and performance subtests respectively. No clearly identifiable third factor was found. Memory-related functions appeared to be contained within the first two factors. However, there were some suggestions that subtests in their analyses did not follow the Wechsler model of verbal vs. performance but that the explanation of Cattell (1963) in relation to 'fluid' and 'crystallised' aspects of intelligence was more relevant.

This model of Cattell has now been applied for many years to the explanation of age-related changes in intellect, from children to the elderly. Cattell suggested that intellect is organised in two main dimensions. The first, fluid ability, involves the immediate adaptive ability of the individual, to perceive relationships between objects and events, to reason, to abstract. The second, crystallised ability, reflects the aggregated experience of the individual, the acquired familiarity with materials and relationships. In the elderly, the model suggests, fluid abilities are more dependent on the physiological and biological integrity of the individual and will be more prone to change. Crystallised abilities may well go on developing into extreme old age.

This model seems to have stood the test of time quite well and appears to have validity in the explanation of aspects of both normal ageing processes and those in abnormal ageing such as dementia. Many studies such as those by Savage's group (1973) and by Horn and Donaldson (1976) have found that Cattell's model provides both an explanation of results on age changes and a useful model for prediction and intervention. Horn and Donaldson (1976) emphasise the individual's approach to a task as combining aspects of both types of intellect. They do not accept decline in either as inevitable in any single individual, but simply suggest fluid intelligence is more likely to decline, and crystallised ability likely to increase, with age.

Alternative models have appeared which are well worth examination. The work by Labouvie-Vief *et al.* (1974), to which we have already referred, prefers an explanation in terms of an operant analysis. They argue that most changes observed in the elderly are a reflection of interaction between environmental changes and the individual. Intellectual behaviour is seen as changing due to changing stimulus or reinforcement patterns in the elderly. Little prompting and poor quality reinforcement of intellectual behaviour lead to an apparent decrement in cognitive function. This model is expanded further into a 'compensatory' model for age-related changes in the book by Hussian (1981). Apparent deficits in intellectual function are viewed as resulting from the person adapting to the natural changes accompanying ageing. The attempt to conserve resources leads to more primitive cognitive styles. The elderly person is seen as attempting to cope with physical changes, changes in the social environment and reinforcement, and differences in responsiveness to stress. Rigidity, less risk taking, withholding of responses and slow response times may be seen as adaptive reactions to these changes.

In similar vein, Baltes and Willis (1982) describe ageing as 'selective optimization'. Ageing is seen as involving increased biological vulnerability and decreased environmental adaptability. This process differs widely between individuals, who differ also in their selective and compensatory strategies. In order to keep up high levels of functioning, more and more effort is required. Accordingly, older people choose to focus on those aspects of behaviour most important for the person's life-situation. This often does *not* include psychometric performance, but given prompting and practice their performance can be improved. Generally, however, the investment of energy required of the older person is too high, or other areas of behaviour are more attractive.

The model proposed by Schaie (1977–8) relates intellectual changes to a broader perspective of cognitive style. He sees cognition as going through a process of development from an acquisitive stage, through achieving, responsible and executive stages to a final, reintegrative stage. He holds that existing tests relate only to the first two stages and that the apparent decline seen in conventional tests of intelligence refers only to these stages. The reintegrative phase, the wisdom of the old, is little mentioned in Western literature and certainly not readily assessed by current tests.

The currently fashionable sociobiological theory is represented by a model proposed by Baltes and Willis (1979). This has three major components, age-graded normative influences, history-graded normative influences and critical life-events (non-normative). The first two represent those environmental and biological events experienced by the majority of individuals in any population, some of which, say education, are related to age, others, say wars, are related to history. Other events such as physical illness, accidents causing head injury, family trauma or redundancy are not related to age or historical experience in any consistent way, and are placed in the third category of influence. The model is intended to reflect the multi-factorial nature of intellectual change with age and emphasis that the observed change in fact results from the *interaction* of a number of influences.

All of these models offer some insights into the explanation of the intellectual decline seen in the elderly. None of them seem at present to give a totally satisfactory integration of the results observed in the previous sections of the chapter. Our knowledge of the nature of intellectual change is at present crude; the following sections of the chapter will illustrate many areas where experimental studies may lead to greater understanding than those studies using global intellectual measures. When we have a clearer understanding of the phenomena involved, we may be in a position to relate them more clearly to the biological, environmental and social changes experienced by the elderly.

Speed of Information Processing

One of the fundamental cognitive functions, information processing, is thought by many to suffer inevitable decline in the elderly. The nature and extent of this decline and its locus within the response train have been the focus of intensive research. This area reflects the increasing sophistication and development of theoretical models extremely well over a 50-year span from Miles (1931) at Stanford, through Welford's important research (see Welford, 1977, for a review) to the more recent contributions of Rabbitt (1980).

The reaction time experiment has provided a focus for much of this research. In such an experiment the response train may be initially broken down into three simple components:

Sensory	Central	Behavioural
input	processing	output

Research has examined the effects of ageing on both the overall sequence and its components. Types of sensory input have varied in sensory modality and in the complexity of the information presented. Similarly the response mechanism, the behavioural output, may vary in complexity and modality.

Early studies, reviewed by Welford (1958), attempted to locate slowing within the response train. The effects of ageing on sensory processes, reviewed above, raise obvious questions about the sensory input stage. If acuity of vision or hearing is affected by age, does this affect speed of processing? It was quickly established that the primary loci of slowing were in the sensory input and central decision-making components. The next phase of research was able to show that, when sensory acuity was clearly compensated for, by stimuli well within the individual's capacity, the locus of slowing was then the central processing mechanism.

These findings may be of great practical importance. A slowing concentrated in the peripheral nervous system, for example visual input or motor output, would not have such severe potential consequences for overall adaptation. A central nervous system slowing could be much more serious. Birren, Woods and Williams (1979) quantify the decrement in response as some 20 per cent between the ages of 20 and 60. In older individuals a more severe decrement may exist. These effects are important since such slowing is held by Birren amongst others to reflect the primary processes of central nervous system ageing which we outlined in Chapter 1. Such slowing is thought by this group to relate closely to a wide variety of cognitive abilities which have a common theme in depending on the ability of the individual to process quickly sequential information (Botwinick and Storandt, 1974).

The results on this type of test have been questioned by many psychologists. Kendrick (1982a) doubts the 'ecological validity' of tests far removed from the day-to-day life expectancies of the elderly. Practice effects may seriously influence the results of studies. Rabbitt (1982b) suggests that 'data collected during a first encounter with a subject are highly unrepresentative of true level of performance, and should usually be discarded'. He also makes the point that instructions given to the elderly are more often misinterpreted, sometimes to a dramatic extent.

These considerations tend to lessen the impact of the general findings in earlier studies of slowing with age. They help to explain the seemingly excessive individual variability seen in elderly subjects on this type of task. Many older individuals perform well within the normal area for younger subjects. Perhaps researchers in this area should look carefully at the composition of their old age-groups. We have seen in previous sections that seeming decrements with age could be attributed to combinations of preserved and significantly deteriorated individuals. Physical health status is again relevant; raised blood pressure, cerebrovascular and cardiovascular disorders and low levels of activity have all been related to slower reaction time (Birren *et al.*, 1979).

The past few years have seen a re-emergence of interest in the investigation of the interaction between speed and ageing. Both theoretical models and experimental procedures have been substantially improved to overcome some of the problems of earlier studies. The advent of microprocessor-based recording mechanisms has facilitated a much more fine grained analysis of such factors as decision and movement times. Tasks have been made much more relevant to the elderly; a good example is the 'supermarket shopping' 'game' devised by Pinkava, reported in Rabbitt (1982b).

Theoretical models have moved far away from simple determination of locus of slowing. Indeed, mean reaction time is now seen as less important than changes in the skew of distributions of reaction time with age (*ibid.*). The large increases in mean reaction times in the elderly reported in earlier studies have been seen to be primarily caused by variations in anticipation of signals and ability to monitor adequacy of previous responding (Welford, 1977). The older person will tend towards accuracy rather than speed, thus artificially raising reaction times. Their strategies in tackling the task may well then differ from those adopted by younger people. Older people seem less able to maintain readiness during the preparatory interval, between the warning signal and the stimulus, and if a fast rate of responding is required may be impaired because they are still involved in monitoring the previous response. Gottsdanker (1982) argues that it is these control processes that are ineffective in older people. He demonstrated only a very slight increase of simple reaction time with age, under optimal conditions. Healthy motivated elderly subjects were used, and preparation for the stimulus made extremely easy. When a larger preparatory interval was used — as in most previous studies — a much larger age difference was noted.

Older people are disproportionately affected by increases in the complexity of the reaction time task (Fozard, 1981), for example if a recoding is required between stimulus and response. Rabbitt (1982a) suggests that one explanation for this may be older people's greater difficulty in using information stored in long-term memory, or in manipulating and indexing information in immediate memory.

Despite the apparent unanimity regarding cognitive slowing with age, controversy remains. Whilst attempts continue to isolate the age deficit (e.g. Salthouse and Somberg, 1982, found impairment at each stage of information processing), or to relate the observed changes to a general, presumably biological, slowing (e.g. Cerella, Poon and Fozard, 1981), there is much to recommend Rabbitt's approach, which concentrates on models of change between and within individuals, and on the control systems used. He suggests 'we require descriptions of the ways in which people actively optimize their performance to cope with changing task demands, to improve with practice, and to circumvent or minimize growing failures in their own efficiency' (Rabbitt, 1982a).

Problem Solving

The ability to solve problems has been the psychologist's laboratory analogue of real-life decision-making. As with the research on speed of information processing, there is an extensive literature on age-related aspects of these more complex tasks. Unfortunately, until quite recently the data on the elderly was sparse. The literature on the development of problem-solving in childhood is vast. The pressure of industrial and organisational psychology, particularly related to retraining the older worker, produced much awareness of strategies in the 40–60 age-group, but little for the older individual.

Again as with speed of information processing, psychology has been trying to systematise and quantify changes which the 'man in the street' assumes do occur in the elderly. There is a general expectancy that both the speed and quality of the solutions of complex problems will reduce in old age. This assumption may well not be quite as true as common myth supposes. With slightly younger persons in industrial tasks, experience may compensate for lack of speed. The work of psychology in recent years has concentrated on an analysis of the strategies of problem solving with various basic aims. Most prominent amongst these are the quantification of the extent of loss in ability, the understanding of the components of tasks and the interrelationships between their decrements in the elderly. Finally, attempts have been made to feed back this information into the modification of problem-solving behaviour, to see whether more efficient, adaptive strategies can be taught.

A very thorough review of the psychology of this area is provided in the book by Botwinick (1978) and chapters by Rabbitt (1977) and Giambra and Arenberg (1980). An examination of the literature suggests that there is support for the contention that the elderly are less efficient at solving complex problems. As with the work on speed of processing and intellectual factors, it is essential to attempt to control for such factors as the relevance of the material to the individual. Tasks developed on university students or for industrial situations may not be seen as relevant by the elderly! A concrete context for the logical operations does help to some extent. The better recent work has controlled for such factors and has continued to verify the previous results showing a general loss of both speed and accuracy in complex problem solving (Arenberg, 1974; Rabbitt, 1980). Arenberg (1982), using a cross-sequential methodology, confirms that problem-solving performance of well-educated older men is poorer than that of younger men, and shows decline over a period of 6–7 years.

The factors influencing problem solving are many. Slower information processing, reduced intelligence, impaired memory, an increase in rigidity and moves towards more concrete thought process are all evidenced in studies and supported in the literature. In particular, the elderly are noticeably poor at organising their attack on a problem and find extreme difficulty when faced with information which is peripheral to the problem under attack. They are far more easily distracted by irrelevant information. The work by Pinkava (reported by Rabbitt, 1982b) using the 'supermarket shopping' task, an innovative task with apparent ecological validity, has confirmed the importance of most of the above variables. As well as simple information on changes in speed of response, many aspects of the strategies used by the elderly in problem solving were investigated. Changes in memory function and the organisation and sequencing of material were found and related to various levels of task difficulty.

One interesting spin-off from this study was its ability (also referred to in Rabbitt, 1982b) to generate under controlled conditions real-life situations such as 'slips of the mind' and 'absent mindedness'.

Analyses of why the elderly fail to solve problems efficiently seem to show that there are several significant components of the task which cause breakdown. When memory becomes less efficient, a reduction in speed of processing may overload memory and cause inability to complete the task. Seemingly random, unsystematic and inappropriate strategies may be the result of task difficulty level beyond the individual's ability to cope. Rigidity and concreteness may relate to the provision of a 'safe', completely predictable option. The elderly will choose the safe option when available but differ little from younger people in cautiousness when no such option is provided. Older people have been shown to have difficulty in using organisational strategies (e.g. note taking). Even when required to keep complete records as part of the task, so that all the current information is available for review, to keep memory load to a minimum, elderly people may still experience information overload (Arenberg, 1982).

Whilst these findings provide some insights, we are not very far along the way towards an understanding of problem-solving difficulties in the elderly which could be used as a clear-cut indication of how to train (or retrain) those who are noticeably deficient.

Some studies have attempted systematic retraining. Labouvie-Vief and Gouda (1976) used four groups. One faced the problems directly, the second were allowed to work with the problems for some time. The two other groups were instructed in the strategies relevant to the tasks with one group having anxiety management training. On immediate testing the latter two groups were superior; but two weeks later there was little difference between these groups and the group who themselves had time to work on the problems. Thus, training seemed to assist the elderly but self-exploration of the task was as effective as systematic training. Botwinick (1978) points out the equivocal nature of these findings and that there is no overwhelming evidence of the efficacy of any specific retraining procedure.

The cognitive ability of the elderly seen in problem-solving tasks is a relatively unexplored area. The findings that exist point to clear-cut deficits, even when tasks are optimally relevant. Why these deficits arise, whether they are general in the population and how to overcome them needs much more investigation.

Memory

The importance of memory in the successful adjustment to age-related changes has been self-evident since psychologists have investigated cognitive abilities. In the preceding sections of the chapter we have seen that, in relation to global changes in intellectual tasks, memory plays an increasingly important part as age advances, as shown by factor analytic studies. Similarly, in problem solving, the ability to retain information is crucial to successful handling of problems and therefore to adaptation.

The topic of memory and memory changes has, like problem solving, occupied and interested many psychologists and a wide range of theoretical models have emerged.

It would appear that three main memory mechanisms may be considered although theorists argue about their boundaries and interrelationships. They are sensory memory, primary (or short-term) memory and secondary (or long-term) memory.

Sensory Memory

Sensory memory is an extremely short-term store (less than a second) which holds information at a sensory, pre-perceptual stage. Visual sensory memory (iconic memory) may be measured in younger people by such tasks as extremely brief tachistoscopic presentation of matrices of letters, or numbers, where the subject is asked to recall part of the matrix (after the experiment of Sperling, 1960). Evidence for age changes in this aspect of memory is rather weak (Botwinick, 1978). Walsh and Thompson (1978) reported that eight out of ten subjects tested were unable to perform the partial report tasks! Walsh (1982) suggests that this is related to other processes — selective attention and pattern recognition — being slower in older people, and so preventing this methodology actually assessing sensory memory. Using a different measure — the longest inter-stimulus interval at which repetitive flashes are perceived as a single persistent display — Walsh and Thompson (1978) estimated that visual sensory memory in younger people is 15 per cent longer in duration than in older subjects. Walsh (1982) comments that there is evidence for older adults being slower in all stages of visual information processing. It seems likely that older people *are* less efficient at this first level of storage, but clearly there are difficulties in finding an appropriate and relevant methodology.

Primary Memory

Primary memory is the ability typically measured by a test such as digit-span or immediate recall of an address. It is a short-term process involving short-term storage and little or no manipulation or processing of the information, just an input–output operation. Many studies in this area, reviewed by Craik (1977), seem to suggest that there is little, if any, change in this aspect of memory in normal ageing. Digit-span, for example, shows little change in older people. Dichotic memory tasks, in which different stimuli are presented simultaneously to each ear for recall, often show a deficit for elderly people in the recall of stimuli from the ear reported second. This has been related to a deficit in short-term storage, although doubts have been expressed about the involvement of other factors, e.g. registration of the stimuli. Parkinson, Lindholm and Urell (1980) have shown that matching old and young subjects on digit-span reduces almost completely the age differences in dichotic memory performance. This suggests dichotic memory *does* reflect primary memory, and so there may be some impairment. Error analysis suggested younger subjects tended to switch attention from ear to ear more than their older counterparts, which could reflect reduced processing capacity in older people. This in turn could be related to reduced auditory acuity (although hearing impairment was minimal) in the older sample.

Related to the short-term level of storage is *working memory* (Baddeley, 1981). Among the components of working memory already identified are a central executive, an articulatory loop (where auditory material may be stored and rehearsed) and a short-term visual store. Digit-span probably reflects largely the function of the articulatory loop. Some evidence that the visual short-term store is working efficiently in older people emerges from Waugh and Barr's (1982) finding that recall of the serial position of the most recently presented item from a series of pictures was unimpaired in older people. Wright (1981) examined the effects of dividing attention between competing tasks on young and old subjects. As task difficulty increased all age-groups were impaired, but older subjects showed a drop in performance at smaller levels of demand for processing capacity. Wright suggests that working memory may change with age such that there is a reduction in automatic processing, so that older adults have to devote more capacity to store small amounts of information; this then leaves less capacity available to operate other control processes. The central executive is then unable to allocate the available capacity as efficiently.

In summary, primary memory is generally considered to be unimpaired in the elderly, except when the reorganisation of stimulus material is required, or attention is divided. These deficits may be related to the normal trade-off in working memory of limited processing capacity between different control processes becoming problematic at lower levels of demand. This may be due to reduced capacity, or the same capacity being less efficiently used. Finally, retrieval time from primary memory has been shown to be increased in older subjects (Waugh, Thomas and Fozard, 1978).

Secondary Memory

Secondary memory, which is the major memory function relevant to day-to-day adjustment, has been the focus of the bulk of research. This research has now become extremely sophisticated in its methodology and has led to interesting insights. Various modalities of sensory input, the relationship between self-organised and externally-organised sorting of material, and various retrieval models, of recall and recognition, have been investigated. The crucial difference between the previous types of memory and secondary memory is in the level of processing: in secondary memory some deeper processing or encoding of the information is thought to have occurred.

There is overall evidence of memory loss with advancing age, which can reach substantial levels, particularly when free recall is required (Botwinick, 1978). However, when the details of such loss are investigated, interesting pointers emerge which are of relevance to possible clinical intervention. If we look at the acquisition of information, there is evidence that the elderly are especially poor when in unfamiliar surroundings and under stress. A study of Leech and Witte (1971) attempted to create a non-demanding but relevant atmosphere and found memory efficiency increased. If some guidance is given on the organisation of the material presented or in developing mediational strategies, it can assist the elderly, particularly if verbal rather than visual mediators are used.

Assessing learning by recognition rather than free recall reveals less deficit (e.g. Perlmutter and Mitchell, 1982) but especially if guessing rates are taken into account recognition memory *is* poorer in the elderly (Harkins, Chapman and Eisdorfer, 1979). Elderly people benefit from cues which assist retrieval (e.g. Laurence, 1967; Hultsch, 1975) but Drachman and Leavitt (1972) were unable to show that older people were differentially helped by them.

Conceptualising the poorer performance of older people on secondary memory tasks as reflecting *either* an acquisition deficit *or* a storage deficit *or* a retrieval deficit is probably not useful. Craik's concept of levels of processing is increasingly used in attempts to describe the impairment (Craik, 1977). The strength of a memory is argued to depend on the strength of processing carried out on it. Shallow encoding would be in terms of the item's physical characteristics; deep levels (semantic encoding) relate to the item's meaning. It has been suggested that younger subjects are superior at deeper levels of processing, as evidenced on tests of incidental learning (i.e. where the memory task is unexpected).

It seems that elderly people are able to encode material semantically (e.g. Barrett and Wright, 1981), however they fail to carry this out spontaneously in an efficient manner. In particular, elderly people encode material more generally, in terms of global semantic features, and less of the specific, unique features of the item or its context are encoded (Rankin and Kausler, 1979; Rabinowitz and Ackerman, 1982). This failure to encode affects both acquisition and retrieval, if it is assumed that retrieval cues are generated at the time of encoding.

It should be pointed out that there are large individual differences. Bowles and Poon (1982) showed a bimodal distribution of scores in the elderly on a recognition task. One group of elderly people had comparable performance to the younger group; the other was markedly impaired (and had lower verbal ability generally). Zacks (1982) similarly found a sub-group of elderly people who performed as well as younger adults; they used active encoding strategies, whereas the relatively impaired elderly subjects passively registered each item as it was presented.

Why do some elderly people *not* actively encode spontaneously? One suggestion is that attentional resources (or 'mental energy') are reduced in some older people; automatic processes are left relatively unimpaired, but deliberate, conscious, effortful processes are much more affected (Craik and Byrd, 1982). On this basis recognition memory is less impaired, as it has a larger automatic processing component (a judgement of familiarity). Tasks involving automatic processing — even at 'deep' or semantic levels — are less impaired than tasks involving effortful, reconstructive processes — e.g. free recall (Howard, McAndrews and Lasaga, 1981).

Remote Memory. Remote (or very long-term) memory has been suggested as a separate process. It may relate to important strategies of adjustment to life events from early in life. Such memories may be of more substantial importance than previously thought since their influence on life satisfaction in the elderly may be great (e.g. Simpson *et al.*, 1981). Reminiscence, the ability to recall and 'mull over' past events, may well be a useful immunising agent against depression. It seems that the small amount of research which exists suggests that such memories remain accessible even into extreme old age. Botwinick and Storandt (1980) looked at memories for past events going back 60 years and found little loss in acuity for major happenings in childhood. There was no difference between age-groups in the greater difficulty of recall as compared with recognition. Warrington and Sanders (1971) covered a more restricted time period, and tested recall of both events and faces from the past, and suggested old people were certainly not superior in their remote memory. There are difficulties in developing adequate tests of remote memory. Matching the difficulty level of events or faces across decades, ensuring equal likelihood of exposure to the event when it occurred, ensuring the memory has not been practised or rehearsed (especially in the case of personal information) can all be problematic.

Metamemory. Metamemory is the person's knowledge of their memory functioning. Several studies have recently examined age-differences in metamemory: Murphy, Sanders, Gabriesheski and Schmitt (1981) found no age differences in the accuracy of predicting what size span of common objects could be recalled. Older subjects were less able however to judge when they were ready to recall items; younger subjects studied the objects longer, and recalled more. When older subjects were forced to study the objects for an extended period, their recall improved greatly. Bruce, Coyne and Botwinick (1982) found that older people overestimated the number of words they could recall, but did not find a greater study time in the elderly. Bruce *et al.* suggest that, despite their own concern about memory decline, their elderly subjects' metamemory had not kept pace with changes in their performance. It is likely that memory-monitoring, judging the optimal amount of time for a study of material to be remembered, is task and material specific. It may vary according to the degree of interest in the material and the subjects' motivation.

Language

Remarkably little research indicates the effects of ageing on language abilities. Walker (1980) reports data on a normal elderly sample on the Schuell Minnesota Aphasia Test. On a number of aspects of the test normal elderly people seemed to be more impaired with increasing age, but much of these apparent deficits could be related to other aspects of function being poorer (e.g. numerical ability).

Albert (1980) suggests a number of changes occur. Speech discrimination and comprehension of spoken language are thought to deteriorate. Older people tend to use longer, more complex sentences. Word finding and naming may also be poorer. In a naming test, Goodglass (1980) showed that elderly people made semantic errors — e.g. giving the name of another object of the same category — and that they tended to be circumlocutory — e.g. saying something about the object when its name was not forthcoming. Misperceptions of objects were also relatively common in older subjects.

Rabbitt (1981a) reports some fascinating explorations of factors influencing older people in group conversations, which particularly reflect the role of memory in natural language interactions. Elderly people remembered what had been said in a small group conversation, but had great difficulty in remembering who said what and to whom. If the older person joined in the conversation they might remember their reply and the question that prompted it, but then be less aware of earlier statements made by other group members. Rabbitt shows how this could lead to the elderly person either dominating the group, changing the topic, ignoring other people's contributions, or, alternatively, remaining a silent presence on the fringe of the group. Dialogues, where the rate of information exchange is under the elderly person's control, are much less problematic, with far fewer problems of attention switching and information overload.

Summary

1. No completely satisfactory methodology is available for assessing 'normal' age changes in cognitive function. Cross-sectional, longitudinal and cross-sequential methods all have drawbacks.

2. Allowing for methodological difficulties, it seems that the extent of cognitive decline with age has been over-estimated in the past. Decline on most functions does not begin until the age of 60 or so, not at the age of 25 as cross-sectional studies might suggest.

3. Individual differences in pattern of change are large. A stereotyped view of inevitable decline in all abilities in all individuals is mistaken. Changes may vary in extent from generation to generation. Different abilities may change at different rates.

4. A number of factors influence cognitive performance. Physical and mental health and sensory loss are of particular importance. Motivational factors related to the relevance of test materials must also be considered.

5. Slowing of speed of information processing is often considered an important aspect of cognitive change with age. The elderly person's control processes are increasingly being seen as relevant to this slowing; strategies for compensating for reduced efficiency are being investigated.

6. Memory changes are relatively small, and particularly affect secondary memory. Primary memory is less impaired and remote memory also seems intact.

7. The causes of reduced function in elderly people are many and varied and cannot be attributed simply to a general ageing process.

3 A HAPPIER OLD AGE — CHANGES IN PERSONALITY AND ADJUSTMENT

Introduction

It is extremely difficult to draw clear lines of distinction between cognitive and personality variables in any age-group. Inevitably, personality characteristics will affect cognitive performance; for instance, cautiousness and rigidity influence performance on problem-solving tasks. Cognitive ability affects the individual's ability to adjust and adapt successfully to their environment. As with cognitive function, myths abound in relation to changes in personality, coping skills and adjustment. Expectancies of an increase in introversion, a withdrawal from the environment, increased emotional instability, all are found in the generally negative evaluation of the elderly personality. Butler and Lewis (1973) have written at length about 'ageism' and the problems of the interaction between a negative evaluation of the aged and their role in society.

As far as the psychologist is concerned, the definition of age-related changes in personality is not at all easy. The same methodological difficulties which arise in relation to studies of cognitive change may influence results (see Chapter 2). It is even more difficult to separate out age-related trends from those with a cohort or cultural influence where the more diffuse variables of personality are concerned. The techniques of personality assessment are subject to problems of validity in the aged. There are few, if any, age-appropriate measures for the elderly, and the existing measures do not easily transfer across age-ranges. Theoretical formulations are also not readily extended to cover the whole age span.

In this chapter we will attempt to outline the work which has been carried out on personality and adjustment changes since they are crucial to the work of the clinical psychologist. Whilst attempts to use techniques grounded in childhood or early childhood may have proved unfortunate, there are interesting developments arising from newer theoretical models combining cognitive and social theories.

59

Personality Change

The literature on personality change with advancing age follows a similar pattern to that on cognitive change. The great majority of studies use cross-sectional methodology. Most use the personality assessment equivalent of the intelligence test, the major personality questionnaires. Most date from before the advent of cross-sequential methodologies. Most studies cover well the adult age-range from 20 to 60, have fewer subjects in the 60—70 group and are very weak in extreme old age (Neugarten, 1977).

How relevant are these major personality inventories to the aged? This topic is discussed in detail by Savage, Gaber, Britton, Bolton and Cooper (1977) and by Lawton, Whelihan and Belsky (1980) and is considered further in Chapter 7. They are generally based on item pools derived from work on normal adults. Most inventories seem to be derived from the same source pool of questions, whether from the Minnesota, Cattell or Eysenck schools. A close examination of the questions used raises many queries about their relevance in extreme old age.

Items are often inappropriate in language or content to the social and environmental context of the aged. The same question could relate to different aspects of personality in different age cohorts. Some of the many factors influencing personality questionnaire responding, such as social desirability biases, may not operate in the same fashion in different age cohorts. Indeed, the general attacks on trait-based measures (Mischel, 1968) may be even more appropriate to assessment in the aged.

The continued use of these questionnaires has been defended, for example by Hogan, De Soto and Solano (1977) and Lawton *et al.* (1980). They emphasise that care is required in interpretation of results, as normative data and validity are either non-existent or less reliable in the elderly.

The results from these studies may be summarised as showing a general stability in personality (Neugarten, 1977). In the few cross-sequential studies age changes have been relatively small (Schaie and Parham, 1976). The changes which do occur tend to be towards social withdrawal and introversion. Once again individual variability in scores is great and tends to increase with age.

On the Minnesota Multiphasic Personality Inventory (MMPI) Calden and Hokanson (1959) found higher scores in the elderly on Hypochondriasis, Depression and the Social-introversion scale.

Swenson (1961) and Britton (1967) present data on non-hos-
pitalised or community elderly which suggest relatively similar
findings of an increased bias towards anxiety-related scales and
more Social Introversion.

Savage (1981) reports very little work with the elderly on the
Eysenck scales. He suggests that the few studies which have been
published tend *not* to support any general swing towards increased
introversion in old age, contrary to the initial finding of Gutman
(1966) on the Maudsley Personality Inventory.

The Cattell scales, notably the Sixteen Personality Factor
Questionnaire (16PF) in its various forms, have been extensively
used in studies on the elderly. One of these is worth specific
comment since it presents rare longitudinal personality data. Costa
and McCrae (1978) administered the 16PF to adult males in a study
where initial assessments were carried out between 1965 and 1967.
Several other scales were also used in this extensive study which
employed the combined A and B forms of the 16PF — a formid-
able array of questions! The 16PF was again included in a ten-year
follow-up of the sample. Analysis of their results suggests an
overall stability of personality. They suggest that 'When longer,
and thus more reliable, scales are used, measuring the broader
dimensions of general anxiety and extraversion, stability coeffi-
cients reach the 0.80 mark'. Savage *et al.* (1977) also report on
16PF findings for an elderly group. Their subjects over 70 differed
from the Cattell norms by a general tendency towards introversion
and social withdrawal. Again, this relatively well-preserved community sample showed very little change in personality across an
age span from 70 to death.

Attempts have been made to use other types of personality
measure with the elderly. An extensive review of the use of projective measures is given by Kahana (1978). Whilst drawing
attention to the difficulties of applying standard administration
and scoring protocols, it is suggested that these tests may be satisfactorily completed by the elderly. Various tests are reviewed and
some studies report age-related trends. As with questionnaire
measures, changes in personality do not appear to be major as age
advances. However, we share the doubts expressed by Savage
(1973) concerning the validity of such techniques.

What may we conclude from these investigations? It would
appear that there is a general stability in personality in the ageing
individual with no gross changes. The personality measures which

have been employed suggest an increase in introversion and a degree of social withdrawal. These may be artifacts of the application of tests designed for younger persons; the questions may be inappropriate. The clinical implications of these results are clear. Excessive change in personality variables is *not* a reasonable expectation in the normal elderly. If such change is observed it is likely to reflect significant abnormality, or perhaps, the total irrelevance of the test to the individual.

This latter point is of importance. The reader will note that there is little or no literature on the use of personality measures in extremes of normal ageing. There is, for example, no literature comparable to the pre-death decline in cognitive function. Personality measures usually break down when faced with acute sensory deficit or motivational problems.

Personality Development, Adjustment and Life Satisfaction

The 1960s saw attempts to integrate the observed personality changes into coherent models. Two main themes emerged and — as is quite common in early developments in theoretical integration — they tended to produce a polarised situation. One emphasised withdrawal from the environment, *disengagement* as a primary need in successful adjustment, the other continued *activity*. Both recognised withdrawal and introversion as being the trend. Activity theory saw this as leading to poor adjustment, whereas in disengagement theory it was thought to lead to increased life satisfaction.

The disengagement theory originated in the Kansas City studies of ageing and emerges in a book by Cumming and Henry (1961). It suggests that the ageing person disengages from active involvement in the environmental and social systems of stable middle age. A new relationship with others is sought which enables greater involvement with the self and less dependence on others, perhaps a reaction to decrease through death in the availability of significant others. This may even commence with the death of parents in middle age. Indeed the process could be seen in a formulation which suggests a transfer from reinforcement and satisfaction from external, overt reinforcers to internal, covert reinforcers (see the section on depression, Chapter 4). The process is seen as being a mutual withdrawal, with society reducing the availability of social roles for the elderly, by forcing retirement, restricting valued roles and so on.

Activity theory relates successful adjustment to the maintenance of activities which characterised middle-life satisfaction and to the development of new activities (Havighurst, 1968; Havighurst, Neugarten and Tobin, 1968; Neugarten, 1977). The stress on continued involvement emphasises a need for continuation of social reinforcers. Studies are quoted in support of activity theory which have found better adjustment in those with continued or developed social links and recreational opportunities in old age. For example, Schneider and Coppinger (1971) found optimal adjustment to be related strongly to the presence of 'people you like'.

Apparent support for various aspects of activity theory appeared in a large number of studies in the 1970s. Life satisfaction was correlated with various indices of involvement in social activities and of integration with the environment. For example, Palmore and Kivett (1977) evaluated participation in various activities, community and religious involvement, sporting interests, care of house and garden and concluded that life satisfaction was closely related to a high level of social activity.

Both theories have been subject to much analysis and criticism. Rose (1968) summarises some of the studies arguing against disengagement theory. He examines the concept of disengagement as a 'new' process in adjustment to the changes of ageing and presents a view which emphasises the continuity of the process throughout adult life. Disengagers may well disengage further in old age. He also suggests that the majority of studies contradict the theory, stressing that the active elderly have been consistently found to be happier. For example, Graney (1975) found well-being strongly correlated with activity measures.

It is probably futile to seek to show that one theory or the other holds for all elderly people. Individual differences have to be considered — both in personality and in circumstances. Most elderly people can be crudely categorised as 'active and happy' or 'inactive and unhappy', in line with activity theory. For a significant minority — probably a quarter — the predictions of disengagement theory seem to hold, with 'happy and inactive' and 'unhappy and active' groups being identified (Neugarten, 1977). Of some importance is to what extent the withdrawal is voluntary, rather, than enforced by circumstances — poor health, insufficient financial resources, death of friends, etc. (Lowenthal and

Boler, 1965). This sort of restriction can prevent elderly people who would like to be active from participating in the activities they would enjoy. Given identical conditions, lifelong personality variables become important in determining adaptation in old age. For instance, the introvert might well adjust optimally towards reinforcement from inner sources, whilst the extrovert may continue to need social stimulation.

The Structure of Personality

The first section of this chapter outlined some of the findings from attempts to apply personality measures to the elderly and the second section looked at some attempts to resolve models of adjustment. As with the study of cognitive change in the elderly, there have been many attempts to apply the statistical techniques of multivariate analysis to produce structures and typologies of personality change in ageing. If some themes could be extracted from the confusion of contrasting studies, then the clinician might be assisted in the identification of target populations for assistance.

This area has also reflected the development of statistical technique. It was even more evident, with the greater complexity of personality and personality measures, that some form of multivariate methodology was necessary to simplify the data and extract salient points. Various techniques of factor analysis have been used, more recently supplemented by cluster analysis. This technique concentrates on producing groupings of similar individuals, a potentially more useful technique to the clinician.

The Berkeley studies (Reichard, Livson and Peterson, 1962) isolated personality patterns in a sample of 87 elderly men, aged 55–84, of whom about half were retired, from 115 personality ratings. They suggested that there were five basic personality types, three of which were considered to be satisfactorily adjusted to age. The three well-adjusted groups were the 'mature', characterised by an integrated, stable personality, capable of adaptation to change, almost a 'supernormal' adjustment. The 'rocking chair' man tends to lie back and let the world go by, withdrawing from activities and relationships. 'Armoured' individuals maintain a satisfactory lifestyle and adjustment by a more positive defence against the changes of ageing, keeping very much to themselves. The two unsuccessfully adjusted groups were described as the 'angry men' and the 'self-haters'. The former were constantly at odds with their environment and others around them to the extent that other people tended to withdraw from interaction. The latter lived in a self-imposed exile of self-hate and depreciation, equally withdrawn.

These findings are reflected in the description by Neugarten, Havighurst and Tobin (1968) of four typologies typical of adjustment in the elderly. They were the 'integrated', 'passive dependent', 'defended' and 'disintegrated'. There are obvious similarities to the Reichard groupings.

Factor-analytic studies of tests such as the MMPI have provided further support for typologies similar to the above. Slater and Scarr (1964) applied the MMPI to a high status group of 211 individuals with a mean age of 66 years. Four significant factors emerged labelled 'ego weakness', 'extraversion/introversion', 'sensitivity' and 'dissociated personality'. When a detailed description of these factors and their constituent scales is analysed, they show similarity to the previous typologies. Britton and Savage (1966a) using the MMPI have also found similar results with a rather older group. One major factor reflected general adjustment, the second factor withdrawal and neuroticism, the third an 'aggressive–defensive' reaction. Similar findings are seen in studies using other measures such as the 16PF (Savage *et al.*, 1977). Gaber (1983) reports data on a community sample of 82 elderly people, with an average age of 80 years, on the 16PF. This sample were slightly atypical, in that they were the survivors of a previous sample drawn some years previously from the elderly population of Newcastle upon Tyne. Using cluster analysis to identify distinct groupings of individuals, four clusters with significantly different personality profiles emerged:

1. The 'normal' or 'silent majority' — roughly 54% who were satisfactorily adjusted to age. When compared to younger people they were more resistant to change, more apprehensive and intense and suspicious of the interference of others in their affairs. They could appear intolerant or calculating but this might represent an adaptive deliberate response giving time for evaluation of the problem, a long cool look before action.
2. An 'introverted' group of 20 per cent, very shy, reserved and self-contained, seeking little help from others. There were some inner tensions and a tendency to self-criticism.

3. A 'perturbed' group of 10 per cent of the population. These were suspicious, awkward people. They tended to have weak ego-strength and to get easily angry and uncontrolled. They had more than average personal problems and did not integrate well with others. In general they were a poorly adjusted, emotionally disturbed group.
4. The 'mature', 16 per cent of the sample, were exceptionally well adjusted. They appeared highly independent and self-sufficient, were very emotionally stable, shrewd and tough-minded.

This study went on to look at the self-concept and adjustment correlates of the above typologies. They found that, as expected, the 'mature' group showed better and more stable adjustment, with a decline in adjustment through to the 'perturbed' group. The normal and introverted groups had similar life-satisfaction scores, but the normal group emerged as being better socially adjusted.

A summary of investigations over roughly 20 years shows a remarkable consistency in findings; Reichard *et al.* (1962), Neugarten *et al.* (1968) and Gaber (1983) (and in Savage *et al.*, 1977) all present a similar picture. They identify a substantial group of the community as satisfactorily adjusted in personality terms (60—70 per cent) with a small, but significant, number who are extremely well adjusted. The poorly adjusted may be characterised by either aggressive outgoing 'hate the world' features or an equally maladaptive withdrawal.

These groupings have a significance for those involved with the aged. One important factor is their ready link with models of cognitive change, and the link with preserved intellectual factors. In most studies where intellectual and personality factors have been investigated, the same persons comprise the well preserved in *both* intellect and personality. It would appear that a balance between preserved and integrated features of long-term development and the ability to continue to adapt to new circumstances is crucial, to optimal adjustment and life satisfaction.

This is emphasised by Birren (1964) who defined personality in the aged as 'the characteristic way in which an individual responds to the events of adult life'. There were two main components of personality, he suggested; stable traits over the life span, and those traits which were capable of evolution and differentiation even into extreme old age. The successful balance between these was the crucial factor in successful ageing. This model has similarities to

Cattell's fluid and crystallised model of changes in intellectual abilities referred to in the previous chapter.

The 'mature' group are readily seen in contact with the elderly. Most workers 'on the ground' have been surprised at the 80-year-old who looks and acts 20 years younger, is the pillar of the community and a catalyst for development of services to the aged. Such people are interesting in their own right, but have a potential value far in excess of their personal features. They are an invaluable tool to the community and voluntary agencies who attempt to provide services to the elderly. In a time of notably reduced resources in economic terms, the elderly, like other groups, may have to be urged to help themselves rather than depending on 'them' or the State. The mature group if identified and recruited are an ideal peer catalyst for self-help groups, clubs and so on.

It is worth noting that the 'normal' group in personality typology are much like they were in late middle age. In personality, as in cognition, there are no dramatic overall changes in all individuals, rather subtle changes perhaps in introversion and rigidity. As with cognitive change there is individual variance which is more marked than in mature adulthood, and which requires further investigation and linking with causative factors. However, most of the elderly are not the self-centred hypochondriacal garrulous stereotype beloved of the myth-makers!

The problem groups identified by personality typology are also familiar to clinical psychologists and others working with the elderly. The perturbed group are usually self-evident. They are constantly around, in and out of surgeries, overtly demanding of care and resources. Indeed, one of their problems is that they may often be overdemanding to the extent that care agencies 'do not want to know' when something really serious happens. On the other hand the 'withdrawn' group are likely to be seriously ill before the milkman or a neighbour finally calls the police to break in. They may well have alienated family, neighbours and past-friends quite some time ago. If not made welcome, people stop visiting; if the invitations to the club are always rejected, they are no longer made. It can be very difficult for the care agent to make and maintain the necessary contact with these individuals.

Attempts to produce typologies of personality have led to consistent and potentially useful findings. The groups consistently isolated by studies have a meaning in practical terms and a link with the adjustment and cognitive literature. The crude typologies presently identified can be a valuable starting-point in our understanding of individual differences in personality among elderly people.

Theories of Adjustment

Some authors have attempted to develop cognitive theories of the ageing process. Thomae (1970) presents an integrative theory which attempts to get away from what he sees as the unfortunate concentration on negative aspects of the ageing process. Instead, he emphasises the positive aspects of individual adjustment and relates them to the person's cognitions, constructs and perceptions of the world around him. Thomae owes much to the background of Kelly, Rogers and others in his model, which unfortunately is not well developed when compared with other cognitive models, particularly those developed in relation to depression. A locus of control model was adopted by Kuypers (1972). He contrasted 'internalisers' and 'externalisers', the former feeling that they had control over life, the latter that 'they' control you. His study found internalisers to be more outgoing and adaptable, and to have higher levels of adjustment.

These approaches suggest a more hopeful model than the earlier restrictive models. The possibility of a positive and successful adjustment dependent on the characteristics of the individual is allowed for, one which takes into account individual need, society and environment. Indeed, it may well be that old age is not a time for defensive reaction to the onslaughts of a hostile world but potentially a time for growth, reconciliation and happiness. The model of Erikson (1963) is one of the few of the general personality theories which explicitly includes an attempt to encompass old age into its overall model. Different developmental tasks are seen as being important during different periods of the life span. For example, the achievement of intimacy is the task of young adulthood, contrasted with isolation if the development does not occur; generativity vs. stagnation is the task of mid-life. Ego-integrity vs. despair is the final of these eight 'stages of man'. This involves acceptance of past life, evaluating and restructuring what has been achieved and accomplished, coming to terms with the failures, disappointments, the missed opportunities that can never be replaced, and acceptance of the inevitability of death.

Recent studies (e.g. Palmore, Cleveland, Nowlin, Ramm and Siegler, 1979) have looked longitudinally at older people coping with common life-events, e.g. retirement, bereavement, illness, etc. A period of disorganisation may occur temporarily after the crisis, followed generally by adaptation to previous levels of functioning. Adaptation depends on the person's resources in a variety of areas — health, social, environmental and psychological. Indeed people with lower resources are generally more likely to experience life-events, at least in the short term.

Similarly Butler (e.g. Butler, 1975) has frequently referred to the considerable ability of most elderly people to come to terms with life-events, physical change, loss and so on, by active cognitive processes, such as reminiscence. The compensatory model is again relevant (e.g. Hussian, 1981). During life the person develops adaptive strategies for coping with stresses and problems. Reduced physical and/or sensory functions may themselves reduce adaptive capacity to some extent, as may social and environmental deprivations. These factors, together with the extent of the stress involved, play a part, then, in adjustment to the vicissitudes of old age. The person's psychological resources, coping skills, compensatory mechanisms and so on, may be sufficient to cope with many life-events, if they are well developed and if the other factors are not too unfavourable. Lazarus and DeLongis (1983) emphasise the importance of a longitudinal, process perspective on coping skills, and suggest that, whilst certain major sources of stress are more common in old age, there is little evidence for age differences in coping mechanisms.

Adjustment, Coping and the Environment

We have indicated previously that there is an interplay between cognitive and personality factors and the physical and social environment. There is little scope for simplistic models of adjustment in the elderly and much to say for the examination of models which examine coping strategies in a variety of circumstances. For example, problem-solving strategies may be relevant, as may the person's strategies for coping with bereavement, depression or possible death.

There has been increasing interest in the interaction between the elderly and their environment (see reviews by Newcomer and

Bexton, 1978; Danford, 1982). Models looking at the congruence between 'environmental press' (the combined influences of all the environmental resources) and the individual's competence, have been developed. Press can be negative (when it is akin to stress), neutral or positive (supportive). High levels of competence can combine with a broad range of environmental stress and produce adaptive behaviour; low levels of competence only produce adaptive behaviour at lower levels of environmental press, and the range of tolerance is greatly reduced. At all levels of competence, levels of press above *or* below the tolerance region can potentially produce maladaptive behaviour. A development of this model is the hypothesis that congruence between the person and their environment may be more important in some aspects of the environment than others, or that a mismatch in one area can be compensated for by a good fit in another.

Newcomer and Bexton (1978) summarise the relationship between the person's behaviour, the environment and their competence in the following equation:

$$B = P + I + N + S + PE$$

where   B = behaviour
        P = personal competence or capabilities
        I = interpersonal environment
        N = social norms, cultural environment
        S = supra-personal environmental features
       PE = physical environment

We shall consider the interpersonal environment later in this chapter. Some studies have examined the physical characteristics of the environment. For example Kazmar (1970) concentrated on the immediate environment (micro-environment), looking at room organisation, lighting, ventilation, heating, etc. Lansing, Maraus and Zehner (1970) moved into a broader environment (macro-environment), looking at the home in its context, the density of dwelling units, occupation by age, access to public transport, etc. Many more of this type of study followed in the 1970s and it became clear that these environmental characteristics were of importance, but that, as the above model indicates, individual differences in cognition and personality were strong determinants to the adjustment of the individual whatever the environment.

In considering the cultural environment, one concept which is currently being transferred from the area of concern with the mentally and physically handicapped to the elderly is that of 'normalisation'. Wolfensberger (1977) outlines a definition of this principle which emphasises the need for an appropriate socially valued environment. In handicap this approach has seen, in many countries, the strong emphasis on integration of the individual in as near a normal environment as follows. This avoids segregation in 'special' hospitals, units, schools or 'homes' often built in the most unsuitable places. Age- and culture-appropriate environments are stressed. A similar approach could be of considerable value in defining the environment of the elderly. Many of the same problems exist in current provision for the elderly. Housing and environment may be designed in a way which acts as a positive disincentive to continued involvement, adjustment and coping. A careful and intelligent application of normalisation principles could have much to offer provided that those involved learn from the handicap literature and avoid some of the perils of facile application of this principle.

The compensatory model has been discussed above, and provides a means of conceptualising how elderly people can cope with environmental change. For example, their micro-environment may change significantly. If moved to a new house, familiar objects may have to be sold, reducing stimulation and reward. Storage may be reduced, inducing conflict and memory load. Unfamiliar cooking and heating controls may be introduced, requiring significant adaptation of life-style. A recent client encountered just such a change from a traditional coal-fired 'range' to ultra-modern electric cooking and gas heating. Cooking required the acquisition of a whole new range of skills. The microprocessor-controlled heating system had a 'user-manual' seemingly written for graduate engineers! Given a systematic retraining within the limits of coping ability, this old lady is now back at home seemingly happy and adjusted. She had been admitted to hospital, depressed, undernourished and cold.

The macro-environment can change dramatically. An elderly man found that the introduction of a new road system and rapid transit railway effectively cut him off from shops and a community centre easily accessible previously. He was discovered by the police trying to cross the new, busy, four-lane inner-city road, a near suicidal move. A detailed analysis of environment enabled him to try alternative routes and shopping strategies leading to eventual readjustment.

There is little doubt that models of behaviour which emphasise the positive aspects of coping and adjustment are of importance in overcoming the common problems of the elderly. The compensatory model provides a useful basis for intervention, accounting as it does for both positive and negative adjustment, the diversity of individual differences, and the variable impact of environmental change.

The Interpersonal Environment and Adjustment

Family Support

In recent years the extent of family support for elderly disabled people has been highlighted many times (see Chapter 10). Current policies emphasise community care, which can become a euphemism for placing greater burdens on families. To what extent can the family be an environmental resource for the elderly?

A number of factors seem to be operating against family support. Smaller families, housing redevelopment that scatters long-established communities far and wide, the apparent tendency for children to live further from their parents, with increased mobility for education and employment, the greater employment prospects for middle-aged women, who traditionally have borne the brunt of caring for the elderly. In addition, with old people now being on average older, their children are themselves often past retirement age; 46 per cent of older people with children are great-grandparents.

There is evidence that despite these changes family support remains generally strong. In the United States, for example, Shanas (1979) reports that the family remains the major social support in times of illness, and that the extended family remains important in linking the elderly person to the community. Families may not live so close together, but very often remain in easy travelling distance, and visit regularly. The suggestion that succeeding generations of children will be less prepared to play a part in the care of their ageing parents is refuted by Brody, Johnsen, Fulcomer and Lang (1983). They report that 'values about family care of elderly adults have not eroded despite demographic and socio-economic changes'. They looked at attitudes of three generations of women (age-range 17–90) to care of the elderly. A majority of each generation agreed that adult children should be expected to help their parents with everyday activities and household tasks if needed. All agreed also that a working daughter should pay someone to help her parent rather than give up her own job. Brody *et al.* describe the notion that adult children do not take as much care of their parents as they did in the past as mythical; all three generations *thought* that this was indeed the trend.

Of course, this resource of family support is not available equally to all elderly people. For some the family may be a stress, relationships may be strained or difficult, there may be long-standing disagreements and feuds that leave scars of bitterness or guilt. A number have few remaining family contacts. Stevenson (1981) points out that Abrams' survey data on over-75-year-olds in England give pause for thought. For example, 45 per cent of those living alone were childless; two thirds of the women were either widowed, divorced or separated, and a further 18 per cent were spinsters. Less than a third had had a visit from any family member during the previous weekend.

The family is not then a panacea for all the problems of all elderly people, but it would be premature to write it off as a major support system, particularly at times of illness. In the UK there may be a slight tendency for there to be more reliance on formal support (social services, home helps, etc.) and less on family care than in the USA (Gurland, Copeland, Kuriansky, Kelleher, Sharpe and Dean, 1983).

Loneliness and Isolation

The extent to which elderly people feel lonely is another aspect of the available interpersonal resources. Generally elderly people do not complain that loneliness is a very serious problem for them. Responses to a national opinion poll in the USA (see Havighurst, 1978, pp. 34–5) showed that less than a fifth of over-seventies reported that not having enough friends was a very serious problem. This was, though, a rather higher proportion than in younger age-groups. Many more younger people mentioned loneliness as being one of the worst things about being over 65 than did the over-65s themselves. Poor health was seen as a much more significant problem by the elderly.

It is important to emphasise that loneliness and isolation are quite distinct concepts (Bergmann, 1978). A person may have few contacts but not feel lonely, or conversely have many social contacts, but complain of loneliness. Liang, Dvorkin, Kahana and Mazian (1980) have, for example, demonstrated that objective social integration (amount of interpersonal interaction, participation in organisations — clubs, churches, etc.) only relates indirectly to the person's morale. Subjective social integration (feelings of loneliness, having significant others) was directly related to morale, however.

The quality of the relationships is, of course, crucial. One close, confiding, intimate relationship may be worth any number of acquaintances. There have been suggestions that having a confidant (Lowenthal and Haven, 1968) or attachment bonds (Bergmann, 1978) may contribute to adjustment to the demands of ageing.

Personality variables are important. There may be aspects of the elderly person's personality or behaviour that have alienated family and/or friends. For example, potentially aggressive or withdrawn behaviour may discourage visits. Only recently have we helped to counsel a distressed relative, criticised by professionals and neighbours for deserting her uncle. The relative had once visited regularly, but eventually had tired of either being shouted at for not coming more often or being totally ignored, and had stayed away after being told 'never to come back'. Some elderly people have always been 'loners', having few social contacts. Gubrium (1975) suggested that single people, who had a long-term adjustment to isolation, may not be as susceptible to the negative effects of old age.

There is a distinct possibility that loneliness when it occurs will result in a reduction of motivation and stimulation which might lead to withdrawal and depression (Wilson, 1955). The Newcastle studies found loneliness to be a common precipitant of psychiatric illness, particularly anxiety states and depression (Garside, Kay and Roth, 1965). Fiske (1980) comments that it is where people blame themselves for their loneliness that mental-health problems are most likely. The person who has tried to form relationships and failed is most at risk. A fuller examination of this area by Ernst and Badash (1977) present a breakup of isolation into emotional, social, sensory and perceptual components. They suggest that different combinations may result in various psychiatric abnormalities.

In recent years sociologists and psychologists have attempted to examine the structure of the social context in detail. Network analysis has been the most common technique used. In such an analysis the focus is on the individual concerned and linkages are built up showing both the quantity and quality of interactions with others. These others include all contacts, formal and informal; doctor, social worker, priest, family, neighbours and friends. Successful adjustment is dependent on a network which provides social support, assistance with normal daily living, and crisis intervention (Snow and Gordon, 1980). The family, when available, has an important part to play but other systems may be necessary in short-term crises or when longer-term support becomes necessary. It is also obvious that cognitive and personality factors influence the individual's social links and eventual adjustment. When faced with a crisis, the elderly must have the cognitive skills to react appropriately and a personality that allows a working relationship to be formed with those who may respond.

Bereavement

Older people suffer multiple losses — mobility, physical health, work and so on. The loss of close friends or family members is particularly significant in changing the person's interpersonal environment. If the relationship has been of an intimate, confiding nature, the impact would be expected to be particularly great.

Most studies of bereavement have specifically excluded the elderly. However, the first report is now available of a longitudinal study of widowhood in elderly people (Gallagher, Breckenridge, Thompson and Peterson, 1983). Two months after the bereavement, levels of psychological distress were higher than in a comparison group, but only a small proportion were in the range consistent with serious psychopathology. Women reported greater distress than men, but this was paralleled in the comparison group. There was then no apparent sex difference related to the bereavement, and certainly no support for the suggestion that men would be differentially impaired. The results of follow-up of this sample at 12 and 24 months post-bereavement will be of great interest.

Other studies (reviewed by Averill and Wisocki, 1981) have suggested that grief tends to be more mild or 'flat' in older persons; that physical symptoms are more common, as are complaints of loss of purpose, and idealisation of the deceased. Heyman and Gianturco (1973) emphasise that adaptation to bereavement in the elderly can be remarkably good, with few changes in life-style and a stable social network. Their sample was, however, fairly small and unrepresentative. Many were greatly helped by their strong religious convictions.

In younger people, adjustment to bereavement is better when the death has been anticipated, rather than when it has occurred suddenly. The opportunity for anticipatory grief is thought to be helpful here. In older people anticipating grief seems to be potentially *harmful* (Averill and Wisocki, 1981); older widows have been found to adjust better to a sudden than to a lingering death. There are several factors possibly contributing to this. Firstly, death in the elderly is seldom a complete surprise; most elderly people anticipate death to some extent, and a 'sudden' death will be much less unexpected in an older than a younger person. Secondly, the stress of caring for a dying spouse may well affect the mental and physical health of the carer. They may throw themselves into the caring task, but in so doing lose many of the social supports that would be of value in adjusting to bereavement later. Caring for the dying spouse may become *the* purpose of life, and so the eventual death will be even more of a blow. Finally, some ambivalence is likely to result from wishing the dying person to be out of their misery, of feeling relief at the end, at the same time as not wanting to lose a lifelong partner. In our experience many of the abnormal grief reactions that we have treated follow a slow, lingering death. The treatment of abnormal grief reactions is discussed in Chapter 7.

Sexual Function

An often neglected aspect of elderly people's interpersonal relationships is their sexuality. Comfort (1980) states that 'human sexual response is normally life-long unless compromised by ill-health, anxiety or social expectation'. The general expectation that elderly people will not be sexually active is seen as a major factor in reduced sexual activity in the elderly. Surveys have suggested that there is a great deal of variation among elderly people in sexual interest and activity. In a longitudinal study (Pfeiffer, 1975a), men's sexual interest remained fairly constant over a ten-year period, whilst their activity level did decrease markedly. The availability of a capable partner emerged as the most important influence on sexuality in elderly females. As there are many more older women than men, this leads to reports of lower levels of sexual interest and activity in older women than in older men. Detailed figures from the various surveys can be found in Corby and Solnick's (1980) review. The interpretation of interview data regarding sexuality is always complicated by response biases, attitudinal factors and so on. Changes in attitudes in different generations render cross-sectional data suspect; even responses given longitudinally may be influenced by changes in prevailing social attitudes, and so may not accurately reflect actual changes in behaviour. What is clear is that sexual function *can* continue into extreme old age (e.g. over 20 per cent of a sample of Danish men aged 80–95 reported continued masturbation), that it does continue for a significant proportion of the elderly, but that for a variety of reasons other elderly people show reduced activity and/or interest. Continuity seems to be the rule in this area, as in others. Past sexual interest, frequency and enjoyment are the best predictors of current function in elderly men. In elderly women past sexual enjoyment is most highly correlated with current sexuality.

Physiological changes do occur (Corby and Solnick, 1980). Hormonal changes in women lead to tissue and lubrication changes that may make intercourse painful, and increase the risk of vaginal infection. No major changes affecting orgasmic capacity have been identified; clitoral response is essentially unchanged. In older men, reaching a full erection takes longer, but once achieved it can be maintained for longer periods before ejaculation occurs. The refractory period, after ejaculation before another erection is possible, is much increased in older men.

Health does affect sexual functioning in men. At least some of these influences are psychologically mediated. For example, many patients with heart disease report abstention from intercourse — in part due to fear of sudden death. In fact the risk of intercourse-related death is extremely slight in these patients. Diabetes does, however, appear to have a direct effect on male sexual function. Various drugs may also impair sexual performance, but these effects are highly idiosyncratic (Comfort, 1980).

There is then generally no reason why, given appropriate circumstances, sexuality cannot continue to be a rewarding part of life for the elderly person. Personality variables will play a part in influencing continued function; for example, men with a tendency to anxiety are more likely to develop impotence through 'fear of failure' following the slower erection reported with age.

Retirement

Work can be a major source of stress or of reward for the older person. Debates concerning flexible vs. compulsory retirement (e.g. Palmore, 1975) seem likely to bear little fruit in the employment market of the 1980s, where there will clearly be insufficient jobs for some considerable time. Flexibility may emerge from being able to retire earlier, but the prospect of significantly more members of elderly people working beyond retirement age seems remote. There is little evidence to link retirement with mental illness, but retirement does seem to lead to a reduction in well-being and morale, usually of a temporary nature (Fiske, 1980). Increased physical health is claimed by some people following retirement. Ekerdt, Bosse and Locastro (1983) demonstrated that this was an increase in functional or subjective health, and was not substantiated by longitudinal data. These reports of increased health tended to be made by men who had had a great deal of strain and many role demands in their jobs. The nature of the work, the person's perception of their job and their health status will all influence adjustment to retirement.

Retirement generally can be planned for; a sudden redundancy may accordingly be much more stressful. Personality variables are again important; a tendency to self-blame or to focus on unattained life-goals have been related to poorer adjustment to retirement. There are some suggestions in the literature that older women may become *more* psychologically stressed after retirement than older men (Fiske, 1980).

Religious Beliefs and Adjustment

For many elderly people religious convictions are an important source of support (Gaine, 1978). Markides (1983) reports that church attendance is significantly related to life satisfaction in elderly people. It is not clear to what extent the social factor implicit in church attendance is of importance. The finding was independent of health status, a factor that often prevents elderly people who have been regular church-goers from continuing. It has been suggested that as people get older and approach death they become more religious. Clearly cross-sectional data cannot confirm this, and only time will tell whether current elderly people have a particularly strong religious commitment.

Most of the world's major religions have an important component related to coping with bereavement and death. This area of attitude and belief is not easy to investigate or define in precise terms, but clinical experience indicates that a religious belief may positively and significantly influence adjustment.

Summary

1. Current models of personality assessment suggest that there are no dramatic changes in personality in the elderly. At most there is an increase in introversion and a degree of social withdrawal. Variability between individuals is likely to increase, however.

2. Models such as disengagement and activity theories related extremes of life-style and coping strategies to successful ageing. They have been replaced by models stressing the diversity of adjustment found among elderly people.

3. Personality typologies of elderly people identify a group of 'supernormal' elderly people. The majority of elderly people have a reasonable level of adjustment. Personality problems and poor adjustment do occur, but are not inevitable.

4. Most current models stress the need for a combination of cognitive, personality and physical/social environment to be considered in any attempt to predict adjustment and life satisfaction.

5. Family support for the elderly remains a major factor, particularly at times of illness. Loneliness is not seen as a major problem by most elderly people; it should be clearly distinguished from isolation; the quality of relationships experienced is of prime importance.

6. Elderly people suffer multiple losses, but bereavement may not have such a great impact on older people as it would on a younger person. The effects of caring for a loved one in a long term terminal illness may be particularly severe for elderly people, however.

7. Physical changes in sexual function are far outweighed by psychological changes. Continuity is important in predicting higher levels of sexual activity in late life.

4 ABNORMAL AGEING

Introduction

In Chapter 1 we reviewed the extent and nature of the major mental-health problems encountered in elderly people. In this chapter we will examine in detail psychological changes associated with the two most common problems — dementia and depression. We will review preliminary formulations of psychological models of these disorders and draw attention to some psychological aspects of other disorders affecting many elderly people. As we have seen previously, these problems are not normal manifestations of an ageing process; elderly people experiencing them are statistically abnormal. The effects of 'ageing' alone cannot be a sufficient explanation for these disorders.

Psychological Functions in Dementia

In Chapter 1 we saw that there are some interesting developments in the neurochemistry and neuropathology of dementia which suggest some models for aspects of the disorder. Psychological research into various types of dementia has been concerned with the definition of the nature, scope and extent of the fundamental cognitive deficits. Interest has moved from the gross aspects of change to attempts to attain a clearer understanding of specific deficits. The ultimate aim is a clarity of definition which will assist in management of the disorder.

Psychological studies of the dementias range in complexity from the straightforward administration of standardised tests of cognitive abilities through to experimental studies. The latter span the various possible functions in ever increasing sophistication, and we will look at their methodology and findings in this section. An interesting aspect of these studies is the lack of interaction, until recent years, between those studying the 'pre-senile' dementias and the 'senile' dementias. There have been gaps in the past in the transfer of ideas and methodology between those working from neurological and psychogeriatric bases in approaching these problems.

Cognitive Change in Dementia

That there is an overall cognitive change in dementia has been known and shown in the literature for many years (Savage *et al.*, 1973). Indeed cognitive deterioration is an essential component of the diagnosis of dementia. The task addressed by investigators over the past 40 years has been to define the details of the changes observed.

The early work in this area is well summarised by Inglis (1958) in a review of work on cognitive deficit in elderly psychiatric patients. He concluded firstly that senile dementia patients have poorer intellectual functioning than normal or psychotic elderly people and that, secondly, there is evidence of a verbal–performance IQ discrepancy in cases of dementia. Verbal and performance abilities were said to change at different rates, performance deteriorating more quickly. A point of interest in many early studies is the evidence that verbal and, particularly, vocabulary abilities were subject to deterioration in dementia (e.g. Orme, 1955). This finding contrasts with those in normal ageing when similar abilities decline but little except in extreme old age or in the pre-death period (see Chapter 2).

Many investigations attempted to define the pattern of change in more detail, but were generally unsuccessful. Brody (1942) and Halstead (1943) showed that the changes occurring were overwhelming and so diffuse that, to quote Brody, 'there is no trace of a specific pattern of abilities in dementia'. Perhaps these studies had run into problems with 'floor effects' in the tests they used. A more experimental study from the same era by Margaret Eysenck (1945) used specific tests related to the low level of functioning expected in the demented group. She showed much poorer functioing in the demented group on tasks such as abstract reasoning and fewer differences on tests involving 'the reactivation of past experiences and knowledge'.

It is useful to look at this early work since many of the more specific and larger scale studies of the past two decades have run into similar problems and produced similar results. Reviews by Savage *et al.* (1973) and Miller (1977a) cover this area in detail, summarising work with both the WAIS and the Raven's Progressive Matrices/Mill-Hill Vocabulary Scale combination. Both suggest consistent patterns of decline with the performance IQ decline exceeding the decline in verbal IQ.

These results have been interpreted in terms of the distinction between fluid and crystallised intelligence. Demented people are seen as being particularly impaired on tasks tapping fluid intellectual ability, tests of abstract reasoning, novel situations involving flexibility of thought and so on. Is the pattern of change then identical to that seen in normal ageing?

As Whitehead (1973a) shows, the *pattern* of impairment on the WAIS subtests is certainly similar to that shown by normal elderly people, and this is supported by the data presented by Savage *et al.* (1973) and Miller (1977a). Vocabulary scores are highest, followed by other over-learned verbal tasks and digit-span. Lowest scores are obtained on performance tasks. One must however be quite cautious about detailed interpretation since the low level of overall performance on some WAIS subtests puts their reliability into doubt.

It is apparent that there is a deficit on *all* subtests, including vocabulary, and this has led some, including Botwinick (1978), to suggest that the patterns of decline in dementia and normal ageing are therefore qualitatively different.

Diagnostic indices based on combinations of different WAIS subtests have sought to use the patterns of subtest impairment to discriminate dementing from normal elderly people. Wechsler's Deterioration Quotient is probably the best-known example (Wechsler, 1958). It is unclear whether these indices were intended to reflect a 'normal' ageing deterioration or a dementia-related pattern of change. Given the similarity between these patterns of change it is not perhaps very surprising that they are in fact unreliable and ineffective diagnostic indicators (Bolton *et al.*, 1966).

The verbal–performance discrepancy might seem to be a more hopeful index, but there is considerable variation among dementing patients (Savage *et al.*, 1973; Semple, Smith and Swash, 1982) and again it proves to be of little use diagnostically. It seems to be only too easy when considering tables of the *average* performance of groups of dementing patients to forget that dementia is a continuing process. Any group of patients will consist of individuals who in earlier life had quite different levels of intellectual function. Many will not have had identical performance and verbal levels *before* the onset of the disease. When assessed, the dementia will have been going on for different amounts of time. The group will probably include a mix of different types of dementia; some patients will have a mixed type of dementia.

There have been surprisingly few attempts to examine cognitive change in dementia longitudinally, despite these considerations, and the clinical evidence that patients change at grossly different rates. Partly this reflects the inadequacy of the available assessment measures, which are often insensitive at low levels of functioning and difficult to use repeatedly. One of the few studies following dementing patients over a time period is reported by Whitehead (1977). Dementing patients showed increasing impairment over a one-year period on several cognitive tests. As yet relatively little is known about the development of various aspects of cognitive dysfunction in the course of a dementing illness, although, as we shall see below, this is of considerable theoretical interest.

Memory Deficit in Dementia

The previous section has suggested that there are specific cognitive deficits in dementia as well as an overall general decline in cognitive abilities. Many have identified difficulties in learning and memory as among the earliest signs of dementia. Study of various aspects of the memory process is leading to a far better understanding of its importance in the pattern of deficit found in the disorder.

Many methodological problems face the investigator in this area. So pervasive are the effects of dementia that most cognitive tests or experimental procedures will show some form of impairment when dementing patients are compared with normal controls. What is of greater interest is the identification of different conditions which facilitate or reduce the dementing person's memory performance. It should be noted that studies typically do *not* include a representative sample of dementing patients. Those with a more severe degree of dementia are often unable to co-operate sufficiently with the experimental procedures employed. Results reported are usually then for less severe cases, in some instances including only younger patients (e.g. many of Miller's experimental studies).

A number of studies have attempted to define the extent of impairment in different aspects of the memory process. The conception of memory prevalent at the time of the study obviously constrains the experimental design. As we saw in Chapter 2, current work seems to accept that short-term and long-term memory represent two separate stages in the handling of information.

Short-term or primary memory is held to have a limited capacity and a limited span of time for which information can be held. Long-term or secondary memory has a greater (possibly almost infinite) capacity and a possibly indefinite ability to hold information over time.

Many early studies assumed a sequential flow of information from the environment, through sensory registers to a short-term store, a temporary working memory. A response could be made from this store and/or information passed into the permanent memory store, long-term memory (Atkinson and Shiffrin, 1971). More recently (e.g. Craik, 1977) the possibility of information passing directly into secondary memory has been recognised, and remote memory, or tertiary memory, has been distinguished as an important aspect of secondary memory. Craik (1977) emphasises that theoretically the length of time elapsed between acquisition and retrieval does not change the properties of secondary memory, whether the memory was laid down ten minutes or ten years ago. Remote memory is of particular interest in cases of acquired memory disorder, where at some point in time the person's ability to acquire new information has deteriorated.

Other conceptualisations and distinctions have been made. Not all are mutually exclusive. Craik and Lockhart's (1972) 'levels of processing' model focuses on the extent of encoding carried out on the incoming information, from the superficial (physical attributes) to the deep (the meaning of the material). There is growing emphasis on the person actively working on the input, not simply being a passive recipient. Working memory (Baddeley, 1981) is seen as the locus for some of this activity. Information is not acquired in a vacuum; the person is seen as relating new material to his/or her current knowledge of the world, his or her semantic memory. Contextual or temporal cues may be 'tagged' to the memory for a particular event, aiding in its later recall, reflecting episodic memory. The research on memory in dementia will be summarised according to the four major stages, with other aspects being drawn out where appropriate.

Sensory Memory. There have been few studies with dementing patients of this pre-perceptual memory store of extremely brief duration. This is probably a reflection of impairment in the other cognitive skills that are required for the person to be tested on the tasks that are usually used with younger subjects. Miller (1977b) used a backward masking technique, where subjects have to report as many as possible of a row of six letters presented tachistoscopically for a very brief time interval (50–250 milliseconds), followed by 'visual noise' (a random array of black and white squares) to prevent a figural after-effect. Dementing subjects needed longer presentation times before any letters could be repeated, and repeated less letters than controls at each exposure period. Moscovitch (1982) also reports data (from Schlotterer, 1977) on a backward masking procedure, comparing patients with Alzheimer's disease with old and young normal controls. Two types of mask were used. One, a flash of light, is thought to act peripherally; the other, a pattern of lines, is thought to operate centrally. Dementing patients showed little impairment when the mask was a flash, compared with normal elderly people. Moscovitch suggests that this reflects the sparing of the sensory cortex in dementia. There was an impairment with the patterned mask in dementia; patients needed longer intervals between stimulus and mask to identify correctly the stimulus letter. This may be due to this mask's effects occurring later in the visual system, closer to those areas of the cortex known to be dysfunctional in dementia. Moscovitch also reports a further experiment indicating unimpaired visual sensitivity compared with normal old people, again emphasising the integrity of the peripheral stages of vision. Similarly colour discrimination is impaired, but brightness discrimination is normal.

The implication of these findings is that, although sensory systems may be intact in dementia, at a fairly early stage in the processing of information impairments may begin to occur. To what extent these deficits contribute to dysfunctions at later stages of processing is unclear.

Primary Memory (PM). Digit-span — the number of digits the subject can recall in correct sequence immediately after presentation — is usually thought to reflect the capacity of primary memory. Most studies indicate that there is some impairment of digit-span in dementia, although compared to other abilities it may appear well-preserved (Savage *et al.*, 1973). Kaszniak, Garron and Fox (1979) confirmed this deficit in patients whose diagnosis of dementia was supported by CAT scan evidence, and Corkin (1982) showed reduced digit-span performance in Alzheimer's disease patients of all severities when compared with normal elderly controls or global amnesic patients. A discrepant finding emerges from Weingartner, Kaye, Smallberg, Ebert, Gillin and Sitaram (1981). Their dementing subjects performed if anything *better* on both digit-span forwards and backwards tasks than normal elderly controls. Sampling differences between the various studies may explain this contradictory result. Matching for pre-morbid intelligence levels is of some importance, but can be difficult to achieve, for instance. Other types of span test have been used. Dementing patients are reported to be impaired on both word-span (Miller, 1973) and block-span — a non-verbal analogue of digit-span (Corkin, 1982).

Dichotic listening techniques have been thought to tap primary memory. Two sequences of digits are presented simultaneously to the subject, one to each ear. The subject is required to recall first from one ear, then the other. Normals and dementing patients show similar recall from the first ear, for lists up to three digits, but recall from the second ear, subject to a greater delay, is less in dementing patients (e.g. Inglis and Sanderson, 1961). Doubt has been cast on whether poor performance on this task does actually reflect a deficient primary memory, rather than a difficulty in divided attention (Craik, 1977).

A further method of investigating the efficiency of primary memory arises from experiments where subjects are presented with lists of words, each to be recalled immediately after its presentation. Normal subjects typically show a 'recency' effect. Words at the end of the list, presented most recently, are recalled more effectively than words in the middle of the list. Miller (1971) showed that, although dementing patients did tend to recall the most recently presented words more effectively than those earlier in the list, the effect was not nearly so marked as in normal controls. Two recent word-list studies have used a slightly different method of distinguishing which items are recalled from primary memory and which from secondary memory. Only words which were recalled before seven other words (presented *or* recalled) had intervened were considered to reflect primary memory. Using this methodology Moscovitch (1982) showed a small, but definite impairment in primary memory in Alzheimer patients. Wilson, Bacon, Fox and Kaszniak (1983a) similarly showed a mild deficit in Alzheimer-type patients. In their patient sample, but *not* in normal controls, primary memory and secondary memory were significantly correlated. Dementing patients performed worse than normals as soon as there were more than three other words between a word's presentation and its recall. Within primary memory there was a direct correlation between this lag and efficiency of recall. These results are interpreted by Wilson *et al.* as indicating that Alzheimer patients are inattentive, and that at least some of the generally much more dramatic secondary-memory deficit (see below) is related to primary memory impairment.

Corkin (1982) reports on forgetting from primary memory, using the Brown−Peterson distractor task. Here, subjects hear a consonant trigram, and recall it after a distraction task, in this case counting backwards for a specified time interval. Dementing patients showed much more rapid forgetting, even with only a three-second distraction period. Global amnesic patients showed significantly less forgetting at most time intervals up to 30 seconds.

Investigations are beginning into what processes underlie this seemingly well-established primary-memory deficit. Miller (1972) suggested that inefficient acoustic encoding may be an important factor. This arose from the observation that control subjects were *more* influenced and confused by acoustic similarities between words than were dementing patients. Unfortunately, the low scores of the dementing group may have led to a 'floor' effect, which could account for the observed interaction between subject groups and degree of acoustic similarity. Morris (1984) using Baddeley's (1981) working memory model has explored this issue further. In one experiment subjects were presented with lists of increasing length made up of letters of the alphabet. Some lists comprised letters with a high level of acoustic confusability; others were much less easy to confuse acoustically. During the presentation of some lists subjects counted repeatedly from 1 to 15. The results indicated that dementing subjects' performance level was worse overall, but that both these patients and normal elderly people were impaired by acoustic similarity and concurrent articulation. Further analysis indicated that the phonemic similarity effect was stronger in the control group, supporting Miller's proposal of inefficient acoustic encoding in dementia.

In a second experiment Morris used words of different lengths in place of letters. Dementing patients, like normal controls, recalled less of the longer words, but were not differentially affected in this respect. In both experiments the detrimental effects of concurrent articulation on dementing patients indicates the integrity of the articulatory loop system in working memory. However again dementing patients are not differentially impaired by concurrent articulation, which is at first sight surprising in view of the demands it makes in terms of divided attention. Possibly this particular secondary task may not be sufficiently demanding to highlight a defective central executive system. Morris points out that there is no evidence that dementing patients rely *more* heavily on the articulatory loop system to maintain performance in memory span tasks.

Secondary Memory (SM). A deficit in secondary memory is a common indicator of dementia. The difficulty in performing actions of everyday life which involve memory processes is a common sign that something is wrong as the individual (or their relatives) see the problem. There is an unexpected inability to recall a telephone conversation; the list is forgotten before the shops are reached; ingredients are omitted from commonly cooked dishes. The clinician and relatives of the dementing person are only too well aware of the insidious appearance and spread of the deficit.

The evidence from a variety of experimental studies converges to support this clinical observation, but goes further in seeking to understand what contributes to the evident breakdown of secondary memory. The serial position curve paradigm has been used a number of times; this was mentioned above in relation to primary memory, where items recalled from a word-list are thought to reflect either primary or secondary memory according to their position in the list. Typically normal subjects show greater recall of words at the beginning of the list, thought to represent words stored in secondary memory. Miller (1971) showed an almost complete absence of this 'primacy' effect in pre-senile dementia patients (as did Gibson, 1981, in older patients). Miller posed the important question of whether this secondary-memory deficit could be attributed, at least in part, to the deficit in primary memory. To test this possibility the experiment was repeated using a slower rate of presentation, to place less demands on the limited storage capacity of primary memory. Control subjects benefited greatly from this change, showing an even greater primacy effect. Dementing patients performed similarly poorly at both presentation rates, suggesting that the secondary-memory deficit is not simply a direct effect of the primary-memory impairment. However, Wilson *et al.* (1983a) did find some evidence relating the secondary-memory and primary-memory deficits. As mentioned above, in their control group primary memory and secondary memory were not significantly correlated, but they were related in the Alzheimer group. It may well be that dementing patients' performance on tests supposedly of primary memory may include a greater relative contribution from secondary memory than in non-dementing people. Also Miller's experiment reflected the then popular theory that information passed sequentially from primary memory to secondary memory, whereas it is now considered that information can also pass directly into secondary memory. The variability of dementing patients must also be emphasised. For example Diesfeldt (1978), in a further serial position curve experiment, showed that half his dementing sample *did* show a primacy effect; these same patients showed relatively good performance on a delayed recognition test, confirming the existence of some secondary-memory storage.

The second type of experiment where secondary-memory deficits have emerged uses 'supra-span learning'. Miller (1973) established each subject's word-span, then gave lists to be learned one, two or three words longer than the span, with up to ten learning trials being given. Dementing subjects were markedly impaired once again.

Paired-associate learning also clearly demonstrates the difficulty in secondary memory. Subjects are required to remember pairs of words, the first member of the pair acting as stimulus or prompt for recall of the second. Dementing patients are impaired on recall and recognition measures, taking more trials to learn to criterion, and are not able subsequently to re-learn identical word-pairs more quickly (Inglis, 1957). Similarly, Corkin (1982) showed Alzheimer patients to be impaired on both verbal and non-verbal paired associates. These deficits are particularly marked with words of low associability (e.g. bottle—comb). Wilson, Bacon, Kaszniak and Fox (1982a) showed that learning of word-pairs that are more closely related (e.g. North—South) taps both semantic memory (the person's network of verbal associations and knowledge) and episodic memory (memory for specific events). Learning of unrelated words tests only episodic memory.

This episodic-semantic memory distinction in secondary memory (proposed by Tulving, 1972) is proving useful in the study of amnesia (Warrington and Weiskrantz, 1982). Several further attempts have been made to apply the concept to memory in dementia. Clark (1980) used a lexical-decision task to assess subject's ability to access information in semantic memory. Dementing subjects were much slower in deciding whether letter-strings were words or not. A similar task was used by Moscovitch (1982) but words and non-words were repeated at varying lags from the initial presentation. Dementing patients showed similar improvements in reaction times to normal controls for lags of up to 29 items, but were quite unable to recognise which letter-strings had appeared previously. There seemed then to be some activation effect in semantic memory, that could not be addressed by episodic memory. Clark also found poor episodic memory, when the words previously presented were re-presented in a recognition paradigm. The suggestion is made that the slower search rate in semantic memory may hinder episodic processes of encoding and storage. Weingartner *et al.* (1981, 1982) provide further evidence supporting this view. They showed that dementing patients were not helped in a free recall task by the words being semantically related rather than being selected at random, even when related words were arranged together in clusters. With repeated learning trials a similar picture emerged, and dementing patients, unlike controls, appeared to impose no organisational structure on the word-lists. Dementing subjects were as able as normal controls to sort the words correctly into categories, but were unable to use these relationships in encoding and organising events in memory. Verbal fluency (see below also) was used as a measure of the extent to which subjects could access semantic memory. Patients produced fewer words starting with a particular letter and words belonging to a particular category (being particularly impaired on the latter task). These measures were highly correlated with the memory measures. Weingartner *et al.* (1981) postulate that dementing patients have difficulty in accessing semantic memory, being unable to produce rich and detailed semantic relationships and associations. Their memory traces are less meaningful or elaborated, and accordingly are weaker, and so more easily disrupted and forgotten.

Encoding by dementing patients has been examined in several studies. Miller (1977a) reports no evidence for distorted encoding in pre-senile patients, but Larner (1977) did find an encoding break-down in older patients. Corkin (1982), employing Craik and Lockhart's (1972) levels of processing model, found, as predicted, that normal elderly subjects remembered more words about which they had previously made semantic judgements, than where sensory or phonological decisions were required. Dementing patients showed no effect of depth of processing, suggesting again a semantic encoding difficulty.

Normal elderly people in a verbal recognition memory task are more likely to recognise correctly rare words than common words, it perhaps being easier to associate relevant contextual cues to words the person is not continually encountering. Wilson, Bacon, Kramer, Fox and Kaszniak (1983b) showed if anything a higher correct recognition for common words in Alzheimer patients, that could not be explained simply by the patients' relatively low level of performance. However, patients also made more false recognitions of common words. Clark (1980), using a signal detection analysis that takes into account both correct answers and false alarms, showed that moderately impaired patients did perform better on rare words, although their performance was much worse than that of normal controls. Whether or not the rare word effect occurs in dementia, it is clear that rare words do not have sufficient impact to bring performance to anything like normal levels in clearly dementing patients.

The use of signal detection analyses of recognition tasks has been mentioned previously. In essence, they allow both measures of memory strength and of decision strategy to be made. The latter indicates how ready the subject is to guess; subjects may vary greatly in this, some only saying they have seen a word previously if absolutely certain, others responding to the faintest degree of familiarity. Several studies have shown that dementing patients adopt decision strategies showing little concern for accuracy (Miller and Lewis, 1977) and tending to be 'liberal' rather than cautious (Larner, 1977).

There has been some interest as to whether a retrieval deficit occurs in dementia i.e. does the dementing patient have difficulty in retrieving information once it is stored. Miller's (1975) demonstration of the contrast between recognition and free and cued recall in pre-senile dementia is a crucial experiment. Miller adapted an experiment of Warrington and Weiskrantz (1970) on amnesic patients. He presented a list of ten common words, three times, to demented and control groups. Following a delay, in which subjects were distracted to avoid rehearsal, there were three types of retention test. Free recall, recognition from ten correct words mixed with ten incorrect and a partial information or cued-recall situation in which the three initial letters of the correct words were supplied. Dementing patients were significantly worse than controls on free recall and recognition tasks but *not* on cued recall. These results have been replicated by Morris, Wheatley and Britton (1983), with older dementing subjects (median age 76), who showed impaired performance on a recognition test, with normal performance on cued recall. Whether this effect would be so marked in more severely demented patients has been queried by Davis and Mumford (1981).

The explanation for this finding has caused some controversy. Miller, following the lead of Warrington and Weiskrantz, has explained the cued-recall advantage in terms of interference effects. It is suggested that information in storage is not inhibited or dissipated normally so competing or irrelevant material interferes in the recall or recognition situation. Cued recall giving partial information reduces the response alternatives and facilitates recall. This interference hypothesis is supported by other experiments which show poorer recognition performance in dementing patients as the number of alternative stimuli is increased from two to eight (Miller, 1978). However, Miller was unable to show a higher proportion of intrusions from prior lists in dementing patients as this interference, or disinhibition hypothesis would suggest. Indeed, dementing patients produced fewer words in free recall, and did not tend to give a higher proportion of incorrect responses as would be predicted. Wilson *et al.* (1983) confirm that dementing patients show *fewer* prior-list intrusions; they showed a similar number of intrusions in total, but the Alzheimer patients' intrusions were predominantly items *not* previously presented. If there is excessive interference it seems not to emerge from the task itself. This was confirmed in the same study. Normally when several word-lists are learned one after the other performance declines as 'proactive interference' builds up, and the subject becomes increasingly uncertain as to which words were heard when. Dementing patients, in contrast with elderly controls, showed no evidence of proactive interference.

In these experiments the dementing patients were performing at a much lower level than controls. Morris (1981), following Winocur and Weiskrantz's (1976) procedure originally used with amnesic patients, ensured that learning level was high in his pre-senile dementing patients by using twelve highly associated word-pairs (e.g. doctor—nurse) repeated four times. After a 30-minute delay, filled with distracting tasks, a second list of word-pairs was presented, again four times, with the same stimulus, but different, though still highly associated, response words (e.g. doctor–patient). Both control subjects and dementing patients learned the first list satisfactorily. Control subjects learned the required reversal within one or two trials; dementing patients showed little sign of improvement over the four trials, continuing to respond with the response from the first list. Interference effects *can* then occur; Morris suggests they arise in this instance from a difficulty in discriminating contextual cues, needed to distinguish two sets of similar material from each other.

An alternative account of the cued-recall effect that has attracted much interest in amnesia research is based on the notion that cued recall may simply be a more sensitive memory test. Material that is encoded more weakly may perhaps be retrieved using this procedure. Other retrieval methods may require more elaborate encoding for correct performance (Woods and Piercy, 1974). For example, Meudell and Mayes (1981) have shown that young normal subjects were differentially impaired on an eight-choice recognition task compared with two choices, when recognition after one week was contrasted with immediate recognition. That is, subjects with a weak memory trace perform more badly on eight-choice recognition. Mayes and Meudell (1981) have replicated the cued-recall effect, again comparing performance in normals at short and long delays (strong and weak memory traces respectively). Subjects scored well on cued recall after six weeks, but felt they were guessing — a feature of amnesic performance in immediate recall!

The cued-recall effect probably does not then imply that the memory problem in dementia is purely one of retrieval, that the information is stored, but cannot be accessed. It is more likely to reflect the weak encoding and poor acquisition of information in dementia. Thus, Davis and Mumford (1984) showed that semantic cueing was *not* helpful to dementing patients. Nonetheless it does have therapeutic implications for the prompting of appropriate performance in dementing patients using various cues.

Non-verbal Memory. Although some studies have used pictorial material, as in Kendrick, Gibson and Moyes's (1979) Object Learning Test (e.g. Gibson, 1981), few attempts to use material more difficult to code verbally have been made. Complex pictures were used by Whitehead (1975), but in contrast to normal people deficits were similar in extent to those found with familiar words. Two reports on facial recognition performance in dementia are available — one of the most pertinent real-life applications of non-verbal memory. Ferris, Crook, Clark, McCarthy and Rae (1980) showed no difference between elderly normals and dementing patients on recognition performance, false-alarm rate or decision strategy, using a signal detection analysis. The two groups did show the customary differences on a verbal memory test, so the groups cannot have been completely atypical. Wilson, Kaszniak, Bacon, Fox and Kelly (1982b) failed to replicate this finding. Their dementing subjects were significantly impaired on facial recognition memory. Although they were also impaired on the perceptual task of matching faces photographed from different angles or with different expressions, neither this nor any response bias could account for the facial memory impairment. However, there did seem to be a dissociation between verbal and facial memory, the former being much more related to subtle linguistic skills. Although it is difficult to match memory tasks across modalities, Wilson *et al.* suggest that the verbal memory impairment was greater than that on facial memory.

Finally, Corkin (1982), as well as showing impairment in dementia on a non-verbal paired-associate learning task (using pairs of complex geometric designs), also reports data on the Gollin incomplete pictures test. Here the subject is shown a number of drawings of common objects and animals in five degrees of fragmentation, beginning with the most fragmented and ending with the complete picture. Normal subjects recognise the pictures at a greater degree of fragmentation when they are re-presented after a delay of one hour or one day. Alzheimer patients — exept where the dementia was extremely mild — showed virtually no savings at all on this task. This is in contrast to the performance of amnesic patients, some of whom show savings even after four months on this test. This suggests that procedural or skill memory, learning a task without awareness, that often seems relatively intact in amnesia, may be impaired in dementia. At best it may be more task specific, as Moscovitch (1982) provides some preliminary data on reading geometrically transformed script (where letters are rotated about their vertical axis), suggesting mildly dementing patients may show some savings over quite lengthy delays.

Remote Memory. Relatives often notice, with puzzlement, that the dementing person seems to remember perfectly events that occurred 50 years ago, but is unable to remember what they had for breakfast. This phenomenon was noted over 100 years ago by Ribot, and his law, that the probability of forgetting an event is inversely related to the time since the occurrence of that event, remains often quoted. However, it may be that it is simply more difficult to check the accuracy of recall of events so long ago, or that the patient only remembers stories that have been well rehearsed over the years, particularly relating to matters of personal significance.

Wilson, Kaszniak and Fox (1981) have given tests about persons and events from 1930 to 1975 to normal controls and dementia patients (mean age 67). They were unable to find any support for Ribot's law. Dementing patients were impaired on all tests, and showed a fairly consistent deficit over the whole time period, except perhaps for very recent events. Their poor performance on these probably reflects their occurrence after the onset of the dementia. These results again differ from those found with Korsakoff amnesics, who showed a clear temporal gradient on the same tests. The performance of these elderly dementing patients is very similar to that of younger patients with Huntington's Chorea (Albert, Butters and Brandt, 1981).

A contradictory finding has been reported by Moscovitch (1982). His smaller group of mild Alzheimer patients did show a temporal gradient on a test identifying famous faces who appeared in various decades of this century; indeed these patients performed as well as normal elderly controls on all decades except the most recent. However, unlike Wilson *et al.*'s study, cues were given to the person if they were initially unable to recall the person, and uncued data is not presented.

Comment on Memory Deficits in Dementia. It is clear that the interest in experimental analysis of memory deficits in dementia is growing rapidly. At present there seems to be little convergence in the findings obtained, once one has accepted that there are both primary- and secondary-memory deficits, the latter dependent to some extent on the former. Perhaps the problems relate to the lack of clarity in some of the theoretical models employed, or to disagreements about which models best apply to normal memory. A major difficulty is the lack of recognition of dementia as a dynamic process of cognitive change, reflecting a variety of diseases. Most studies use dementing patients sufficiently unimpaired to manage the experimental procedure designed for other patient groups and so exclude many more severely dementing patients (Davis and Mumford, 1981). Comparability of patients between studies is difficult.

Future studies should be much more closely linked to bio-chemical, physiological and post-mortem information than in the past to clarify problems of the definition of the nature and extent of dementia in the groups used. We need specific investigations using sophisticated experimental techniques on well-defined sub-groups of dementia, of defined severity, rather than adaptations of techniques devised for other target groups applied to heterogeneous groups of dementing patients. In this way results will emerge with clearer implications for those caring for dementing people.

Conditioning in Dementia

Very few studies have examined classical or operant conditioning in subjects with dementia. What evidence there is suggests that classical conditioning is slower in dementia (Solyom and Barik, 1965), but that operant conditioning can be relatively unimpaired if appropriate rewards for each patient are used (Ankus and Quarrington, 1972). The rate of increase of the ratio of lever-pulls required for each reward had to be kept very gradual for dementing patients.

Information Processing in Dementia

Very few studies have used information theory methods to quantify performance on simple tasks in dementing subjects. Hibbard, Migliaccio, Goldstone and Lhamon (1975) showed that a group of patients with dementia were impaired on a measure of informa-tion–transmission in a sensory discrimination task; subjects were required to discriminate between tones of different temporal durations.

A number of reports of a slowing of performance in dementing subjects have appeared, with a wide range of tasks being affected. These include naming common objects (Lawson and Barker, 1968), transferring pegs from one set of holes to another (Miller, 1974a), copying digits (Kendrick, Gibson and Moyes, 1979) and identifying tachistoscopically presented pictures (Neville and Folstein, 1979).

Reaction times are generally increased. Miller (1974a) using a five-choice reaction time task, reported that both the time to execute the movements and the time to make the decision were impaired in a sample of patients with pre-senile dementia.

Movement times seemed to show the greater impairment, the converse of the usual findings in relation to normal ageing. Miller (1977a) points out that this retardation of movement is too large to be explicable in terms of the delays in motor nerve conduction that have also been reported in dementia.

The effects of increasing cognitive load have been highlighted by Ferris, Crook, Sathananthan and Gershon (1976), with a sample of older dementing patients. These patients were differentially impaired when the reaction time task involved a choice, rather than being the simple reaction time paradigm of one stimulus and one response.

This is reinforced by data from a card-sorting task, giving a measure of continuous choice reaction time, reported by Woods (1981). Again both movement times and decision times were impaired in elderly dementing subjects, compared with normal elderly people. As the number of choices to be made increased from two to four to eight, with a corresponding increase in information load, the dementing patient's decision times increased much more steeply than the control subjects'. An important finding of this study — that cannot be over-emphasised in psychological research on dementia — was the greater variability in the dementing group. This was seen both between patients, who showed a massive range of function, and within the performance of individual patients, who varied greatly from trial to trial. It is this variability and fluctuation in function that may well emerge as being just as characteristic of dementia as the actual level of performance.

Language in Dementia

Conversational Speech. Some dementing patients show clear-cut dysphasic symptoms, but often deficits in language are not so immediately apparent. Some studies have examined certain features of conversational speech in dementing patients. Miller and Hague (1975) examined 2,000 word samples of speech in five patients with pre-senile dementia in order to test whether they used rare words less frequently than normal, or whether they used a more restricted range of words. No evidence for either possibility was found, suggesting that, at least in these relatively early cases, there was no significant loss of words from their vocabularies.

Forty-five minutes of conversation with an experimenter for five older dementing patients and five controls were analysed by Hutchinson and Jensen (1980). Dementing patients elaborated much less on each topic, making fewer distinct utterances in each of their 'turns' in the conversation. Analysis in terms of the distribution of types of speech acts showed no differences in the frequency of statements of belief or assertions, or in expressions of feeling, promises, etc. Dementing patients' speech more often had the aim of directing the listener to do something. These were often requests for confirmation, identification or explanation based on events or objects that had transitorily entered the patient's immediate consciousness. They were thus often irrelevant or tangential to the topic of conversation, preventing the progression of the topic. New topics were introduced much more frequently by dementing patients, who violated conversational rules for the continuation of their own and their partner's topic much more frequently than controls. Nearly a third of dementing patients' utterances were judged to be inappropriate to their conversational context.

These problems in conversational speech may be attributed to the other cognitive impairments, especially in recent memory, associated with dementia. Another explanation is in terms of dementia involving increased egocentrism. It is possible that — perhaps because of these cognitive changes — dementing patients assume their words convey more meaning than they actually do. Dementing patients seem to assume much greater shared knowledge than actually exists, and so fail to elaborate their speech adequately. This egocentrism is reflected in the emphasis on what is in the immediate environment, in the lack of concern for the progression of the discourse and in the violation of conversational rules. In children, it has been suggested that egocentric speech reflects a lack of communicative intention, but it is not clear from this study whether dementia also involves a lack of social will to communicate.

Aphasia Tests. A less naturalistic approach to the study of language in dementia has involved the application of standard tests for dysphasia. For example, Walker (1981) administered Schuell's Minnesota test for differential diagnosis of aphasia to 20 patients with dementia as well as to 70 normal elderly people. Dementing patients appeared most impaired on subtests involving numerical ability and calculation and where visuo-motor ability or writing was involved. On all sections they made more errors than both normal elderly people and a group of mildly dysphasic patients who had suffered strokes. Dementing patients showed a higher incidence of both semantic and phonological irregularities. Walker (1980) comments that, whilst the Schuell is formally presented as a test of language function, examination of the tests used indicates that other cognitive abilities — particularly memory — are involved to a considerable extent (particularly in the numerical section where dementing patients showed their worst performance). This raises the issue of the extent to which the dementing patients' failing cognitive abilities can be analysed independently of each other. Certainly if distinct functions can be conceptualised, purer tests of each would be required than are presently available.

Three further aphasia tests have been used with a small sample of nine dementing patients by Semple, Smith and Swash (1982). Four patients performed extremely poorly on the Token Test, which is intended to assess the patient's ability to understand and respond to verbal commands of increasing complexity. Nearly all patients were severely impaired on the Reporter's Test, which is derived from the Token Test, but requires expressive ability. This pattern of greater expressive difficulty was repeated on an aphasia screening test, covering a range of language functions. Patients had particular difficulty in describing action pictures and in describing a composite picture as an integrated whole; they tended to describe the various parts in apparent isolation from each other. Again, other cognitive impairments — memory and apraxia particularly — were thought to account for some of the 'language' problems encountered, especially on the Token Test.

Albert (1980) summarises language disorders in moderately advanced cases of dementia as follows: 'disorganisation of syntax, loss of words, paraphasias and neologisms, and perseveration interact with memory disorders to such a degree that coherence of thought or coherence of expression is severely impaired. As a result, comprehension becomes difficult to evaluate.' He suggests that the combination of apparently impaired comprehension and fluent, but incoherent, output gives a presentation similar to that seen in Wernicke's aphasia. He argues that the difference lies in the general intention of the utterance being retained in Wernicke's aphasia, whereas with the severely dementing patient both specifics and the intention of the communicator are lost.

Naming difficulties. A difficulty in word finding and naming has often been reported in dementia. There are at least three stages involved in naming an object. First, the perceptual task of recognising the object; secondly, the semantic task of searching for the word, and the specific name; thirdly, encoding of the phonemes of the name into a motor articulatory sequence (Kirshner, Webb and Kelly, 1984). The third stage generally is thought intact, as evidenced by spontaneous speech, oral reading and so on being preserved.

Rochford (1971) carried out a comparative study, contrasting the naming disorder in dysphasics and dementing patients. He suggested that dementing patients were impaired more in recognition (despite adequate vision) than in naming. This was supported by the great improvement in the naming performance of patients with dementia when the objects were familiar (body parts). Dysphasics' naming ability did not, however, improve, suggesting their impairment lies at the second, word-search, stage. As mentioned above, Lawson and Barker (1968) found dementing patients were slower to name objects, especially when the name was a low-frequency word. Dementing subjects were helped in identifying the object when its use was demonstrated, but controls' performance was not similarly facilitated in this way. The word-frequency effect suggests an impairment at the word-search stage, but the effectiveness of demonstration for both high- and low-frequency words again implicates the first, perceptual stage.

A recent study by Kirshner *et al.* (1984) similarly indicates that *both* first and second stages of naming are impaired. Their dementing subjects named the actual objects more accurately than photographs of the objects, which in turn were more often identified than line drawings and masked drawings, suggesting a perceptual element. High-frequency names were more frequently identified, reflecting a word-search difficulty. This naming difficulty was present even when no other language problem could be identified, but worsened when overall language performance was lower. Naming impairment seemed to correlate well with degree of dementia, and Kirshner *et al.* suggest it is evident early in the course of the dementing process. Most of the errors made by both patients and controls were perceptual — the name of an object similar in appearance to the stimulus being given. Patients did not make a greater proportion of semantic errors, although it has been suggested they tend to loosen the semantic boundaries of a specific name e.g. describing all small animals as 'dogs'.

Verbal Fluency. This aspect of language has been extensively studied. It involves the subject giving as many words as possible beginning with a given letter or belonging to a particular category (e.g. animals) in a certain time. Depending on how much time is allowed, this could be thought of as a test of speed. For example, Miller and Hague (1975) reported that both their pre-senile patients and normal controls could have produced more words given more time; the patients were much slower at producing words.

This finding of impaired verbal fluency is widely reported. There is some disagreement as to which type of task is more impaired in dementia. Weingartner *et al* (1981) report their dementing subjects to be more impaired on giving category examplars, than on giving words beginning with a certain letter. Rosen (1980) found no difference between the tasks in patients with moderate/severe dementia, but a clear superiority on the category task in mildly dementing patients. There were several differences between the studies. Weingartner *et al.*'s patients were much younger, of previously superior intelligence. Rosen's patients *and* normal controls were all residents of a nursing home. Different categories, with possibly differing numbers of examplars, were used in the two studies.

The difference between the two types of tasks is of some theoretical interest. For example, Rosen argues from her findings that in mild dementia the 'clearest cases' for a particular category can be given relatively normally; this gives an advantage to 'animal names' over words beginning with 'C', the latter having few obvious examples. Producing words beginning with a letter quickly involves entering into subsets phonetically or semantically related, as does retrieving animal names, once the clear-cut cases have been given. In mild dementia this ability would be seen as impaired, from Rosen's results.

Miller (1984) suggests that the impairment of verbal fluency in dementia can be accounted for by general verbal intellectual deterioration. The impairment may then be different in nature from that seen in patients with focal frontal lesions, where verbal intellectual level and verbal fluency are unrelated. Weingartner *et al.* (1981) similarly have shown in their dementing subjects a strong relationship between verbal performance and verbal fluency.

Reading. The ability to read individual words aloud is generally thought to be unimpaired, to the extent that word-reading ability forms the basis for an index of pre-morbid intellectual ability, the

National Adult Reading Test (Nelson and Mckenna, 1975; Nelson, 1982). Deriving *meaning* from what is read does show more impairment.

Conclusion. Language in dementia can remain deceptively intact. Speech can remain spontaneous and fluent, with grammatical form and articulation little affected till late in the disorder. However, the person's use of language becomes less elaborated, perhaps because of other cognitive problems, and his or her comprehension is reduced likewise. Naming problems occur early on, partly because of difficulties in recognising the object as well as in word finding. The relationship between language impairment and impairment in other cognitive functions remains a key issue. Ultimately a more detailed information-processing task analysis may prove more fruitful than simply dividing cognition conventionally into language, memory and so on.

Perceptuo-motor Ability in Dementia

Despite well-established deficits on the Block Design subtest of the WAIS, reflecting perceptuo-motor problems, the nature of these deficits has not been extensively elaborated. As with language, some patients with clear dyspraxic symptoms are seen, who, for example, are unable to begin a digit-copying task, as their hand–eye co-ordination will not allow them to place the numbers they write anywhere near the correct position. Semple *et al.* (1982) report that most of their small group of extensively assessed Alzheimer patients showed some difficulty in copying geometric designs. Performance on this test correlated highly with scores on the Block Design subtest. Moore and Wyke (1984) report an analysis of drawing ability in elderly dementing patients. Subjects were asked to draw a house, a cube, a human face and a clock face, to copy drawings of a house and a cube and to copy solid models of the same two objects. The dementing patients' spontaneous drawings were impoverished, lacking essential details in comparison with those of control subjects. When a drawing was given to copy, more details were included, but they were incorrectly positioned in space. Providing a solid object did not improve performance. Drawing performance was related to degree of dementia and to intellectual function, but did not resemble that of patients with any specific focal lesion or that of young children.

Adaptation and Behaviour Change in Dementia

Personality and adaptive behaviour in dementia has been little investigated. A review of what little specific information is available has been given by Savage *et al.* (1977). Their own work attempted to apply various personality tests and adjustment measures such as the Eysenck and Cattell Inventories and the Life Satisfaction Index to this population. They found such problems of relevance and administrative difficulty that either the tests could not be given or their interpretation was extremely dubious.

There is a need for some appropriate and specific measure of personality change in dementia. Reports and personal observation suggest that personality changes do occur, but there is little evidence of a pattern of change. Some dementing individuals show exaggeration of previous features, some quite severe changes in personality. In some, insight into failure is preserved, in others absent. Some show catastrophic reactions, a massive emotional reaction to stress; others are more placid. Some are disinhibited in their behaviour; in others social graces seem well preserved. Systematic longitudinal observational assessment of dementing patients is probably required to clarify this area.

One of the first signs of dementia may be in the loss of adaptive ability. In Chapter 6 we discuss the assessment of such abilities and suggest that there are now a variety of measures which can be appropriate to the range of deficits seen, from slight to severe dementia. Whilst such measures in various forms have been available for some time, there are few studies which have looked at the developmental progress of dementia on a longitudinal basis. Such studies might indicate a developing pattern of impairment and, particularly, suggest early indicators of dementia.

Ferm (1974) conducted a cross-sectional study in which 136 elderly psychiatric patients (mainly with dementia) were assessed by nurses and rated on eleven areas of behaviour. The following rank order of loss emerged:

1. Hobbies
2. Participation
3. Ability to wash
4. Ability to dress
5. Orientation in space
6. Recognition of persons
7. Ability to communicate
8. Bladder control
9. Bowel control
10. Movement
11. Eating.

This study concluded from the rank order that complex life skills were the first to be affected in dementia, survival skills (eating, moving, elimination) the last to go. Such a finding, attractive as it is, seems perhaps premature and we await further research with more sophisticated methodology. In particular, such research should follow the natural history of the dementing process in individuals, and take account of other important factors such as immobility (which has a relatively low correlation with severity of dementia) and the extent to which independent behaviours of various types are encouraged in the patient's environment.

A rather more sophisticated approach is that of Pattie and Gilleard (1979) who factor analysed the rating scale component of the Clifton Assessment Procedure for the Elderly (CAPE: see Chapter 6). They isolated three major factors: first, physical disability/communication disabilty; secondly, apathy; and finally social disturbance. They have attempted to derive Guttman scales on these factors (Gilleard and Pattie, 1980), reflecting different aspects of the dementing process. Follow-up of the sample over a two-year period indicated that change in the three factors was dissimilar as the dementia progressed. Whilst the physical and communication disability factor showed a linear trend, social disturbance did not, change being related to initial level. Apathy and withdrawal reached a peak early in the disease process, and is perhaps akin to Ferm's finding of loss of hobbies and participation in activities occurring early on in dementia. This particular factor solution — like any other — is limited by the scale items making up the test, which may or may not adequately cover the required area of behavioural function. Gilleard (1984b) discusses in detail the convergence of content of a number of rating scales. It does seem reasonable to assume that dementia is not a unidimensional process, and particularly that dependency and disruption can be distinguished from each other. Thus a patient may be highly dependent with a great deal of impairment in physical abilities and in communication, but not be disruptive, aggressive or disinhibited. Conversely, a patient may be extremely disruptive, but have relatively preserved self-care skills. To see dementia as a uniform universal path of decline in all aspects of functions is almost certainly mistaken.

Psychological Models of Dementia

Introduction. This section is extremely speculative; the quest for a satisfactory psychological model of dementia has a considerable way yet to go. *Descriptive* models are the focus here. There is little to suggest that psychological factors *cause* dementia, although some rather unsatisfactory causative psychological models have been developed (see Miller, 1977a, pp. 92–5, for a review of these). A good descriptive model would help in the integration and understanding of the diverse findings reviewed above, would generate hypotheses for further research into the psychological features of dementia, and could lead to suggestions regarding the psychological management of the disorder. The models to be discussed here have often not been propounded at length, some are implicit in current research directions, or are widely held assumptions.

Heterogeneity. In much of the above discussion we have used terms such as 'patients with dementia', as if dementia is a single entity. There is no doubt at all that there are several types of dementia, at a pathological level. In terms of psychological function some differences have already been reported e.g. between Alzheimer's disease and multi-infarct dementia (Perez, Rivera, Meyer, Gay, Taylor and Mathew, 1975) and between Alzheimer's disease and global amnesia (Corkin, 1982). Most of the studies discussed previously have focused on the so-called Alzheimer's disease type of dementia, excluding probable cases of multi-infarct dementia. Even if it were possible to make this distinction reliably during life (as opposed to using pathological evidence at post-mortem to make the definitive diagnosis), a heterogenous group of patients would remain. McDonald (1969), for example, identified two distinct subgroups. One showed parietal lobe symptoms (apraxia, right–left disorientation, dysphasia, etc.), was younger on average, and had a worse prognosis. The second group, who survived relatively longer, showed few parietal lobe symptoms, and had a higher mean age. Recent evidence suggests that dementing patients showing language disorders and apraxia may have Familial Alzheimer's disease with a much higher genetic loading (Breitner and Folstein, 1984). Other workers (e.g. Diesfeldt, 1978; Rosen and Mohs, 1982) have commented on the variability in performance within their dementing samples. Whether this is related to patients being at different stages in the disease, or to different levels of pre-morbid abilities, or to different distributions of the characteristic Alzheimer pathological changes remains to be seen. One distinction often emerging clinically is between patients where it is mainly memory functions that seem to be impaired, and those showing more widespread deficits, as in McDonald's two groups. The unresolved question remains as to whether these are different stages of the same process or distinct processes. Longitudinal studies of the evolution of dementia are needed, but will have to develop ways of identifying possibly dementing individuals early in the disorder. Age differences may also be relevant. Although the pathological evidence suggests that pre-senile and senile dementia of the Alzheimer type are identical, it is conceivable that their psychological and behavioural manifestations might be different in different age-groups. Clearly any successful model of dementia must account for the observed heterogeneity of function.

Accelerated ageing. This model sees dementia as representing a more rapid version of the normal ageing process, and has been postulated to include both physiological and psychological mechanisms (Miller, 1974b, provides an excellent review). Thus memory changes in a 'normal' 80-year-old would be seen as quantitatively but not qualitatively different from those in a 70-year-old dementing patient.

Some pathological evidence lends support to this view. The 'characteristic' Alzheimer changes are seen in the brains of normal elderly people, but there are far greater numbers of plaques and tangles in the brains of dementing patients at post-mortem. Psychologically, there are similarities in the patterns of deterioration observed in normal ageing and dementia on the WAIS.

It is clear that there is a large range of rates of change among normal elderly people in cognitive and other functions. If these rates of change were normally distributed, could dementia not then represent the extreme portion of the distribution, including those showing the fastest rates of change? If this were the case, it would have ramifications for the 'disease' concept of dementia, and for the early identification of cases. As tests for early dementia became more 'sensitive' they would include an increasing area under the normal distribution curve, as any cut-off point would have to be arbitrary.

Miller (1977a) argues that testing the accelerated ageing hypothesis is methodologically quite complex, and probably has yet to be accomplished. It would involve the use of control groups of 'normal' elderly people *older* than those in the dementia group, although cohort problems might then arise to some extent. One experiment that does include an older control group is reported by Kaszniak *et al.* (1979). They included groups of younger and older people, with and without dementia, and showed that one memory test (paired-associate learning) was impaired both by dementia and ageing, whereas another (digit-span) was impaired only in dementing patients. This, and other studies showing qualitative differences in function between dementia and normal ageing, imply the model is unlikely to hold in its simplest form. Qualitative changes could be explained if a threshold effect occurs — where the brain only shows dysfunction where a certain level of structural damage has taken place. The assumption would be that the brain could compensate for lower levels of damage. This model would not then require a smooth gradation of dysfunction with only quantitative differences between normal ageing and dementia. It would however be even more difficult to test!

Sensory deprivation. In this model an analogy is drawn between the behaviour of young volunteers following a period of acute, intense sensory deprivation and that of dementing people (Inglis, 1962; Bower, 1967). The sensory deprivation is thought to arise from three factors. The elderly person has losses in sensory activity, possibly in visual, auditory and tactile modalities. Secondly, the person may be in an unstimulating environment, perhaps in an old people's home, or alone and housebound at home. Finally, the person may have become withdrawn, perhaps as a way of coping with a large, unfamiliar environment that appears strange and threatening. These aspects of sensory deprivation are seen as interacting with and exacerbating early memory loss to produce confused behaviour. Clearly, a person with memory loss is particularly dependent on environmental input to keep in touch with reality (Woods and Britton, 1977). Some experimental support for this model is provided by Cameron's (1941) classic investigation of nocturnal confusion. He suggested that this was related to reduced sensory input, rather than to fatigue, by showing that patients became more confused and wandered more when placed in a room with a reduced level of illumination earlier in the day. As Hodge (1984) points out, the manipulation may also have involved social as well as sensory deprivation.

It must be said that the analogy on which the model is based is fairly loose, with a chronic process of deprivation being compared to an acute intense experimental situation. The model has led to some intervention studies (see Chapter 8), with the effects of increased stimulation being studied. However, the stimulation used has been of a fairly general nature, so it is not clear these studies could give support to the model. Also the model takes the dementing person's recent memory loss as a 'given', and fails to elaborate on the nature of the loss.

Arousal. Is the dementing person's level of cerebral excitation lowered, and could this account for the observed cognitive dysfunction? The development of this model is particularly associated with Kendrick (1972). The model was based on the then popular two-arousal system hypothesis. One (AS1) was based on the reticular activating system, and related to 'drive', the other (AS2) was based on the limbic system, and related to 'incentive'. Kendrick argues that AS1 is involved in short-term memory, with AS2 being involved in reinforcement.

In dementia both systems are seen as dysfunctional, whereas in some depressed patients AS2 only would be impaired. Kendrick has related various tests in the Kendrick Battery to the two arousal systems, and had to modify the theory (as it relates to depression) in the light of data from the Revised Kendrick Battery. The effects of activity level and medication are now also taken into account (Kendrick and Moyes, 1979). Drug-induced pseudodementia is now postulated as accounting for reduced performance in depression on the Digit Copying Test (reflecting AS1) with normal performance on the Object Learning Test (reflecting AS2).

The model has probably had much more elaboration in seeking to account for cognitive changes in elderly depressed patients than it has in describing dementia. An arousal model may have some applicability to dementia, but Miller (1977a) cautions against the use of single behavioural indices to measure arousal systems.

Developmental reversal. As seen above, there have oeen suggestions that the pattern of behavioural deterioration in dementia represents a reversal of the development in behaviour in childhood (Ferm, 1974). This has been elaborated further, in relation to Piaget's stage theory of development (Constantinidis, Richard and de Ajuriaguerra, 1978; Rosen and Mohs, 1982). There probably are some parallels between order of development and order of deterioration, but these may relate as much to the difficulty level of the various tasks involved as to the loss of particular types of cognitive abilities. In development there is a goal to be attained, a peak to be reached; it is unlikely that deterioration can be ordered in precisely the same way, given the acquired knowledge and over-learned skills the dementing person brings into the process of decline. Whether there are aspects of this developmental approach that can be clarified to generate useful insights into the patterns of impairment in dementia remains to be seen.

Other models. In normal ageing there have been attempts to account for a whole range of dysfunction from changes in a single aspect of function, namely speed (e.g. Birren, Woods and Williams, 1979). Could a single dysfunctional system account for the pattern of impairment in dementia? Memory would be an obvious choice, and clearly many other cognitive tasks have a memory component. Biochemical and pathological evidence might also lend some support, with structures and neurotransmitter systems thought relevant to efficient memory showing greater probabilities of involvement in Alzheimer's disease. The existence of global amnesia, where severe memory deficits coexist with intact functions in other areas of cognition, suggests either it is a different sort of memory that is involved (although quite what this would be is hard to define using current conceptions of memory), or that a different underlying function is involved, or that the pattern of dementia impairment arises from a combination of dysfunctional systems. Speed of information processing is again a possible unitary dysfunction that could account for wide-ranging losses of cognitive function. Dementing patients show reduced speed on a number of tasks, but to what extent this is task specific is not yet known. The emergence of a speed factor from a number of tasks, related to extent of, say, memory loss, would add weight to this notion. Certainly, reduced speed of information processing if related (simple-mindedly) to increased 'neural noise' could account for the increased variability in function in dementia. If the 'noise' fluctuates randomly then on occasions it will be low, and performance will be good, and at other times it will be high and performance will be poor.

Neuropsychological ideas are beginning to be applied to dementia (Moscovitch, 1982; Rosen and Mohs, 1982). Attempts are made to relate particular dysfunctions to particular areas of pathological involvement, with more severe dementia being attributed to more widespread pathological changes. Thus, Moscovitch describes the sensory cortex as being spared in dementia, and Rosen and Mohs suggest frontal, temporal and parietal areas are all dysfunctional to some extent in early dementia. There are some dangers in assuming that, because there is impairment on a particular test that is thought to reflect a focal lesion in a defined cortical area, that area is damaged in a diffuse process like dementia. Performance on most psychological tests is not governed by a single cortical area — although a lesion in one area may impair it. Functional systems are involved in any task performance, and damage to other parts of the functional system could also explain the impaired performance. An illustration of this is Rosen and Mohs' conclusion that poor verbal fluency in dementia indicates frontal lobe involvement. Miller (1984) shows clearly that, although in focal cases verbal fluency is indeed a good indicator of a frontal lesion, in dementia the verbal fluency impairment is attributable to impaired verbal intelligence, i.e. other parts of the system are dysfunctional, and so frontal lobe pathology cannot be assumed. However, Rosen and Mohs' suggestion that some of the observed heterogeneity in dementia may be attributed to differential distributions of the pathological changes in different regions of the brain could be valid.

Comment. We would like to see a compensatory model being applied more fully to dementia (cf. Hussian, 1981). How does the person suffering from dementia seek to cope with the changes occurring, changes that are of course affecting the efficacy of the person's habitual coping mechanisms? What strategies does the person adopt in order to maintain function at some level? How are cognitive resources conserved or expended? What control systems are used to cope with information overload, when speed of processing information is reduced? How does the person seek to make sense of his or her environment? Some of the variability seen in dementia may be attributed, in part at least, to individual differences in coping under conditions of great pressure, stress and overload, with repeated exposure to tasks of great difficulty level. Some patients deny any problems, some become anxious and tearful, some withdraw into their own inner world, some become angry and blame others, some feel guilty and worthless, some become agitated and restless, some use a social façade to cover their deficits or confabulate. All are ways of coping with extremes of pressure. We do not know as yet whether dementing patients use strategies similar to those used earlier in life, and to what extent these strategies influence cognitive performance. If the variability and fluctuation in dementing patients is to be understood, these issues need to be explained — too often the importance of the reaction of the dementing person to the disorder is underestimated (Cohen, Kennedy and Eisdorfer, 1984).

Psychological Function in Depression

In recent years there have been welcome attempts to develop integrative models of depression (e.g. Akiskal and McKinney, 1975). The causes of depression can only be understood in terms of a multivariate analysis, emphasising the interplay and interdependence of a number of factors: genetic mechanisms, biochemical factors, social influences, physical health, life experiences and so on. In Chapter 1 the relevance of social influences, in the form of life-events, to depression in the elderly was mentioned, and in Chapter 7, the complicating role of physical health in the presentation of depression in older people will be described. In focusing here on psychological aspects of depression, we are not wishing to minimise their interrelationship with other factors. Before considering the applicability of various psychological models of depression to the elderly, we will present details of the findings on cognitive change in depressed elderly people. This is a topic that has preoccupied psychologists working with the elderly for some years, in the hope of identifying differences from dementing patients to aid in the differential diagnosis of depression and dementia in the elderly. This is in some ways a futile exercise (see Chapter 5), but has provided some data on cognitive function in depressed elderly people that may have other applications.

Cognitive Changes in Depression

In a few patients, cognitive change is so profound that a condition of 'depressive pseudodementia' has been described. The person seems disorientated and to have some memory loss and reduced awareness, possibly with impaired self-care ability. The person's cognitive function improves as the depression lifts. Most patients show much less marked clinical impairment although, on detailed cognitive testing, some deficiency may be apparent. Most studies have included patients whose depression was severe enough to warrant admission to hospital; less severely depressed people might be expected to show less cognitive dysfunction.

On testing of intellectual functioning — using the WAIS — Savage *et al.* (1973) showed that depressed patients had lower verbal *and* performance IQs than normal controls. Subtests failing to show impairment were Comprehension, Digit Symbol, Block Design and Object Assembly. Interestingly, three of these are timed tests with bonuses for speed, where depression might have been thought to have had a particular impact. This finding may, however, relate as much to the difficulty of some of these subtests for the normal group. A similar finding of verbal and performance impairment emerged in a community sample of 'neurotic' patients, including many depressed subjects (Nunn, Bergmann, Britton, Foster, Hall and Kay 1974). From following up this sample, evidence emerged that those with poorer intellectual ability had a greater susceptibility to depression. The deficits in these comparatively mild cases did not seem to be related to test-anxiety, poor motivation, physical illness or social class, or to represent the early stages of a dementing process. Whitehead (1973a) comments on the similarity of the pattern of impairment in normal ageing, depression and dementia. In this study early dementia cases scored overall lower than the depressed patients, whereas in Savage *et al.*'s (1973) study, differences were more patchy, being particularly evident on performance subtests.

Most research studies have concentrated on memory and learning difficulties, particularly on tests involving paired-associate learning or the learning of the meanings of words. Detailed consideration of various aspects of memory has seldom been attempted. Primary memory — as measured by digit-span — was impaired in Savage *et al.*'s hospitalised sample. Whitehead (1973b) argues that digit-span is not impaired in depression, but used only forward digit-span, which is easier than the WAIS subtest where recall of digits in reverse order is also required. Also no normal control group was included in Whitehead's study, where performances before and after the depression remitted were compared.

In this study also a number of tests that would reflect secondary memory were administered. Most did *not* show improvement as the depression lifted (including paired-associate learning; memory passages recalled immediately or after a delay, and a recognition test), but two tests did, and so were assumed to have been impaired by the person's depression. These were a serial learning test (where words have to be learned in correct sequence) and the Synonym Learning Test (SLT; where meanings of words have to be learned;

part of the original Kendrick Battery).

The interpretation of these results is, however, complicated by the failure of Davies, Hamilton, Hendrickson, Levy and Post (1978) to replicate significant improvements in performance on psychological tests following remission of depression. Their depressed patients were impaired compared with normal controls on both paired-associate learning and serial learning. Normals and patients were not well matched in this study, differing also in verbal IQ, and possibly in social class and lifelong intellectual level.

Further evidence on paired-associate learning is conflicting. Irving, Robinson and McAdam (1970) showed no difference between normals and depressed patients; whereas Savage *et al.* (1973) showed their depressed patients did not differ significantly from those with dementia on this test. On the Modified Word Learning Test (a fore-runner of the SLT), the affective group were less impaired than the dementing group, but were still significantly worse than normal controls.

Free recall of pictorially presented material seemed intact in Neville and Folstein's (1979) experiment, but Kendrick *et al.* (1979) have shown a clear-cut deficit on the Object Learning Test (OLT) in comparison with a large group of normal subjects, well matched for verbal IQ.

To summarise these disparate results is difficult. Memory and learning deficits *can* occur in depression, but much less consistently than is the case in dementia. Differences between tasks and samples also have more effect in depression. In several instances the depressed group occupies an intermediate position between normal and dementing elderly groups. This is reflected in the findings on more physical measures of cortical function, for example the evoked potential measure from the EEG (Hendrickson, Levy and Post, 1979) and measures from CAT scanning (e.g. Jacoby and Levy, 1980b). Whether these reflect changes generally in depressed patients or impairment in a sub-group of depressed patients with cortical or other physical dysfunction remains open to question (cf. Jacoby, Levy and Bird, 1981).

A few studies have attempted to define the nature of memory deficits in depression in more detail. Familiarity of material to be learned seemed not to influence the deficit (Whitehead, 1974). Depressed patients make more errors transposed from other parts of the task, whereas dementing patients show more random errors, even when error level is held constant (Whitehead 1973b). Both groups showed many omissions; depressed patients reduced their level of non-response when the depression improved. That depressed patients' tendency not to respond reflects increased cautiousness is supported by their more conservative decision strategies, when a signal detection analysis is applied to a recognition memory task (Miller and Lewis, 1977; Larner, 1977). Miller and Lewis's depressed and normal groups did not differ in memory accuracy on the non-verbal task used; both were better than a dementing group. Part of any memory or learning problem in depression is then likely to be the depressed patient's strategy of responding only when fairly certain a word was one of those to be memorised. Lower intelligence is probably another factor; performance on many of the learning tasks is related to IQ (Whitehead, 1974), and, as mentioned above, lower intellectual function may lead to greater susceptibility to neurotic disorders. Weingartner, Kaye, Smallberg, Cohen, Ebert, Gillin and Gold (1982) comment that depressed patients tend to be impaired when the task requires sustained motivation and effort.

Retardation is often a clinical feature of severe depression, the person appearing slower in thought and movement. This is reflected psychologically in slowness in crossing out target letters from an array of other letters (Neville and Folstein, 1979) and slowness in simply copying digits (Kendrick *et al.*, 1979). Again, depressed patients fall between normals and dementing patients, and are significantly different from both on digit copying. Davies *et al.* (1978) report digit copying to be the only psychological test to improve with the remission of depression, but this may be a practice effect as normals also improve on re-test at a similar rate (Kendrick and Moyes, 1979).

Kendrick and Moyes (1979) suggest that, where performance on the Digit Copying Test is very poor, this may be related to the effects of the medication the person is receiving for their depression (a 'drug-induced pseudodementia') or to the effects of lowered physical activity. Certainly, these factors must be taken into consideration in understanding cognitive function in depressed elderly patients, although the exact nature of their influence remains to be clarified. Many depressed patients are receiving various types of medication, sometimes over considerable periods of time, and often before admission to hospital is considered. Although Kendrick and Moyes (1979) have shown an association between medication and impairment, the possibility remains that it is the most severely depressed patients who both receive most drugs *and* show most cognitive change.

Perhaps the most important feature to emerge from this review is how inconsistent and patchy cognitive impairments in depression actually are, especially when the extent of agitation, anxiety, retardation and depressive preoccupation is considered, together with the stressful nature of many of the tests used. Depressed patients are more likely to complain of memory problems than dementing patients (Kahn, Zarit, Hilbert and Niederehe, 1975), but the evidence seems to indicate that these may reflect the person's increased cautiousness and uncertainty about the efficiency of their memory rather than a genuine loss in memory accuracy. This may form one aspect of the depressed person's negative view of themselves and of their abilities and resources. Negative self-statements also tend to reduce cognitive function, of course (Bellucci and Hoyer, 1975). It really is remarkable how *well* depressed patients do manage to function cognitively!

Psychological Models of Depression

As discussed above, psychological models of depression must be seen in the context of the genetic, biochemical, social and environmental context of the individual. Nevertheless, there are some highly relevant models in the current psychological literature on depression which can be applied to the elderly.

The range of psychological models of depression is vast, covering most possibilities from dynamic to strictly behaviourist. Some psychologists confine themselves to the observable, outward behaviours, other have extended their interests to the cognitions of the individual. The latter are undoubtedly important but being covert behaviours are far less accessible to definition and analysis. Their importance is shown in the literature in the increasing viability of cognitive therapy which, despite its title, is a combination of behavioural and cognitive approaches to depressive problems (see Chapter 7).

Beck's Cognitive Theory. The work of Beck has had a profound influence on our understanding of depression. His books (Beck 1967, 1973) are extensive accounts of his position which a brief review can do little to reflect adequately. Beck presents an integrative model covering symptoms and behaviours in depression including both overt behaviours and covert (cognitive) aspects of the disorder. Depressed mood is seen as being related to negative cognition. The person has a pessimistic view of themselves, of the world and of the future. They over-generalise from a failure in a specific instance, so that, for example, a single mistake in a difficult task becomes an indication of their uselessness as a human being. They see only the negative aspects of an experience; even an obvious success will be down-rated — 'I should be able to do better than that'. A person who has some difficulty getting off to sleep may say 'I can't sleep at all', overstating the negative aspects of an experience. As well as these cognitive distortions, the person may have dysfunctional attitudes and beliefs, which result in information being evaluated and structured in this negative manner. Mis-attributions occur — the person will blame himself or herself for events outside his or her control, or assume the worst on the flimsiest of evidence. The depressed person may initially be hardly aware of his or her negative cognitions, the repeated 'automatic thoughts' that help to maintain depressed mood.

As we shall see in Chapter 7, attempts are beginning to apply these concepts to treatment of depressed elderly patients, and there are already encouraging signs of their usefulness. As a theory, some questions remain. These features undoubtedly occur in depressed elderly people (e.g. Vezina and Bourque, 1984), but whether they lead to, or are simply associated with, depressed mood is not clear. Many depressed older people become depressed for the first time in later life. Why do they develop a negative cognitive shift at that particular time? How does physical health and loss relate to the theory? Finally, as we shall see in Chapter 6, some doubts have been expressed regarding the Beck Depression Inventory, with which severity of depression is defined. Many of the items have a strong association with somatic physical symptomatology, which, of course, has a higher incidence in the normal older person.

Behavioural Models. Behavioural models of depression have their roots in studies of behaviour and are based on an increasing under-standing of some of the features which facilitate or inhibit behaviour in both animals and humans. These models make much of the importance of reinforcement as a central feature in depression.

Simpson (1979) identified six major approaches to behavioural models. They can be isolated, but are more often seen in combina-tion in a particular theoretical model. They are shown in Table 4.1.

Table 4.1: Behavioural Models of Depression

Depression is a function of:	
1. Reduced reinforcement	Lazarus (1968)
2. Reduced social reinforcement	Liberman and Raskin (1971); Lewinsohn (1975)
3. Loss of reinforceable behaviour	Ferster (1973)
4. Loss of reinforcer effectiveness	Costello (1972)
5. Aversive control	Moss and Boren (1972)
6. Learned helplessness	Overmier and Seligman (1967); Abramson, Seligman and Teasdale (1978)

Source: Adapted from Simpson (1979).

This emphasis on reinforcement as a crucial variable in the depression has considerable relevance to the elderly. It is possible that, following retirement or physical illness, there will be significant changes in some aspects of reinforcement noted above. Reduction in physical mobility may reduce opportunity for both general and social reinforcement. A slower pace of life may reduce the number of reinforceable events, previously pleasurable activities may lose their impact as reinforcers. Faced with changing ability to adapt to the environment the elderly may feel impotent to influence events, and helplessness may result. More negative experiences may occur; with physical illness there may be more pain and discomfort, with the simplest activities perhaps becoming an effort, and losing any pleasure they once held.

It is not possible here to review all the above models in detail; the references quoted will assist the reader requiring a more detailed review. However, it is of some value to look at two of the most influential theoretical approaches. Since it has been applied to several specific studies with the elderly, Lewinsohn's (1975) model will be considered first. Lewinsohn's model incorporates aspects of the first five of the features of theories noted in Table 4.1 excluding only a detailed consideration of helplessness. A particular emphasis is placed on the importance of social reinforcement and the role of social reinforcers. The model seeks to explain both the development and maintenance of depression.

A reduction in the availability of reinforcement in the environment, or reduced activity, or reduced intensity of potentially reinforcing events result in the person receiving a low rate of positive reinforcement. This leads to 'depressed' behaviour, which may attract some social reinforcement (sympathy), and includes social avoidance, thus maintaining and exacerbating the initial precipitants.

A study of this model will suggest at least that it has relevance for the elderly. Potentially reinforcing events may well be less readily available, environmental reinforcement may well be greatly reduced through bereavement and environmental change. Lewinsohn and MacPhillamy (1974) suggest a comparison between the behaviour of many normal elderly people and people with depression. They point to low self-esteem, loss of interest, feelings of emptiness and hopelessness, depressed libido and appetite, feelings of rejection, psychosomatic symptoms and complaints and a progressive reduction in the rate of behaviour as support for this position. They compared non-depressed elderly with depressed and non-depressed younger people and found a similar lack of engagement in potentially pleasant activities in both elderly and depressed groups. However, the elderly group did *not* report the loss of subjective enjoyment of these activities which the younger group experienced. This suggests that *quantity* of engagement may not be crucial in the elderly, but that the quality, or perceived value of the event, may be much more important.

We do not accept that Lewinsohn and MacPhillamy's comparison between the normal elderly and depressed people in general has any validity. Enough of the 'supernormal' elderly was seen in Chapter 3 to make it clear that such a comparison is a massive overgeneralisation from the minority sub-group of elderly people who themselves have depression. However, the study is of interest in that it raises the issue of the relationship between activity and depression, and the possibility of this relationship differing between younger and older people.

Two studies have explored this relationship further. Davies and Gledhill (1983) found no significant correlation between degree of depression and disengagement in elderly people attending a day-centre. This replicated Simpson, Woods and Britton's (1981) findings with residents of an old people's home. In both cases the type of engagement proved more important. Simpson *et al.* showed that non-depressed residents were more likely to engage in activities they preferred and Davies and Gledhill found a relationship between level of depression and 'onlooking', a passive form of engagement, where the person is attending to something or someone, but is not participating fully.

Apart from the possibility of an age difference, Davies and Gledhill point out there are at least two other explanations of these findings. Firstly, that depression in the elderly may be more labile than in the young, so that being at the day-centre may have been sufficient to raise the mood and engagement level of people who the rest of the time in their own homes were much more depressed and less active. Simpson *et al.*'s findings in a residential setting suggest this cannot be a sufficient explanation. Secondly, the relationship between activity and mood may be similarly weak in younger subjects and there are certainly some indications that this may indeed be the case (Davies and Gledhill, 1983).

We can conclude that a simplistic activity model of depression in the elderly is untenable. Indiscriminate activity programmes are not the cure for depression in the elderly! Engagement *per se* does not lead directly to reinforcement. The perception of the activity by the elderly person is most important. Covert behaviour, reminiscing, and other internal activities, may be preferred by some older people to more active pursuits or to social interaction. Lewisohn's model would need to take these cognitive components into account if it is to add further to our understanding of depression in the elderly.

Learned helplessness. The second behavioural model to be considered sees depression as 'learned helplessness' (Seligman, 1975). This model has often been cited with respect to its relevance to depression in the elderly (e.g. Bergmann, 1978). In its original form, depression was thought to arise from a perceived loss of control over reinforcers. The patient comes to believe that nothing in his or her power will make any difference or bring any pleasure or enjoyment. This belief in the uncontrollability of reinforcement may lead to the person giving up activities of which he or she is quite capable, and which could potentially have provided disconfirmatory evidence for the belief. The experiences on which this belief is based might, in the elderly, relate to loss of a partner, of mobility, of health, of his or her own home, of worthwhile occupation, and so on. All reduce the controllability of the environment and are likely to have occurred almost independently of the person's actions.

The theory has been re-formulated to account for the variability in helplessness encountered (Abramson *et al.*, 1978). It now includes a strong attributional component. The cause to which the

Table 4.2: Attributional Analysis of Learned Helplessness

Three key orthogonal dimensions along which attributions are made, and their implications:

1. Internal–external	: affects self-esteem
2. Stable–unstable	: affects long-term consequences
3. Global–specific	: affects generalisation to other situations

Source: adapted from Abramson *et al.* (1978).

person attributes his or her helplessness following say, a stressful life-event, influences how drastic and long-standing its effects will be (see Table 4.2). If the cause is seen as a global inner failing, then the effects will be worse than if a transitory external influence affecting only the specific situation is blamed. Mood changes are greatest when the desirability of the situation that cannot be controlled is high and when the certainty of uncontrollability is strong. Clearly the losses mentioned above would be likely on this basis to produce large changes in the person's mood.

Evidence that a lack of sense of control is an important contributor to depression in the elderly is reviewed by Schulz (1980). Several studies (e.g. Langer and Rodin, 1976) have shown improved adjustment when more control or choice has been given to elderly people. These studies have mainly been on residents of institutions, and follow-up studies have not always been as encouraging as the initial interventions. Using a specially developed locus of control measure, Reid, Haas and Hawkins (1977) and Ziegler and Reid (1979) have shown a negative relationship between the extent to which people feel they attain the control they desire and depression in both institutional residents and in elderly people living in the community. Similarly Hanes and Wild (1977) report an association between depression and perceived lack of control in a community sample. These workers noted a sex difference, the association being stronger in elderly men.

There is then support from both intervention and correlational studies of the relevance of control and predictability to depressed mood in the elderly. Even the varying long-term results of the interventions can be explained within the context of Abramson *et al.*'s (1978) attributional framework (Schulz, 1980). It would be interesting to explore the relationship between Abramson *et al.*'s internal–external dimension of attributional style and the internal–external locus of control dimension. Do people's beliefs that they can generally influence their environment lead to them also selecting an internal cause for helplessness, for example? Brewin and Shapiro (1984) suggest that attributions for positive and negative outcome are separate dimensions, and need to be distinguished in locus of control research.

There are clearly areas of overlap between this model and Beck's cognitive theory — which perhaps has more to offer regarding the negative view of the world that leads to global and stable attributions of helplessness being made. Together they lead to a much more useful framework for working with depressed elderly people than any of the simpler lack of reinforcement models. The cognitive component is essential — as we saw above, the *meaning* of the loss of reinforcement, or activity or whatever to the individual must be included in a behavioural analysis of depression. Together the cognitive and the helplessness models provide a clear mechanism for understanding how stressful life-events, like a bereavement or physical ill health, can lead to depression in elderly people.

Other Disorders

The progressive and pervasive nature of dementia and the prevalence of depression in the elderly focus attention on them, and have prompted research into their cognitive and other psychological effects. There are a number of other problems which arise in the elderly which can also have a profound effect on similar functions. We will not be able to consider each of these in detail but will attempt to direct the attention of the reader to some important disorders.

The use of alcohol and its effects will be considered, along with the problems of Korsakoff's disorder, closely associated with alcohol consumption, but in reality a nutritional disorder. Parkinson's disease has been the subject of increasing psychological interest of late as its neurochemical basis has been better understood. The specific problems caused by neurological trauma, cerebrovascular accidents, strokes and tumours in the elderly need consideration, as do the consequences of physical illness particularly to the cardiovascular system. In most of these areas there is even less psychological research and theoretical sophistication than was the case with dementia or depression.

There are still many problems potentially affecting the psychological adjustment of the aged which have had precious little research investigation. Specific disorders such as diabetes and arthritis are likely to produce psychological problems; infections may cause temporary cognitive impairment more readily than in younger people. There has also been little consideration of the effects on the elderly of some of the drugs used to combat either mental or physical illness.

Alcohol-related Problems

Interest in the use and abuse of alcohol by the elderly has grown of late. The book of Mishara and Kastenbaum (1980) is an overall summary of this area and, perhaps, a reflection of the seemingly growing problem of alcoholism in the older person in the USA. A similar review by James (1983) suggests that alcohol may result in more problems in the elderly in Britain than had been realised. The real problem in most cases is identification of the presenting problem as alcohol-related. Memory problems in a Korsakoff patient may have an initial presentation little different from that of Alzheimer's disease or a drug-induced problem. Depression, of course, may be either cause or effect of alcoholism. It is clear from the literature that alcohol must be considered seriously when investigating any client presenting with even mild memory or learning difficulties; the presentation may not be similar to that of the younger alcoholic.

Psychological studies of old alcoholics suggest that intellectual deficits are apparent on a wide range of tasks. Overall global intelligence test performance is impaired compared with both younger alcoholics and age-peers. Specific neuropsychological assessment on the Halstead–Reitan Battery shows areas of deficit particularly implicating the frontal lobes (Ron, 1977) and more experimental studies of memory and learning processes reflect specific problems (Cermak and Ryback, 1976).

Cutting (1978) distinguishes alcohol-related dementia — where cognitive impairment is more global — from Korsakoff's syndrome, which affects the person's memory, but not their general intellectual level. Korsakoff's syndrome is thought to be associated with a nutritional deficiency (depletion of thiamine, Vitamin B.12). This finding is both interesting in relation to that specific disorder, but also has raised the fascinating possibility that some of the more subtle changes in mental state in the elderly may have a link with changed or disordered nutrition or metabolism.

The Korsakoff patient presents to the psychologist with much of the symptomatology of a dementing patient whose memory is primarily affected, without the progressive element of the disorder. In fact, in Korsakoff's syndrome some remission is possible if the nutritional deficit is rectified at an early stage. The affected individual is alert and aware and their amnesia — obvious on testing — may be obscured on interview by their ability to confabulate.

There is no doubt that groups of Korsakoff and dementing patients differ psychologically (see Butters and Cermak, 1980). For example, Neville and Folstein (1979) showed both groups were impaired on a recall task, but Korsakoff patients performed normally on a test involving the tachistoscopic recognition of objects. Dementing patients were significantly slower on this task.

Differences between dementia and global amnesia reported by Corkin (1982) were mentioned previously. However, these amnesias were not of Korsakoff aetiology and there is some controversy as to whether amnesia of differing aetiologies do produce identical psychological deficits. Several recent reviews have attempted to integrate the extensive (and rapidly growing) literature on amnesia (e.g. Squire, 1980; Stern, 1981; Warrington and Weiskrantz, 1982). Broadly speaking, episodic memory is particularly impaired, with some suggestion of unimpaired learning on skill- or motor-learning tasks. Most of the amnesia research has not specifically concerned itself with more elderly Korsakoff patients, however.

Parkinson's Disease

Parkinson's disease is interesting in that it is one of the few neuro-psychological disorders of the elderly for which a specific treatment has been found, although a number of causes have been implicated (Rosin, 1982). The biochemical finding of a neuro-transmitter deficit related to dopaminergic neurones is capable of substantial amelioration by the administration of a drug (L-dopa). However, recent findings suggest that, whilst L-dopa may relieve symptomatology, it does not arrest the progress of the disorder. It is thus possible that other mechanisms may be involved and that these are related to the development of dementia in a proportion of the Parkinson's patients (see Rosin, 1982). The prevalence of the disease increases with age, and — as with dementia — there has been speculation as to whether it represents a form of accelerated ageing (Calne, 1981).

Controversy has surrounded the presence or absence of specific psychological deficit in Parkinson's disease. The obvious motor disorders may have masked less evident cognitive change. On the WAIS, Loranger, Goodell, McDowell, Lee and Sweet (1982) found general cognitive deterioration, particularly affecting perceptual organisation, and increased scatter of subtest scores in patients with Parkinson's disease. Although performance tests were particularly impaired, this could not be wholly explained by the person's tremor or slowness.

The Wechsler Memory Scale has also been used. Heller (1979) found the memory deficit to be mainly in new learning. The ability to use and recall old information and to preserve orientation for time and place was relatively unimpaired. The deficits were much less marked than in dementing patients. The Parkinson's patients adopted a relatively cautious decision strategy in the memory task — this feature, at least, being more akin to the psychological deficit in depression than in dementia.

Experimental studies have shown deterioration in problem solving and perceptual-motor co-ordination. Reitan and Boll (1971) and Flower (1978) support these findings and further suggest that the Parkinson's patient is more seriously affected when there is a need to co-ordinate input from various sensory pathways and when feedback control of ongoing behaviour is involved. These studies also suggest an increasing correspondence between Parkinsonism and Alzheimer-type dementia from a cognitive point of view as the disorder progresses.

The situation is further complicated by the effects of the various pharmacological treatments currently being employed. Some cognitive deficits could potentially arise as side-effects of these drugs. Conversely, L-dopa has been shown to *reduce* a number of cognitive deficits in Parkinson's patients. Thus, Rosin (1982) reviews reports of improved cognitive function, following the administration of L-dopa. These include a reversal of the phenomena of lengthened articulation of syllables in speech and of briefer pauses between words shown by Parkinson patients; a reduction in the length of time from start to finish of a movement (but not a reduction in their lengthened reaction time); as well as more general improvements in intellectual performance and learning ability (e.g. Fisher and Findley, 1981).

To what extent some of the deficits that are identified can be attributed to the coexistence of Alzheimer's disease and Parkinson's disease in the same individual remains unclear. Both are common disorders in the very old, and so are likely by chance alone to occur frequently together. There is support for both processes occurring together from pathological evidence, and some suggestion that this happens more frequently than chance alone would predict (Rosin, 1982). For example, in a ten-year follow-up study of Parkinson's patients, half the survivors showed evidence of dementia. In a pathological study 29 of 30 Parkinson's patients showed some Alzheimer features. Further studies will need to clarify this overlap between the two diseases.

Depression also is often reported in Parkinsonism, and is thought to be alleviated by L-dopa. On the other hand, L-dopa may cause depressive episodes! The cognitive deficits noted above are probably not simply related to depressed affect, as some studies have used depressed elderly patients as a control group, but in the individual case depression could well be a factor contributing to an apparent deficit.

Cognitive impairment in Parkinson's disease has then been shown on a number of occasions. Most evidence points to it not being simply attributable to other aspects of the disease — e.g. slowness or tremor or rigidity or depression. Whether the deficit occurs in all Parkinson's patients or whether there is a close relationship between Parkinson's and Alzheimer's diseases remains to be clarified. L-dopa treatment ameliorates the intellectual impairments to some extent, but long-term studies of its effects are needed to establish whether they can be arrested completely.

Cerebral Trauma, Physical Illness and Drug Effects

There is not space in this book to outline all the general effects of these factors on the elderly. In many cases the overall effects have a marked similarity to those seen in younger clients. However, some caution is needed to avoid facile extrapolation from studies with younger groups. Cerebral trauma, stroke or similar conditions relate to an already ageing organism which may have lost adaptive potential. Effects can thus be different in some respects from those expected in younger clients.

Strokes occur most commonly in older people. Seventy per cent of the victims of strokes are over 65 years old (Mulley, 1981), and increasing age is related to a reduced probability of long-term survival (Wade, Skilbeck, Wood and Hewer, 1984). The psychological effects of the stroke depend largely on the site and extent of the lesion. Dominant hemisphere lesions often lead to speech and communication problems. Walker and Williams (1980) describe a consecutive sample of elderly patients (nearly all hemiplegic) referred for speech therapy. About a quarter were dysphasic only, whilst a further quarter showed evidence of dyspraxia in addition to their dysphasia. Most of the remainder were dysarthric only, although a few patients were dysphasic and dysarthric. Powell, Clark and Bailey's (1979) study of dysphasic patients (many of whom were elderly) suggests that the classical distinctions between, say, expressive and receptive dysphasia are less relevant than the severity of the dysphasia in routine practice. Walker and Williams (1980) comment that even dysphasic patients who were showing little improvement on standardised assessment procedures 'devised effective compensatory mechanisms i.e. sophisticated gesture or interactional patterning codes for relating to family and environment'. The learning potential of elderly patients with focal lesions has been demonstrated experimentally with respect to the conditioning of verbal responses (Halberstam and Zaretsky, 1969) and avoidance learning of motor responses (Halberstam, Zaretsky, Brucker and Gutman, 1971). Patients showed clear learning but were generally slower to learn, and benefited greatly from extended practice over-learning the response required.

Several workers have commented on the importance of the stroke patient's motivation in predicting their progress in rehabilitation (e.g. Suchett-Kaye, Sarkar, Elkan and Waring, 1971; Wade *et al.*, 1984). Mulley (1981) cautions that the effects of non-dominant lesions may be wrongly interpreted as 'poor motivation'. Unilateral neglect, with denial of the damaged limb, for instance, can wrongly be attributed to the patient's attitude, rather than to their focal brain damage. Depression is also viewed as a barrier to rehabilitation, although it is, of course, an understandable reaction. This may be one element in the pain expressed by some hemiplegic patients in the disabled half of their body (Evans, 1982, p. 117). Social factors — especially with respect to the patient's family — are also of significance (Mulhall, 1978). From a controlled trial, comparing the management of stroke in the elderly in a special rehabilitation unit with the conventional medical care, Garraway, Akhtar, Hockey and Prescott (1980) suggested that over-protection of the patient by their family counteracted many of the stroke unit's achievements at follow-up. There is great scope for increasing exploration of these psychological and social factors in stroke rehabilitation.

The interaction between physical illness, drug treatment and psychological factors is also of interest. Drugs prescribed to assist in cardiac insufficiency may react with an ageing brain to produce bizarre effects. Some of the standard psychoactive drugs prescribed for anxiety or depression may have effects on memory or learning processes which can be adapted to by the younger adult, but which cause noticeable difficulties with the elderly. Evans (1982, p. 134) lists some of the drugs which may lead to acute confusional states in elderly people. A number of physical illnesses may also lead to this state of delirium. Psychologically, the person is unable to maintain attention, and so may become disorientated. The patient is less alert and may show considerable cognitive fluctuation. It has been speculated that anxiety-prone or field-dependent elderly people may be more likely to develop a delirious state. Field-dependence implies a reliance on the immediate perceptions of the person, leading to more likelihood of misinterpretations of dreams, illusions and so forth. Dementing patients' memory problems similarly render them field-dependent and so more susceptible to delirium, superimposed on their dementia. Evans puts forward a 'neural noise' model of delirium. The final common pathway of a large number of disorders is an increase in neural noise, so that environmental stimuli are harder to perceive against the noisy background, which may itself at times be mistaken for reality. When environmental stimulation is at its lowest — at night — delirium often becomes more pronounced. Evans (1982, pp. 135–7) demonstrates elegantly the importance of an understanding of the psychological aspects of delirium in its management.

Summary

Dementia

1. Despite agreement regarding the major deficits of intellectual function, memory and learning ability, considerable controversy remains regarding details of the pattern and progression of impairment. Cross-sectional studies of possibly heterogeneous groups of dementing patients have added to the conflicting evidence available.

2. Language and perceptuo-motor problems in dementia are

now being investigated more fully, and deficits in, say, naming and drawing ability are well established. However, other aspects of cognitive dysfunction may be relevant, with the naming disorder, for example, being at least partially related to difficulties in object recognition.

3. The deterioration of behavioural function in dementia is emerging as a multi-dimensional process, with dependency and disruption, for example, being distinguishable from each other.

4. A satisfactory psychological model of dementia has yet to be developed. It must take account of the heterogeneity and variability of function observed, and it may be that several subtypes of dementia need to be more precisely identified.

Depression

1. Cognitive impairments in depressed elderly people are patchy. Increased cautiousness may contribute to the memory and learning problems observed. Retardation of motor function has been noted, but has been attributed by some researchers to drug effects or to a reduction in activity.

2. Beck's cognitive model and behavioural learned helplessness models have much to contribute to our understanding of the maintenance of depression in the elderly, although the causal mechanisms need further exploration. They also have direct therapeutic implications, which is of great importance in a condition where pharmacological and other physical treatments have many unwanted side-effects, cannot always be used safely in the long term, and are often ineffective in bringing about complete recovery or preventing relapse.

Other Disorders

Psychological aspects of other disorders, whether alcohol-related or usually falling within the remit of geriatric medicine and neurology (strokes, Parkinson's disease, delirium) could profitably be evaluated more extensively. In several instances cognitive dysfunctions and depressed mood may coexist, and may interact with social factors such as family support. To treat these disorders simply as physical problems is misguided.

5 COGNITIVE ASSESSMENT OF THE ELDERLY PERSON

Until the mid-1970s the sole involvement of many clinical psychologists with the elderly had been in response to a request from some source for cognitive assessment. The reason for the request might be that deterioration had been suspected and an 'IQ' had been assumed to be an essential part of the diagnostic process, or commonly that it was thought useful in the differentiation of dementia and depression. However, we have seen in Chapters 2 and 4 that the psychological processes of cognition in normal and abnormal ageing are extremely complex. It is therefore unlikely that a straightforward assessment on, say, a global measure of intelligence, will yield much of value for the patient, or the referring agent.

This chapter will look at some of the issues surrounding the use of psychometric and other cognitive assessment techniques with the elderly. Some strategies will be introduced and examined which promise more than just a quest for ever-increasing diagnostic precision. The reader will be introduced to tests which have been extensively used with the elderly, both for overall cognitive assessment and for investigation of specific facets of cognitive behaviour. The clinical use of these tests will be illustrated by case studies. Lastly, we will review the new and exciting possibilities raised by the interaction of three recent advances. These are the developments in our understanding of aspects of cognitive behaviour in the elderly, a greater emphasis on the use of relevant materials, and developments in current technology such as microcomputers which allow new methods of presentation and recording of responses.

Why Assess the Elderly?

Psychologists have in the past been primarily associated with assessment in the elderly as a diagnostic tool. Tests have been used as discriminators between normal age changes, dementia and depression. Patients have then been placed in diagnostic categories according to their test results. Such cognitive assessment is held by the authors to be rarely, if ever, justified. Assessment of this type should always be seen as a means to an end, not as an end in itself.

In the elderly, as in other client groups, cognitive assessment must lead to a definition of the client's resources in a way which will assist in care and rehabilitation. Too often in the past the mere suspicion of deterioration in cognitive ability has led to the emergence of the 'dementia' label with all its negative implications including potentially a switching off of the 'patient support system' by care-staff or family. In the recent past one of the authors has come across a remarkably well-preserved lady in her mid-eighties, whose medical notes contain a seemingly clear-cut diagnosis of dementia based on IQ assessment some 20 years previously. Despite the obvious contradiction of the diagnosis in her life and behaviour, inspection of her medical notes revealed the 'dementia' tag appearing at regular intervals, undoubtedly influencing care and treatment. Similar cases exist only too often in the experience of these concerned with the elderly.

How did this diagnostic use (or abuse?) of cognitive tests emerge? If one looks at most of the commonly used global tests of intelligence, age-related trends seemed to emerge in their normative data. These trends were apparent in both overall level of functioning and in differences in subtest or subscale patterns. As we have shown in Chapter 2, methodological factors probably mean that many of these trends were spurious. However, a great deal of effort was expended on their identification and their interpretation (Savage *et al.*, 1973).

Interpretation of changes in overall level of IQ in the individual has proved difficult, since it is not easy to obtain a baseline of previous functioning. Very rarely has a comparable global assessment been carried out when the client was younger which remains accessible on file. Usually any comparison is based on an *estimate* of previous ability from life history, occupation, educational attainment, etc. Such a comparison is prone to error, especially when, for sociocultural reasons, the client may well not have been able to reflect their potential in life achievements.

Verbal IQ or vocabulary level has also been used to give an estimate of lifelong intellectual function, on the basis that these are least affected by deterioration. Thus, the verbal–performance IQ discrepancy, found in the WAIS to increase as age advances, has been used as an index of deterioration (Matarazzo, 1972). A parallel development is the comparison of Mill-Hill Vocabulary Test scores with attainment on the Raven's Progressive Matrices Test. However, the decline that does occur in verbal function in dementia leads to a reduction in their accuracy as diagnostic indices. In addition, the assumption that the normal person will have identical scores on each component of the index is of course in error for many individuals.

Similar problems apply to the Deterioration Quotients (DQ) which compare performance on subtests thought to 'hold', being insensitive to cognitive decline, and on the 'don't hold' subtests, those most susceptible to the effects of decline. Savage *et al.* (1973) review the use of a number of these quotients, the most often used being Wechsler's own DQ. Their data — both on hospital and community samples — show clearly that the variability is so large that a high misclassification rate is inevitable. The DQ difference between dementing patients and normal controls holds for groups but *not* reliably for the individual case. Similar data were obtained for the verbal–performance discrepancy.

In Chapters 2 and 4 we referred to the interpretation of differences in subtest scores on tests such as the WAIS. Bolton *et al.* (1966) question the use of the WAIS in this context and more recent attempts by Crookes (1974) to develop an index to differentiate elderly dementing people and depressives may be of similarly doubtful value, as a universally applicable diagnostic index.

More recently, word-reading ability has become popular as a guide to pre-morbid intellectual level (Nelson and McKenna, 1975; Nelson, 1982). It would be foolish to expect the discrepancy between this and current IQ to be a perfect diagnostic indicator, useful as it may be in other respects.

A significant problem which underlies all of these models is the inappropriate use of both the tests involved and their normative data. Global tests of intelligence were devised to assess cognitive ability in the general population. Their use in diagnostic prediction or as measures of subtle changes in specific populations may be a valuable spin-off, if it is justified. However, tests devised to tap abilities in the average range are unlikely to produce satisfactory discrimination at the extremes of ability where few questions on each item are answered.

Whilst we have concentrated on the use of global intelligence tests, similar difficulties are apparent in the use of more specific measures. The 1950s and 1960s saw a rapid development of tests involving new learning ability. Many of these tests presented difficulties in their use with the elderly. Their derivation was often in relation to diagnostic criteria rather than definition of the process involved. In many cases they were unsuitable in design or level of difficulty for the client groups. Any clinical psychologist who has used the Walton–Black Modified Word Learning Test (Walton and Black, 1957) or the Synonym Learning Test (Kendrick, 1965) will be aware of the severe motivational problems which can arise in repeated administration of such tests to the elderly. They expose patients to repeated, overt failure, and are extremely stressful for patient and psychologist. Their usefulness with patients of low IQ has been questioned, and in fact their misclassification rates may often be high (Irving *et al.*, 1970; Savage *et al.*, 1973).

Several other difficulties with tests used diagnostically should be noted. Their standardisation data should be examined. Many are standardised on unequivocal cases of dementia and depression; in practice these would be the cases where the tests would not be used. In our experience, where the diagnosis is not clear-cut the psychological tests results may reflect and not resolve this uncertainty. A good illustration of the importance of the standardisation sample is provided by the Revised Kendrick Battery. Although near perfect discrimination of clear-cut acute cases has been demonstrated (Kendrick *et al.*, 1979), Gibson, Moyes and Kendrick (1980) report that nearly half of a sample of long-stay psychiatric patients were misclassified.

If diagnostic tests are simply validated against psychiatric diagnosis, some error is inevitably introduced. Severe dementia may be relatively simple to diagnose, but mistakes are made in less severe cases. For example, Ron, Toone, Garralda and Lishman (1979) followed up cases diagnosed as having pre-senile dementia. Five to fifteen years later nearly a third were judged to have been misdiagnosed.

Diagnostic testing must also take into account the problem of base-rates — how common the alternative diagnoses are in the actual population to be assessed. If one diagnostic category predominates then the tests will have to discriminate extremely accurately to be of greater value than simply 'guessing' the more common diagnosis each time. Tests like the Revised Kendrick Battery which provide cut-off points for various diagnostic groups assume particular base-rates for the diagnoses involved. Ideally, cut-off points for each test should be determined locally, according to the referral practices operating.

At present, the diagnosis of dementia and depression have quite different consequences. Depression can be treated; dementia typically leads to therapeutic despair. If it is present, in time the diagnosis will become clear. If the person is only depressed, however, appropriate treatment will usually resolve the concern about their cognitive function. If the person is both depressed and dementing, treatment for their depression may well enhance their quality of life and again in time their dementia will become self-evident.

We are not here arguing against diagnosis *per se*. Rather we would emphasise that diagnosis involves bringing together a variety of types of information about a person. Cognitive test results are only one source of information. Other features such as mood, history of the disorder and behavioural function will be as relevant as cognitive function in the process of differential diagnosis. Where diagnosis remains doubtful, the consequences of each alternative for the patient must be carefully considered, and likely costs and benefits of each treatment option be evaluated. Using psychological tests to provide a diagnostic category allocation devalues the careful, wide-ranging, multi-disciplinary assessment that is required for appropriate treatment decisions to be made.

If diagnostic testing is not to be recommended, what reasons are there for assessing the elderly person's cognitive function? Several suggestions have been made recently. Kendrick (1982a) proposes that cognitive assessment would be useful in the early detection of Alzheimer's disease and in exploring the relationship of cognitive function with depression, certain drugs and activity level. Miller (1980a) suggests it could be of value in evaluating treatment programmes, in identifying suitability for particular treatments and in measuring the occurrence and extent of decline in cognitive function. Volans and Woods (1983) point out cognitive assessment can help in examining questions of prognosis and placement. In addition, from the person's pattern of abilities and dysfunctions, and changes in their pattern over time, treatment strategies can be generated, and counselling undertaken with the patients themselves and/or their carers.

It is our view that psychological assessment of the elderly person should aim primarily to *describe* rather than to *discriminate*. For many of the above purposes description of the person's pattern of abilities and impairments is exactly what is required. For others, where the primary aim is a category assignment (e.g. placement, diagnosis), descriptive assessment can still be useful as one part of the information about the person leading to the decision. The emphasis here is away from proceeding immediately from a test score to a category assignment. Instead the test results are interpreted in the light of other information about the person; hypotheses regarding poor performance on certain tests are examined; the cognitive function data is then integrated with other types of information in making the categorisation. Our assessments and our decisions must reflect the complexity inherent in the functioning of the elderly person. The tests currently available are not ideal for this type of descriptive assessment, particularly where changes over time are to be monitored, but by explicitly adopting this approach it may prove possible to avoid the mistakes of the past when new tests are developed.

Descriptive Assessment

Cognitive assessment should be seen as only part of an overall psychological evaluation. Coping strategies, morale and behavioural functioning, for example, should also be considered. In the cognitive realm, it is important to consider which aspects of cognition need to be covered. The depth, degree of detail and structure of the assessment are also pertinent. Currently available tests allow only a limited range of functions to be assessed readily. This probably results from the emphasis on diagnostic testing. The relationship between test results, and real-life behaviour is usually not well established. For many tests the effects of repeated assessment have not been ascertained, so that the assessment of rate of change or changes over time can present difficulties.

A framework for descriptive cognitive assessment has been proposed by Savage *et al.* (1973) and elaborated more recently by Savage (1981). This model for assessment evolved from research on normal and abnormal elderly groups in a variety of settings. Savage and his co-workers found a consistent trend towards a distinction between the person's *level* of functioning and their *learning* ability for new information. There was a further distinction, between verbal and performance tests of both level and learning. They suggested that initial assessment should be carried out with a measure of general intellect such as one of the global intelligence tests, for example the WAIS. This assessment would give a measure of overall ability and some indication of verbal and performance abilities.

Such assessment must then be supplemented by a cascade process of further investigation of specific functions, such as verbal and performance learning parameters. Initially, this may be carried out by procedures which use part of the initial measure such as the Vocabulary or Block Design subtests adapted as learning measures. Optimally, such assessment should be supplemented by specific experimental tests of these parameters.

Whilst such a model has validity and potential there are some major problems. The tests such as the WAIS which form the backbone of this framework are flawed in their application to the elderly by dubious validity when operating at the lower end of their range with few responses to each subtest. There is a clear need for more appropriate and age-relevant tests with this group, as for children. The use of the verbal/performance distinction may be less useful than the concept of crystallized and fluid intelligence (see Chapter 2). The WAIS subtests fall into different categories dependent on which of these models are used. A further problem is the use of WAIS-subtest-based learning tests. These are notorious for producing poor motivation in the elderly and there may be serious doubts over the reliability of results obtained. A further problem is the time taken for a full assessment, which may lie well beyond that available in the practical situation. In general such a model has obvious potential but requires some modification to be widely applicable for use with the elderly.

Some attempts have been made to produce revised models which may overcome some of these difficulties. Savage (1981) refers to developments which utilise the short form of the WAIS (Britton and Savage, 1966b). These reduce the time taken whilst still allowing estimates of deficit in both level and learning potential. This approach does not overcome the problem of the relevance of the measures used. Kendrick (1982a) has drawn attention to the concept of 'Ecological Validity'. He points out that tests like the WAIS do not appear relevant to the elderly person's everyday life, and so reduce motivation and co-operation. Clearly questions about being lost in a forest, or putting blocks together to make patterns, or assembling a jigsaw do lack immediate relevance for most elderly people. This whole area requires further clarification however; simply using tasks conceivably performed in everyday life does not guarantee the acceptability of the test, as the difficulty level and degree of abstraction are also relevant (Volans and Woods, 1983). Contrary to Kendrick's argument, the WAIS has been shown to be associated with a measure from the elderly person's environment — their competence in spontaneous discourse (North and Ulatowska, 1981). We certainly need tests that have relevance for behaviour in everyday life, but this involves more than a simplistic face validity; if the test is not acceptable to many elderly people, its value will be extremely limited.

Models are certainly required that allow the evaluation of change over time. As Kendrick points out, tests like the WAIS are difficult to use repeatedly, as a fairly long interval (a year or so) is usually recommended before re-testing. The length of such tests also is likely to reduce the motivation of elderly patients for repeated testing. Rabbitt (1981b, 1982b) argues that experimental cognitive psychology has been slow to develop models for changes in performance, and draws attention to control system models which are better able to describe changes over time.

Until such models become more fully developed a strategy with much to recommend it is to reserve detailed cognitive assessment for 'special' cases, where a particular question needs exploration and investigation. At present the advantages of detailed testing with the present inadequate tests (e.g. in predicting outcome, Kuriansky, Gurland and Cowan, 1976) are far outweighed by the cost and time involved. The time can be far better employed in other aspects of the psychologist's role (see Chapter 11). We would argue, however, that each patient should be cognitively assessed on brief screening measures that may be administered by other staff. Memory and information tests are particularly valuable (see below) and have been validated against a number of external criteria. These include pathological changes (Blessed, Tomlinson and Roth, 1968), measures of atrophy on computed tomography (Jacoby and Levy, 1980a, 1980b) as well as outcome (Whitehead, 1976). Ideally other aspects of cognitive function could be assessed similarly, although as yet fewer measures are available. 'Parietal lobe' tests assessing constructional skills, naming ability, calculation ability and left–right discrimination are frequently used (McDonald, 1969).

A need for more detailed assessment can often be identified from these tests, where their results perhaps apparently conflict with clinical data, or in the ranges of function where these tests are at their least predictive, namely those patients with lifelong high intellectual levels (who may have deteriorated from their peak but still appear 'normal') and those with lifelong low intelligence, who may perform misleadingly badly. Bergmann, Kay, Foster, McKechnie and Roth (1971) showed that subjects with a lower level of intellectual function were occasionally misdiagnosed as having dementia on a one-off assessment. A reading test (such as the National Adult Reading Test, Nelson, 1982) will often help to clarify this particular issue. The tests used in a detailed assessment should be selected so as to provide information relevant to the clinical questions being posed — by the patient or by carers or staff — and often a sequential process occurs, following up questions arising from an initial assessment. If change is to be monitored, tests must be selected that can be used repeatedly, for which the effects of practice can be estimated and on which the person scores in the middle of the possible score range — allowing scope for change in either direction.

Any model for assessment must ensure that there is an adequate means of recording other, significant, aspects of the status of the client. For example, physical health may influence the results in a wide variety of ways. There may be interference from drug effects, both from prescribed drugs or more subtle influences from use of alcohol or other agents. It is not unknown for alcohol to have been taken to provide enough courage to attend a psychologist's appointment; the effects on cognitive tests may be severe long before the behavioural effects are apparent! We have also referred to the problems of adequate motivation. There is a clear need to monitor and *record* such information assisting in the interpretation of results.

Our suggested strategy for cognitive assessment would then involve the widespread use of brief, reliable, validated screening measures of cognitive function, in order to quantify in a replicable, objective, communicable form what is often collected as clinical data or as subjective impression. Detailed cognitive assessment is seen as a back-up to this routine screening, to be used where the results actually would contribute to the management of the case, where specific questions arise from the brief screening tests and from other information on the patient. Used thoughtfully in this way we would suggest that — despite all the problems with current tests — cognitive assessment does enhance the distinctly psychological contribution to the care of the elderly patient.

Cognitive Tests and the Elderly

Provided that care is taken with their selection, administration and interpretation, there are a number of tests of potential value in the cognitive assessment of the elderly. A thorough review of these tests is provided by Miller (1980a) and Kramer and Jarvik (1979).

Brief tests of Cognition

A great many of these have been developed. They typically focus on areas such as current orientation (what is the name of this place? what day is it today? what year is it now?), current information (who is the Prime Minister (or President in USA)?), personal information (how old are you now? where do you live?), personal remote memory (where were you born?) and non-personal remote memory (when did the Second World War finish?). They differ most obviously in length — ranging from 10 to 35 items. Of the shorter tests Pfeiffer's (1975b) Short Portable Mental Status Questionnaire and the Abbreviated Mental Test (Hodkinson, 1972) are frequently used. Gurland (1980) compares the content of a number of brief tests. Some measures of other cognitive abilities are included in some tests. For example, the 25-point Memory and Information Test devised by Blessed *et al.* (1968) has an additional three items assessing concentration and attention (e.g. counting backwards from 20), as well as asking for recall of a name and address after a five-minute interval, to assess new learning ability. The extensively researched Clifton Assessment Procedure for the Elderly (CAPE: Pattie and Gilleard, 1979) includes brief tests of reading and writing ability and a psychomotor test as well as tests of information/orientation and attention/concentration. The combination of these cognitive tests with a behaviour-rating scale (see Chapter 6) thus providing a well-rounded assessment, has led to it becoming a deservedly popular instrument in the UK. With this combination of measures there is less risk of mistakenly expecting information/orientation performance to predict accurately self care ability (Winograd, 1984); they are distinct — and only partially related — areas of function.

These tests have usually been shown to have satisfactory reliability (see Holden and Woods, 1982, pp. 109–11) and are usually straightforward enough for an inexperienced tester to be able to use with a minimum of training. The major problem in their administration comes from patients objecting to being asked 'silly questions'. These patients may be unimpaired, seeing the items as an insult to their intelligence, or impaired with sufficient insight to realise the questions may expose their deficits. Presenting the tests in conversational manner, providing face-saving excuses for failure where appropriate and apologising for the silliness of the questions may help in this situation.

The validity of these tests is well established, as discussed above; often their validity is at least as good as more detailed memory testing (Pattie and Gilleard, 1979). They are likely to be influenced by educational level, motivation, mood and so on; score ranges should be interpreted as indicative rather than definitive. The choice of test will be determined by the purpose; the brief tests are ideal for screening purposes, but more items are required if, say, the rate of change over time in a dementing patient is being monitored.

Brief tests of 'parietal lobe' functions are much less well researched, although examples are available (McDonald, 1969). Normal data on these tests are needed in addition to clinical data. Moore and Wyke (1984) illustrate, for instance, a high failure rate among normal elderly subjects on a test often used clinically (drawing a cube). Whether these tests do reflect parietal lobe dysfunction specifically, or more generalised impairment remains open to question.

Intellectual Function

Without doubt and not withstanding the problems we have referred to in Chapter 2 and in the previous sections of this Chapter, the WAIS is the most commonly used global intellectual measure. Various investigators have found that its validity and reliability remain reasonably adequate into old age (Savage *et al.*, 1973) and that the USA standardisation is appropriate to the UK. It should be noted that norms of over-75-year-olds in the WAIS manual were collected separately from the main standardisation sample, and are much less representative. The recently published revised form of the WAIS, the WAIS−R has norms up to age 75, for a US population. In view of the effects of cohort differences (see Chapter 2) this more recent standardisation makes the WAIS−R preferable for assessing subjects who are 75 years old and younger. The various revisions carried out on many of the subtests are likely to increase the acceptability a little. For patients over the age of 75, or where a previous WAIS has been carried out, the original WAIS remains worth considering. Its norms on the over-seventy-fives are the best available current guide.

As noted above, the length of the WAIS with consequent problems of motivation led to the development of a short-form for the elderly (Britton and Savage, 1966b). This consists of the Comprehension, Vocabulary, Block Design and Object Assembly subtests. Scores are pro-rated and give verbal, performance and full-scale IQs. Correlations with the full WAIS are highly satisfactory and normative data are presented by Savage *et al.* (1973). Whether the same subtests of the WAIS—R would be as accurate in predicting verbal, performance and full-scale IQs requires evaluation before a short form of the WAIS—R could be used confidently.

The major alternative to the WAIS as a measure of global intellectual function is the combination of Raven's Coloured Progressive Matrices and the Mill-Hill Vocabulary Scale (Raven, Court and Raven, 1976). Indications of both verbal and performance levels are given, and the tests are fairly simple and quick to administer. They relate clearly to the fluid and crystallised model of intelligence described in Chapter 2. Some old-age norms are available (Orme, 1957). One of the advantages of using them is also paradoxically a disadvantage; a highly trained tester is not required to administer them, and so the psychologist is less likely to observe the patient's approach to the tests, and to generate alternative hypotheses for apparent deficits. The full WAIS taps a much wider range of skills and abilities, of course.

The diagnostic failure of the verbal—performance discrepancy and deterioration quotients has been documented above. These indices can be used descriptively, by comparing the patient's performance with norms provided by Savage *et al.* (1973). They provide one means of describing the pattern of the patient's current intellectual performance. The person's verbal—performance discrepancy may be described, for example, as being over a standard deviation greater than the norm for elderly people of a similar age. The reason for this, which could be dementia, a lifelong pattern, or a severe physical disability affecting motor movements, then needs to be explored. The verbal—performance discrepancy is thus an indicator of the persons's current intellectual function rather than a diagnostic index.

Memory and Learning

Erikson, Poon and Walsh-Sweeney (1980) pointed out that 'no

comprehensive and well documented memory battery has been developed'. At present it is necessary to make the most of the existing tests, whilst recognising their limitations.

The Wechsler Memory Scale (WMS: Wechsler, 1945) remains the most widely used, and the most extensively criticised (e.g. Prigatano, 1978). As with the WAIS, Wechsler assembled a variety of subtests to form a global test, giving a Memory Quotient (MQ). Doubtless its association (by name) with the WAIS and its rapid coverage of a number of areas of memory function in its seven subtests have led to its continued popularity. To use it simply to provide an MQ is probably mistaken, but a fair amount of information can be gleaned from the test as a whole; indeed some subtests have served as tests in their own right (e.g. logical memory, digit-span, information and orientation).

The norms provided in the test's manual are woefully inadequate, only going up to the age of 49 years. Fortunately norms for elderly people are to be found in reports by Hulicka (1966), Klonoff and Kennedy (1966), Cauthen (1977) and Whitehead (1973b). From these norms the most appropriate comparison for the individual patient must be selected, taking into account their age, sex and lifelong intellectual level. As the test stands, scores on the different subtests are not directly comparable. Osborne and Davis (1978) provide formulae for calculating age-corrected scale scores for the various subtests. An alternative procedure for comparing different aspects of the patient's memory performance is to calculate factor scores on the three components of the scale reliably identified in a number of studies on younger patients (Kear Colwell, 1973). These are new learning, attention/concentration and information/orientation. In older patients the factor structure may change slightly, with visual reproduction becoming a component in its own right, and information/orientation combining with new learning to form a single factor (Skilbeck and Woods, 1980). Attention/concentration remains the other factor. Although the test as a whole bears little obvious relationship to current conceptions of memory, this factor structure could be interpreted as representing non-verbal and verbal secondary-memory and primary-memory functions respectively. The secondary-memory aspect becomes clearer if a test of delayed recall is introduced (Whitehead, 1973b; Russell, 1975). This is usually achieved by asking for recall of the logical memory passages a second time, after a period of 30 or 60 minutes has elapsed. The same can be done for the Visual Reproduction subtest, but it is important here to ascertain whether the patient can actually copy similar designs, before assuming a visual memory problem.

There are many more specific tests of memory function, some developed specifically for the elderly and some which may be usefully applied to this age-group. In the previous section we referred to the model proposed by Savage *et al.* (1973) which incorporates measures of verbal and performance learning. Verbal learning may be assessed using a test such as the Walton–Black Modified Word Learning Test (Walton and Black, 1957). This test utilises the Vocabulary subtest of whatever intelligence test has been administered and attempts to assess ability to learn words above the ceiling attained on the test. In this way, there is some control for level of ability. Normative data are available for the elderly (Bolton, Savage and Roth, 1967). A similar measure of performance learning was developed from the WAIS Block Design subtest by Savage and Hall (1973) who provide some normative data for its use. Whilst these tests have some potential, problems can arise in practice as the difficulty level involved often leads to undue anxiety or poor motivation. They should only be used with selected patients, when other tests cannot provide similar information, where the patients' motivation is good, and their anxiety level low.

The other type of test where learning — in the sense of repeated trials to criterion — is assessed involves the paired-associate paradigm. Although Inglis (1957) originally used various modalities of presentation and response, most tests have been based on auditory presentation of the pairs of words to be learned, with learning tested by recall of the second word of the pair when given the first word. The difficulty level of the test depends on the degree of association between the words, and the test can again be stressful when there is no apparent connection. Including pairs of words with a higher level of association (e.g. Irving *et al.*, 1970; Whitehead, 1973b; Davies, Hamilton, Hendrickson, Levy and Post, 1977) increases the acceptability of the test greatly.

The battery of tasks proposed by Williams (1968) has been used in some centres for assessment of memory problems in the aged. Included are tests, some similar to those in the WMS, which measure aspects of learning and recall. One of the more useful aspects of this battery is the distinction between various modalities (verbal and non-verbal) and in the ability to compare and contrast recognition and recall, including cued recall. A study by White, Merrick and Harbison (1969) commends the use of this battery with the elderly.

The Benton Visual Retention Test is probably the most useful test of immediate visual memory for use with the elderly (Crookes and McDonald, 1972). Some normative data for older subjects is included in the test manual. The copying version of the test, where the design is left in front of the subject, instead of being removed after the ten-second inspection period, provides a much-needed control for the effects of perceptuo-motor, rather than memory, impairments.

The Object Learning Test from the Revised Kendrick Battery (Gibson and Kendrick, 1979) has a useful role in assessing secondary memory. The test involves free recall of a number of common objects presented pictorially and has a much higher degree of acceptability to patients than other learning tests. It has two parallel forms and data on six-week re-test enable it to be readily used longitudinally. An Object Learning Test Quotient expresses the person's performance in relation to their age-group, and enables comparison with other areas of cognitive function. It could benefit from further development, perhaps using a cued-recall or recognition format and certainly making use of the data from repeated presentation of some items, and of the different category groupings into which the items fall.

Finally, all these tests are intended to be objective measures of aspects of the person's memory. There is increasing interest in examining more precisely the person's subjective memory, or their knowledge of their own memory (meta-memory). Some questionnaires have been devised (e.g. Bennett-Levy and Powell, 1980; Broadbent, Cooper, Fitzgerald and Parkes, 1982) but have not yet been widely used with elderly patients. Having such questionnaires completed by both patients and their relatives may show some discrepancies, especially with dementing patients who may show little awareness of their memory problem (Baddeley, Sunderland and Harris, 1982). Using such measures may draw attention to the gulf between current memory testing and the demands on memory in everyday life.

Speed

The other test from the Revised Kendrick Battery — the Digit Copying Test — measures speed of performance simply and acceptably. The task is to copy printed digits as quickly as possible. A quotient may be again calculated, facilitating comparison with other areas of the patient's function, and re-test data give some indication of the extent of practice effects when it is used repeatedly. It is preferable to the WAIS Digit Symbol subtest, as it is less complex and relies less on memory and on the comprehension of instructions. Severe perceptuo-motor difficulties can produce impaired performance on these tests, with the patient being unable to follow the sequence of digits across the page.

Language

A number of aphasia batteries have been developed, for the identification and description of language dysfunction. None have been specifically designed for use with older people. The Schuell Minnesota Aphasia Test covers a wide range of functions, and has been standardised on normal elderly people (Walker, 1980). A useful short form has been empirically derived (Powell, Bailey and Clark, 1980). This comprises subtests of the Schuell assessing word-reading ability, writing ability, naming ability and the comprehension of simple instructions. The Token Test (De Renzi and Vignolo, 1962) tests comprehension of increasingly linguistically more complex instructions (from 'touch the red circle' to 'put the blue circle under the white rectangle'; it can be useful in describing the extent of a receptive deficit. With the greater length of the more complex instructions and increased processing required a greater load is placed on memory span. This should be taken into account when interpreting results on the test of patients with memory impairments. Walker (1980) showed that normal elderly people performed poorly on the Weigl Test, which involves sorting different coloured shapes sequentially first on one dimension (shape or colour), then the other. The Token Test uses similar material — tokens of various colours, shapes and sizes. However the difficulty experienced on the Weigl Test may well be more one of changing set than of a difficulty in using shape and colour concepts. Walker's results do not then necessarily invalidate the Token Test. Semple *et al.* (1982) have used an expressive version of the test, the Reporter's Test, successfully with cognitively impaired elderly patients.

Albert (1981) states that language assessment should 'include an evaluation of language comprehension, repetition, reading, writing and naming'. Specific tests of certain functions are now becoming available to supplement the measures available in the various batteries. For example, McKenna and Warrington (1983) have developed a naming test, with items of graded difficulty. Reading could be assessed by the National Adult Reading Test (Nelson, 1982), mentioned above. This is designed primarily to give a guide to lifelong intellectual level, and so includes words that are unlikely to be read correctly unless the person is familiar with them. The ability to read and understand words in sentences would need to be evaluated as well as the ability to read words alone.

Finally in this language section, tests of verbal fluency should be mentioned — although they might be considered tests of semantic memory or of speed of processing as much as of language. Typically they involve asking the patient to name as many words as possible in a certain time beginning with a particular letter (Whitehead, 1973b) or to give as many names as possible belonging to a particular category (e.g. animals, towns; Isaacs and Akhtar, 1972).

Neuropsychological Assessment

Batteries developed for use with younger patients should be used with caution, unless old-age norms are available. A number of studies (reviewed by Klisz, 1978) have shown that normal older people perform poorly on certain parts of the Halstead–Reitan Battery, and similar results emerge from other neuropsychological tests (e.g. Benton, Eslinger and Damasio, 1981). Probably the length and difficulty level of these batteries contribute to their unsuitability for elderly people. Whether such batteries could be amended to increase their applicability — as has been the case for their use with children — remains to be seen.

One method of testing elderly people neuropsychologically is to use very simple clinical tests, utilising everyday objects and materials. Holden and Woods (1982, pp. 113–29) describe such an approach that could help in identifying common neuropsychological deficits. Another is to use the various tests described above to draw up an overall neuropsychological profile. For instance, Albert (1981) suggests five areas should always be investigated; attention, language, memory, visuo-spatial ability and cognitive flexibility and abstraction. Language and memory tests have been detailed above. Attention tests include digit-span and crossing out particular letters from an array; cognitive flexibility and abstraction may be assessed by tests like the Wisconsin Card Sorting Test, where the person's ability to change set, and not persevere with a particular strategy when it becomes inappropriate, is evaluated. Visuo-spatial ability has been mentioned in relation to the copying version of the Benton Visual Retention Test. Spontaneous drawing and copying of simple shapes and a house have been used by Moore and Wyke (1984), who provide useful data on the performance that might be expected of normal elderly people.

From these measures some indication of strengths and weaknesses can be obtained. Where an area in particular is impaired, it may be possible to relate the dysfunction to a specific focal lesion. Where impairment is more general, it may be inadvisable to describe the impairment as the sum of a number of specific problems. For example, verbal fluency does not seem to be related to frontal lobe dysfunction in patients with dementia (Miller, 1984) and the drawing disability in dementia seems quite different from that seen in patients with focal parietal lobe lesions (Moore and Wyke, 1984).

Special Considerations in Cognitive Assessment of the Older Person

There are a number of basic steps that can be taken, whether the assessment is brief or very detailed, that can help the elderly person to perform as close as possible to their potential. These involve reducing the stress level and maintaining the person's attention and motivation.

Sensory deficits

These must be corrected as far as possible with spectacles, hearing aid and so on. For deaf patients specially designed amplifiers with microphone and headphones are available that can be helpful in some instances. Severe deficits that cannot be corrected require careful selection of tests that can be presented through less impaired sensory systems. For some tests instructions and items can be written out to aid deaf patients. Testing visually impaired patients on performance tasks presents great difficulty as most involve visuo-motor skills. Occasionally increasing the size of the stimulus material is of help; alternatively simple tactile tests may have to be used.

Rapport

Older subjects generally require more than a passing comment regarding the weather before pressing on with the tests! Time must be allowed for the patient to become comfortable with the assessment situation, and for initial anxieties to subside. The purpose of the assessment must be explained carefully and straightforwardly. Its relevance for the elderly person should be emphasised (a good discipline — if it has no relevance why is it being done?) Where possible the assessment should seek to mesh in with the elderly person's own concern. If their memory bothers them for instance, then the assessment may help identify what sort of memory problems are occurring, and may suggest ways of overcoming some of them. It is worth mentioning at the outset that the items vary greatly in difficulty — some will seem ridiculously simple, others impossibly difficult. Everybody will fail some items, because of the design of the test.

Pacing

Sessions must never be rushed; a time-limit increases everyone's anxiety. The session must be gently paced, with opportunities for a rest and a chat between tests. Sessions should be relatively short; two brief sessions are always preferable to a lengthy attempt to do all the tests in one go. Fatigue reduces cognitive performance, and the patient should be carefully observed for signs of tiredness. Where further sessions will be needed it is particularly important to end the session on an apparent note of success. Even the most demented patients seem to retain an awareness of situations that have previously proved stressful, and will be reluctant to return where this has been the case.

Encouragement

Most tests do not allow specific feedback on the patient's responses. There is no reason why supportive encouragement of a generalised nature cannot be given. Most elderly people find this helpful, particularly if it is given in a realistic fashion. There is no point telling the patient they are doing well when they have clearly just failed an item. It is preferable then to talk of how difficult the failed item can be, how many patients find it similarly difficult, and so on. Patients often underestimate their performance level, and realistic positive evaluation can often be given, e.g. 'You're doing better than most people of your age'.

Test selection

Overt, obvious, glaring, persistent failure has to be avoided if the patient's co-operation is to be retained. A few failures that can be perceived as difficult can usually be tolerated. Selection of appropriate tests is most important in this regard. A good strategy is to begin with relatively simple tests, and to gauge from the patient's responses what order of difficulty level would be appropriate later. Tests can also be selected so that the testing time is kept to a minimum, by using short forms and tests covering a wide range of functions briefly. From results on these tests decisions as to the usefulness of more in-depth assessment of particular functions can be made.

Examples of Cognitive Assessment

Some aspects of the use of assessment techniques are illustrated in the following case outlines which represent typical situations for the application of cognitive assessment.

Case 1. Mrs B., in her early seventies, was referred by her general practitioner for advice on coping with memory loss caused by depression. She had been a capable professional whose husband had been killed in the Second World War. She had not remarried but built up a substantial professional career, from which she had retired some ten years previously. Soon afterwards her mother died, and she had moved into the family home and had looked after her father (now in his nineties) since then. The remainder of the family had had little contact, except 'when they wanted something'.

Clinical tests of memory suggested some short-term memory loss. Further investigations commenced with the WAIS, which showed a full-scale IQ in the 105 region with verbal IQ around 115 and performance IQ 95. Subtest scores were widely scattered, Arithmetic and Digit Span very low, but Vocabulary excellent. More intensive memory assessment suggested a substantial deficit in short-term verbal memory, some deficit in short-term visuo-spatial memory, but little problem with long-term functions.

Her behaviour was interesting with little suggestion of depressive problems in motivation and concentration. In addition current life-style did not suggest the usual associations of early dementia. To cut a long story short, a brief home visit followed, when her elderly father sent her to get some tea then quite bluntly said, 'You know she drinks my vodka — all the time'.

This provided a fresh and unexpected (in view of the seemingly extensive medical and social reports) twist to the story. Control of alcohol intake produced a dramatic improvement in ability (including WAIS scores in the 120s), indeed far better than expected. She was helped with some advice on home and personal organisation to assist memory functions. Some five years later the GP reports she has adapted well to the death of her father and is helping with a local self-help group for the elderly.

This case provides an example where intelligent use of assessment techniques and their interpretation produced some valuable insights from results which had an unusual flavour in relation to the presenting problems. The need to integrate results with background information and treatment is shown.

Case 2. An 85-year-old man, living on his own, was referred by an orthopaedic ward. A broken leg, caused by a fall on the ice, had resulted in admission, and slow but complete recovery from the break. However, he had refused to go home and was acting in a very depressed and dependent way on the ward. Basic self-care and even toileting had caused problems.

A thorough assessment was planned with evaluation of behavioural, cognitive and adjustment functions. Before coming into hospital there had been no apparent problems, as related by the patient, his home help, neighbours, etc. Clinical assessment showed some orientation problems but nothing as severe as his behaviour indidicated. More formal assessment was very patchy with major problems of motivation and concentration on WAIS and other formal tests. However, when he 'co-operated', scores were well within average ranges for his age.

It was decided to send him home with support from local authority and voluntary agencies who were cued to encourage the re-emergence of his previous coping behaviour. In a short while he readjusted and was able to live his previous life.

This case illustrates the ability of formal cognitive assessment to suggest that capabilities remain (when problems of motivation and co-operation are overcome), even although behavioural functioning may suggest otherwise.

Case 3. This 62-year-old lady had become very concerned about her memory since her husband's death twelve months previously. She was referred to a consultant psychiatrist, and told him her memory was extremely poor. A provisional diagnosis of pre-senile dementia was made, together with a request for psychological assessment. This assessment aimed to describe the patient's strengths and deficits, in order to feed back realistic information about her memory and to advise on any appropriate strategies to maintain memory function.

The WAIS and Wechsler Memory Scale were used as the basis of the initial assessment. The WAIS verbal subtests showed considerable scatter, with high scores on Comprehension, Similarities and Vocabulary, and much lower scores on Arithmetic and Digit Span. The difference between verbal and performance levels (108 and 95 respectively) is reliable, but not abnormal; it is within a standard deviation of the mean verbal–performance discrepancy for normal elderly people under the age of 75 reported by Savage *et al.* (1973).

The patient's performance on the Wechsler Memory Scale was generally at least average for her age, when compared with Hulicka's (1966) or Cauthen's (1977) norms. Her orientation and personal information were good, as was her delayed recall of the logical memory passages, and her visual memory. Her learning of the paired associates was outstanding, whether the word-pairs had a high or low degree of association. Using Kear Colwell's (1973) factor scores, the attention/concentration factor seemed to reflect the patient's weakest area of memory function. This ties in with the WAIS results — Arithmetic and Digit Span having the largest primary memory component of the WAIS subtests.

It was possible to feed back to the patient that generally her memory was as good as, if not better than, most people of her age. The only area where impairment might be detectable was in concentration/attention. This led on to a discussion of the impact of emotional upset on concentration, and the patient began to talk about her as yet unresolved grief over the loss of her husband. Previously she had maintained adamantly that this was not a problem for her. A series of guided mourning sessions were agreed, and the patient made considerable progress.

Case 4. This charming 78-year-old lady was referred to a psychiatrist when her general practitioner realised how much of the physical symptoms of which she complained had no basis in reality. Following a gastric operation 20 years previously, when she suffered hypoxic cerebral damage, she had partial amnesia. Psychological assessment was requested to assess the extent of the memory problems. Discussion with relatives indicated that the problem was static, and in fact became less when her sleeping tablet medication was reduced (she had acquired these from several doctors, none realising someone else was also prescribing them!) Her son confirmed that she filled gaps in her memory using her vivid imagination — fuelled doubtless by a rich, varied (and at times harrowing) life.

On the WAIS, her overall intellectual level remained in the bright normal/superior range, on both performance and verbal scales. Her speed of information processing (on Kendrick's Digit Copying Test) was normal, but on the Object Learning Test, as on other memory tests, impairments were evident. This applied to both verbal and visual memory, and regardless of whether retention was assessed by free recall or recognition. Deficits were more apparent after a delay — immediate recall being less impaired. Despite this severe memory problem, some evidence of patchy new learning ability was evident. This, together with her well-preserved general intellectual function, suggested that some work on introducing, and reinforcing the use of, memory aids might be beneficial. These included an electric clock giving day, date and time — previously she had woken her teenage grandchildren at 4.00 a.m. to ask what day it was! She was encouraged to use a diary to keep track of appointments, to avoid her arriving on the wrong day, which had become a common occurrence. This patient proved able to make use of these memory aids to some extent, and seemed better able to accept their introduction from a psychologist than from her family, who had suggested them previously.

Cases 3 and 4 illustrate how cognitive assessment can contribute to psychological intervention with elderly patients.

Developments in Cognitive Assessment

We have tried to show in this chapter that cognitive assessment is an aspect of psychological work with the elderly that can have a valuable contribution to make, provided it is used appropriately.

However, we are under no illusions as to the deficiencies of the tests currently available, which are summarised in Table 5.1.

Table 5.1: Problems with Current Cognitive Tests for the Elderly

1. Designed to show *failure* in dementing patients
2. Difficult to use repeatedly to monitor change
3. Each test involves a number of cognitive processes (e.g. Digit Symbol subtest of WAIS involves speed, comprehension, memory and visuo-spatial skills)
4. Often stressful
5. Often seem irrelevant to 'real life'
6. Doubtful relationship to 'real-life' skills and function
7. Can be time-consuming, for information produced

Three major areas of development seem to be occurring at present, which have the potential to produce methods of assessment that can overcome these problems to some extent. These three areas have considerable overlap, and show some signs of eventually converging.

Cognitive models

Increasingly tests are being based on current conceptions of cognition from experimental psychology, rather than on items that traditionally seem to discriminate particular diagnostic groups. This gives hope that a patient's ability — rather than only their deficits — may be assessed, and that a broader range of function may be covered. At present, for example, widely used tests of remote memory, or of secondary memory tested by recognition methods are not available. Such methods might also be better suited to giving specific measures of particular processes. If cognitive processes underlying performance in real life are identified and can be assessed, the void between performance in the test situation and performance where it really matters might be reduced.

Among those proposing this development are Kendrick (1982a) and Cohen and Eisdorfer (1979), who suggest experimental paradigms that could be of value in assessing a number of areas of cognition including the control process as the person uses in carrying out cognitive tasks. Rabbitt (1981b, 1982b) acknowledges the deficiencies of psychometric models, but points out current cognitive models cannot be simply transposed into the clinical arena as straightforward measures of function. A major problem is that models developed in cognitive psychology have not addressed themselves to issues of individual differences and of change over time. Rabbitt similarly draws attention to the importance of control system models, that can describe how improvements with practice occur, how patients adjust to changes in task demands and overcome limitations in their function. He points out for example that mean reaction time would be a poor measure of cognitive performance; practice effects may reduce differences between young and old subjects in mean reaction time considerably. Variability in reaction time might be a more useful index, reflecting the way in which the subject employs their cognitive resources throughout the task. It is important to recognise then that cognitive psychology does not have immediate 'off the shelf' solutions to assessment of the elderly. Many experimental paradigms are simply too difficult for elderly people (although ideal for undergraduates!); some involve processes automatic in the young and fit that cannot be taken for granted in the dementing elderly person. What is needed is collaboration between experimental cognitive and clinical psychologists to explore the complex issues involved.

Relevance of materials

The concept of 'ecological validity' has been mentioned previously. There is certainly increasing concern to use age-appropriate and relevant materials, and to select tests of appropriate difficulty, to reduce stress and increase motivation as much as possible. For example, Crook, Ferris and McCarthy (1979) have devised the Misplaced-objects Task as a brief test of memory dysfunction for elderly patients. The test has a game-like structure and involves the subject placing pictures of everyday objects in particular 'rooms' on a board laid out as a representation of a seven-room house. After a delay of 5–30 minutes the subject is asked to replace the objects in the room previously chosen. Crook *et al.* report that the test was more acceptable than conventional psychological tests. Rabbitt (1982b) mentions a simulated 'supermarket shopping' task (presented on a microcomputer) that similarly seeks to assess aspects of the person's cognitive function in a manner that seems directly relevant to a real-life situation. Whether these simulations do indeed have greater validity in relation to real-life performance, as well as greater face validity, remains to be seen.

Automated assessment

Automation of cognitive tests for the elderly has a surprisingly lengthy history, dating back to at least the mid-1960s when a teaching machine was used to assess change in cognitive function in geriatric patients (Gedye and Miller, 1970; Wedgwood, 1982). Miller (1980a) comments that automated tests 'have proved very acceptable to old people and are capable of satisfactory use with many who would be unable to cope with the more usual psychometric tests'.

Most of these early studies used the Pictorial Paired Associate Learning Test (see Thompson and Wilson, 1982). This involved a matching to sample task, and was individually tailored, returning to previous items when an item was failed. However, this test has been shown to be very susceptible to practice effects, to have an uneven rise in difficulty level and to have too restricted a range for more able subjects (Levy and Post, 1975; Volans and Levy, 1982). In addition, its use of a projection system driven by an on-line mainframe computer has now been superseded by more portable, flexible microcomputer systems.

Perez, Hruska, Stell and Rivera (1978) also report the use of an automated matching to sample task with elderly dementing subjects. Their task incorporated a delay of variable intervals (filled with a distraction task), giving an index of memory performance. Both visual and verbal materials were used. By adjusting the delay interval on each trial according to performance on the previous trial, the maximum delay for the subject reliably to be able to perform correctly was identified. If the patient was correct the delay increased on the next trial, if incorrect the delay was reduced. The hardware used again involved a projection system, but in this case controlled by a mini-computer.

Microcomputer systems are now becoming extremely popular. They are much cheaper, more reliable and flexible than previous systems. Several batteries of cognitive tests are already available. For example, Acker (1980) has developed the Bexley–Maudsley Automated Psychological Screening Tests. These include a vocabulary test, visual and verbal memory tests, a perceptual test and a choice reaction time test. Beaumont (1981) is also automating a number of conventional tests (including Raven's Matrices and Digit Span). These systems have a number of advantages over conventional tests. They can accurately time response latencies; this means that a range of performance can be obtained on items which all subjects perform correctly; failures are not necessary to produce a range of scores! As noted above, speed of response (and variability in this) is a particulary important variable with elderly people. The microcomputer can potentially record times for each part of a task that has several components. Secondly, they can precisely control the important parameters of the task. The stimuli can be presented for an exact period of time, as can delay intervals; feedback is given in a standardised and replicable fashion. In other words, the computer is more likely to give the test exactly as intended than the conventional tester! Also the precise control allows small variations in, say, delay interval, to be programmed into the test. Thirdly, the computer can generate random stimuli, given certain constraints. For example, it can produce lists of digits of a given length, randomly selected and in random order. Or it could select a list of twelve words to be learned at random from a larger pool of words of similar difficulty. This should enable automated tests to be used repeatedly more readily than conventional tests, which seldom have more than one parallel form. Finally, automated assessment promises to save time, freeing the psychologist from some of the more mundane aspects of test administration.

It might seem that if automated assessment could incorporate relevant materials and insights from cognitive psychology (as in the 'supermarket shopping' simulation mentioned above) that all the problems of current cognitive tests would have been overcome. A great deal of development work remains to be done, however. For example, Carr, Wilson, Ghosh, Ancill and Woods (1982) administered a memory and information test to 24 psychogeriatric patients both conventionally and using a microcomputer system. Although correlations between total scores on the two forms were high, patients achieved significantly higher scores with conventional testing, and agreement on answers on the two forms was only around 60 per cent.

Several points emerged from this study that highlight some of the difficulties of using automated tests with this population. Firstly, five patients were unable to read the questions which were presented verbally on a TV screen. Visual, as well as cognitive, problems were important here. Some patients were able to read the individual words, but not able to comprehend the meaning of the sentence as a whole. A voice-over, presenting the question to the subject auditorially may be feasible as speech synthesis devices become more sophisticated, and would certainly help with this problem. One patient was completely unable to grasp the link between the three alternative answers offered on the TV screen and the three response buttons provided. Many others gave a correct verbal response, and then pressed the wrong button. Verbal response, as required in the conventional test, seemed to be the natural mode for most patients. The additional step of translating this into a motor response presents an extra burden. Translation from the screen to the buttons could be overcome using a touch-sensitive screen, where the subject simply has to point to the correct answer on the screen. In many conventional tests questions are open-ended, the subject has an unlimited choice of responses; correct answers may be expressed in several different ways. In the automated test presented by Carr *et al.*, a forced-choice format was imposed (given that subjects are unable to use the computer keyboard, there is little alternative). If the answers seemed all equally likely, or if none of the given answers seemed reasonable to the patient, subjects occasionally became overcome by indecision. In the conventional test subjects avoided this by simply giving any apparently likely response, and so were not confronted by their lack of certainty.

Kendrick (1982a) argues that automated testing with the current generation of elderly people is not worth pursuing, because of their relative unfamiliarity with TV and video games. However, as Carr *et al.* (1982) point out, if hardware is specially developed giving large, clear displays, a natural, straightforward response device, and a small number of response alternatives, and if software is creatively devised to make use of the computer's potential for graphics and for motivational aids (like music), worthwhile systems may be possible. They will need to be flexible and wide-ranging, to take into account the large variability in cognitive function found in elderly people. It will probably not be sufficient simply to use the automated tests that have been devised for younger patients; considerable modifications may be needed before they can be used with the elderly.

Conclusion

It is our hope that the current wave of enthusiasm for automated assessment will not simply result in the computer administration of a number of the conventional tests. The opportunity exists to make use of the potential of the micro computer *and* to develop new methods of assessment that incorporate materials relevant to the lives of elderly people, and that are based on current concepts from cognitive psychology. It must be recognised that even the most flexible system will not be able to assess a proportion of the most severely disabled elderly. Observational measures will produce more useful information in these cases.

Summary

1. Traditionally cognitive assessment has been used *diagnostically*, resulting in allocation to a particular category. We argue that assessment should be descriptive of the person's psychological function, and this information can be useful in a number of practical situations.

2. Diagnostic indices, such as the verbal–performance discrepancy or the Deterioration Quotient, have proven imperfect predictors for the individual case. Diagnostic tests have many problems; some are very stressful, many are not standardised on the type of patients they will actually be used with, and so on.

3. Descriptive assessment is not without its own problems: repeated assessment is often difficult, current tests are unsuitable on many grounds, including that of 'ecological validity'. Detailed assessment should be reserved for particular cases where an important question arises from the brief cognitive screening tests that should be routinely carried out, by members of the clinical team other than the psychologist.

4. As well as brief tests of cognitive function, useable tests are currently available to assess aspects of intellectual function, memory and learning, speed, language and neuropsychological function. Great care must be taken in their selection and administration for them to be useful with regard to the particular purpose of the assessment for the individual patient.

5. Developments in cognitive assessment are badly needed. Ideally they should use much more relevant materials and tasks, and be based on developments in cognitive psychology, which is beginning to develop control system models for individual differences and for change over time. Microcomputer technology is encouraging a great deal of interest in automated assessment. Developing systems suitable for the elderly calls for considerable ingenuity in both hardware and software design. It provides a good

opportunity to make progress also with the other two areas already mentioned.

6 THE ASSESSMENT OF ADAPTATION

Personality Assessment

Introduction

In Chapter 3 we reviewed some of the characteristics of personality in the elderly. The models reviewed in that discussion were based on studies which had two major approaches — the projective and the psychometric. Assessing personality in the elderly presents some particular difficulties which — in our view — render both of these approaches less than satisfactory. In this chapter we will direct the reader's attention to how these approaches have been applied to the elderly, before going on to look at the applicability of a wider range of techniques for investigating this contentious area of functioning.

Projective Measures

There is an extensive literature on the use of both the Rorschach and Thematic Apperception Test (TAT) with the elderly (Kahana, 1978; Savage, 1973). Indeed versions of the TAT specifically for the elderly have been developed — the Senior Apperception Test (SAT: Bellak and Bellak, 1973) and the Gerontological Apperception Test (Wolk and Wolk, 1971). These tests adapt the scenes depicted on the cards, using situations more appropriate to the elderly and portraying older people. They are thus intended to be more acceptable and to elicit more appropriate responses.

Kahana (1978) points out supposed advantages of projective tests with the elderly; they are said to be more readily understood by the elderly person, do not require a high degree of literacy, and do not require decisions between complex alternatives as in pencil and paper multiple-choice testing. In addition they are administered in a face-to-face interview and so the clinician is able to observe more closely how the person responds.

Whilst there is little doubt that a perceptive clinician will be able to make useful observations of an elderly person's functioning by watching them respond to the stimulus of an inkblot or of an appropriate scene, their usefulness as *tests* is limited. There is no universally accepted scoring system for the TAT, still less the SAT, although Lawton *et al.* (1980) review evidence suggesting a scoring system with acceptable inter-rater reliability may be feasible. They also point out that, far from being helpful, the versions specially designed for the elderly may simply remind the patient of negative stereotyping of older people and their environment. The responses may then reflect this bias rather than the personality of the individual concerned. Research on the Rorschach with the elderly is extremely limited and of very poor quality. Most work is of dubious methodology and, if anything, suggests that there is more association between test results and intellectual ability, rather than adjustment.

There do not seem to be any clear grounds for the use of these measures of personality with the elderly. They have an apparent acceptability to elderly individuals and seeming ease of administration, coupled with the opportunity to observe the client in the assessment situation. However, these factors do little to compensate for a lack of theoretical basis and psychometric adequacy.

Objective Tests

The Minnesota Multiphasic Personality Inventory (MMPI) has been described as the most frequently used test of personality for older clients (Lawton *et al.*, 1980). Yet the original version of the test consists of 550 items, and in fact was designed to diagnose psychopathology, rather than to give a personality profile. Not surprisingly shorter forms have been developed — Lawton *et al.* (1980) comment that the full scale is only for the above average in intellect, vigour and motivation! The Mini-mult is a 71-item version. It forms part of the Duke University Older Americans Resources and Service assessment materials (Pfeiffer, 1975c). Fillenbaum and Pfeiffer (1976) found that the re-test reliability of some scales was rather low (median scale reliability r = 0.38, range 0.10 = 0.75). Evidence for its validity was mixed, with it perhaps tending to overestimate pathology. The validity of the full MMPI in distinguishing 'pathological' and normal elderly groups is better established (Savage *et al.*, 1977). A brief form for screening purposes in the elderly was produced by Britton and Savage (1966a).

The reliability of the full scale with the elderly is not known, and the validity of each scale is open to question. The MMPI is perhaps best viewed as a diagnostic aid, using single score measures rather than the typical MMPI profile generally used.

In research studies on younger people the Maudsley Personality Inventory (MPI) and its developments the Eysenck Personality Inventory (EPI) and Eysenck Personality Questionnaire (EPQ) have often been used. A few studies have examined its applicability to the elderly, and Gutman (1966), for example, provides data on 200 older subjects (60–94). Savage *et al.* (1977) report results of the MPI with normal elderly people and with elderly psychiatric patients. Their (small) sample of normal elderly did not differ on either of the two scales measured, extraversion and neuroticism, from those of normal younger age-groups. Generally age changes seem to be small on this test, with a trend towards greater introversion with increasing age. Savage *et al.*'s elderly hospital psychiatric patients included a number having senile or arteriosclerotic dementia, who were able to complete the MPI. Is this then a personality test that can be recommended for use with a wide range of elderly patients?

A detailed examination of the use of the MPI with 100 normal elderly people living in their own homes (Gilmore, 1972) is instructive — and has implications for the use of other similar measures. Firstly, Gilmore points out that the questions had to be read out to the elderly subjects, instead of them completing it for themselves (largely because of frequent sensory and/or physical disabilities). Secondly, despite this modification to the standard administration of the test, 37 per cent could not complete the test due to lack of comprehension of some items. Nearly all were able to understand the items, and finish the test, when explanations were given. Those unable to comprehend some items had lower scores on a verbal intelligence test than those who were able to understand immediately all of the items. Gilmore accordingly then used a form of the EPI devised for people with lower levels of intelligence as a basis for modifying the MPI. When this was given to 75 normal elderly people, there were now no difficulties in comprehension. Certain items such as those concerning making new friends or being quick to act were however seen as irrelevant or affected by physical disabilities. In these studies Gilmore used a twelve-item short form of the MPI, with simplified wording. She concluded that five out of six of the extraversion items were 'inappropriate to the old person's personal and social context'.

Other similar — and generally longer inventories — have been used. Savage *et al.* (1977) report the use of Cattell's Sixteen

Personality Factor Test (16PF), together with some data on a small sample on the more recent Clinical Analysis Questionnaire (CAQ), which extends the 16PF by adding clinical or psychopathological scales to the existing normal personality factors. Gaber (1983) reports in more detail on this work adding a cluster analysis to an appraisal of the utility of the 16PF as an assessment measure. He concludes that the measure was valid with this group, although he was forced to exclude the use of factor B, the intelligence factor, which was found to be 'confusing and frustrating'.

A number of other researchers have also used the 16PF, e.g. Botwinick and Storandt (1974), and it has become clear that the norms for younger people cannot be used with older people as a number of age differences emerge. There is some agreement about the direction of these differences for most — but not all — scales (see Lawton *et al.*, 1980). It should be emphasised that age differences are as likely to be cohort effects as the effects of ageing *per se*. Some evidence for the validity of the 16PF with the elderly is emerging (Costa and McCrae, 1977–8).

The Edwards Personal Preference Schedule (EPPS) is another lengthy (225 items) inventory that has had some use. Lawton *et al.* (1980) consider its length and its paired-comparison format make it a difficult test to administer to elderly people.

Finally, Savage *et al.* (1977) report a study using the Tennessee Self-Concept Scale (TSCS) with a sample of 82 'normal' elderly people. A number of age differences emerged — but it should be emphasised that this group were in a sense 'super-normal', all having survived seven years from the time the sample was identified to the time when the scale was administered.

There are then at least five 'objective' personality tests that have been used with the elderly and for which some information is available to guide interpretation of the scores of elderly people. For some (MPI, 16PF) reliability data is available; generally evidence of validity is limited in relation to the elderly. The MMPI has been criticised for being wholly concerned with clinical features, the 16PF for not being clinically relevant (although the CAQ could potentially overcome this), the MPI/EPI cover a more limited range of personality traits; the EPPS and TSCS cover what seem initially quite different aspects of personality — the latter emphasising how the person views him or herself, rather than describing underlying traits.

All will undoubtedly prove difficult for many elderly people to complete themselves — the transfer of response from answer book to answer sheet may pose sensory, physical or cognitive difficulties. Reading out the items and the response alternatives can be a lengthy and tedious process — taxing the concentration and attention of elderly person and tester, complicated by any hearing difficulties. An increase in socially desirable responses may also be likely to result from this departure from the standard administration procedures. The older person is likely to be slower in completing the test, to tire more quickly and is more likely to choose non-committal responses, in tests where these are supplied. Personality tests are more familiar to younger people generally, with older people at present being less used to them, and potentially less aware of their 'usefulness'. They may reject the whole test if they feel items are irrelevant or inappropriate or incomprehensible (cf. Gilmore, 1972) or if they deal with areas considered taboo by some cultural groups.

What then are the advantages in using such tests? If the elderly person is cognitively, physically and sensorily unimpaired and has above average verbal skills then one of the tests might be appropriate, depending on the particular areas of interest. In research studies where some indication of broad personality types is needed, a short version of the MPI/EPI (with simplified wording) may be acceptable — particularly for the neuroticism score. However for quantifiable assessment of general psychopathology in a research setting the short forms of the MMPI could also be considered. In each case care will be needed to explain the value of the test and to counter as many of the above administration problems as possible.

In the UK at present few psychologists working with the elderly routinely use such tests. Apart from the usual dissatisfaction with theories as well as measures of personality, an important consideration is that often evidence is available from other sources as to the person's life-style and ways of coping with various situations. There is almost literally a lifetime of experiences that may give a far clearer indication of the older person's personality than measures devised specifically with younger people in mind.

Adjective Checklists

In this technique of assessment clients are asked to 'check out' adjectives most appropriately describing themselves and their behaviour. It is possible to structure this task so that the elderly may quite readily understand both the words and the instructions.

A less demanding task, such as this, may produce greater reliability and validity. Studies which report the use of this methodology have shown that the technique is acceptable and that consistent and meaningful data may be obtained (Apfeldorf and Hunley, 1971; Tobin and Lieberman, 1976).

Life Satisfaction and Morale

A great many scales measuring morale, life satisfaction and well-being have been developed, as gerontologists have sought to explore factors contributing to happiness and adjustment in older people (see Chapter 3). Fortunately many of the items seem to have been drawn from the same pool, so there is considerable overlap. For practical purposes it is desirable to identify scales that are brief and simple to understand and complete, and that show evidence of reliability and validity.

Obviously a unidimensional scale can be much briefer than a test assessing a number of distinct but related themes. Whilst some workers have contended that morale is unidimensional, there is general agreement that it is made up of several distinct aspects. Lawton (1975), for example, has shown the Philadelphia Geriatric Center (PGC) Morale Scale to contain three stable factors: agitation, attitude towards own ageing and lonely dissatisfaction. These have been replicated in several studies on large numbers of elderly people. However, factor analysis of other scales, for example the Life Satisfaction Index A (LSI-A) (Adams, 1969), does produce other additional factors (e.g. congruence between desired and achieved goals) and Lawton recognises that full coverage of morale may well need broader item pools. Recent factor-analytic studies involving elderly subjects (Hoyt and Creech, 1983) and subjects from age 25 upwards (Carp and Carp, 1983) have added to the controversy surrounding the underlying factor structure of 'morale' or 'well-being' and of the scales that have been developed to measure them. Hoyt and Creech identified three factors on the LSI-A: satisfaction with the past, satisfaction with the present and future orientation/optimism. They point out however, that different subgroups of their large sample, divided by race and sex, had slightly different factor structures. Carstensen and Cone (1983) provide a further cautionary note. They showed a relatively high correlation between the PGC and LSI-B (r = 0.64), but both scales correlated at a similarly high level with a measure of social desirability. Strong response biases may then be operating with this type of measure.

Can a useful brief measure then be possible? Fortunately, for many practical purposes, a global measure will suffice and where more detailed information is needed this may be obtained through the use of several measures in combination or obtained by other means or by interview.

The two major scales that have been extensively used are those mentioned above, the PGC Morale Scale and the LSI. The 17-item revised form of the PGC covering the three factors mentioned above (which show a high degree of internal consistency) presented by Lawton (1975) is recommended. It is simply worded, with dichotomous response choices (normally 'Yes' or 'No').

A number of forms of the LSI exist, e.g. LSI-A (20 items; agree or disagree); LSI-B (12 open-ended questions and checklist items scored on three point scales); LSI-Z (13 items; agree; ?; disagree; Wood, Wylie and Sheafor, 1969); Bigot's Life Satisfaction Index (8 items; true; cannot say; false; Bigot, 1974). The two briefer indices of Wood *et al.* (1969) and Bigot (1974) are probably most useful for routine purposes. Bigot's scale has two subscales: 'Acceptance–contentment' and 'Achievement–fulfillment'. Gilleard, Willmott and Vaddadi (1981a) suggest the latter subscale may reflect a more stable attitudinal component of morale, this aspect of life satisfaction being based on past life achievements and experiences. Bigot (1974) showed that other indices of life satisfaction (LSI-A and LSI-Z) tended to relate more to present life circumstances, whereas this overall index relates to both aspects. He also presents evidence that this eight item index may have greater reliability, although Wood *et al.*'s split-half reliability coefficient for the LSI-Z of 0.79 is reasonable. More recently Stock and Okun (1982) support this estimate of LSI-Z's reliability (r = 0.80).

The PGC Morale Scale and the LSI then are both worth considering; the former is slightly simpler in wording and format, but is twice as long as the Bigot LSI. Linn (1979) recommends both scales as good measures of well-being in the elderly, and reviews evidence that they have a reasonable inter-correlation (0.57). While this confirms that there is a fair amount of overlap, there is also sufficient variance specific to each measure to suggest that it would be valuable to use both measures where brevity is not of overriding importance.

How do the concepts of life satisfaction and morale relate to clinical populations? Do these general evaluations of 'happiness' with life past and present relate to clinical features of mood and affect? Some indication of the answers to these questions emerge from studies inter-correlating these measures with scales specifically devised to assess depression. Morris, Wolf and Klerman (1975) inter-correlated the PGC with two depression inventories, one of which was the Zung Self-rating Depression Scale (see below), on a sample of state mental hospital patients. They report considerable overlap between the three scales, with a common depression factor emerging. The Zung and PGC showed evidence of themes specific to each — self-satisfaction and life progression respectively. Savage *et al.* (1977) similarly report that the low energy depression scale of Cattell's Clinical Analysis Questionnaire is highly related to LSI-A and LSI-B scores. Gilleard, Willmott and Vaddadi (1981a) used both Bigot's LSI scales and a depression scale (Schwab, Holzer and Warheit, 1973) in comparing elderly depressed patients with normal elderly people. Both LSI and depression scales significantly differentiated between the two groups and were related to ratings by ward staff of overt depressive signs. Both scales also showed changes in the anticipated direction when readministered at the time of the patient's discharge. Interestingly on Bigot's LSI most change was on the contentment factor, with the past achievement factor showing little change, being significantly lower than that of the normal elderly. This could reflect a personality predisposition to depression in the elderly.

These two measures may then be suggested as brief, simple ways of assessing morale and well-being in elderly people. They will be particularly useful in monitoring depression. Although they have been used with elderly demented people, they can only be satisfactorily used with elderly people with little or no cognitive impairment. Useful normative data on Bigot's LSI is presented by Gilleard *et al.* (1981a). Although Lawton (1971) suggests score ranges for the PGC indicative of psychological distress or of a person 'badly mismatched with his total environmental situation', these are for an earlier, slightly longer form, with later research not presenting data in a form from which norms can be derived. In contrast to many of the measures mentioned, at least these have been devised specifically for the elderly, and so their acceptability is correspondingly higher.

Depression Scales

We have shown above that some morale scales can be useful measures of depression in the elderly. Are there any useful scales specifically designed to measure depression that are applicable to the elderly, or indeed have any such been specifically designed for the elderly?

Some scales have already been mentioned above and have clearly found some use with the elderly — the Zung in particular. In Gilleard *et al.*'s (1981a) study the Schwab Depression Scale was effective in distinguishing depressed elderly patients from normal elderly people, and was sensitive to change as the depressed patients improved. It also successfully discriminated depressed patients showing severe overt depressive behaviour from those who did not.

Gallagher, Nies and Thompson (1982) report data on the reliability of the Beck Depression Inventory in samples of elderly community volunteers and depressed out-patients. Re-test reliability (at an interval of 1–3 weeks) for the whole sample was excellent (r = 0.90), although considering the depressed group separately reliability was a little lower (r = 0.79). The internal consistency of the scale was also satisfactory. The normative data in this report (on 82 normal elderly people and 77 depressed patients) gives a guide to score ranges that might be of use clinically.

Despite such promising evidence of potential acceptability, reliability and validity with elderly depressed patients, the use of these self-report measures of depression with the elderly has been criticised. For example, Plutchik (1979) in a critique of the Zung SDS pointed out that in addition to a confusing format a number of items were inappropriate or might be affected by something other than depression in elderly patients — particularly items concerning health. The Beck Depression Inventory could be similarly criticised.

Indeed a major issue is the relation of physical ill health to old-age depression. Physical symptoms that might be associated with depression in younger people are much more common in older people with and without depression, but also physical ill health is an important factor leading to depression in elderly people (Bergmann, 1982). Certainly, over-emphasis on physical aspects of depression in a depression scale will lead to overrating of the level of depression in the elderly. However, in correlating physician's ratings of health and scores of elderly people on the Zung SDS,

Steuer, Bank, Olsen and Jarvik (1980) found no evidence of a significant relationship between physical health and total score on the Zung. Only three of the individual items on the scale were related to physical health ratings — fatigue, loss of libido and diurnal variation. It may be then that the problem of symptoms of depression and physical health being confounded in self-rating scales in the elderly has been overstated. Steuer *et al.*'s sample were however relatively young (median 64.5 years) and in relatively good health, so there must still be some doubt regarding the use of these scales with older, less healthy samples.

Adjective checklists again provide an alternative format. For example, Davies and Gledhill (1983) used items from the Multiple Adjective Affect Checklist (MAACL) (Lubin, 1965) with elderly people living in the community to asses level of depression. Scores on this measure correlated well with a psychiatric structured interview scale and a symptom checklist.

Observer rating scales are widely used, e.g. the Hamilton Depression Rating Scales (Hamilton, 1960). The ratings are made by a clinician interviewing the patient. In younger patients it correlates with the Beck Depression Inventory ($r = 0.68$, Bailey and Coppen, 1976), although for a sizeable group of patients (about a third) there were notable discrepancies between the scales. Kearns, Cruickshank, McGuigan, Riley, Shaw and Snaith (1982) have compared several self-rating and interviewer-rated scales. The latter (including the Hamilton) performed better in distinguishing different degrees of severity of depression in a sample of depressed in-patients (including some who were elderly). These authors recommend the Montgomery–Asberg Scale (Montgomery and Asberg, 1979) as an interviewer-rating scale where there is likely to be concurrent physical illness (as is probable in older samples). There is much to be said — particularly where milder degrees of depression are involved — for using both self-rating and interviewer-rating scales, as potentially tapping different, but overlapping, domains of depression in the elderly person. A semi-structured interview technique, as used in the Geriatric Mental State Depression Scale (Gurland *et al.*, 1976) may be a way of combining both self-report and observational measures.

In the previous section the overlap between life-satisfaction measures and depression scales was pointed out. There is some concern (e.g. Gurland, 1980) that depression should be distinguished from demoralisation in elderly people — a temporary state from a more permanent attitude. It may be here that the morale and depression measures part company. Although as we have seen they have much in common, each has some specific features not accounted for by a common factor — the life-progression factor in the morale scales (things get worse as you get older) and a self-satisfaction factor in the depression scales.

Other Measures of Adjustment

There are a number of other ways of looking at adjustment that have not been extensively used with the elderly, but potentially could be valuable. These include measures of locus of control, repertory grids and personal questionnaires.

The locus of control measure gives an indication of the extent to which the person perceives his environment and events within it as being within his control. The contrast is between the person who sees themselves as master of their own destiny with the person whose self-perception is as a victim of circumstance. Clinically this is an important aspect of how the person perceives and copes with their environment, and, although it has been used in some studies (e.g. Hanes and Wild, 1977), Rotter's (1966) original 23-item measure may be criticised as being too general and not relevant enough to elderly people. Reid *et al.* (1977) accordingly devised a more situation-specific measure for use with elderly people in residential care. They assessed not only whether the person felt a certain outcome was controllable, but also the desirability of the outcome for that person, controllability being irrelevant if the outcome is not reinforcing to the person. Both controllability and desirability were assessed using four point scales on seven outcome areas. Although Reid *et al.* used the scales with elderly people both in the community and in residential care (reliability coefficient (homogeneity) 0.66), they recommend it being extended to include more outcomes appropriate to community elderly if it is to be used there (see Ziegler and Reid, 1979).

The Repertory Grid (Fransella and Bannister, 1977) is a powerful technique for analysing and monitoring the way in which an individual perceives their environment in general as well as specific components such as relationships. The grid can be made specific to the individual reflecting their own personal interests, needs or problems or can reflect a facet of personality such as self-concept. Several 'self'-directed concepts could be included in a grid (e.g. self-now, self-before illness, ideal-self, etc.). There is little evidence in the literature of the use of the repertory grid with the elderly. However, use with children and the mentally handicapped (Gowans and Hulbert, 1983) suggests that the technique can be modified and successfully used even with those with cognitive loss.

The Personal Questionnaire (Shapiro, 1961) is particularly useful in monitoring changes over time in an individual. A different questionnaire is constructed for each person using the person's statements about their problems in an extensive interview as a basis. Having constructed the questionnaire, it is extremely easy to use repeatedly — the person having to choose between pairs of statements derived from the original problem items, expressing graded improvement. The Personal Questionnaire is applicable to the elderly, and has been used with a number of depressed elderly patients (Volans, 1981, personal communication). The questionnaire construction is a time-consuming process, but Mulhall (1976) has derived the Personal Questionnaire Rapid Scaling Technique (PQRST) which uses a standard item set, but the same basic approach, to overcome this problem.

As clinical psychologists become increasingly involved in the treatment of depressed elderly patients (see Chapter 7), it is likely that these, and other, as yet little used techniques will be applied to the elderly.

An Alternative Approach — Life History or Biographical Assessment

It could be argued that many of the previously mentioned questionnaires and other techniques would be redundant if the response of the subject to a large variety of circumstances and situations was known. With elderly people there is literally almost a lifetime of evidence potentially available as to their style of personality, coping strategies and so on. This forms the basis for an alternative evaluation approach, based on a life history or biographical assessment (Thurnher, 1973; Johnson, 1976; Bromley, 1978). In order to overcome problems of bias by the elderly people and/or their relatives, a composite picture may have to be formed from a variety of sources. Of particular interest will be how they coped with various points of transition and critical incidents in their lives — in their work, relationships and family for example. The coping strategies — cognitive and behavioural — the person employed to help them get through times of change and stress need to be identified. It is important not simply to establish a chronicle of events —

pleasant or distressing — but to aim at exploring how elderly people *perceived* these events, while they were occurring as well as in retrospect.

This is obviously not a quick, simple task to achieve. A number of interviews with the elderly person concerned and other informants may be needed. Conflicting reports may need to be reconciled; the person may — for whatever reason — not be able to recall certain potentially important events. An overwhelming amount of detailed information may be obtained, particularly if the emphasis is not kept firmly on examining the person's transition points. In any therapeutic endeavour with elderly patients, however, it cannot be stressed too strongly that having an awareness of the person's previous experiences and life-style is essential for work with the elderly person in his or her current circumstances.

Behavioural Assessment

For a number of purposes it is thought desirable to assess what a person actually *does* (or sometimes, is capable of doing). An example of this would be in relation to decisions concerning suitable placements for an elderly person needing residential care; different institutions might be more appropriate for different patterns of self-care ability or for elderly people having particular kinds of problems. Similarly, in providing appropriate services to an elderly person living in his or her own home, careful assessment would be needed to ensure that gaps in the person's abilities were overcome without making redundant the abilities still retained. Treatment interventions aimed at increasing certain types of behaviour (e.g. self-care) also need measures of these behaviours to identify areas of deficit and any changes in them. As well as behavioural deficits, in many situations behavioural excesses will be of interest, for example, high frequency of asking questions, excessive shouting.

Here we will discuss three distinctive ways of assessing behaviour, each particularly appropriate for certain purposes. Examples of useful measures will be given, as well as some indication of their possible areas of application.

Rating Scales

These are probably the most widely used method of assessing

elderly people's behaviour. People who know the elderly person well (members of the care-staff, a relative or occasionally the person him or herself) assess the person's functioning from their general unsystematic, day-to-day, observations of his or her behaviour. A bewildering variety of scales have been developed — none of the existing ones ever seem quite to fit another worker's requirements! They differ most importantly in the areas of behaviour assessed, but also in terms of numer of items, the time period to which observations relate, the number of rating points, and so on. Even where two scales cover the same area of behaviour they often differ greatly in the depth in which that area is assessed.

A number of reviews of behaviour-rating scales are available and are recommended for those wanting more details of other scales, as only a selection will be considered here (e.g.Salzman, Kochansky and Shader, 1972; Goga and Hambacher, 1977; Smith, 1979; Gilleard, 1984b). The review by Hall (1980) is particularly recommended, and in addition gives valuable advice on devising scales.

Among the most commonly used scales in the UK covering general aspects of behaviour particularly relevant to impaired elderly people are the Crichton Geriatric Rating Scale (Robinson, 1977), the Clifton Behaviour Rating Scale (formerly the Shortened Stockton Geriatric Rating Scale: Pattie and Gilleard, 1979), and the Psychogeriatric Dependency Rating Scales (PGDRS) (Wilkinson and Graham-White, 1980). The Crichton and Clifton scales are often confused; they are different scales!

In the USA the Physical and Mental Impairment of Function Evaluation (PAMIE: Gurel, Linn and Linn, 1972), the Physical Self-maintenance Scale (PSMS: Lawton and Brody, 1969) and the Geriatric Rating Scale (GRS: Plutchik, Conte, Lieberman, Bakur, Grossman and Lehrman, 1970) have been developed and cover similar ground. The areas covered by each are summarised in Table 6.1.

Despite the apparent similarity in content, several important differences should be emphasised, and will perhaps aid the selection of the correct scale for a particular task. Firstly scores are derived in different ways on different scales. The PAMIE, GRS and Clifton BRS have a total score and sub-scale scores based on factor analysis of the performance of the elderly people on the measure. The other scales impose a structure to the profile of subtest abilities by virtue of their design.

Secondly, the PSMS has no items relating to problem behaviour

Table 6.1: Six Behaviour-rating Scales Frequently Used with Elderly People

(1) Modified Crichton Geriatric Rating Scale — 13 five-point scales. The original scale included ratings of the patient's subjective and objective mood in place of scales 6, 7, 8 and 13.

1. Orientation	8. Social behaviour
2. Mobility	9. Restlessness
3. Feeding	10. Co-operation
4. Dressing	11. Sleep
5. Continence	12. Communication
6. Interest in environment	13. Complaints
7. Interest in others	

(Robinson, 1977; modified by Woods, 1979)

(2) Clifton Behaviour Rating Scale (Clifton BRS) — 18 three-point items, yielding a total score and four factor scores.

1. Physical disability	3. Communication difficulties
2. Apathy	4. Social disturbance

(Pattie and Gilleard, 1979; part of the Clifton Assessment Procedures for the Elderly — CAPE)

(3) Psychogeriatric Dependency Rating Scales (PGDRS)
   1. Orientation — 10 two point items
   2. Behaviour — 16 three-point items (largely problem behaviours)
   3. Physical (a) Hearing — 1 four-point item
               (b) Visual — 1 four-point item
               (c) Speech — 1 four-point item
               (d) Mobility — 1 six-point item
               (e) Dressing — 1 four-point item
               (f) Personal hygiene — 5 two-point items
               (g) Toiletting/continence — 5 three-point items
               (h) Feeding — 1 three-point item

(Wilkinson and Graham-White, 1980)

(4) Physical and Mental Impairment of Function Evaluation (PAMIE) — a 77-item scale, producing 10 factor scores.

1. Self-care dependent	6. Behaviourally deteriorated
2. Belligerent/irritable	7. Paranoid/suspicious
3. Mentally disorganised/confused	8. Sensori-motor impaired
4. Anxious/depressed	9. Withdrawn/apathetic
5. Bedfast/moribund	10. Ambulatory

(Gurel *et al.*, 1972)

(5) Physical Self-maintenance Scale (PSMS) — 6 five-point scales.

1. Toilet	4. Grooming
2. Feeding	5. Physical ambulation
3. Dressing	6. Bathing

(Lawton and Brody, 1969)

Table 6.1 — *continued*

(6) Geriatric Rating Scale (GRS) — 31 three-point items, yielding total score and three factor scores.
1. Withdrawal/apathy
2. Anti-social disruptive behaviour
3. Deficits in activities of daily living
(Plutchik *et al.*, 1970; Smith *et al.*, 1977)

while the Crichton and Clifton scales have relatively few. Wilkinson and Graham-White (1980) point out that the inter-rater reliabilities of their problem behaviour items were much lower than those found for orientation or physical functioning, perhaps emphasising the greater element of subjective judgement involved in rating these behaviours. This problem has been found in similar scales for the mentally handicapped.

Thirdly, an illustration of the differences in depth of coverage is the contrast between the Crichton's coverage of continence (1 five-point scale) with that of the PGDRS which has 5 three-point items covering this aspect of behaviour.

This type of scale is of most use in providing information as to the level of care or services the elderly person requires, and may be of some help in identifying specific areas of difficulty. The length of the scale is often of some importance for this purpose — it must not be so long that hard-pressed care-staff become reluctant to complete it carefully. For this reason, and because of its fairly wide coverage and extensive UK validation, the Clifton BRS has much to recommend it. For use in survey work an even briefer form, consisting of the Physical Disability Scale together with a brief information/orientation test, has been developed (Pattie, 1981).

Activity Scales. The above scales are ideally suited to those aspects of behaviour of impaired elderly people that determine the level of care and support needed in an institutional setting. They reflect little or nothing of other important aspects of the behaviour of less impaired elderly people, which may be important in determining the type of services they require or the goals of rehabilitation. Fewer scales to meet this need are available. Lawton and Brody's (1969) eight-item Instrumental Activities of Daily Living (IADL) is probably the best known, covering areas such as food preparation, laundry, financial responsibility and so on. Pfeffer, Kurosaki, Harrah, Chance and Filos (1982) have developed the Functional

Activities Questionnaire (FAQ — ten items) having some additional and more complex activities included. They claim it to be more sensitive than the IADL Scale, with which it shows a fairly high correlation (r = 0.72).

Holbrook and Skilbeck (1983) report the development of the 15-item Holbrook Activities Index, originally devised for patients who had suffered a stroke, but which seems likely to be more generally applicable to elderly people. Factor analysis revealed a three-factor structure, so that scores can be calculated for domestic, leisure/work and outdoor activities. This brief scale may be particularly useful in monitoring change in activity level over time in relatively unimpaired elderly people.

In therapeutic intervention with depressed elderly people it may well be relevant to have a measure of the patient's participation in pleasant and unpleasant events. Teri and Lewinsohn (1982) report a modification of the Pleasant and Unpleasant Event Schedules for use with the elderly. A number of items in the version used with younger adults occur with extremely low frequency in elderly patients (e.g. rock climbing, experiencing child birth!), and both are extremely long (640 items altogether). The abbreviated and adapted forms are still fairly long (114 items pleasant events, 131 items unpleasant), but may well be useful with more able, moderately depressed patients. If should be mentioned that for all four of these activity scales sex differences, at least in the current generation of elderly people, are likely to be relevant.

Future Developments. In the next few years there are likely to be further developments in these scales, some of which are already apparent from preliminary reports of continuing research.

Firstly, in developing treatment plans and in monitoring progress of treatment, more detailed and specific scales are likely to be necessary. A promising example of this is Cornbleth's (1978) Geriatric Resident Goals Scale, which consists of a number of behavioural 'goals' (e.g. 'Washes own face'). These are intended to be specific, unambiguous, observable behaviours, the occurrence of which may be readily ticked 'yes' or 'no', and requiring the minimum of subjective interpretation. The published form contains 85 such goals, based on staff's opinion of what desired behaviour would be. Evidence that this form has high inter-rater and re-test reliability (r = 0.95) is available. This format could readily be adapted and extended or modified to suit the desired outcomes in any particular setting. A similar attempt at rating a person's positive behaviour resulted in the Brighton Clinic Adaptive Behaviour Scale (available from R. Woods). It is long and detailed and attempts to break down behaviours into their component parts and in several settings has formed a good basis for developing care plans for particular patients. Its completion necessitates the care staff engaging in directed and precise observation of the individual's abilities. It is based on the Adaptive Behaviour Scales used for some years in mental handicap facilities (Nihira, Foster, Shellhaas and Leland, 1974).

An alternative approach is to examine one area of behaviour in greater detail. A general scale might suggest a problem with, say, dressing, that could then be evaluated further with a much more detailed rating. Few examples of this type of scale exist as yet, perhaps reflecting the relatively little headway a positive goal-planning approach has made on care of the elderly. An exception is Holden's Communication Scale (Holden and Woods, 1982), which assesses the person's speech, conversation and general awareness, and has proved useful in the evaluation of intervention programmes which focus on social behaviour rather than self-care functioning, e.g. Reality Orientation (RO) and reminiscence.

Secondly, there will be more emphasis on assessing the behaviours that relatives find difficult to cope with in the elderly person at home. These may not of course be identical with the behaviour that interferes with the smooth running of a ward that has been traditionally emphasised! Relatives, for instance, are likely to be much more concerned with the elderly person's repeated questioning or failure to recognise them, than would be a team of care-staff in an institutional setting, with considerably lower emotional involvement. Different types of behaviour may be relevant according to whether the relative lives with the elderly person or visits regularly. In the latter case questions of risk may outweigh the irritating repetitions that can be left behind. One scale devised for relatives is Greene, Smith, Gardiner and Timbury's (1982) Behaviour and Mood Disturbance Scale. Three factors emerged when this scale was used by relatives living with a dementing elderly person. These related to mood disturbance, active disturbed behaviour and apathy/withdrawal. Other scales have been developed by Gilleard, Watt and Boyd (1981c). An important issue here will be the reconciliation of frequency and severity of problems. There are some behaviours that may be seen as so difficult to cope with that even one occurrence will be a crisis (e.g. leaving gas on unlit, or, for some relatives, faecal incontinence). Others may not be seen as severe (e.g. asking the same question again and again), but may occur so frequently during the 24-hour period that they become a major source of strain. It may be necessary to adopt Sanford's (1975) approach, by first establishing the frequency of occurrence of a behaviour, and then the relative's attitude to it. How a particular behaviour affects their ability to continue caring is likely to vary from one relative to another according to their particular circumstances.

Thirdly, scales will be improved by the adoption of more rational and systematic procedures in their development, rather than the traditional trial and error approach. Techniques such as Guttman scaling have a great deal to offer, and have already been applied to some general behaviour rating scales (Volans, 1979, personal communication; Gilleard and Pattie, 1980; Lyle, 1984). The basis of a Guttman scale is that items are statistically selected and ordered so that if a person is able to perform a particular item then it is highly probable they will also be able to be successful at all lower items of the scale. Ideally the scale forms a hierarchy of skilled performances. An immediate advantage is that such scales can be more efficient than a traditional scale of similar length, as it should be possible to predict unobserved behaviour from performance on these items. Scales can then be briefer, and sub-scales have a more rational structure than simply combining items which seem to be superficially alike. The scale may also give some indication of the possible pathway of deterioration in behavioural functioning.

Practical Use of Scales. How can rating scales be used most beneficially in the practical situation? A rating by a group of nurses is likely to be more reliable than that by a single member of the care team. The scale should only be as long and as detailed as is necessary for the particular setting and purpose; motivation of the rater decreases if large numbers of irrelevant items have to be rated routinely for each patient. The amount of detail required should not be more than the staff levels of the setting or the patient-contact available to the staff member allow, or ratings will be based on guesswork. Senior staff will not always be in a good position to comment on, say, incontinence. The period over which observations should be based — the last week, month or whatever — should also be clearly specified. Whether the patient's *optimum* or *usual* performance is to be rated should be clarified. Staff should be trained in the use of the scale, and should rate the same patients as other staff independently as part of this training, to highlight any misunderstandings or differences of interpretation. These can be minimised by the use of simple unambiguous terminology, a clear, straightforward format and clear instructions. Items should be specific, with a minimum of subjective interpretation required. Items should avoid mutiple definitions (e.g. 'misidentifies persons and surroundings but can find way about') which cause difficulties for patients who meet some but not all of the given definition!

Finally it is tempting to assign from these scales a functional level to a particular elderly person. It should be remembered that what is being rated often depends to an extent on what the institution or relatives allow of the person, as well as their capabilities. If in a particular institution time is short patients may be dressed, or fed, simply because it takes longer if they are allowed to be independent. In many settings patient's behaviour fluctuates a great deal — one of the many reasons for this may be the different expectancies and attitudes of different staff. Behavioural functioning then is the end-product of the person–environment interaction, not an inherent quality of the individual in isolation.

Direct Observation in a Structured Setting

This type of behavioural assessment is analogous to traditional cognitive assessment. The person is asked to perform a particular task. Task performance is then rated in this structured situation. It is the basis of most traditional occupational therapy assessment, for example, where the person's cooking ability is assessed in the Occupational Therapy training kitchen. The major disadvantage of this type of procedure with dementing patients is immediately apparent; assessing them out of their familiar surroundings may well *not* be an accurate predictor of competence in their own home. The home may contain many familiar cues which prompt over-learned sequences of behaviour that may be absent elsewhere.

However, one measure has been developed which has been extensively used with both intact and impaired elderly subjects in the UK and the USA, and which succeeds to some extent in reducing interfering effects. It is the Performance Test of Activities of Daily Living (PADL: Kuriansky and Gurland, 1976). It consists of 16 tasks — drinking from a cup, combing hair, eating, locking a door. By using a portable kit of props (cup, spoon with sweet, door lock) it is possible for these tasks to be carried out in an interview situation in a standardised fashion. Performance is rated according to successful completion of defined component parts of the task, so that partial success is rewarded and some analysis is possible of where performance breaks down (see Table 6.2). Prompts and cues may be given, but are not specified.

Table 6.2: Example of Rating a Task on the PADL

Drinking

Rater places cup in front of subject and says 'Show me how you would drink from this cup'

Components of task — each scored according to whether achieved with/without prompting.

Grasps cup in hand
Lifts cup upright
Touches cup to mouth
Tip cup as if drinking

To reduce anxiety and increase motivation, simpler tasks are given first. The whole test takes only about 20 minutes to administer and is said to be generally acceptable to patients. Inter-rater reliability is high (r = 0.90) and Kuriansky *et al.* (1976) present evidence of its validity in that it is strongly related to physical health, mental state and prognosis. Its relationship to other indices of behavioural functioning has not as yet been established. An advantage over rating scales is that it may elicit positive behaviour not encouraged or prompted on the ward. Unfortunately, against the PADL's possible detection of under-functioning on the ward, a number of further possibilities arise for patients under-functioning on the PADL itself. As well as the problem of unfamiliarity mentioned above, the structured situation is more likely to give rise to problems of anxiety and motivation than would observation in the person's natural environment. Also some patients may have difficulty in comprehending the task and/or the instructions when they are taken out of their natural environment and placed in an inevitably artificial context. Why should I eat a sweet from a spoon? Why should I take my jacket off and put it on again? may be unspoken questions affecting the confused person's response. In planning treatment or in the assessment of change the subdivision of tasks may be useful, but the narrow range of tasks sampled lessens this potential application. The relationship of the test to a wide range of measures of cognitive and behavioural functioning might be of interest — it is conceivable that PADL is largely a test of constructional apraxia, and its relationship to general level of behavioural functioning may be less than anticipated. We would recommend its use alongside ward-ratings rather than in place of them.

Direct Observation in the Natural Environment

The observation of the elderly person's actual behaviour in their natural environment (home, day-centre, hospital ward) seems the most obvious method of assessing behavioural functioning. However, in practice, a number of issues make direct observation a rather complex task.

Firstly, there is the problem of privacy and related to this the effects of the observer on the behaviour. It is one thing for a nurse to rate a patient on their toileting or whatever from their general observation and knowledge of the patient; quite another for a psychologist armed with clipboard to follow the patient to every part of the ward or home. Families and police forces may be able to behave 'normally' with a four-man film crew recording their every move, but will elderly people learn to ignore the quiet man with a clipboard who pointedly ignores any comments directed at him, even in the 'public' area of the home or ward? As the design of care settings evolves with more emphasis on private areas, 'natural' observation becomes even more problematic. In using these observation methods this issue of privacy for the elderly people involved must be examined closely, and explanations given to them and to their relatives of the observations that are being carried out and their purpose.

It is of course not only the behaviour of the elderly people that will be observed, and which may be influenced by the presence of an observer. For example, in the pilot phase of an observational study we recorded very low levels of staff–resident interaction. In discussing this with staff, we discovered they had kept out of the lounge where the observations were being carried out so they would not influence the residents' behaviour that we were monitoring! Watson (1979–80) attempted to use a fixed video camera in a home for the elderly to collect data on staff–resident interactions. He discovered staff employed a number of strategies to defeat the purpose, for example, leaving a door open which then obscured the camera's line of vision! Generally, staff may feel considerably threatened when their behaviour is being closely monitored, and their behaviour may be influenced by this knowledge. This would particularly apply where the observation seems to carry with it an implicit criticism of the staff's performance — that they work inefficiently, do not talk to the residents enough, or where it seems to be forced upon them by their managerial 'superiors', rather than being requested by the care-staff as helping to meet their own needs and aspirations. Staff need clear explanations of the purposes of any observational work carried out, and an adaptation period is essential.

Secondly, direct observation produces a potentially huge amount of data; how can this be reduced to manageable proportions? Frequently this is achieved by time-sampling — observing the person's behaviour every minute, five minutes, 30 minutes, or whatever, depending on the frequency of the behaviour to be recorded. Enough behaviour has to be observed for it to be assumed to be a representative sample of the person's behaviour. Either the particular behaviour the person is exhibiting at the sampling point is recorded or all the behaviours occurring during a specified time period (say 10–30 seconds) might be recorded at each sampling point. Alternatively certain behaviours may be discrete and frequent enough for all occurrences in a certain time period to be counted at various times of the day (e.g. how many times the elderly person shouts in a ten-minute period).

Thirdly, some decision needs to be made about which behaviours to record, and with what level of precision. Ethological studies might generate categories of behaviour from detailed observational work; generally studies with elderly people have used predetermined categorisations of behaviour. Having decided which area of functioning is of interest the range of detail is vast — for social behaviour it might extend from recording each change of direction of gaze and its duration to only recording behaviour as 'engaged' or 'disengaged'. If detailed recording is desired, then the observer may be attempting to use a long and unwieldy behavioural coding schedule.

Fourthly, behaviours must be unambiguously defined, and inter-rater reliability checks should always be carried out to ensure this has been achieved. This is carried out by other raters independently, but simultaneously, making the observations. The calculation of inter-rater reliabilities has been the subject of some controversy — see Hartmann (1977), Harris and Lahey (1978).

The important point to emphasise is that direct observation is a potentially valuable technique in assessing the behaviour of elderly people. In practice it requires a great deal of consideration and preparation, depending on the behaviours to be observed, their frequency (if they only occur once or twice per day time-sampling will be tedious and unproductive — record keeping by care-staff would be preferable here!) and the nature of the setting (if all residents to be observed spend most of the day in one area time-sampling is much easier than if they are spread about the home!). Adaptation periods — for both elderly people and staff — are essential, of course.

Some examples of the use of these methods will be given. Probably the simplest (and thus potentially the most reliable) is the application of the concept of 'engagement', used previously in mental-handicap research. Jenkins, Felce, Lunt and Powell (1977) used this method in a study of activity in old people's homes. Residents are rated as engaged if they are interacting, either with people or materials; disengaged if they are doing nothing. A detailed manual is available with full definitions. The method they used was to enter the room where the residents were to be observed, count the number of people who were engaged and then count the total number of people present. The percentage of those present who are engaged is calculated, giving a group level of engagement at that point in time. Simpson, Woods and Britton (1981) and McFadyen, Prior and Kindness (1980) (see also McFadyen, 1984) have extended the method by recording engagement levels for individuals and by breaking down the definitions of engagement and non-engagement into their component parts (e.g. self-care and social engagement). This is the form in which Jenkins *et al.* (1977) present their definitions of engagement and non-engagement. McFadyen *et al.* (1980) made observations on every patient every 30 minutes over a 2½-day period. Inter-rater agreement was higher than 90 per cent on simultaneous observations of 20 patients. Engagement correlated significantly with lack of self-care impairment in both a psychogeriatric ward and an old people's home. Burton (1980) used six categories of patient behaviour and two categories of staff behaviour in observing activity sessions in a psychogeriatric ward. Patients were observed for 5 seconds at 15-second intervals for about an hour. Godlove, Richard and

Rodwell (1982) give details of a system for categorising their direct observations in day-care and residential settings, where they recorded a person's behaviour for a whole day, rather than using a sampling method.

Burrows *et al.* (1981) used a time-sampling technique, observing each resident for 15 seconds, completing a behavioural checklist in the next 15 seconds, observing the next resident for 15 seconds and so on for 15-minute periods. The checklist included waking state, position and activity, each item having two or three choices in which to place the resident's behaviour. Inter-rater reliability ranged from 97 per cent agreement to 100 per cent agreement for the different items.

Finally, Baltes, Burgess and Stewart (1980) have examined sequential relationships between resident and staff behaviour — of great importance in understanding the behavioural contingencies operating in these settings. The study concentrated on self-care in a nursing home. Residents' behaviour was coded as 'independent', 'dependent' or 'other' and staff behaviour as 'independence-supporting', 'dependence-supporting', 'no response' and 'other', each category being defined according to observable acts. Observers followed each staff member throughout the early morning round of waking residents and helping them prepare for breakfast. Every behaviour occurring for over five seconds in the first five minutes of each staff–resident interaction was recorded in sequence. Sequential recording was facilitated by the use of the Behavioural Observation Scoring System (BOSS) which electronically records data, fed in via a small portable keyboard, for later computer analysis. The mean inter-rater reliability coefficient was 0.95 (see also Baltes, Honn, Barton, Orzech and Lago, 1983).

This type of sequential recording may prove one of the major contributions of the direct observation approach, allowing the analysis of aspects of staff–resident interaction leading, say, to dependent behaviour, that would be inaccessible by other means of behavioural assessment. As we have seen this is an area abounding with methodological pitfalls. However, the extensive use of these techniques to aid effective assessment in work with children and the mentally handicapped point to a considerable potential. The keynotes to successful use would appear to be clear and explicit definitions of behaviour, simple error-free recording techniques and keeping the observations as unobtrusive as possible.

Assessment of the Environment

An important aspect of psychological intervention with the elderly is facilitating changes to the environment that increase the quality of life of the elderly people in that setting. This raises two assessment issues not previously discussed here; these are, firstly, how to identify the changes needed in a particular environment and, secondly, how to show whether any changes have occurred.

Relatively little attention has been given to these issues as yet — perhaps partly because of the problems in even defining 'environment', let alone measuring it! Here we will provide an indication as to what has been done, and how this is likely to be developed.

One method — mentioned briefly above — has been 'borrowed' from mental-handicap research. This is based on the notion that a good institutional environment offers and encourages many opportunities for residents to be engaged. The hallmark of a good environment then is that levels of engagement will be high (Jenkins *et al.*, 1977). Positive environmental changes will be accompanied by an increase in engagement; relatively less appropriate aspects of the environment may be identified by lower levels of engagement. There are substantial drawbacks to this attractively simplistic approach, as will become apparent in Chapter 9, but, perhaps in combination with other measures, it may be one way of tackling this area. One could of course envisage a number of other aspects of residents' functioning that similarly *indirectly* relate to the hypothesised quality of the environment. Life satisfaction, locus of control and depression measures might provide general indices of environmental quality, but lack the sensitivity of the engagement measure to different aspects of an institutional environment, i.e. different lounges, different times of day, different staff, and perhaps fall too far on the resident side of the resident–environment interaction that we are currently exploring.

One of the first attempts to develop a direct assessment of the environment in homes for the elderly was the Home for the Aged Description Questionnaire (Pincus, 1968; Pincus and Wood, 1970). This consisted of 36 statements describing various aspects of life in the home, covering staff and resident behaviour, the physical setting and programme and policies. Five dimensions emerged from factor analysis — privacy, freedom, resources, integration and personalisation. The questionnaire was designed to be completed by both staff and residents, and Pincus and Wood

(1970) describe some differences between them in their perception of the environment.

Recent years have seen an upsurge in comprehensive environment analysis in settings for the mentally handicapped. These techniques have some links to the 'normalisation' movement although their development contains many influences. Typical examples are the National Development Group's Checklist in the UK and the Program Assessment of Service Systems (PASS) in the USA, which could potentially be adapted for use in old-age settings. Moos and his colleagues (Moos and Lemke, 1979) have evolved a Multiphasic Environmental Assessment Procedure (MEAP) for elderly settings. They attempt to identify crucial aspects of the environments provided for the care of the elderly and to provide a framework for their assessment. The diffuse global concept of 'environment' is broken down into physical and architectural features, programmes and policies, the 'human aggregate' (staff, residents and their interaction) and the social climate.

The MEAP consists of five instruments which may be used in conjunction or separately, which aim to define these physical and social aspects of the environment.

They are:

1. Part A: Physical and Architectural Features Checklist (PAF)
   146 items, ranging from 'Are there lights in the surrounding streets' to 'Is there a pool or billiard table'.
2. Part B: Policy and Program Information Form (POLIF)
   129 items, covering rules, policies, expectations, resident participation, and decision-making, services and activities available, etc.
3. Part C: Resident and Staff Information Form (RESIF)
   70 items, covering residents' background, abilities and activities and staff and volunteers' characteristics.
4. Part D: Rating Scale (RS)
   27 items to provide a picture of four general aspects of the environment — the overall site, the physical environment, the residents and the staff.
5. Part E: Sheltered Care Environment Scale (SCES)
   63-item yes-no questionnaire devised to measure three areas of social climate — relationship, personal growth and system maintenance and change, designed to be completed by both staff and residents.

A great deal of development work has gone into the MEAP, and scores obtained can be compared with normative data on 93 facilities, including nursing homes, residential homes and apartment facilities. Some changes, of a relatively minor nature, would be needed for its use in the UK, and fresh norms would be desirable for this context. It may be particularly useful in giving feedback to staff in a particular environment, and facilitating their efforts to improve its quality. Its usefulness for monitoring change needs to be evaluated — not all aspects of the environment monitored by MEAP are potentially changeable of course. It may also be of use in comparing and contrasting different facilities, and in looking at the impact of aspects of the environment on the residents, e.g. do environments differing in amount of control allowed to residents show differences also in the mood or morale of the residents? Clearly, even if the whole MEAP is not used, there is much within it that may prove valuable for more specific purposes.

An important aspect of the environment of course is the attitude and morale of those caring for the elderly person(s). The home setting, where a relative is caring for the elderly person, is attracting particular interest at present (see Chapter 10). In a number of research studies attempts have been made to assess the degree of strain felt by the relative. This differs from the amount of burden or stress, as different relatives have different capacities to cope with the same stress — one may be overburdened by demands that another could take in their stride. One of the instruments used for this purpose is the General Health Questionnaire (GHQ: Goldberg, 1978) originally designed as a screening instrument for distress associated with psychiatric disorders. It has been used by both Gledhill, Mackie and Gilleard (1982) and Levin (1983). Greene *et al.* (1982) have devised their own 15-item Relatives Stress Scale; factor analysis suggested this contained three factors — the relative's personal distress in relation to the elderly person; the degree of life upset produced by having to care for the elderly person, and thirdly, the relative's negative feelings towards the person, of embarrassment, anger or frustration. The scale is reasonably reliable ($r = 0.85$), but so far data is only available for 38 relatives of patients suffering from senile dementia. A 13-item Caregiver Strain Index has been described by Robinson (1983). Some evidence for its reliability and validity is available, but not, as yet, for carers looking after elderly dementing people.

Assessing attitudes of staff in institutional settings is to some extent accomplished by the MEAP, which at least examines that part of staff attitudes that are a function of the policy and practice of the institution. This enables a distinction to be drawn, say, between task-centred and client-centred care. Less well covered are the attitudes of individual staff members to the elderly for whom they care. Do they see all old people as needing care and protection, not differentiating individual needs? Do they see getting tasks done as more important than the elderly person accomplishing the tasks themselves? Do they feel helpless in the face of chronic, deteriorating diseases? There have been attempts to measure such attitudes — e.g. Smith and Barker (1972) used Oberleder's (1962) Attitude Scale to assess positive attitudes to the elderly, although the original scale needs some adaptation for this purpose. Gale and Livesley (1974) assessed the attitudes of medical students to the elderly, and similarly attempts have been made to assess nursing staff attitudes (e.g. Heller and Walsh, 1976, using Kogan's 1961, attitude scale). As yet no acceptable and widely used staff attitude or morale measure has emerged.

The concept of staff 'burnout' is however being increasingly used (Quattrochi-Tubin, Jones and Breedlove, 1982). It refers to a state of exhaustion and demoralisation in the staff member, where the demands of working with difficult clients, often without much support from colleagues or superiors, become so overwhelming that the staff member avoids contact with clients wherever possible, develops physical symptoms, and other problems both in the work setting and outside. This approach could lead to useful measures of staff morale being developed.

Summary

1. A wide range of techniques for the assessment of adaptation in the elderly are in use, from personality tests to direct observation of behaviour. There has been a noticeable increase in attempts to find culturally, ecologically and practically valid measures of adaptation.

2. Traditional assessment of personality through projective or psychometric questionnaire methods seems to have relatively little to contribute. These methods are often difficult to use in practice.

3. Several methods of assessing depression/life satisfaction are available that will be of value in monitoring response to psycho-

logical and pharmacological treatment of depression in the elderly.

4. Scope exists for applying techniques used with younger clients — like the repertory grid — to aid in analysing and treating the psychological problems of elderly people. Biographical assessment would also be worth developing further.

5. Many behaviour-rating scales have been developed, and their design is now becoming more sophisticated and empirically derived. Great care is needed to select the appropriate measure for any particular purpose.

6. Direct observation — whether in a structured setting or the natural environment — has much to recommend it. Again the technique must be carefully chosen to match the reason for assessment and the resources available.

7. Measures for the assessment of the environment are beginning to be developed. Here it is important to ensure that all the important areas of the environment are covered by the measures used. The morale of staff, relatives and other carers is an important aspect of the environment for many elderly people.

7 TREATMENT APPROACHES FOR AFFECTIVE DISORDERS

Introduction

In earlier chapters we have outlined the ways in which the affective disorders — notably depression and anxiety — may appear in the elderly. If mild levels of these problems are included, perhaps up to 25 per cent of the elderly population may at some time experience an episode which could and should be treated. These figures do not differ greatly from those with younger people. However, there has been much less effort to treat these disorders when they occur in the elderly. There is little specific literature on, for example, the application of psychotherapy or behavioural therapies to this group.

The reasons for this apparent lack of interest are complex. Perhaps, the elderly may have been 'written off' as though it were natural for them to be depressed and miserable. Kay *et al.* (1964) found a marked reluctance amongst doctors to treat affective disorder in the community. Twenty years later many cases of depression are still untreated. The problems of idiosyncratic drug reactions in the elderly, particularly to anti-depressants, may have prompted caution in some doctors but should have encouraged the exploration of alternative treatments.

Apart from any other considerations, elderly people deserve at least a fair share of resource as their suffering may well also influence members of their families and use up other types of medical services if not recognised in its own right. Indeed the high rate of suicide amongst elderly people is often attributed to their depression not being recognised, despite recent contact with their family doctor (Barraclough, 1971).

Factors Influencing Treatment Strategies

In general the techniques of therapy appropriate to the adult population are equally relevant to the elderly. The strategies developed for the 30-year-old anxious patient are equally applicable to the 70-year-old, although the targets and treatment goals may differ considerably. For example, the treatment goal for a 75-year-old agoraphobic treated by one of the authors was being able to shop at the local shop 5 minutes' walk away; a younger patient might well have been much more ambitious. Treatment goals always need to be set individually, according to the person's needs, aspirations, life-style, resources and so on — regardless of age. Commonly used questionnaires for aiding therapy, e.g. the Reinforcement Survey Schedule, may need considerable adaptation for elderly patients, to include the interests of older people as well as those of students!

The most significant special consideration is, however, the person's physical health. Depression and physical ill health are closely related in older people (Bergmann, 1982). On the one hand, physical illnesses may precipitate, or even present as, depression. On the other hand, the person may present as physically ill, with a number of somatic symptoms, which in fact are manifestations of depression. For example, an elderly person may have a physical disability of recent onset, which has restricted their activities and led to depression. Or, a severe pain is reported with no apparent physical cause which responds to anti-depressant therapy. On occasions a depressed patient may appear physically fit, but over the months, or sometimes years, a serious illness, perhaps a carcinoma, may become manifest. It is almost as if the person's general feeling of malaise was a precursor of the illness, long before it was medically detectable. It should be noted that patients' judgements of their physical health are often more accurate than those of physicians in predicting survival (Kay, Bergmann, Foster and Garside, 1966).

A further complication of the presentation of affective disorders can be the effects of medication — prescribed or otherwise. It is common for the elderly to be taking a range of medication even if no supposedly psychoactive drugs are prescribed. Amongst the non-prescribed drugs idiosyncratic use of analgesics is quite common. Information on the effects of these drugs is crucial in the analysis of the problems. A common example would be a patient on diuretics who doesn't like being away from home for long, which on closer examination may be related to a drug-induced increased frequency of micturition. The final physical factor often encountered is sensory loss, which may relate to affective disorders, through reducing social contact, and which may make therapy more difficult in a number of ways. For example, it is extremely hard to sound empathic while speaking very loudly for the benefit of the deaf patient; teaching materials used with younger patients may not be so easy to read for visually impaired patients; deaf patients find group therapy very difficult.

The above reflect some of the many physical factors which must be taken into account in the analysis of a patient's problems and in the setting of goals; with elderly patients it is important to work closely with a medical colleague who can advise on the presence and the likely effects of the various physical disorders, and of medications. Should one encourage the agoraphobic patient with gout to exercise? Do steroids lower mood? are among the many questions about which the authors have needed to seek a medical opinion.

A further important difference from the younger client is likely to be the experience of loss. The older patient is more likely to have undergone a number of losses than his counterpart. These losses may be physical or sensory, as mentioned above, or the loss of significant relationships in the person's life. In examining the patient's difficulties, these losses, and the way in which the person has attempted to cope with them, must be given careful attention. These real-life hardships mean that care is required to distinguish the patient's cognitive distortions from a realistic recognition of their limitations.

These two factors — physical health and cumulative losses — are always likely to be important influences on older patients. The third factor may to some extent be a cohort or generational effect that in years to come may cease to be a special consideration with the elderly. This is what is referred to by Emery (1981) as 'treatment socialisation'. The patient is not used to a 'talking' therapy, and may be expecting more medication or other physical treatments. The patient may have misconceptions about therapy, or have been coerced into coming by another family member. The patient may perceive his or her symptoms as part of ageing, rather than as a depression. Emery recommends an educational model to socialise the patient into treatment.

Finally, it is sometimes argued that the treatment of older people needs to be modified in view of 'normal' cognitive loss with the 'ageing process' (e.g. Church, 1983). For example, a difficulty with abstract thinking may lead to problems in the understanding of some aspects of cognitive therapy. However, the variability in 'normal' ageing is such that it is probably inadvisable to make hard and fast rules about this. The authors have successfully treated patients who have perhaps had a small stroke, and whose thinking was less organised than previously and in whom cognitive change was evident; most patients show no obvious impairment. In general treatment does need to be practical and relatively concrete for patients of all ages (e.g. Structured Learning Therapy: Goldstein, 1973) and this issue is best resolved on an individual basis.

Psychotherapy

The development of psychotherapy with the elderly has been haunted by Freud's contention that older patients are too rigid for the necessary shifts in personality to be brought about by psychotherapy. A number of reviews have since indicated that therapeutic nihilism is unnecessary, but little in the way of a coherent model for psychotherapy with the elderly has emerged (Rechtschaffen, 1959; Gottesman, Quarterman and Cohn, 1973; Bergmann, 1978; Sparacino, 1978–9; Knight, 1978–9; Verwoerdt, 1981). Here a few emerging themes will be described, with readers being referred to the above reviews for more detailed expositions.

The 'gerophobia' of the therapist often receives comment. It is contended that psychotherapists avoid elderly patients, perhaps because they feel improvement will be limited, or that it is more economical to work with younger patients, with longer to live, or because of the low status of the elderly, or at a deeper level perhaps because of the therapist's own unresolved fear of ageing and death.

The therapist–patient relationship is often seen as differing from that in psychotherapy with younger people. For example, the age difference may lead to different transference patterns, perhaps even grandparent–grandchild at times, if the therapist is young. An older therapist may be seen as belonging to the generation of the patient's children. Some degree of dependence and attachment may need to be encouraged, giving the person confidence to face external difficulties and his or her own deficits in an adaptive fashion. The sense of control thus experienced by the patient in the therapeutic relationship may help combat fears of helplessness, and enable a feeling of safety. In this type of relationship feelings of anger and resentment may be safely expressed, without fear of reprisal.

The content areas of therapy may also differ. No attempt may be made to change long-standing personality patterns, or necessarily to trace all dynamics back to childhood patterns. Bergmann (1978) summarises the major tasks faced by elderly people, that will form, the focus of psychotherapy.

1. Accepting the proximity of death.
2. Coping with and adjusting to physical disabilities and ill health.
3. Achieving a rational dependence on medical, social and family support, and identifying and exercising available choices to maximise satisfaction.
4. Sustaining mutually emotionally gratifying relationships with friends and relatives.

Coping with the closeness of death relates to 'life-review' (Lewis and Butler, 1974), achieving an overall view of one's life, making sense of what has happened, seeing successes and failure in perspective. Here patients are encouraged to describe their lives in some detail using photo albums and other memorabilia, with the therapist assisting in encouraging the recall of feelings as well as facts and in drawing attention to integrative themes. The patients may feel the need to prepare for death, practically and emotionally. Elsewhere elderly people may find this whole subject taboo, skirted around — in the therapeutic relationship it needs to be discussed openly and readily.

'Reminiscence therapy' is discussed in more detail in Chapter 8. At least one controlled trial of its effects on depression in older people is available. Perrotta and Meacham (1981–2) compared structured reminiscing with a current events discussion and a no-treatment control group. The two treatment conditions consisted of five sessions of 45 minutes each. No changes in depression or self-esteem were found — although the elderly people involved were by no means severely depressed. These disappointing results cast doubt on the effectiveness of reminiscence in the short term, although there may be scope for evaluation of variations of the techniques (e.g. using prompts, more sessions and so on) with clinically depressed patients.

In relation to the second task, it should be noted that physical ill health may well be genuine. The term 'hypochondriac' is a dangerous one to use with the elderly. In adjusting to and coping with disability and ill health some of the features of loss may be seen. Guilt or anger and resentment may be apparent, perhaps directed at the medical profession. There may be an all-consuming search for a cause ('If only I knew why it happened'), which it soon becomes apparent does not respond to rational information.

For many elderly people the fact that *independence* is an unattainable state becomes only too clear, and lifelong *interdependence* becomes more explicit. The elderly person maintaining a fierce 'independent' stance (often at some cost to a supporting relative!) may be aided through the development of a protective therapeutic relationship.

Interpersonal issues may frequently arise; a son who is a disappointment; a friend who has proved unreliable; a husband who is unhelpful. There is much to be said for family sessions where these are possible. Some marital problems arise where couples spend more time with each other than at any other point in their lives. Sexual issues should not be a taboo topic in psychotherapy with the elderly.

Finally Sparacino (1978–9) lists five modifications to psychotherapy when applied to the elderly:

1. Increased activity — therapist assumes greater initiative, even extending into direct intervention in the patient's life.
2. Symbolic giving — the therapeutic relationship is offered as a partial substitute for some of the cumulative losses the person has experienced. The therapist is more prepared to talk of his or her patient's own life, family, etc.
3. Limited goals.
4. Need to anticipate and discuss with colleagues the particular transference and counter-transference problems arising.
5. Empathy with patient — need to have repeated contacts with older people to identify with their problems and to gain greater familiarity and comfort with the ageing process.

It can be seen that recent reviews have given some credibility to the use of psychotherapeutic models with the elderly. There is an obvious need for further specific exploration of their use and effectiveness, particularly in relation to affective disorders.

Behaviour Therapy

Anxiety Reduction

There is regrettably little reported in the literature on work with the applications of behaviour therapy to the majority of clients with affective illness, those who live in the community. The studies reported tend to concentrate on institutionalised clients in various care settings. One problem group often met in practice are those patients with a fear of leaving home and going out alone. The onset of the problem may be traced to a specific incident, perhaps a fall or a 'funny-turn' when outside. These can lead to depression where the people's avoidance prevents them from receiving previously enjoyed reinforcement.

Such fears can be tackled as with younger patients using systematic desensitisation, or graded exposure utilising anxiety management procedures, including relaxation. For example, Garrison (1978) describes the use of 'Stress Management Training' with elderly patients — an educational approach using relaxation and other anxiety control techniques. A case report is given, and the use of the procedure in groups is described. Woods (1982) describes the treatment of a patient who was too anxious to go out of the house or do housework, using graded exposure with anxiety management. Again a group approach was used — in this case a small group where all the members lacked confidence in going out alone. The group met weekly, learnt anxiety management together, set themselves homework tasks which were reported back at subsequent group meetings, and went together on a graded series of excursions — the first literally a few yards from the day-hospital, the final one a visit to the city centre by bus, for coffee and cream cakes!

Relaxation techniques often have to be more flexibly taught to elderly patients, taking into account any physical problems, with particular emphasis on slower, deeper breathing and mental relaxation. Care must be taken that the exercises are not seen as a form of physiotherapy, with the tension element being emphasised more than the relaxation! The following case illustrates the use of graded exposure with an elderly patient agoraphobic.

Case 1. Mrs P. was a 64-year-old widow, living in a comfortable ground floor flat, where she was seen. She stated her main problem as being unable to go out. This had developed over two years previously and seemed related to two incidents — a mild heart attack and an attempted burglary. Her extensive family were extremely supportive, did all her shopping and ensured Mrs P. had many social contacts without leaving the comfort of her living-room. Mrs P. was extremely overweight, to the extent that her mobility was in any case reduced. A behavioural test indicated that Mrs P. literally was unable to cross her front door step, becoming extremely fearful and anxious. Before commencing treatment Mrs P. was asked to commit herself to working to overcome her problems — this was particularly important in view of the reinforcement her family was providing for the *status quo*.

Treatment consisted of regular sessions in Mrs P.'s home, in which, following some simple relaxation instructions, Mrs P. was encouraged to walk gradually increasing distances from her home. Her family were enlisted to help Mrs P. to go out between sessions, and she kept detailed records of her activities. Mrs P.'s fear ratings (on a personalised fear questionnaire) are shown in Figure 7.1. Most items concerned her difficulties in going out, and it can be seen that her progress in this area was excellent. By contrast her fear of heights, which was not tackled in therapy sessions, showed little change, until it was specifically targeted so she could travel in a lift to her daughter's flat.

Mrs. P.'s progress was self-reinforcing as it allowed her to attend various family occasions and social events. At the termination of therapy (after eight months and twenty-two, 30-minute sessions) Mrs P. could still not travel on public transport (and had no desire or need to), but could visit friends, local shops and a local bingo session, and plan a family holiday. Her weight incidentally showed little change, but it was now possible for her to attend a hospital out-patient department regarding medical investigation for this problem.

Thyer (1981) reports the treatment of a 70-year-old woman with a debilitating fear of dogs subsequent to being attacked by a large St Bernard. Prolonged *in vivo* exposure to dogs was used, with the woman's anxiety dissipating satisfactorily within half an hour or so in the first two sessions. After five sessions her phobic symptoms — which had led to her not going out, and experiencing insomnia and nightmares — had disappeared. This improvement was maintained at six months' follow-up. The patient had previously had three years' verbal psychotherapy, which had not led to any symptom alleviation.

A report by Hussian (1981) of the treatment of four residents in an institution indicated success in using 'stress inoculation training' to overcome anxiety concerning lifts. An important aspect of this training was the construction of positive coping statements which

Figure 7.1: Fear-rating Scores for Mrs P. on a Personalised Fear Questionnaire

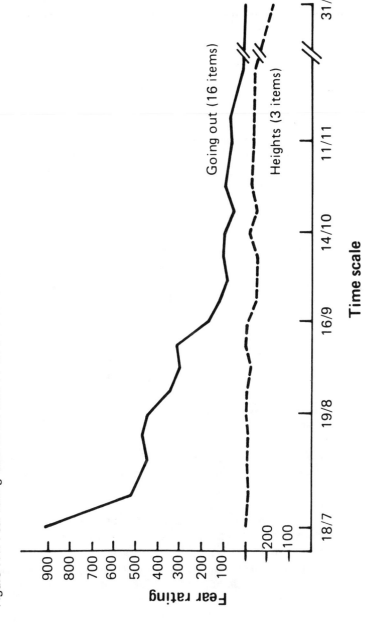

residents practised aloud and covertly, e.g., 'If the doors stick, I will not panic but will press the red button until help arrives.' Residents were encouraged to imagine themselves going into the lift whilst practising these positive self-statements. This procedure was needed before any of the residents could enter a lift to begin the process of graded exposure, and shows that imaginal procedures can be used with the elderly. Hussian also reports the treatment of a resident who became anxious in the proximity of other residents showing 'crazy' behaviour. Again both imaginal and *in vivo* exposure were used, and rational coping statements served as a major means of anxiety control, e.g. 'I will not allow my fears to prevent me from enjoying the activities here.'

Cognitive Therapies

Although the above treatment approaches clearly include a strong cognitive component, reports of the clinical applications of cognitive therapy, as developed by Beck and Ellis, are only just beginning to emerge. Earlier reports of rational-emotive therapy with older people (e.g. Keller, Croake and Brooking, 1975) used apparently 'normal' elderly people.

Emery (1981) provides some useful illustrative case histories of patients living in the community. The techniques he describes include helping patients become aware of and examine their automatic thoughts, evaluating cognitive distortions and misattributions and using positive coping statements to counter negative cognitions. For example, an elderly patient with a tremor from some organic cause (e.g. the side-effects of medication) may misattribute this to anxiety and this mis-labelling may lead to further anxiety. Similarly, Steuer and Hammen (1983) report four cases treated in cognitive therapy groups. Here the techniques included behavioural activation and problem solving as well as cognitive restructuring.

There are a number of methodological and practical problems to be overcome in carrying out controlled trials of cognitive therapy with elderly people (Mintz, Steuer and Jarvik, 1981). Gallagher and Thompson (1983) have been able to complete a comparative study. Depressed out-patients received one of three therapies for 16 individual sessions over a three month period. The therapies compared with cognitive therapy were insight-orientated psychotherapy and behavioural therapy. The latter was based on Lewinsohn's (1975) model of depression (see Chapter 4 and below), and involved encouraging patients to take part in more activities they found pleasant. The results indicated that all three therapies were equally effective in reducing depression at the end of the treatment period. Patients treated with insight-orientated therapy tended to be more depressed and to relapse more often during the one-year follow-up period. Depressed patients who showed less endogenous symptomatology generally showed more recovery, but some patients with endogenous symptoms did improve. The study confirms the validity of cognitive therapy with older patients, but clearly its comparative efficacy with different types of depressed patients needs to be explored further. The distinction between 'cognitive' and 'behavioural' treatments may well, in practice, be rather artificial.

Case 2 demonstrates the use of cognitive-behavioural treatment with a depressed elderly man.

Case 2. Mr M. was a 68-year-old widower, living alone in a large house. He had been admitted to hospital with depression. The major feature of his depression were his negative thoughts, e.g. 'I can't cope with the house, it's like a huge burden to me'; 'aren't I stupid, I should be able to do this'; 'I've let the house and garden get in a dreadful mess'; 'I'll never put it right'; 'I've got so many things to do and I can't do any of them'. Over a period of some months he was encouraged to carry out a series of graded tasks devised to break down his apparently overwhelming problems into small manageable steps, each of which he could at least successfully attempt, e.g. in dealing with his financial affairs one task would be paying a bill, or writing a cheque. Each task served as an opportunity to test against reality the validity of his negative cognitions. Before the task Mr M.'s predictions concerning his performance would be elicited, and then discussed with him in the light of his subsequent success. This often involved Mr M. decrying the success e.g. 'I didn't do it as quickly as I used to', giving more negative statements to challenge in the light of the evidence from the task successfully completed. This was a slow process, but ultimately improvements were seen, particularly when progress could be made to achieve goals that Mr M. perceived as important and satisfying. At this point Mr M. became much more active in planning subsequent tasks and in evaluating his negative automatic cognitions. Mr M. was finally discharged, and now again copes independently with his financial affairs, enjoys his large house, does gardening for his neighbours, and carries out voluntary work for the elderly!

Problem Solving

An approach which is often an important component of cognitive therapy and which is also based on an educational model of treatment involves the teaching of problem-solving strategies and skills. The aim is to teach the depressed patient skills that will be generalisable to any number of current and future problems they experience. Patients are typically taught to define problems concisely and succinctly, then to generate a number of alternative solutions in 'brainstorming' manner, and to consider the likely consequences of each, before choosing the most favourable option. Finally, the patient is taught to evaluate solutions and to repeat the problem-solving process if a solution is not successful.

Hussian and Lawrence (1981) describe an evelution of this approach with 36 depressed nursing home residents, their degree of depression being evaluated using the Beck Depression Inventory. In addition to comparing individual problem-solving training with a waiting-list control and an information-placebo control (where patients discussed changes accompanying ageing with a therapist), some patients participated in a social reinforcement condition. These patients were prompted to participate in activities such as craft classes or art sessions, and were reinforced during the sessions when actually actively participating in the task, or interacting with other patients. Initially both problem-solving and social reinforcement groups showed lower levels of self-rated depression; subsequently results favoured the problem-solving treatment, which showed superiority at the end of the two-week treatment period and at a two-week follow-up, although the difference was not significant three months later. Although the treatment period was short, five 30-minute sessions were held each week. The design used allowed some comparison of combined treatment — some patients had two weeks' problem solving, some two weeks' social reinforcement and others one week of each. Generally the group having two weeks' social reinforcement fared worst of the treated groups. A check that problem-solving subjects improved in problem-solving ability and social reinforcement subjects improved in activity level in comparison with the alternatively treated group also adds credibility to the treatments evaluated. It should be noted the improvements were mainly on self-rating scales — an adjustment scale completed by staff members for each subject showed less significant differences, although those obtained were in line with these findings. The authors comment that adjustment to the environment will be related to other variables than the person's level of depression, and so this measure would not be so sensitive to the changes related to the experimental treatments.

Activity Programmes

The relative ineffectiveness of the social reinforcement condition is of considerable theoretical interest. Depression has been related to reduced activity levels (Lewinsohn, 1975), with the implication that increasing activity levels will consequently reduce depression. Several other lines of evidence, in addition to the Hussian and Lawrence (1981) results, emphasise that activity programmes alone are likely to be insufficient to reduce depression in elderly patients. Firstly, Lewinsohn and MacPhillamy (1974) showed that elderly people like (younger) depressed people show a reduction in participation in pleasant activities, but unlike depressed people show no reduction in reported enjoyment of these activities. Thus in older people inactivity is not necessarily related to loss of reinforced effectiveness as is the case with younger depressed people. Secondly, Simpson *et al.* (1981) have shown there to be no relationship between level of activity and level of depression among residents in an old people's home; there was a strong relationship between low levels of depression and engagement in the activities subjectively reported as most enjoyable by the resident. This study emphasises that overt activity is not the only source of reinforcement available to elderly people, for whom covert activities (e.g. reminiscing) may have considerable significance.

How their activity is perceived by different people is important; clearly, the same activity will not be seen as equally reinforcing by all elderly people. Very active people may see their activity in such negative terms that little positive reinforcement results from it. Indiscriminate activity programmes are not likely to reduce depression in the elderly; an individualised approach, exploring the meaning of the activity for the individual and working at this cognitive level, is much more likely to be fruitful (Power and McCarron, 1975); Gallagher and Thompson, 1983).

Sense of Control

Hussian and Lawrence (1981) argue that a problem-solving

approach may serve to increase the person's subjective control over the environment and the problematic situations encountered there. Several studies have shown elderly community and institutional residents' sense of well-being or contentment to be related to their sense of control over their environment (Reid *et al.*, 1977; Ziegler and Reid, 1979), and the well-established negative effects of relocation on elderly people (with increased mortality rates when the residents of one home have to be moved to another) have also been related to lack of control and predictability over the move or a difference in controllability in the new environment (Schulz and Brenner, 1977). This relates of course to Seligman's (1975) 'learned helplessness' model of depression, with the elderly person's loss of control over their environment leading to the helplessness position of withdrawal, lack of response and activity. This may relate to survival; MacDonald and Dunn (1982) have shown a strong relationship between lack of will to live and death. The following case report illustrates the importance of a sense of control in coping with pain.

Case 3. Mr R. was an 80-year-old man whose major complaint was of throbbing pain and tinnitus in one ear, which had led to a depression severe enough for in-patient treatment, and which one morning had seemed so unbearable that he attempted to take his life. Drug therapy brought a remission of his depression, but he continued constantly to monitor the throbbing, and was still extremely distressed by it. Behavioural treatment attempted to use distracting activities to prevent him focusing on the pain, by using relaxation or self-distraction (carrying out domestic tasks or listening to favourite pieces of music). He was encouraged to construct and practise positive self-statements, stressing the controllability of the pain. For example, he replaced 'The pain will be getting really bad in a few minutes, it always does after a meal' with 'If the pain begins to increase I'll go and listen to some music'. These procedures proved effective, so that two years after discharge he now says 'I have the pain quite badly at times, but I can take my mind off it; I'm the boss now, not the pain'.

Most of the studies that have attempted to increase the person's sense of control have been carried out in institutional settings. Langer and Rodin (1976) showed that an intervention designed to increase residents' sense of responsibility for themselves led to increased well-being compared with a group where the staff's responsibility for the residents was stressed. The interventions were relatively minimal — a talk by an administrator, and plants which either residents were encouraged to look after or, in the low responsibility group, were cared for by the staff. Schulz (1976) showed that residents' well-being improved more when they were able to control or predict the frequency and duration of visits to them by volunteers than when they were visited randomly. In a further experiment (see Schulz, 1980) some new residents in an institutional facility received an individualised programme to inform them about relevant aspects of the home and to orient them to it. Others received information not directly relevant to their situation in the home, to control for the effects of increased attention, or no additional orientation programme at all. The results showed a clear difference in favour of the group who were informed about relevant aspects of the home, for whom the environment thus became more predictable and controllable. However, Schulz presents some evidence suggesting that initially less-depressed residents benefit most from these interventions, and so they may be viewed as preventative measures rather than as treatment for depression, which would probably need to be much more intensive to achieve success with more severely depressed residents. Certainly procedures effective in the long term need to emphasise the person's control over a range of events and situations and outcomes, and not simply one specific event (Rodin and Langer, 1977; Schulz and Hanusa, 1978).

Skills Training

A further method of increasing the elderly person's control over the environment is to increase their level of skill, by skills training procedures. For example, an elderly man's wife dies, who has always done the cooking. One 'solution' is to provide meals-on-wheels, which removes the person's control over choice and so on; training the person to cook for himself reduces dependence and increases his sense of control and responsibility. At a severe level of depression, Burton and Spall (1981) successfully used operant procedures to reinstate self-feeding skills in a depressed patient. Several studies have trained elderly institutional subjects in social skills (e.g. Berger and Rose, 1977; Lopez, Hoyer, Goldstein, Gershaw and Sprafkin, 1980). Skills such as 'starting a conversation' have been taught, with evidence of generalisation to new situations in some, but not all studies. Corby (1975) describes the use of group assertion training in a retirement home, increasing interpersonal disclosure markedly after only four 1-hour sessions. The findings of these studies closely parallel early studies on the teaching of skills to the mentally handicapped. The emphasis in early studies is to produce behavioural change with later sophistication in methodology leading to more effective generalisation. As methodology in skills training of the elderly improves, we may expect more efficient generalisation and maintenance of new behaviours.

An important issue in institutions is the extent to which additional social skills are needed in view of the size and layout of the environment and the social climate; much could be achieved by designing environments where natural social interaction is encouraged and facilitated using small living groups, with common tasks, reduced resident−staff distance and so on, without necessitating the teaching of extra social skills. However, these studies do illustrate what might be possible for the individual depressed patient with an identifiable social-skills, or assertion problem (e.g. Emery, 1981, p. 97).

Loss and Grief Therapy

Loss is a common feature in elderly depressed patients; often multiple losses are experienced — work, the family home, loved ones, mobility, physical health, etc. The treatment of loss, grief and bereavement is then of particular significance with the elderly. Parkes (1972) provides an excellent description of the features of bereavement — anger, guilt, searching for the lost person, a tendency to idealise the dead person, etc. One should be wary of assuming that all bereaved people *have* to pass through *all* these stages in a given sequence; in reality patients may show these features more or less strongly, alone or in combination at various times in their bereavement. In a useful review article Averill and Wisocki (1981) suggested a model with four basic components: shock; protest and yearning; disorganisation and despair; detachment and reorganisation. They suggest that these are not sequential stages of a process but, rather, components which may occur in any order, or perhaps simultaneously in the grief process.

Behavioural models of abnormal bereavement reactions have identified at least two possible patterns (Gauthier and Marshall, 1977). One is where the normal grief reaction is extended by family and friends. They are seen as continuing to pay attention to grieving for too long, rather than helping and encouraging the bereaved person to take up old activities again or starting new activities and friendships. The other is where the normal grief reaction, far from being extended, is in fact avoided. A 'conspiracy of silence' may occur, with family and friends not mentioning the loss to avoid 'upsetting' the bereaved person and perhaps discouraging them from attending the funeral. This is akin to Ramsay's (1977) comparison of an unresolved grief reaction to a phobia; the distressing emotional response is feared and avoided, thus not allowing the emotional processing to occur that would be necessary for a disturbing emotional experience to be successfully absorbed (Rachman, 1980).

These models have led to the development of therapeutic techniques; in the former case family and friends would be instructed to encourage alternative, more adaptive behaviour and to pay less attention to the person's grieving. In the latter pattern the person would be exposed to the stimuli that spark off grief, pictures and other reminders of the dead person, then encouraged to think and talk about them. The aim would be to produce the full emotional response until it subsides in the presence of the stimuli, as in flooding. Ramsay and Gauthier and Marshall claim some therapeutic success with these methods, and recent studies by Hodgkinson (1982) and Mawson, Marks, Ramm and Stern (1981) of this 'guided mourning' technique have also been encouraging. These studies have not specifically been on elderly patients, and in many instances it will be important to develop a supportive therapeutic relationship to create a safe setting for the grief to be eventually experienced. This relationship can be used also to encourage the development of more positive and appropriate activities. In some instances it may be important to provide feedback to the person regarding the 'normality' of their experiences, e.g. 'seeing' a lost partner in their accustomed armchair; 'talking' to the same partner in the kitchen; sensing their partner at their side in bed, etc. Case 4 illustrates bereavement counselling with an older person.

Case 4. Mrs H., aged 73, had been a widow for six months when she was referred via a voluntary agency. Guilt was a prominent feature; she blamed herself for her late husband's cancer, as before she realised about his illness she 'made' him walk long distances with her, when he was unwilling; she blamed herself for leaving the hospital, as it transpired, a few minutes before he died — although the nurses had told her to go home and rest. She lived alone in a large house, and felt extremely nervous to be alone there. She felt unable to mix with other people, her major social contact being occasional visits to her son and his family. During sessions Mrs H. went over and over the events leading up to her husband's death, and her sense of guilt, 'If only' being her major opening gambit. Gradually she was encouraged to evaluate alternative perceptions of what had happened from a rational perspective, and to discuss other aspects of her relationship with her husband, positive and negative. This was facilitated by her bringing in mementoes of her husband — the emotional response to these gradually subsiding more quickly. She was encouraged to say the things she would have said to her husband and to consider how he would have responded to her, and would have understood the way in which she had acted. At the same time her family encouraged her to be more independent and she began to mix with other older people. Disorganisation and despair no longer predominated and Mrs H. seemed well on the way to a satisfactory resolution of her grief without further professional help.

We have so far emphasised procedures for cases of 'abnormal' grief, i.e. where the unresolved grief has extended over a period of at least a year, perhaps more (although this distinction is somewhat arbitrary). There has been increasing interest recently in making bereavement counselling more widely available, at the time of bereavement or soon after, with the partial aim of preventing abnormal reactions developing. Raphael (1977) reports the use of bereavement counselling (consisting of specific support for grief and encouragement of mourning) with widows (under 60 years old) with a high risk for abnormal grief reaction, which was successful in reducing problems over a year later, in relation to an untreated comparison group. Most impact was achieved with widows who felt their family and friends were non-supportive during the bereavement crisis. A review by Parkes (1980) of a number of similar studies including some for elderly people, concludes that supportive counselling can reduce the risk for a high-risk bereaved person to that of a low-risk person, and that a trained and experienced volunteer counsellor can often provide such a service at least as well as many professional workers. Factors leading to high-risk, other than an unsupportive family or social network, are a particularly traumatic bereavement, a highly ambivalent relationship with the deceased, and the presence of another major concurrent life-crisis. There is here some encouragement then for the development of bereavement counselling services for the elderly. This could perhaps be staffed by volunteers, and offer a befriending and counselling service, preferably in the bereaved person's home, for those bereaved people most at risk. It would serve the function family and friends fulfil for most bereaved people.

Other Issues in Treatment of Functional Disorders

Relationship Problems

Even where the presenting problem does not include a relationship component, it is important, where possible, to see relatives or other significant people in the patient's life. They can often throw light on some of the problems being experienced, and, with the patient's consent, act as an auxiliary therapist, e.g. accompanying an agoraphobic patient on short journeys. Fairly often a relationship problem only comes to light when other family members are seen. For example, an elderly lady living with her sister was referred for 'lack of self-confidence'. Only when the sister was seen did it become clear this included making it difficult for the sister to go out to her own activities and to leave her alone for any length of time, problems that needed to be tackled by both sisters together.

Relationship problems generally are tackled as for younger people, emphasising open communication, exchange of reinforcement, using behavioural contracts where appropriate, and other established techniques. Particular points to note are the need to identify each person's expectations of the other, especially in the parent–child relationship, where parents may expect the child to take them into their home, as if this were the norm for our society. Conversely children may expect that parents will need looking after, say after a bereavement, when in fact they are capable of remaining independent. In the instance of a longstanding difficult relationship, goals may have to be quite limited, e.g. ensuring a couple have time apart may be more realistic than seeking to alter the quality of interaction when they are together.

Sexual Problems

Often the whole area of sexual functioning is ignored in relation to the elderly, although it is debatable whether it is more embarrassing for the professionals than the patients. At the very least, it should be recognised in evaluating a case that this area may be of importance. Our knowledge of sexual functioning in elderly people is increasing (Corby and Solnick, 1980; Baikie, 1984) and this provides a basis for appropriate feedback to patients with particular concern about their sexual functioning. Good medical advice is desirable as physical factors or medication may contribute to sexual dysfunction. Psychological treatment may involve giving 'permission' to continue sexual activity (Comfort, 1980), or helping the development of new strategies for sexual enjoyment, where disability or other factors have prevented the continuation of a previous pattern. As yet little is known of the effectiveness with the elderly of sex therapy techniques that have proved useful with younger clients.

Sleep Problems

Many elderly people complain of sleep problems; sleep disturbance is generally thought to increase with age. Many elderly people regularly take medication to help them sleep. This not only alters the person's natural sleep pattern, leading to problems of dependence as tolerance increases, but also can lead to health problems through interaction with other drugs or through overdose, accidental or otherwise.

A number of behavioural treatments for insomnia have been developed with younger people, and these are beginning to be applied to older people. Stimulus control treatment involves establishing a regular sleep schedule and using the bed only for sleep, going to bed only when drowsy, not to read or lie awake. Progressive relaxation has also been used in a number of trials with younger people.

Puder, Lacks, Bertelson and Storandt (1983) report the successful application of stimulus control therapy to elderly people with problems getting off to sleep. The gains were maintained at a six-week follow-up, despite the treatment period being relatively brief (four weeks). This could prove to be a valuable area of application of psychological techniques with elderly people.

Paraphrenia

Other functional psychiatric disorders do occur, of course, apart from depression and anxiety. Obsessional disorders seem to be rare, but paraphrenia is relatively common, characterised by paranoid delusions, generally fairly circumscribed, typically in a deaf, isolated person with difficulty in forming close relationships. The usual treatment is pharmacological, with the delusions not being thought to be amenable to correction. However, several recent case studies suggest that an approach in which feedback is given on misinterpretations can be successful in some cases (Carstensen and Fremouw, 1981; Hussian, 1981, p. 175). The patient is trained to substitute rational statements for the paranoid ideas, and is reinforced for positive behaviour. Relaxation training may also help in reducing the person's level of arousal.

Rambling

A problem occasionally encountered in individual therapy sessions with elderly patients is a difficulty in focusing on the salient points, a refusal to be hurried through a particular (often well-rehearsed and sometimes repeated) tale. Emery (1981) suggests establishing a specific agenda for the session, with the therapist informing the patient at the beginning of each session that they will be interrupted if they wander from the topic. This needs to be performed sensitively to avoid reducing the patient's self-esteem, and is dependent on the therapist's careful initial identification of the patient's problem areas.

Practical Help

Many depressed elderly patients have practical as well as emotional problems; to what extent should the therapist remain aloof from them? A primary aim should clearly be to help the patient to be able to tackle the problem as far as possible independently, and so each practical problem provides a useful concrete focus for the person to learn problem-solving skills. The therapist can assist by being familiar with services and provisions for elderly people in the locality, so the patient can make more informed choices and decisions, and by providing sufficient prompting and encouragement to enable the patient actually to face up to and tackle the problem.

Occasionally a fairly small practical step can relieve much

anxiety for the patient, and boost self-esteem. However it must be emphasised that not all emotional problems can be overcome by practical means, e.g. patients who attribute their unhappiness to their house or flat and want to be re-housed may well be as unhappy when they move, if their attribution has been faulty. In this instance a problem-solving analysis might have revealed a problem in getting on with neighbours rather than a housing problem *per se*. It is important to take a longitudinal view — if the person has been happy in the house for 20 years, why are they unhappy now? Therapists must also beware of imposing their own values and standards in some situations — to say 'no wonder she's depressed, I would be in her situation' is to ignore the compensatory mechanisms adopted by the majority of elderly people. It is important that therapists identify their own dysfunctional beliefs (e.g. 'old people are all depressed and miserable; you can't expect to be happy at 90; all old people deteriorate', etc.) and check them out by frequent contact with healthy well-functioning elderly people (Emery, 1981). Seeing depressed elderly people recovering their former skills, drive and interests is of course also a valuable and rewarding rejoinder to such erroneous attitudes and over-generalisations. To add life to the years that remain is a worthwhile, and for many patients, an attainable, aim.

Group-work

Many of the therapeutic methods described can be used in group settings, and in various centres problem-solving groups, cognitive therapy groups and graded exposure groups have been carried out. Generally groups need to be fairly small. Deafness or other communication problems are the most frequently encountered difficulties. Patients may have to be encouraged actively to listen to each other (e.g. by having to tell the group something about another member), and often some sort of life-review is appropriate to help members to know each other better in the context of their previous life as well as their present problems. As with any group, group cohesion has to be developed, perhaps using exercises that help members be more aware of positive aspects of other members. As with younger people one of the leader's tasks in a behavioural group is to prevent particular members monopolising the discussion, and to bring in quieter members. Each of the groups mentioned above would be fairly directive, using an educational model. Homework tasks are extremely valuable, with group members encouraging each other to generalise new-found skills. Having a specific number of sessions encourages members to focus on their problems and encourages attendance. Two therapists are always needed so that at any time one can concentrate on the leadership task and the other on observing and recording members' contributions and reactions.

Alcohol Problems

Few treatment studies of elderly people with drinking problems have been reported. Mishara and Kastenbaum (1980) review surveys suggesting that older people tend to drink less than when they were younger and that there are fewer drinking problems with increasing age. Of course this may reflect an age *difference* rather than an age *change*, and future cohorts may show a different pattern (Wattis, 1983). This trend to reduced consumption has however been consistent for around 30 years or so. Other explanations suggested include the possibility of alcoholism being a self-limiting disorder, with problem drinkers not surviving to old age (in fact the increased mortality could not explain the size of the reduction), or that alcoholics spontaneously improve with age. Because of physiological changes elderly people may *need* less alcohol than younger people to produce the same effect. The effects of financial restrictions experienced by older people, or fears of a detrimental health effect from excessive drinking may also be relevant. It is also possible that older respondents may show a higher social desirability response set, tending to play down their level of alcohol consumption for a variety of reasons. A further relevant point is that in younger adults problem drinking comes to light through a whole range of related problems: health, financial, family problems and so on. As some of these related problems occur more commonly with elderly people for other reasons, it is possible that a problem with alcohol may be overlooked as a contributory factor. Certainly, the elderly form a very small proportion of those treated in alcoholism units.

To what extent are elderly problem drinkers continuing a lifelong pattern, or does the drinking become heavy in later years, perhaps as a way of coping with loss of a partner, or a role-loss? In fact both patterns occur with the former probably being more common (Rosin and Glatt, 1971). Bereavement was the most common factor related to the onset of problem drinking in old age, with retirement, loneliness, physical and mental infirmity and marital stress also being implicated. The importance of cultural and social factors is emphasised by Mishara and Kastenbaum (1980). For example, French rest homes for the elderly have a high prevalence of alcoholism, with drinking being the major form of recreation.

Can problem drinking in elderly patients be successfully treated? The relatively few outcome studies that give details for different age-groups suggest that improvement is achieved at least as often as with other patients, if not more so. This may be related to the group of elderly problem drinkers starting late in life having less entrenched drinking habits and psychological difficulties and a history of good psychological adjustment. There is little information available as to the most effective forms of treatment for elderly problem drinkers. Each case requires a careful analysis of the exact nature of the problems, of what has led to and is maintaining the problem drinking. This can then lead to a rational treatment plan, perhaps involving work with the family, bereavement counselling, developing alternative strategies to cope with loneliness, or using covert aversive conditioning by pairing in imagination drinking and unpleasant feelings. Little guidance is available as to whether treatment should aim for total abstinence or for controlled drinking with elderly patients. Again an assessment of the individual patient and their circumstances will be needed. A major problem for the future will be to identify elderly people with drinking problems — Mishara and Kastenbaum (1980) comment that at present elderly clients receiving help may represent only the tip of the iceberg. Wattis (1983) comments that heavy drinking may be more common in older women than was previously thought, especially as the definition of 'heavy' drinking may need to be different in older people.

Crisis Intervention

Whether behaviour therapy or psychotherapy is being practised, it is tempting and convenient with functional patients to see the patient alone in the hospital consulting room for the statutory hour at regular intervals. One of the drawbacks of this model is that it is possible to lose sight of the interpersonal and environmental aspects of the person's problems and of the importance of formal and informal social supports. A further disadvantage in certain situations is that by the time therapy gets underway the point of crisis has passed, and an opportunity for constructive change in the person and their social network may have been lost.

There is much to be said for dealing with 'crisis' referrals as quickly as possible, seeing the person in their own home, together with relatives, neighbours and so on who may be involved. This home assessment allows ready assessment of the person's social support and resources, which is likely to lead to a more accurate definition of the person's problems. Garrison and Howe (1976) describe a behavioural problem-solving approach that is applicable in such situations. The therapeutic potential of relatives and friends can be harnessed immediately and their own needs, difficulties and fears about the situation explored, acknowledged and incorporated in the agreed contract between therapist, 'patient' and significant others. Having defined problems in specific terms, all the alternative courses of action can be listed, and a choice made as to which are to be tried in the first instance, with all parties including the therapist agreeing to carry out specific tasks. The progress with these is then reviewed at the next meeting.

Such an approach may save considerable time at a later stage, for example when, perhaps after some months, it becomes apparent that the patient is not making progress because relatives are not reinforcing the changes in the patient's behaviour being worked on at the out-patient clinic. The mutual expectations of relatives and therapist are much better established at the outset, and treatment goals are likely to be much more relevant to the real-life needs of the situation if this approach is adopted. By making explicit the establishment of a therapeutic contract the patient's sense of control is enhanced and the responsibilities of patient, therapist and of the others involved in the treatment plan are emphasised, serving to encourage an adult-level therapeutic relationship.

Summary

1. Affective disorders are common in the elderly, in mild forms affecting a significant proportion of the elderly (perhaps 25 per cent).

2. Idiosyncratic reactions to psychoactive drugs may make these disorders less easy to treat pharmacologically, increasing the need for and relevance of psychological treatment.

3. Most psychological therapies used with younger individuals are applicable to the elderly, with appropriate adaptation.

4. Psychotherapeutic techniques may be of some relevance to

the elderly, recent advances in conceptualisation replacing the earlier nihilism of Freudian approaches.

5. There is increasing evidence in the literature for successful behavioural treatment of the elderly with affective disorders. Most studies concentrate, however, on institutionalised clients with a slow growth in reports of community work.

6. There are reports of success in depressed individuals with a range of behavioural techniques from simple work on skills to complex cognitive restructuring.

7. Current efforts concentrate on working at an earlier stage of the problem (in the community or institution), on cost-effective treatment (use of volunteers or relatives as co-therapists, or use of groups), and on effective maintenance and generalisation of behaviours.

8. Among the major influences on affective disorders in the elderly are physical health and multiple losses. These factors are important to consider in any treatment plan. For the current generation of older people 'treatment socialisation' may be needed, educating the patient regarding the nature of psychological treatment.

8   TREATMENT APPROACHES FOR ORGANIC DISORDERS

Introduction

The most exciting development in clinical psychology with the elderly in recent years has been the rapid growth of interest in approaches to working with elderly people suffering from dementia and other organic disorders. The need for such approaches is evident. Although hopes for a pharmacological treatment of dementia are growing (e.g. Levy *et al.*, 1983), the prospect of a complete reversal of the dementing process seems a long way off — if indeed it can ever be attained. Relatives and care-staff, in the absence of any guidelines or management principles, have been left in the dark, to manage alone as best they could the often difficult problems associated with dementia.

In this chapter we will review many of the approaches that have been developed, and the evidence for their effectiveness. There are problems in evaluating the efficacy of 'treatments' applied to a chronic, deteriorating condition. Is it realistic to expect a reversal of the natural history of dementia? In Figure 8.1 'a' represents 'usual' deterioration in dementia; 'b' represents stabilisation of self-care ability at an intermediate level; 'c' represents a slowing down of deterioration resulting in a higher quality of life for 'c' as compared with 'a' for the period of time $X-Y$. It is evident that the lesser aim of maintaining skills and slowing down the deterioration could be said to improve the patient's quality of life, in terms of postponing the point where basic nursing care is required. An alternative model is to consider improvements in particular limited areas, i.e. modifying some of the manifestations of dementia, rather than reversing the whole process. This might apply also to 'excess disabilities' (Brody, Kleban, Lawton and Silverman, 1971) where a particular area of the person's functioning seems disproportionately dysfunctional — although allowance must be made for the influence of focal organic lesions.

These models, and much of the research to date, focus on change or rate of change in the dementing person. There is surely justification for a broader evaluation of these methods. Do they alter

Figure 8.1: Schematic Graph of Self-Care Ability in Dementia, Illustrating that Halting or Even Slowing Down Deterioration Can be Useful Aims

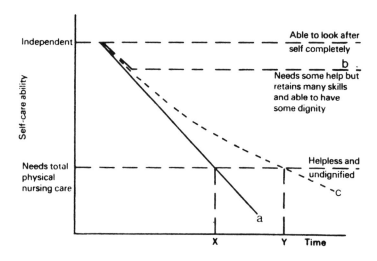

Source: Holden and Woods (1982), pp. 203, with permission of Churchill Livingstone.

the behaviour, or attitudes or morale of the carers? Whether they be relatives or nurses, their influence on the dementing person's quality of life is potentially enormous. They may govern and control every area of the patient's life; they may be worn down by the strain of care (see Chapters 9 and 10); they may feel helpless and inadequate to cope with the problems of dementia. Whether the approach then helps or changes the carer is an important issue.

The final method of evaluation is as yet lacking in rigour, but worthy of development. It is based again on the admittedly nebulous notion of 'quality of life', already invoked twice above. Could not approaches be evaluated in terms of the quantity and quality of life-enriching experiences that they provide for the dementing person? The experiences are not assumed to have any cumulative effect or to have more than a transitory impact on the person. The approach does not have to change the patient, but rather to increase the person's involvement in fulfilling life-events. Problems of definition and values abound in such an approach;

concepts of 'normalisation' (see Chapter 9), of what experiences are valued by society, or were valued by the person previously, may be of assistance. If psychological approaches are to be applicable to the most profoundly dementing patients, where the most basic person-to-person contact — a smile, a touch, a greeting — is an achievement, we need to break away from our preoccupation with treatment in the sense of cure and recovery, and be aware of the different types of goals that are feasible, and the value of some of the more limited goals in improving the patient's quality of life.

A number of previous reviews of this area are available (e.g. Woods and Britton, 1977; Miller, 1977c; Holden and Woods, 1982; Leng, 1982a).

We will discuss the major approaches, concentrating on the most recent research, before attempting to outline a practical psychological approach to the management of organic brain disorders, integrating the most useful features of various approaches, which in fact have a great deal in common.

Stimulation and Activity Programmes

These programmes owed their theoretical base to one of the models of dementia described in Chapter 4. If dementia can be seen as arising from the interaction of impaired recent memory and deprivation of sensory stimulation and environmental input, then increasing the amount of stimulation and activity may be a means of reducing confused behaviour.

A wide range of stimulating activities — physical, social and psychological — were used leading to some improvements compared to control groups in the early studies in this area. More recently, there has been increasing concern to specify the type of activity or stimulation used, to adopt a more focused approach, or to examine how the patient's involvement in activities can be increased. These studies will be discussed below, where it will be apparent that many approaches could be loosely described as activating or stimulating the dementing patient.

Many activities include some physical component. There is a little evidence that physical exercise may increase cognitive function in dementing people (Diesfeldt and Diesfeldt-Groenendijk, 1977). The failure of that most active and energetic group of dementing people — the so-called 'wanderers', who appear to be on their feet all day long — to treat themselves by this continual exercise (Cornbleth, 1977) suggests that the structured component of exercise sessions may be important. Physical exercises are a relatively simple activity for these patients, and the patient's participation is easier to monitor by the staff member leading the session than in more complex social activities.

Environmental Modification

The approaches included in this section have a variety of theoretical roots — social psychology, ego psychology and ergonomics for example. What they have in common is the explicit manipulation of the person's environment in order to bring about more appropriate behaviour *without* an explicit reinforcement system. This separation from the behaviour modification approach may well be more related to different conceptualisations employed by different workers than to a major difference in practice.

Changing the Physical Environment

Probably the most frequently applied change is the rearrangement of chairs in the day-room from their typical round the wall placement to small groups around coffee-tables. Sommer and Ross (1958) were the first to report this change, and their study has been replicated by Peterson, Knapp, Rosen and Pither (1977). Figure 8.2(a) shows the traditional situation; chairs were firmly against the walls. Normal social interaction is only possible for a few residents in the corners of the room. Other residents have either to shout across the room to residents sitting against the opposite wall, or to strain to turn to their neighbour. This is not a natural position for conversation — eye contact is difficult, and many of the chairs used have 'winged' backs, presenting yet another barrier to conversation. Sommer and Ross described the arrangement as being like a waiting-room with residents being observers, waiting 'for a train that never comes'. The sort of rearrangement shown in Figure 8.2(b) almost doubled the level of social interaction. It places residents in natural positions for conversation, facing each other at an angle of about 45° and within the normal social distance for comfortable interaction. The tables are resting places for magazines, flowers, etc., which may prompt further conversation. Peterson *et al.* (1977) similarly found this arrangement facilitated

Figure 8.2: Day-room Seating Arrangements

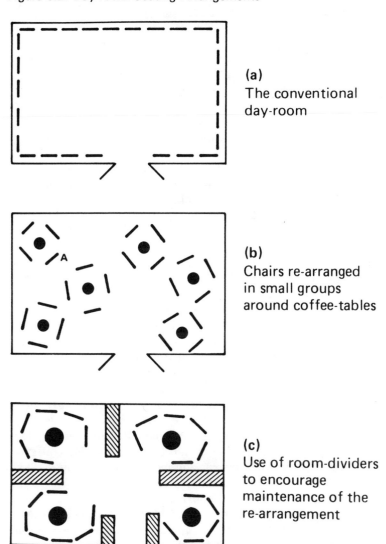

(a)
The conventional
day-room

(b)
Chairs re-arranged
in small groups
around coffee-tables

(c)
Use of room-dividers
to encourage
maintenance of the
re-arrangement

interaction. In both studies it proved difficult to maintain the rearrangement — the chairs kept finding their way back to the walls! There are several possible reasons for this. Domestic staff find the new arrangement makes cleaning more difficult. Care-staff may find it difficult to adjust to a less tidy, more cluttered room, with access to some parts likely to be impeded. Patients may feel less secure without something 'solid' behind them; patients seated in a chair such as that marked A on Figure 8.2(b) have a much more limited view of their surroundings — they can no longer observe all that is happening, everyone who comes in or goes out as they did previously. Figure 8.2(c) shows one way, suggested by Marston and Gupta (1977), of maintaining the new arrangements. Small permanent room-dividers — partitions or pieces of furniture — prevent the chairs being moved back, and allow every chair to have something solid behind it.

Other aspects of the physical environment may also serve to increase patient's dysfunction. Lengthy corridors, shiny floors (despite being officially 'non-slip'), high beds, long distances to be traversed to reach the toilet, lack of stable furniture to assist in walking, all serve to demonstrate any disability the patient has. There has been some talk of 'prosthetic environments'. Lindsley (1964) in his classic paper suggested that the environment for elderly people should be designed for any disabilities, just as prostheses are available for a range of physical impairments to restore competent performance, e.g. hearing aids, spectacles and dentures.

The prosthetic environment is not a retraining environment — it compensates for disabilities rather than seeking to modify them. Some prostheses might require the person to learn how to use them before they could be effective, e.g. a coloured line on the floor leading to the toilet (Pollock and Liberman, 1974); different coloured doors for toilets; signs and memory aids (Hanley, 1981). Other examples of prosthetic aids include Velcro fastenings instead of buttons, for those with poor dressing skills; special plates, utensils and non-slip mats for those with feeding difficulties. New technology is beginning to be applied to tackle some of the problems of dementing patients. For example, some wards now have a system where nursing staff are alerted by an alarm sounding when a patient wanders off the ward. This enables the ward door to be kept unlocked, with those patients not at risk of getting lost being free to come and go as they please. The alarm is triggered by a small tag fitted to the clothing of the patient who would get lost outside, or who would be at risk on the roads outside the ward.

Little evaluation has been carried out of aspects of prosthetic environments (except for signposting — see section on Reality Orientation (RO), in this chapter), and this is an area where there is a great deal of scope for development, utilising appropriate and effective methodologies.

Changing the Regime

Other environmental changes have focused on the regime, the structure of care, the expectations of staff and patients, seeking to create a milieu where patients have normal social roles, and have choices and some control over their environment. Many of the early accounts concerned the rehabilitation of chronic psychiatric patients who had reached old age in the psychiatric hospital. Sheltered workshops, where the elderly person can continue in the role of worker, producing something of quality and value, often were an important aspect of this 'milieu therapy'. The earnings from the workshop also allowed the elderly person to continue to function as a consumer, purchasing desired items. MacDonald and Settin (1978) reported that nursing home residents showed an improvement in life satisfaction and social interest following participation in a form of sheltered workshop, compared with residents taking part in a basic RO group or a non-treatment control. The activity involved was making gifts for a children's home. Unfortunately the degree of dementia — if any — of the residents was not indicated (they were certainly young — mean age 64.4 years). For most patients with more than a mild degree of dementia the activities would need to be extremely simple.

Some studies have evaluated the effects of allowing more choice and independence in wards including dementing patients. From Sweden, Gustafsson (1976) and Melin and Gotestam (1981) report an intervention study in three parts, using a multiple baseline design and direct observation of time-sampled behaviour to monitor change. The first phase was a change in afternoon coffee. Previously this had been a passive affair, with coffee (already with sugar and cream added) and cake being brought to the patients in their seats. The situation was changed so that the patients went into another room where coffee, cups, etc. were laid out on two tables. No staff were present, so patients had to fend for themselves, to choose what they wanted, and where to sit. Thus a social situation was created, allowing more independence and choice. Social interaction did increase dramatically during afternoon coffee.

The second phase involved mealtimes. Unlimited time was

offered — previously patients who were slow at feeding themselves were fed by staff. Freer choice of food and accompaniments was also offered. An increase in eating skills was observed following these changes.

Finally activity materials were provided on the ward — games, books, puzzles and so on. For the first week these materials were available for patients to use under their own initiative; in the second week, staff encouraged patients to use them, but again in the third week no encouragement was given. In this final week activity levels showed an increase, compared with the control group, who had received no encouragement at all to use the materials (but had access to them).

In a geriatric ward in the UK, Davies and Snaith (1980) were successful in increasing social interaction at mealtimes, by creating a more normal social situation. Instead of patients sitting around the walls, they were placed around tables in groups of six. Table cloths, water jugs and so on were provided, and efforts were made to reduce the background noise level, to facilitate interaction. These changes produced an immediate increase in social interaction, particularly between patients, who in fact began to help each other.

Group Living

An increasingly popular concept involving changes to both the regime and the physical environment is 'group living'. This concept derives in part from social psychological theories of groups — that they are most effective when having eight to twelve members, with a shared purpose. This contrasts with the typical ward or old people's home where 30, 40 or more residents share a space, but little else. It is hard enough for a normal person to adjust to living with 30 other people, to get to know them and build relationships with them — for the dementing person this must seem like an impossible task. It is argued then that a small group of people living together, with shared activities, will be more effective in preventing loneliness, apathy and institutionalisation in residential settings.

Each group of eight to twelve residents (Marston and Gupta, 1977) has its own living area, with the shared purpose being the basic domestic activities that form part of the daily routine for most elderly people. Residents help themselves to breakfast; other meals are provided, but residents serve themselves, clear up afterwards, wash the dishes and so on. They participate in the choice of furniture and decor of their rooms, and choose when to have drinks and snacks. They can entertain visitors — and even offer hospitality to staff! Less able residents are helped by the able, each helping with the various tasks according to their skills. Clearly a mix of abilities is desirable, but the approach has been implemented in hospital settings (Adams, Davies and Northwood, 1979) as well as in residential homes. Anecdotal reports have been encouraging, with many dormant abilities being demonstrated by residents previously written off as 'confused'. The transition from conventional care to group living does need a great deal of preparation and consultation with both staff and residents and their relatives, as the pattern of care is so fundamentally different. It is not enough to allocate residents to groups and expect the system to work immediately; staff need to be able to work with the groups, helping them arrive at solutions to any difficulties within the group, and helping them to take responsibility again. Many residents may feel they have surrendered control over their lives before coming into the old people's home (Tobin and Lieberman, 1976).

Controlled evaluations of this approach are badly needed, and indications of the range of dementia that could be accommodated would be valuable. An observational study of one old person's home where a number of residents had dementia showed a marked increase in purposeful activity following the introduction of group living (Rothwell, Britton and Woods, 1983). Self-reports of life satisfaction suggested residents were generally more content under the new system; there was no evidence of any improvement in verbal orientation.

Finally, an important aspect of group living is that the extra activity is mainly centred around domestic tasks. It is not activity for the sake of activity, merely to fill in some time, but has a clear purpose and benefit for those concerned. Group living and the other environmental approaches have demonstrated that people with dementia may well be under-functioning in many situations, simply because the environment is not structured in such a way as to elicit all the person's residual skills and abilities, or to compensate for the person's deficits. This applies both in institutions for the elderly (Chapter 9) and in the community (Chapter 10).

Reality Orientation (RO)

What is RO

The development of RO can be traced back to 1958 when Dr James

Folsom set up an 'aide-centred activity programme for elderly patients' at the Veterans Administration Hospital in Topeka, Kansas, USA. The first published descriptions appeared in the mid-1960s, by which time Folsom was at the VA Hospital in Tuscaloosa, Alabama (Taulbee and Folsom, 1966; Folsom, 1967).

Three major components of RO were identified. Informal, or 24-hour, RO involves staff presenting current information to the patient in every interaction, a commentary on what is happening and reminding the patient of the time, the place and of the identities of those around them. Confused, rambling speech is systematically not reinforced. Signs and other memory aids around the environment reinforce the reorientation process.

RO sessions (or as originally conceived, classes) were intended to supplement the 24-hour approach. These groups typically meet daily for 30 minutes, and consist of three to six patients with one or two members of staff, according to the patients' degree of dementia. Staff members do not need particular qualifications to lead these groups, but do require specific training, enthusiasm and a positive approach. One of the innovative aspects of RO was its involvement of all grades of staff in group-work. In the group, sessions are varied according to the skill and interests of the partici-pants. Current information is usually discussed initially, using some sort of board as a focus for details of date, place and so on. Other activities also tend to have a definite focus — a picture, object, some music or whatever — that helps the group members retain a common topic despite their memory difficulties. Whatever the activity, through cues and prompts and careful selection of the difficulty level of the task the patient is helped to experience success.

The third aspect involved staff maintaining a particular attitude to each patient, according to the patient's personality and needs. This involved staff in identifying the person's mechanism of coping with their memory loss (e.g. blaming others, self-blame, denial or withdrawal) and responding appropriately. Whilst the individuali-sation of care has continued to be emphasised in RO, this 'attitude therapy' aspect seems not to have been developed or investigated further.

In the last ten years or so there has been a huge growth of interest in RO. Indeed Hussian (1981) claims that in facilities for the elderly in the USA it has replaced 'custodial care' as the norm! In the authors' experience in the UK this cannot be said to be the case;

psychological needs are still, by and large, ignored (cf. Godlove *et al.*, 1982). RO has, even so, certainly been the most written and talked about of the various approaches reviewed here. A number of recent reviews are available (e.g. Burton, 1982; Schwenk, 1981; Powell-Proctor and Miller, 1982; Woods and Holden, 1982; Greene, 1984; Hanley, 1984) and a recent book serves both as a practical manual and a guide to the research on RO (Holden and Woods, 1982). Other practical manuals have recently become available (Hanley, 1982; Rimmer, 1982).

Research on RO

Here only the most recent research will be reviewed, before considering some of the criticisms that have been levelled at RO. Earlier research is comprehensively described by Holden and Woods (1982, Chapter 3).

With regard to evaluative research, recently published studies (Hanley, McGuire and Boyd, 1981; Johnson, McLaren and McPherson, 1981; Zepelin, Wolfe and Kleinplatz, 1981; Greene, Timbury, Smith and Gardiner, 1983) confirm Holden and Woods's conclusion that verbal orientation is most frequently found to be improved by RO, with much less evidence for more generalized behavioural change. A controlled study not reporting an improvement in verbal orientation (Hogstel, 1979) had only a three-week experimental period. Another recent study (Wallis, Baldwin and Higginbotham, 1983), using patients with chronic psychiatric disorders as well as those with dementia, found marginally more cognitive improvements in patients participating in RO sessions than in similar patients attending diversional occupational therapy.

Relatively few studies have identified positive changes in the patients' general functioning following RO — despite many anecdotal accounts. For example, Zepelin *et al.* (1981) carried out a very thorough and detailed study of RO over a twelve-month period, attempting to implement 24-hour RO and attitude therapy as well as RO sessions. Additional staff and volunteer resources were provided so the programme could be carried out. Yet such behavioural changes as were found favoured the untreated control group, who were residents of a similar nursing home to where the RO programme was implemented.

Why does RO achieve so little impact where it really matters, in the patients' ability to function independently, or to socialise or to communicate, despite its undoubted success in improving verbal orientation slightly? Behavioural change is more difficult to assess objectively and consistently. Zepelin *et al.* (1981) had to abandon two behavioural measures because their inter-rater agreement did not reach statistical significance. Behavioural ratings depend on observation over time, rather than in a straightforward structured verbal orientation interview, and are more likely to be influenced by other factors in the setting — staff changes and shortages, slight changes in regime and so on. Many scales have very few points and are insensitive to small amounts of change. Zepelin *et al.* (1981) describe a floor effect on some of their ratings with controls having less scope for decline.

24-hour RO

The respective roles of 24-hour RO and RO sessions also need to be clarified. A number of studies have included only RO sessions, although these were intended to be supplementary to the basic 24-hour approach. It is the 24-hour approach that is seen as crucial for behavioural change to occur (e.g. Hanley *et al.*, 1981); it is here that appropriate behaviour is cued and reinforced. If all the disabilities of the dementing person are considered, it is surely unreasonable to expect that placing them in a different context for 2½ hours or so a week will produce dramatic behavioural changes (although this is indeed the implication of Brook, Degun and Mather's, 1975, pioneering study).

Hanley (1984) points out that, whilst there is some evidence for RO sessions being carried out as planned (Holden and Woods, 1982, p. 58), no evidence that staff actually do put 24-hour RO into practice has emerged. Indeed Hanley showed that no change was detectable in the quantity or quality of staff–resident interactions following a training programme that marked the implementation of 24-hour RO in a particular setting. This was despite the staff's apparent enthusiasm for the programme. Direct observation of staff behaviour produced findings in marked contrast to the staff's own beliefs about the way in which they interacted with patients. Staff in any setting may carry out 24-hour RO to some degree — the question is to what extent it actually occurs. This lack of attention to evaluating and changing staff behaviour may account for some of the disappointing results so far reported with regard to general behavioural change. Twenty-four-hour RO has not been tried and found wanting — indeed it may never have been fully tried!

Developing RO

To date, the typical RO research study has compared patients attending RO sessions (with or without some back-up training for staff in 24-hour RO) with control patients (often having no treatment) on a verbal orientation test and a behaviour-rating scale. Future research needs to tackle the question 'does RO work' from a much broader basis. Changes in staff behaviour and attitudes need to be evaluated (Greene, 1984). Particular components of the RO techniques need to be studied and refined. At present, as Hanley (1984) comments, 'RO can be all things to all people'. Methods are required that ensure that high quality RO is practised, that it is developed to incorporate psychological findings on memory, learning and behavioural functioning (Carroll and Gray, 1981; Hanley, 1984), that it does not become mechanical or depersonalised (cf. Buckholdt and Gubrium, 1983), or applied in a context of inappropriate attitudes (Holden and Woods, 1982, p. 152).

Ward Orientation Training

A good example of the systematic investigation of parts of the total RO approach is provided by recent research on ward-orientation training. Hanley *et al.* (1981) demonstrated that a relatively straightforward training procedure was effective in increasing dementing patients' ability to find their way from one location to another on the ward. Predictably RO sessions alone had no effect on ward orientation (see Figure 8.3). The training procedure involved a staff member accompanying the patient twice around the ward seven times over a two-week period. The patient was asked to show the staff member to the next location on a set route; if correct, the patient was reinforced verbally; if not, appropriate information and cues were given for the patient to be able to find the location requested. Training did not generalise to untrained locations, and the effects of training were gradually lost over time. Hanley (1981) showed that the introduction of large pictorial signposts, clearly labelled, did not in itself have any effect on ward orientation. However, in combination with the ward-orientation training procedure, the signs were effective, and seemed to assist in the maintenance of the improvements from training (see Figure 8.4). Similar findings are reported by Gilleard, Mitchell and Riordan (1981b).

Figure 8.3: Change in Mean Verbal Orientation (VO) and Ward Orientation (WO) after Classroom Orientation (CO) and Ward Training (WT)

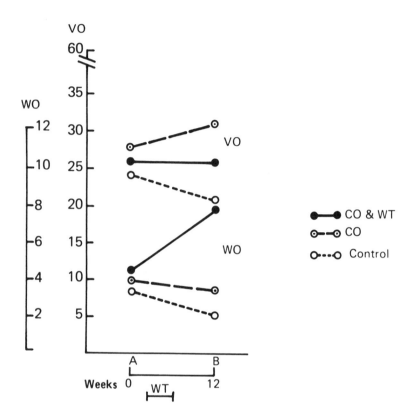

Source: Hanley *et al.* (1981), with permission of the *British Journal of Psychiatry* and the authors.

Verbal Orientation Training

A further example of the examination of one aspect of RO is seen in the highly structured verbal-orientation training used in the single-case studies reported by Greene, Nicol and Jamieson (1979) and Woods (1983). Greene *et al.* reported three cases, showed a clear learning effect, using an ABAB design, with some generalisation to OT performance, but not to social behaviour in OT. Woods

Figure 8.4: (a) Ward Orientation Scores for Two Patients as Examples of the Effects of Ward Training on Individual Dementing Patients

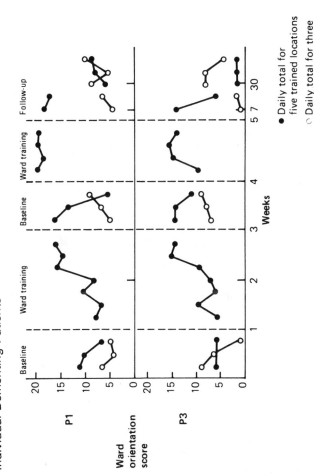

Source: Derived from Hanley (1981).

Figure 8.4: (b) Ward Orientation Scores for Two Dementing Patients, Showing the Effects of the Combination of Training and Signposting in Individual Patients

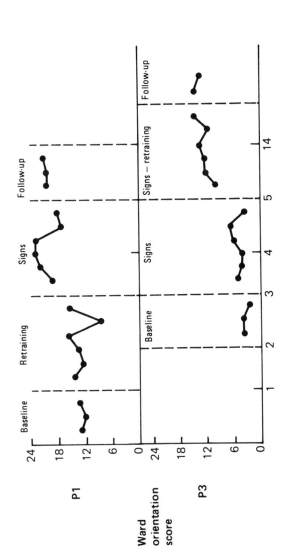

Source: Derived from Hanley (1981), reprinted, with the permission of the author and the *Journal of Behaviour Therapy and Experimental Psychiatry*, copyright (1981) Pergamon Press Ltd.

used a multiple-baseline design and showed a specific learning effect in a single-case, with learning being confined to items that were specifically taught.

How Does RO Work?

These examples lend weight to the suggestion that what positive results RO does achieve are related to re-learning. As Hanley (1984) points out, the use of cued recall, regular practice and increasing motivation by the use of meaningful and enjoyable materials and activities contribute to this re-learning process. Another important mechanism that should be considered involves the possibility that some dementing patients under-function. This may arise from anxiety concerning their performance, based on some awareness of their deficits, actually exacerbating their dysfunction. Or it may be related to a more depressive withdrawal, a feeling of helplessness following repeated failure at tasks that were previously relatively easy for the person. In both instances RO may be effective by taking pressure off the person, by helping them, through cues and prompts, to experience some success and to enjoy some of the social reinforcers still available to them. It could serve to reassure and to calm and to help them function closer to the limitations placed by their degree of dementia. The evidence for these mechanisms is almost entirely anecdotal, but they may well account for some of the more dramatic changes occasionally seen following RO. The best evidence for their importance emerges from Greene *et al.*'s (1983) recent study of RO sessions in a day-hospital with dementing people living with relatives at home. As well as the usual increase in verbal orientation during RO phases there was a significant improvement in one aspect of the patient's behaviour as rated by the relative, namely mood stability, see Figure 8.5.

Of great interest is that the relative's mood improved also during the RO phase (although relatives were 'blind' as to the phases of the study). Exactly what the causal relationship is between the three improved areas — verbal orientation, patient's mood and relative's mood — remains open to doubt (Greene, 1984), but it may well mean that a re-learning mechanism alone is insufficient to account for the limited improvements related to RO.

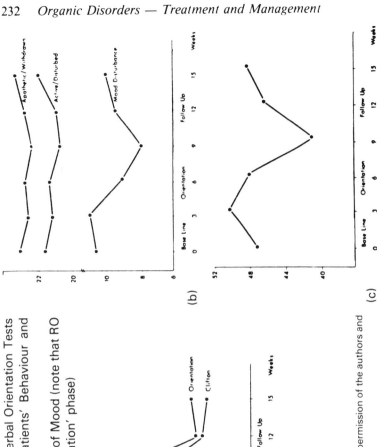

Figure 8.5: (a) Patients' Mean Scores on Verbal Orientation Tests
(b) Mean Scores on Sub-scales of the Patients' Behaviour and
Mood Disturbance Scale (rated by relative)
(c) Mean Scores of Relatives on Self-rating of Mood (note that RO
sessions only took place during the 'orientation' phase)

Source: Reprinted from Greene *et al.* (1983), with the permission of the authors and
Age and Ageing.

Reminiscence Therapy

Life-review

In the last few years reminiscence has been increasingly popular as a therapeutic approach. It is often linked theoretically to Butler's (1963) concept of 'life-review'; elderly people were seen as looking back at their life, evaluating achievements, disappointments, successes and failures; arriving ideally at an acceptance of what has been done and what has been left; in a sense finishing the business of life, before reaching the ultimate developmental stage, death. This tied in with Erikson's framework, where this stage is seen as ego integrity vs. despair — the latter being the result of a life-review leading to a conclusion of life having been useless and worthless. It is now recognised that life-review occurs not only in old age, but at other points of transition during life.

However, this life-review process, involving the evaluation and analysis of life-events, negative and positive, is only one form of reminiscence (Merriam, 1980). Two other types should be identified: *simple* reminiscence, the recall of the past, and *informative* reminiscence for education or retirement, 'telling a story' about the past, past events and experiences. Different applications of reminiscence therapy almost certainly include differing proportions of these different types of reminiscence.

Reminiscence as Therapy

In the UK the growth of reminiscence therapy has been facilitated by the production of the 'Recall' pack (Help the Aged, 1981), a set of six tape-slide sequences, depicting events and experiences relevant to current elderly people, drawing on resources such as pictures, music and archival recordings, to provide a range of stimuli designed to prompt and facilitate reminiscence. These are intended to be used as a starting-point, to encourage others to gather locally relevant materials, souvenirs, mementoes, etc. For many towns a 'then and now' book is available, showing landmarks of the town at the turn of the century contrasted with the present day. Many patients and their families have items such as photo albums, dating back to the patient's childhood. TV programmes show aspects of life years ago. A wealth of material is potentially available — but takes some work to unearth and collate. If this is not done, an unfortunate temptation to use the published materials over and over again with the same patients arises, and an opportunity to use more individually meaningful material is lost.

What is reminiscence therapy as applied to patients with dementia? A description of one implementation is provided by Norris and Abu El Eileh (1982). They describe twice-weekly groups for six patients, meeting over a five-week period, each session lasting for 30 minutes. At first a particular theme for the session was suggested, e.g. families or places where members had lived, backed up with appropriate reminiscence aids. In later sessions topics emerged from the members' reminiscences. With some more confused patients a group setting may not be feasible, and a brief one-to-one session may be more appropriate. The pace of the session is important, giving the patient time to look at and appreciate the materials, making sure their contribution is heard and acknowledged, not rushing through an entire tape-slide sequence, when a couple of pictures or a piece of music might have generated a whole stream of memories, or been enough for the attention span of the patient. It is worth noting that for the most severely demented patients a piece of music from their youth may elicit a response where little else does.

Effectiveness of Reminiscence Therapy

Little in the way of controlled research evaluating the effectiveness of reminiscence therapy on dementing patients is available. Kiernat (1979) reports on a 20-session life-review activity group, with life-events discussed in chronological order up to the present time. Residents who attended most sessions showed most behavioural improvement. Other reports (e.g. Lesser, Lazarus, Frankel and Havasy, 1981; Norris and Abu El Eileh, 1982) have given positive anecdotal evaluations.

It is to be hoped that the evaluation of reminiscence, which will undoubtedly mushroom in the next few years, will benefit from the RO literature. Research should look at the effects on staff, their behaviour and attitudes, at changes in patient behaviour in group sessions as well as outside, at patient's preferences for different types of materials and different modes of presentation, at changes in the patient's quality of life and simply at their enjoyment of reminiscence sessions. To what extent is *analysis* of events and experiences needed? Is simple *recall* of events/experiences sufficient?

For example, Norris and Abu El Eileh describe a number of changes resulting from reminiscence groups — increased participation in discussion in the groups, more spontaneity and enjoyment; what type of materials/discussion/leadership facilitates this? Nurses came to know each patient better as an individual, and were helped to form relationships with them; how can this be evaluated/encouraged? Would a life-history book for each patient, made up of photos, etc., be an effective means of encouraging this process? An activity programme was begun as a direct consequence of the reminiscence group, based on the activities and interests expressed by the group members in their past life. A broad-spectrum approach to programme evaluation is obviously indicated — a behavioural-rating scale and a memory test are not appropriate if such effects are to be monitored.

Reminiscence is a popular idea. It enables patients to give something back to the staff, telling them about events and experiences which for once the patients know about. It is an activity which normal elderly people enjoy, and so is age appropriate, unlike some activities offered to dementing people. It potentially helps staff to see the patient as a whole person, rather than as the shadow of their former selves that is so often evident. It has already found much use in RO as a means of facilitating communication, as a way of bridging the past and present. Research-based guidelines on its use, on its limitations and on its effects are urgently needed if it is to find continued use, and not written off as yet another 'therapy' that does not achieve the (probably impossible) goal of reversing dementia.

Behaviour Modification

Unfulfilled Potential

Holden and Woods (1982) conclude their recent review: 'In relation to dementia at least, behaviour modification is an extremely promising approach, but as yet there remains a lack of convincing evidence for its effectiveness'. They pointed out that a major problem in evaluating behavioural treatment studies in the elderly was the lack of precise details given concerning the patients involved. Together with diagnostic differences between the UK and the USA (where organic brain syndromes appear to be over-diagnosed), this made it difficult to be certain that the studies reported showing the success of behavioural treatment had actually involved any patients suffering from dementia. Has more recent evidence suggested that the behavioural approach is at last fulfilling its potential in dementia?

Increasing Activity Levels

The flow of studies involving elderly patients or nursing home residents continues. They have been taught the skill of 'starting a conversation' (Lopez *et al.*, 1980), and have increased their participation in activity programmes when prompts and/or reinforcements have been provided (Konarski, Johnson and Whitman, 1980; Quattrochi-Tubin and Jason, 1980). None of these studies, however, has specifically included dementing patients — indeed Lopez *et al.* specifically excluded those with severe organic impairment. There are, however, at least two reports from the UK showing that the participation of dementing elderly people in activities can be increased behaviourally. Burton (1980) showed that, when staff consistently prompted patients to use materials and reinforced them they did so in OT sessions, then patients' appropriately materially directed activity increased. Patients also slept less in the OT sessions! Jenkins *et al.* (1977) similarly reported increased activity levels in dementing elderly people when the use of activity materials was prompted and encouraged.

Improving Self-care

Increasing and maintaining self-care skills is a major consideration with dementing patients. Again, there are relatively few behavioural studies showing successful intervention on self-care skills with elderly patients clearly having dementia. Rinke, Williams, Lloyd and Smith-Scott (1978) evaluated the effects of prompting and reinforcement on self-bathing in six nursing home residents, diagnosed as having chronic brain syndrome, ranging in age from 67 to 90 years. The target behaviour, self-bathing, was broken down into five components: undressing, soaping, rinsing, drying and dressing. A multiple-baseline design was used, with the experimental intervention being applied to each of these components in turn. Two residents remained under baseline conditions throughout the experimental period; they showed little systematic change. Data on the remaining four residents show clearly the effects of prompting and reinforcement, with each aspect of behaviour increasing to near maximum levels when it was prompted and reinforced. Prompting included verbal instructions, and a physical prompt, such as handing the resident a bar of soap, where necessary. Reinforcement included verbal praise, visual feed-back on a wall-chart and a choice of things to eat or of 'grooming aids' (e.g. powder or lotion) contingent on a set number of responses. Although the respective contributions of prompting and reinforcement were not systematically investigated, there were some indications that prompting alone or reinforcement alone might have been sufficient in some cases to bring about or maintain the behavioural change.

Improving Continence

Incontinence is often seen as a major problem in the care of dementing patients. There have been a number of attempts to reduce its frequency or, more constructively, to retrain appropriate toileting skills necessary for continence to be achieved. The early literature is reviewed by Holden and Woods (1982) and Tarrier and Larner (1983). Behavioural methods have generally been successful in reducing incontinence in elderly chronic schizophrenic patients, but, at best, only partially successful with dementing patients.

More recently Hussian (1981) reports results from a urinary incontinence programme with twelve 'regressed institutionalized geriatric patients'. A regular toileting programme, with prompts and reinforcement for toileting and praise for being dry, reduced incontinence dramatically in two weeks. This improvement was maintained when reinforcement and feedback were no longer given — presumably indicating the effectiveness of prompting in maintaining this behavioural change.

Sanavio (1981) reports an application of Foxx and Azrin's (1973) rapid toilet-training method (developed for use originally with the mentally handicapped) to two elderly patients. Both had been incontinent, day and night, of urine and/or faeces for over two years. Neither showed any independent toileting. The first patient, a 60-year-old, with alcoholic dementia, showed a rapid decrease in number of accidents per day following four days of the Foxx and Azrin procedure. This was accompanied by a dramatic increase in the number of occurrences of independent toileting (initially zero). A reversal phase (where reinforcement and punishment were given non-contingently) led to a deterioration in behaviour, which improved again when treatment was reinstated. Improvements were maintained at eight-week follow-up. A second patient was treated for faecal incontinence. This patient was 77 years old, and had a long psychiatric history, though was now thought to have senile dementia. The frequency of faecal incontinence was reduced to near-zero, and again self-initiated toileting regularly occurred. It is important to clarify the aims of these retraining programmes. Ideally, complete continence and independent toileting, as in Sanavio's study, might be the aim. For more deteriorated or physically disabled patients, remaining dry might be a more attainable goal, perhaps with regular prompting, as in Hussian's procedure. If the patient has to be taken to the toilet, it is desirable that the number of occasions when voiding does not occur is kept to a minimum — perhaps by developing an individual programme based on the person's pattern of micturition. Tarrier and Larner (1983) report an intervention with a group of four immobile stroke patients. Nursing staff complained that many of their requests to be toileted were false alarms, often occurring at busy times on the ward. The intervention involved staff giving attention when the patient was behaving appropriately — rather than only in response to toileting requests. 'False alarms' reduced significantly, and patient-initiated contacts were also reduced. Despite these objective changes, nursing staff did not perceive that behavioural change had in fact occurred.

It should be emphasised that appropriate toileting is a complex process requiring a number of skills — dressing, mobility, ability to find the toilet, recognition of the toilet, etc., as well as a degree of social awareness. Each incontinent patient needs a careful behavioural analysis to identify the particular behavioural difficulties involved (see Turner, 1980, Hodge, 1984). This needs to consider institutional and attitudinal variables, which form part of the person–environment interaction, leading to the observed behaviour. Medical and nutritional variables are also relevant, and a multi-modal approach (e.g. King, 1980) is needed to deal with this complex, difficult problem.

Behavioural Problems

Some work has sought to reduce some of the behavioural excesses that occur occasionally in dementing patients. Birchmore and Clague (1983) report treating a 70-year-old blind woman suffering from senile dementia, who shouted constantly. This was viewed as being a means of exerting control over her environment, providing stimulation, and inadvertently reinforced by nursing staff and other patients. The intervention consisted of providing reinforcement for being quiet. A number of potent reinforcers were tried; touch, in the form of rubbing the patient's back, proved most useful. Shouting was reduced by this procedure, with the effects of a treatment session lasting for some time afterwards.

Hussian (1981) similarly discusses the self-stimulatory aspects of some repeated, apparently meaningless behaviours of dementing patients. Hussian and Hill (1980) showed that a small group of dementing patients spent 87 per cent of their time when not eating or sleeping engaged in stereotyped self-stimulating behaviour — rubbing part of the body, nonsensical vocalisations, manipulating nearby objects, etc., and Hussian suggests it may even be a useful diagnostic indicator, as it so frequently occurs in dementing patients. It is not clear, however, at what stage of dementia it occurs, or whether it may also be related to an unstimulating environment or the effects of medication.

In an intervention study, each of three patients' most frequent stereotyped behaviour was targeted (Hussian, 1980). For two patients the target behaviour was the stereotyped manipulation of objects; these patients received positive practice training, involving being reinforced for a similar, but appropriate behaviour (clay moulding). The third patient's repeated vocalisations were tackled by providing reinforcement for an entire ten-second period without a vocalisation occurring. Neither of these interventions reduced the frequency of the targeted behaviour unless an artificial discriminative cue was present, when significant reductions occurred. This cue was simply a red cardboard circle, 18 inches in diameter, which had been associated with positive reinforcers in 4 three-minute training sessions with each patient. Exactly how this cue operated is not clear; it may have signalled that reinforcement could be forthcoming; it may have aided attention and concentration. In this study it seemed to enhance greatly the effectiveness of the behavioural procedure employed, which alone did not produce the desired reduction in stereotyped behaviour.

Hussian (1981) reports a similar procedure in reducing the frequency of inappropriate sexual behaviour. The treatment of a 62-year-old male nursing home resident who frequently masturbated in public is described. He was prevented from masturbating except in the presence of an artificial cue (a large orange disc), which was placed in his room and in the bathroom. If observed publicly masturbating, he was taken to his room. It proved possible gradually to reduce the size of the cue, and finally to remove it, as the behaviour came under the control of the room. Here the patient was taught to discriminate between locations where the behaviour was acceptable and those where it was not, and again the use of the artificial cue seems to facilitate other behavioural techniques (Hussian, 1980).

A third application of these artificial stimuli has been in reducing wandering (Hussian, 1980). Here two types of stimuli, e.g. orange rectangles (or arrows) and blue circles, were used. One type is again paired with positive events in individual training sessions, the other is paired with noxious stimuli (a loud hand-clap). These latter cues would be placed at potential danger points — stairs, exits, etc. The others would lead to the patient's room, and would be placed strategically in those areas where the patient habitually wandered. Data on three dementing patients suggest a marked reduction in entries to hazardous areas, maintained when the cues were gradually faded, by being reduced in size. Booster-training sessions were required for all three patients within a few months, however. Further application and evaluation of these artificial 'supernormal' discriminative cues would be of great interest, particularly if they could be used in rebuilding skills, as well as in reducing and redirecting behavioural excesses.

Modular Treatment Programmes

Finally, in this section on behavioural modification, mention must be made of an extensive behavioural treatment and rehabilitation programme for elderly psychiatric patients described by Patterson (1982). The programme was aimed at placing in the community elderly people in state hospitals and at maintaining in the community elderly people at risk of being hospitalized. Both day-care and residential facilities were used, to provide 'short-term intensive restorative treatment of a behavioural nature aimed at community placement'. Entry criteria for the programme excluded those thought unlikely to attain placement in the community. Mobility and continence were prerequisites for acceptance; patients were excluded if they needed one-to-one supervision in an open setting, of if they were considered a danger to themselves or others, of if in need of skilled nursing care. It is difficult to be certain what proportion of the patients suffered from dementia — despite extensive descriptions of client characteristics, diagnostic details are not given. Certainly some clients were chronic psychiatric patients — some had been in hospital up to 30 years. It seems possible from the data given (p. 249) that up to a third might have had dementia — but the entry criteria must have excluded those with a severe degree of dementia.

Treatment programmes consisted of a number of modules, covering the major problems experienced by the clients, together with individualised treatment programmes using single-case designs where a patient had particular less common difficulties, perhaps interfering with modular treatment. Clients entered only those modules where they showed deficits, and left them if and when they reached a set level of performance. Each client then had an individualised programme from among the modules available. The modules described were as follows:—

Personal Information Training	: a structured verbal-orientation training programme.
Activities of Daily Living I	: personal hygiene, dressing, eating, etc.
Activities of Daily Living II	: higher level skills — telephone, laundry, money, etc.
Activities of Daily Living III	: housekeeping, budgeting, etc.
Social Skills — Conversation	: to increase frequency of conversation.
— Communication	: to teach appropriate expression of pleasure and displeasure.
Self-esteem Training	: to improve client's psychological support system, by reinforcing positive self-statements.

The programme also included a number of non-modular activities, including exercise, muscle relaxation, rational-emotive therapy, etc.

Evaluation of the programme is complex, as for ethical and practical reasons a straightforward comparison with a control group was impossible. Each module is evaluated, showing significant improvement among clients receiving modular training; there was some evidence that the training had specific effects, and that general exposure to the programme as a whole did not simply produce generalised improvements. For example, clients receiving communication training improved much more on ratings of expression of affect than clients in the conversation training group. Four clients with a diagnosis of organic brain syndrome showed a specificity of learning in the Personal Information Training session, similar to that described by Woods (1983) in RO sessions.

The programme as a whole did seem to have encouragingly positive effects, in behavioural improvement, community placements and reduced relapse rates. How effective it was for clients with dementia is difficult to assess, as results are not reported for different diagnostic groups. However, it does seem that poor initial performance on a ten-item test of current information does relate to slower rates of learning skills in the various modules and to greater chance of relapse (p. 271); this may reflect poorer prognosis in more demented clients. The overall programme probably has application to patients both with organic and functional disorders; it is impressive in its in-depth application of behavioural principles over a broad range of real-life problems in a genuine attempt to provide restorative rehabilitation. There is a great deal to be learned from the programme's use of multi-disciplinary teamwork, case-management, use of objective assessment procedures and of record-keeping related to, and influencing, practice.

An Integrative Approach

In 1977 we suggested that much of the literature on psychological approaches to treating the elderly could be understood in a behavioural framework. We see no reason to change this view, as long as a behavioural approach is adopted that encompasses the elderly person's ecology, that does not treat the elderly person in isolation from their environmental, institutional, family or social context. There is much to be drawn from the various approaches reviewed above which can be interpreted and developed usefully in behavioural terms. Hussian (1981) gives an example of this in his suggested modification of RO and Rebok and Hoyer (1977) similarly draw attention to the need to incorporate insights from the various approaches in their discussion of behavioural ecology with the elderly.

RO and reminiscence can both involve environmental change — in terms of physical features as well as the regime. The dividing line between environmental and behavioural modification was stated earlier to be rather arbitrary; much environmental change is designed to prompt appropriate behaviour. RO has been seen as a model for the behavioural re-learning potential of dementing elderly people (Woods and Holden, 1982), showing that change can be achieved in areas where specific training is given.

Individual Programme Planning

The application of an integrated approach must be centred on individual elderly people. For each, an individual plan is needed. This ideally would incorporate all aspects of the person's life; medical, physical, social and psychological aspects can only be separated artificially. A multi-disciplinary team is then the ideal group to develop such a plan with the person and their carers.

The plan should emphasise the person's assets and resources, and not concentrate only on their problems and needs. Looking at the person in the context of their whole life, their interests, achievements, habits and background, is important if the person is to be seen as a complete individual. However severely demented they may be, they will be better understood and cared for if the experiences, attitudes and events that have shaped their lives are known to the carers.

Holden and Woods (1982) suggest that four questions need to be posed in the development of a care-plan.

1. What does the elderly person want?
2. What assets, abilities and interests does the person have?
3. What problems does the person have?
4. What inconsistencies are there in the person's behaviour?

They emphasise the often forgotten right of the person and their family to have their views taken into account in drawing up a plan, together with the use of the person's assets to build up positive behaviours incompatible with any problem behaviours. The person is *not* regarded simply as a list of problems, with the plan defining ways of removing these problems. Rather the person's resources are developed by the plan in directions that will enhance the quality of his or her life and — often indirectly — lead to a reduction in the frequency of any problems. A similar way of tackling this task of collecting the basic information required for care-planning is to draw up lists of the person's strengths and of needs, insisting that the former be the longer!

Behavioural Analysis. In this assessment process it is important to work towards an understanding of the dementing person's behaviour. As Hodge (1984) points out 'the same problem may occur in the same person at different times for different reasons'. For example, Snyder, Rupprecht, Pyrek, Brekhus and Moss (1978) identified at least three types of wandering behaviour, with single individuals showing more than one pattern at different times. Careful behavioural analysis and behavioural definition is essential, if appropriate strategies for working with the dementing individual are to be developed. Generalised descriptions of behaviour such as 'attention-seeking', 'confused', 'wandering', 'incontinent' and so on have to be replaced by specific descriptions of the actual behaviour, its frequency, the circumstances in which it occurs and its consequences for the patient.

Neuropsychological Assessment. Dementing patients differ greatly in the extent to which they show focal neuropsychological deficits — constructional dyspraxia, visual agnosia and so on. Awareness of some of the person's specific deficits will assist in understanding why particular difficulties are occurring. Incontinence provides a good example (see Hodge, 1984). Among the many factors contributing to incontinence, the person may fail to recognise the toilet as a toilet, if they have visual agnosia; or be unable to cope with the necessary dressing/undressing skills, if dressing dyspraxia is present.

This is not to say that every dementing person should have a full neuropsychological assessment. Neither the skilled resources nor the appropriate measures are available. The important consideration is that the person's behaviour is not simply a product of the environmental antecedents and consequences; the changes in the person's cognitive function must be taken into account. Holden and Woods (1982, Ch. 5) describe some straightforward methods for examining these focal deficits in dementing people.

The discovery of focal deficits need not lead to therapeutic pessimism, but to the development of ways of overcoming the effects of these problems, and of methods for compensating for the dysfunction. For instance, Walker and Williams (1980) have shown — in a non-dementing population — that many elderly patients with dysphasia resulting from a stroke *do* improve over a period of time. Even where speech had stopped improving, many patients developed effective ways of communicating with those around them.

Other aspects of the person's function also need to be evaluated in the care-planning phase. Their health status, medical needs and their medication (Hussian, 1981) may all have an impact on the observed behaviour. This emphasises the importance of multi-disciplinary care-planning.

Goal Planning. The next stage is to use the information gathered in the assessment phase to draw up a plan consisting of specific performance goals. These may be specific expressions of more general aims with the patient, or sub-goals of longer-term targets. Holden and Woods (1982, Ch. 10) give examples of a number of such plans. Davies and Crisp (1980) define the important characteristics of performance goals. Which people will take which actions should be made explicit. The circumstances under which the action will be taken, the resources required and the conditions under which it will be carried out should be specified. The criterion for successful completion of the goal should be carefully set to be realistic, attainable and observable, and the consequences of success or failure should also, they argue, be spelt out.

This should assist in the identification of the most important goals to be set, in a situation where a plethora of possible goals present themselves.

The care-plan should never be seen as complete or final. It must be regularly reviewed and modified as targets are achieved or as it becomes clear that a target was set too high. The clear specification of goals greatly facilitates the review and evaluation process.

Effectiveness. This sort of multi-disciplinary care-planning approach, with specific goals (Brody, Cole and Moss, 1973) was evaluated by Brody *et al.* (1971, 1974) at the Philadelphia Geriatric Centre. It formed the basis for their individual treatment programme for 'excess disabilities' in mentally impaired elderly people. Patients benefited from this approach, improving more than matched controls, over a period of a year. Nine months later, after the treatment programme was discontinued, the experimental group slipped back. Even during the treatment phase only areas directly treated showed any improvement. Clearly it is an approach that has to be applied continuously and consistently to be effective, and must directly address the areas of most significance for each individual patient.

Behavioural Procedures

This section has focused on the development of individual care-plans; little has been said about the use of behavioural procedures in achieving behavioural goals. Holden and Woods (1982, Ch. 10) describe these briefly, and many more detailed manuals are available. From the behaviour modification studies reviewed above it seems that often simple specific prompting and reinforcement of the behaviour will be sufficient, perhaps with the addition of clear discriminative stimuli, as used by Hussian (1981). Kennedy and Kennedy (1982) make some useful observations about the retraining procedures that may be involved in many dementing patients' care-plans. They suggest there is a need to be careful regarding the manner in which reinforcement is given. For instance, if effusive praise is given when the person achieves something that clearly has been very simple for them all their life (e.g. putting on a shirt), this may in fact reinforce the person's awareness of their failing abilities, and may not have the desired effect of increasing the probability of success occurring again. A straightforward 'OK' or 'that's right' may be more appropriate, and run less risk of infantilising the patient. Defining *appropriate* reinforcement for particular individual patients that allows dignity and encourages self-esteem is a challenging aspect of care-planning. Similarly when correcting a person, who is, for example, getting into difficulty with dressing, the phrase 'try another way' may be more helpful than manual correction or telling the person what perhaps is obvious, that they are doing it incorrectly.

The Environmental Context

Where do the environmental change and group-treatment approaches fit in with this individual-centred model? Certainly the person's environmental situation is considered as part of the behaviour analysis (Rebok and Hoyer, 1977). There is much to be said also for developing an environment for the dementing patient that is rich in natural prompts of normal valued behaviours. For instance, it should facilitate normal social interaction by its physical arrangement, and recreation by the ready availability of appropriate materials. These might include personalised reminiscence aids, appropriate music, and age-appropriate craft materials and games adapted for the patient's ability level. Certain themes may recur frequently in individual care-plans, e.g. a need for social activity, for orientation, for dressing practice, or whatever. It would then be possible to set up group or modular treatments, as in Patterson's (1982) programme, which combined modular and individualised approaches. These should arise from a recognition of the need of a number of individuals, from the care-plans, rather than fitting in patients to existing groups which may not meet their defined needs, simply because the group or module is already established. Within each group or module there will of course be a great deal of individualisation, according to the person's abilities and interests.

Other Organic Disorders

This chapter has focused on dementia, as being the most challenging of the organic disorders from the point of view of treatment. Other disorders do occur of course; many elderly people suffer strokes or have other forms of static brain damage; Parkinson's disease is common in the elderly; elderly people are more vulnerable to acute confusional states. For patients with strokes and other static lesions, rehabilitation does not differ in principle from that with younger patients (Miller, 1980b; Powell, 1981). 'Memory Therapy' — developed for younger brain injured patients — may have applications for the elderly (Wilson and Moffat, 1984). Neuropsychological rehabilitation is, of course, itself at an early stage of development, although speech therapy for elderly dysphasics has been available for some years (Walker and Williams, 1980). For some patients with such problems depression, frustration or anxiety may be hindering the development of compensatory skills or further recovery of function. Some of the methods described in Chapter 7 may be applicable, modified appropriately. For example, Damon, Lesser and Woods (1979) taught anxiety management skills to an elderly patient with speech problems, whose anxiety prevented her from using her remaining speech ability to the full. Wisocki and Mosher (1980) have used sign-language training with elderly aphasic patients, and Burnside (1979) reported the use of bio-feedback for neuromuscular re-education in elderly stroke patients. Doubtless there is considerable potential for psychological help for Parkinson's disease sufferers. Evans (1982) outlines some psychological aspects that may be of help in the management of acute confusional states. Whatever the disorder, the individual care-planning approach is likely to be of value in identifying the person's whole range of needs — medical, physical, social and psychological — and to lead to appropriate psychological interventions, where there is acceptance of the patient as a whole person.

Summary

1. Evaluation of treatment methods should be more broadly based than simply looking for overall improvement in the dementing patient. The person's quality of life, 'excess disabilities' and the carer's attitudes and feelings of strain should also be considered.

2. Stimulation programmes aimed at reducing dementing patients' stimulus deprivation have become more focused and specific. Structured physical exercise may be beneficial.

3. Environmental modification, of both the physical setting and the regime, has proved successful in a number of evaluative studies. Group living is a particularly promising approach. Prompting appropriate behaviour using natural discriminative stimuli often seems sufficient to produce behavioural change.

4. Reality Orientation (RO) sessions usually lead to small improvements in verbal orientation, but not general behavioural change. Twenty-four-hour RO may well never have been adequately tested, although the success of ward-orientation training suggests it could be an effective approach.

5. Reminiscence is a popular approach and is probably a valuable means of facilitating communiction. There is a scope for a great deal of development of the concepts and methods employed, before it is evaluated as another 'therapy'.

6. The evidence for the applicability of behaviour modification techniques with *dementing* patients is beginning to grow (at last), with attention now being given to the particular difficulties of working with dementing patients. Some successes in the areas of self-care skills and toileting are emerging, and some innovative methods for the reduction of problem behaviours have been reported.

7. An individual care-planning approach has the potential to integrate the various methods that have so far proved of value in working with dementing patients. It should be multi-disciplinary, involve a wide-ranging and detailed assessment including the person's health and neuropsychological function, be based on the person's strengths rather than his or her problems, set and review specific goals, and involve the patient and his or her family in

decision-making.

8. Psychological treatment for organic disorders other than dementia has considerable potential, but little work has yet been reported with elderly patients.

9 INTERVENTION IN INSTITUTIONS

Introduction

We have seen in the previous two chapters that most of the intervention studies published to date have been carried out in institutions for the elderly. This is despite the fact that only a minority of elderly people with organic disorders live in such settings. There are several reasons for this emphasis on work in institutions. These include the concentration of professional resources in these centres and the magnification effect of grouping people with similar problems together. For example, 30 people in one ward with incontinence seems a huge problem compared with a similar number of people scattered in the community with the same level of disability. There is the tendency for problems to be only too apparent in institutions, but, perhaps conveniently from the point of view of service provision, to be 'hidden' in the community.

Institutional residents also, of course, form a convenient 'captive' population for intervention studies. The degree of control staff have over every aspect of residents' lives, the availability of large numbers of residents of similar disability levels and the ease of behavioural observation make institutions attractive, superficially at least, for psychological intervention studies. There is a considerable danger that many of these treatments will have only a marginal effect on the quality of life of residents if they ignore wider issues of the effect of the institution on the individual resident. For example, some of the very factors that make the intervention feasible — staff control, large size and lack of privacy — may influence quality of life more powerfully than the planned treatment programme.

In this chapter we will discuss how the institution can influence psychological intervention, and how intervention needs to be adapted to maximise residents' quality of life in these settings. Firstly, we will try to give an overview of the nature of institutions for the elderly.

Type of Institutions

Institutional Settings in the United Kingdom

Administratively speaking there are a variety of types of institutions catering for the elderly. In the UK these include:

Geriatric hospital wards
Psychogeriatric hospital wards
Residential homes for the elderly
Nursing homes.

The geriatric and psychogeriatric hospital wards are run by the National Health Service (NHS). They differ mainly in degree of physical infirmity, psychogeriatric wards tending to take *mobile* dementing patients. They are occasionally found in general hospitals, but more commonly these long-stay geriatric wards are in separate (and often geographically isolated) geriatric hospitals. Psychogeriatric wards are usually in large psychiatric hospitals, which are often again isolated from the area they serve. They are staffed by nurses, some of whom will have a general or psychiatric nurse-training and qualification. Other NHS provision is for elderly mentally handicapped people — becoming an increasing proportion of those remaining in mental handicap hospitals — and for chronic psychiatric patients who have grown old in the psychiatric hospital (the so called 'graduate' population). NHS long-stay facilities for the elderly are generally old, converted buildings. Some of these buildings arouse considerable negative emotional reactions in current elderly people as they previously housed the local workhouse (see below) or lunatic asylum.

Most residential homes are run by local authority Social Services departments, who have a duty under Part III of the 1948 National Assistance Act to provide 'residential accommodation for persons who by reason of age, infirmity or any other circumstances are in need of care and attention not otherwise available to them'. Hence these homes are often referred to as 'Part III' homes. They are staffed mainly by care-attendants, who usually have no particular qualifications or training; senior staff may have a nursing or a residential social work qualification. Generally, these homes are intended to be in the community from where the residents come, but this is by no means always the case.

Prior to 1948, for many years elderly people needing care would often be admitted to the local workhouse. These were large, crowded, extremely authoritarian establishments. They were based on the premise that conditions should be unattractive enough to discourage anyone from staying a moment longer than absolutely necessary. The implication was that anyone needing such a place must be responsible for their failure to provide for themselves independently. Inmates were subject to strict rules, and disobedience led to the removal of the few privileges allowed. Inmates would have various duties to perform daily. The physical facilities were generally spartan and inadequate, with no simple comforts or amenities.

Against this background there was a laudable desire to create small comfortable homes where elderly people could live pleasantly and with dignity. The homes were intended to have 25–30 residents, and the change in regime is expressed in the desire to change the 'Master–inmate' relationship into one resembling that of an 'hotel manager and his guests'. Townsend (1962), in his report of a national survey of old people's homes, *The Last Refuge*, shows clearly the lack of progress at that time in implementing these policies. There were still a number of adapted workhouses in operation and the quality of the new homes varied greatly. In the last 20 years the number of very old and infirm (physically and/or mentally) residents has increased dramatically (at least partly because psychiatric hospital beds have decreased — Jolley, 1981), so that a massive expansion programme would have been needed to maintain the *status quo*. Many residential homes now have residents as infirm as those in geriatric wards, as demented as those in psychogeriatric wards. Some authorities have sought to cope with the difficulties arising from such high levels of disabilty by designating certain homes for the confused elderly (Elderly Mentally Infirm homes) or for the physically frail, usually with slightly better staffing levels and resources. Other homes have a particular wing or unit so designated.

Part III of the 1948 Act also required local authorities to inspect and register homes run by voluntary agencies and private individuals. Many such homes have been established. Townsend (1962) noted they varied enormously in quality, with the *good* private and voluntary homes being excellent. They vary in level of disability accepted, and in the number and training of staff. Some take very disabled people and have a staff of trained nurses; others have unqualified staff and admit only elderly people independent in self-care.

Currently there is much interest in the establishment of nursing homes — residential homes with a higher level of qualified nursing staff, able to care for severely infirm elderly people outside a hospital setting. Whether these will be run by the NHS or Local Authorities or jointly remains to be seen.

There is considerable overlap between these facilities in terms of the type and level of functioning of their residents. For example, a mildly demented person admitted to an old people's home will probably remain there despite their deteriorating function, particularly if the person shows few problem behaviours; staff are prepared to offer more care to an established resident than would be acceptable for a new resident. The result is that, even if the facilities could be clearly distinguished on their admission criteria (which are in fact infrequently made explicit), the changes in residents following admission contribute to a blurring of any clear divisions. For example, a demented person in a psychogeriatric ward who for one reason or another loses their mobility may not be readily accepted by a geriatric hospital.

Institutional Settings Outside the UK

Millard (1983) contrasts long-term care provision in the UK with services in other European countries — particularly France and Denmark. He comments that in France services for acute, medium and long-stay patients are separate, which can cause difficulties if the patient changes categories. Long-stay beds are controlled by social services, rather than medically. In Denmark, Millard was impressed by the extent to which the long-term care environments were personalised, and privacy emphasised. Combined sheltered housing units with nursing wings on the same site are being developed, often by voluntary organisations, with social services controlling admission. However, despite this high standard of care, rehabilitation and discharge have not been provided for, so long-term care is for life. A new speciality of long-term medicine is developing to undertake the rehabilitation of elderly patients, which often takes longer than acute medical services allow.

In the USA, as described by Hawley, Hirschland, Williams and Vincent (1983), the situation differs in various parts of the country. Generally there are 'domiciliary care facilities' or 'personal care facilities', which provide meals and some supervision, but are not intended to provide any nursing or health-care facilities. Two levels of long-stay care involving health-care services are identified — 'intermediate care facilities' and 'skilled nursing facilities'. Regulations requiring nursing inspections and requirements for recreational, social and rehabilitation staff become more stringent as the level of nursing care increases.

A direct comparison of long-term care in New York and London has been reported by Gurland *et al.* (1979). They show that there are a comparable number of elderly people in both cities, and a similar number of long-term beds — although there are nearly four times as many institutions in London, those in New York being generally much larger. Table 9.1 indicates that hospital provision is

Table 9.1: Comparison of Institutional Care for the Elderly in New York and London

	New York % of total beds	London % of total beds
1. *Skilled nursing care facilities*		
Psychiatric hospitals	3.7	16.9
Non-psychiatric hospitals	2.2	17.4
Private nursing homes (UK)/ Skilled Nursing Facility (SNF) beds	60.9	1.5
	66.8	35.8
2. *Not intended for skilled nursing care*		
Health Related Facilities /HRF) (intermediate care facility)	21.3	N/A
Homes for Adults (domiciliary care facility)	11.9	N/A
Social Services 'Part III' homes	N/A	41.0
Other residential homes (voluntary and private)	N/A	23.2
	33.2	64.2

Source: Adapted from Gurland *et al.* (1979).

much smaller in New York, where many more chronic hospital patients have been discharged over the years, often to nursing homes. However in New York two-thirds of the long-term beds are in settings offering skilled nursing care, whereas in London only one-third fall into this category. The majority of London long-stay beds are in residential homes. A further difference is that in

London three-quarters of the beds are publicly owned, in New York more than half are privately owned, with less than one in twelve being in the public sector. Through Medicare and Medicaid most of the New York elderly are in fact supported by public funds. A 0.5 per cent random sample of the elderly in each city had a mean age of 81, and was nearly three-quarters female, with 80 per cent of residents being 75 or over. The two samples had identical median scores on a mental status questionnaire. In New York dementing subjects (defined from the MSQ score) were concentrated in SNF facilities, whereas in London they were more evenly distributed across the different types of institution (see Table 9.2). Thus in

Table 9.2: Proportion of Severely Demented Residents in Different Types of Care in New York and London

New York	%	London	%
Skilled Nursing Facilities	57	Psychiatric hospitals	47
Health Related Facilities	10	Geriatric hospitals	25
Homes for Adults	13	Social Services Part III	36
		Voluntary residential homes	23
		Private residential homes	21

Source: Adapted from Gurland *et al.* (1979).

London the problems of severe dementia will be encountered in a variety of institutions, whereas in New York the proportions outside the nursing homes are relatively small.

Godlove, Dunn and Wright (1980) have shown that similar people are employed in London and New York to provide basic care services, but that there is much more in-service training in New York, and more emphasis there on technical nursing care, such as changing catheters, taking temperatures and so on.

Models of Institutional Care

As well as the various administrative categories for institutions for the elderly, a number of frameworks have been suggested to draw attention to important aspects of institutions. For example, Pincus (1968) presents such a structure combining four dimensions of the institutional setting with three aspects of the environment (see Table 9.3). This framework exemplifies the differences between institutions acording to differences on these dimensions claimed by Pincus to be of particular value in the study of institutional environments.

Table 9.3: Examples of Aspects of Institutions Related to Four Important Environmental Dimensions

Aspects of the Institutional Setting	Dimensions of the Institutional Environment			
	Public–Private	Structured–Unstructured	Resources sparse–Resources rich	Integrated–Isolated
Physical	Proportion of single/double rooms. Number of day-rooms.	Signs displaying rules and regulations.	Facilities for meal or snack preparation by residents.	Distance from shops, transport.
Rules, regulations and programme	Rules requiring residents to keep doors to their rooms always open.	Rules regulating bedtime.	Regular jobs around the home performed by residents.	Restrictions on visiting hours. Frequent trips out of home.
Staff behaviour	Extent to which staff knock on doors before entering residents' rooms.	Extent to which staff decide TV programmes.	Extent to which staff encourage residents' participation in activities.	Extent to which staff help residents make phone calls or write letters.

Source: Adapted from Pincus (1968).

A similar typology of institutional settings is outlined by Clough (1981), who concentrates on the style and regime of the institution rather than its formal administrative category (see Table 9.4).

Table 9.4: Typology of Old-Age Institutions

Control of life-style by resident	Model of Ageing		
	Activity	Disengagement	Socio-environmental
Minimal control by resident	Nursing Home	Institution	Home
Some control	Therapeutic Unit	Hotel	Hostel
Maxium feasible control	Retirement Community	Flatlets	Supportive Unit

Source: Clough (1981).

Clough seeks to characterise nine distinctive types of institution. The model of ageing underlying the institution's regime reflects the attitudes and assumptions of the staff (although there may be discrepancies among the staff). The activity model implies an emphasis on the residents participating and being involved in some form of activity; the disengagement model is used here to indicate that staff see activity as not to be encouraged, serving no particular purpose. The socio-environmental model sees individuals as having different needs and abilities and allows different expectations of different residents. The interaction with degree of control suggests that for activity and disengagement models the communal living arrangement has to be much more tenuous if the resident has maximum control. It can be seen that the 'hotel' model that was desired for the Part III accommodation in the UK tends towards an 'institutional' model if sufficient control is not released to residents, and emphasises that it involves a giving up of roles and activities.

There are of course other ways of categorising these institutions. The point being stressed here is that there is considerable scope for overlap both in the level of disability catered for and in the style and regime of the institution between administratively distinct facilities.

The Quality of Institutions

Assessment of the quality of life in such settings has become an increasingly sophisticated process. No longer is it deemed remotely satisfactory to have the guided tour by a senior member of staff or a cosy chat with staff asking 'what goes on' in their unit. The views of residents must be sought and what actually does happen day-by-day in the unit carefully observed before an honest appraisal can be obtained. An increasing number of accounts exist of life in such settings. We have already referred to the work by Townsend (1962) which provides a national picture of UK provision in the late 1950s. Meacher (1972) focused attention on the issue of whether or not confused residents should be segregated. In the USA Tobin and Lieberman (1976) followed a group of elderly people from the community into the old people's home, looking at changes in adjustment before and after admission. In the UK, Peace (1983) reports findings from a national consumer study of 100 old people's homes. Clough (1981) and Godlove *et al.* (1982) report in detail on residential home settings, in the latter case offering a comparison with day-care facilities. These studies cover many aspects of service provision; a resumé of some features especially relevant to psychological components of care is of particular interest here.

Effects of Institutional Living

Townsend (1962) lists six different effects of institutional life upon elderly people from his survey:

1. Loss of occupation — many residents want to occupy their time more fruitfully.
2. Isolation from family, friends and community — related to both geographical isolation and the emotional difficulty for relatives/friends in visiting these homes.
3. Tenuousness of new relationships — only about 20 per cent make friends with another resident.
4. Loneliness — nearly half of new residents say they are lonely.
5. Loss of privacy and identity — many miss their own clothing, furniture and possessions, few have single rooms.
6. Collapse of self-determination.

Twenty years on these remain relevant issues.

Activity Levels

Several recent studies have looked at levels of activity in institutions covering both home and hospital environments in different areas

Table 9.5: Summary of Activity Level Studies

Godlove et al. 1982
Local authority homes
Hospital wards

% of observation time spent in each type of activity (10.00 a.m.–4.00 p.m.)
N = 15   Age 83   61.9% 'sitting or lying and doing nothing else'
N = 17   Age 83   68.5% 'sitting or lying and doing nothing else'

Galliard 1978
Psychogeriatric ward

% of total observations (day-time, evening and weekends; 2,356 observation periods)
N = 22F 22M (no age given)   F54% M57% 'no constructive activity'

McFadyen et al. 1980
Psychogeriatric ward

% of total observations (9.00 a.m.–8.00 p.m.)
N = 30F   Age 80   35% 'non-engagement' — doing nothing or asleep
                        24% watching

Old people's home

N = 19F 5M   Age 84   21% 'non-engagement' — doing nothing or asleep
                        9% watching

Jenkins et al. 1977
Local authority home (physically frail)
Local authority home (mentally frail)

% of residents engaged (during free time)
N = 17F 2M Age 85   81.5% 'not engaged'
N = 19F   Age 80   93.6% 'not engaged'

McCormack and Whitehead 1981
Long-stay geriatric ward

% of patients engaged (2.00–4.00 p.m.)
N = 16F   Age 82.6   71.25% 'not engaged'

of the U.K. Their findings are summarised in Table 9.5.

Whilst this table brings together results from many studies it is worth noting that the methodologies used were often quite different. Godlove *et al.* observed each subject for a whole six-hour day, thus having exact figures for the amount of time spent on each behaviour by each person. Galliard, and McFadyen *et al.* used time-sampling techniques, each subject being observed for 30 seconds each half-hour, over a more extensive time period (see also McFadyen, 1984). Their results indicate the proportion of observation intervals when particular behaviours were observed. Jenkins *et al.*'s results are for a restricted time period — 'free-time' in the morning and afternoon, and represent the average proportion of residents engaged of those present in a lounge area.

Direct comparisons between studies cannot be made. What is clear is that in each case doing nothing appears to be the norm, whether in terms of proportion of total time, or of observations, or of residents present. The apparent exception is McFadyen *et al.*'s study. Here only 35 per cent of the time is spent doing nothing or dozing in a chair in the psychogeriatric ward, and 21 per cent in the old people's home; however these workers have excluded 'watching' — showing passive interest in some aspect of the physical or social environment, from non-engagement, unlike the other three studies. Including this category gives a figure for non-engagement of 59 per cent in the psychogeriatric ward, but still a fairly low figure of 30 per cent for the old people's home.

Figure 9.1 shows that Godlove *et al.*'s figure for non-engagement for old people's homes may well be an underestimate, as for 16.5 per cent of the time subjects in their sample could not be observed. Despite the different methodologies, McFadyen *et al.*'s results seem at odds with Godlove *et al.*'s for this group. One explanation of this discrepancy may simply be that the home studied by McFadyen *et al.* was much more stimulating than those included in Godlove *et al.*'s work — certainly their location could not be more different: rural North Scotland and urban London. Another possibility to be considered is that the individual residents studied were different in some way. McFadyen *et al.* included a random selection of the residents of one particular home, Godlove *et al.* studied a few residents from several homes, excluding those who had only a mild degree of impairment. Their sample was then biased by selection towards a higher level of impairment. McFadyen *et al.* showed that active engagement is negatively correlated with dementia-type

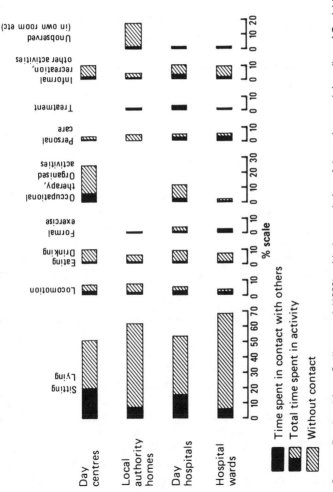

Figure 9.1: Mean Percentage of Observation Time Spent in Each Type of Activity in Four Different Environments

Source: Reprinted from Godlove *et al.* (1982), with the permission of the authors and the editor of Social Services Monographs, University of Sheffield.

impairments, and similarly Godlove *et al.* found that their more impaired subjects tended to be less active, and so it would be anticipated that their more impaired subjects would show a lower level of active engagement.

An interesting finding from McFadyen *et al.*'s study is that more impaired subjects, while not being so frequently actively engaged, may still be judged as taking an interest in their environment by watching what is happening around them. In most studies this is included in 'doing nothing', but perhaps it should be distinguished from a complete lack of contact with the environment. A crucial point in relation to intervention is the effect of the regime of the institution on activity levels. For example, Hitch and Simpson (1972) carrying out a comparative study of three homes with residents thought to be comparable but with different regimes found large differences in the percentage of residents observed to be 'doing nothing' (21 per cent, 57 per cent and 76 per cent respectively), a 'group living' home having the lowest level of inactivity. Similarly Rothwell, Britton and Woods (1983) found an increase in observed activity in an old people's home, following the introduction of group living, from 25 per cent to 31 per cent of the residents being engaged. In both Jenkins *et al.* (1977) and McCormack and Whitehead's (1981) study, engagement levels increased when activities were provided and encouraged, emphasising again their environmental responsiveness.

Social Interaction

Levels of social interaction in institutions for the elderly have similarly come under close scrutiny (see Table 9.6). A fairly consistent level of overall verbal interaction in institutions for the elderly emerges — in between 12 per cent and 17 per cent of the observations or observation time some interaction occurs (although in Godlove *et al.*'s study 'contact' was defined as including both physical and verbal contact). Of some interest is a further analysis of these findings in terms of with whom the elderly person is in contact. Godlove *et al.* showed a different pattern in their homes, where contact with other residents predominated over contact with staff, from their hospital wards, where contact with staff was over three times as frequent as contact with other patients. Galliard's results showed a sex difference with men's lower level of overall interactions being attributable to a much lower level of interaction with other patients (3.9 per cent, 11 per cent for women). Most

Table 9.6: Summary of Social Interaction Studies

Godlove et al. 1982	% of observation time in contact with others (10.00 a.m.–4.00 p.m.)			
Local authority homes	N = 15 Age 83	12.2%	with staff 3.3%	with residents 5.3%
Hospital wards	N = 17 Age 83	15.8%	with staff 10.6%	with residents 2.9%
Galliard 1978	% of total observations			
Psychogeriatric ward	N = 22F 22M	F 17.2%	M 12.4%	
McFadyen et al. 1980	% of total observations			
Psychogeriatric ward	N = 30F Age 80	12%		
Old people's home	N = 19F 5M Age 84	13%		

interaction initiated by nurses occurred during 'physical' nursing duties, and staff other than nurses were much more likely to talk to patients. McFadyen *et al.* found that, in both the hospital and the home, interactions with other residents or visitors greatly exceeded those with staff (in the proportions 72:28 and 87:13 respectively). In the ward more interactions were one-way, particularly those of staff with patients, which were usually instructions.

The average elderly person in an institution then has about eight minutes per hour social contact, mostly with other residents. Contact with nursing staff will be largely related to physical care.

The *quantity* of interaction is not the only relevant consideration; *quality* is also of importance. Lubinski (1978–9), while confirming the limited quantity of verbal communication in an institution in the USA, reports that residents perceived what communication did occur as 'meaningless', 'disparaging' and 'of no value', while staff felt they were too busy to talk with patients. Lipman, Slater and Harris (1979) have analysed verbal interactions in a number of old people's homes in the UK. They looked at the proportion of interactions classifiable as 'supportive–acceptive' (including all positive, supporting, accepting and caring comments) and 'instrumental' (functional comments, unaccompanied by affective content, dominated by a physical care task). The proportion of supportive interactions between residents was generally high (and in every home the great majority of interactions were between residents). On the other hand the extent to which staff–resident interactions were more likely to be supportive varied greatly from home to home, ranging from 22 per cent to 70 per cent being classified supportive. In many of the homes instrumental staff–resident interactions predominated. The supportive quality of resident–resident interactions was related to the mental status of the residents involved, with confused residents being involved in less supportive interactions. Staff–resident interactions did not seem to be differentiated according to whether the person was confused; confused residents did not receive a greater proportion of supportive comments from staff than rational residents.

Once again differences in regime and attitudes of staff are relevant. Davies and Snaith (1980) observed mealtimes in two similar long-stay geriatric wards. One ward had twice as many interactions as the other; a third of the interactions in one ward were patient-initiated, none were in the second. In the first ward patients exercised many more choices — on the other ward there were a number of instances of patients' expressed choices being refused, or of self-help being reprimanded.

Dependence

Many examples are available of independence being discouraged in institutions for the elderly. A comparative study by Rogers and Snow (1982) showed how three different nursing home facilities in the USA differed in their approach to mealtimes. In one the residents were encouraged to feed themselves as much as possible, at their own pace, with spillage, etc., being tolerated. In a second home residents were expected either to be totally independent or to need help only at the start of a meal — otherwise they were fed throughout. In the third home residents who were slow to feed themselves were fed for the sake of 'efficiency'. Baltes *et al.* (1980), again in a US nursing home, showed that staff typically failed to respond to independent behaviour by residents but strongly supported dependent behaviour, e.g. 'Good girl, . . . you waited for someone to help you', or 'see, I told you, you spill when you eat by yourself'. Baltes, Honn, Barton, Orzech and Lago (1983) argue that these residents do not experience 'learned helplessness', which involves objective or subjective lack of control over reinforcement. By exhibiting dependent behaviour they are systematically reinforced, with dependence being seen as an instrumental behaviour, controlling reinforcement.

Restrictions

Institutions are also places where 'the normal everyday freedoms of adults are eroded'. Godlove *et al.* (1980) listed rules and restrictions reported by care staff in institutions for the elderly in New York and London (see Table 9.7). Generally of course staff may have a

Table 9.7: Rules and Restrictions Reported by Care-staff

Residents *not* allowed to:	%
Smoke in their own rooms	89
Change TV channels (on communal TV)	36
Bring radio into the institution	6
Bring TV into the institution	12
Bring any furniture	64
Bring pictures (to hang on walls)	26
Visit the rooms of residents of opposite sex (or see each other privately)	41
Keep their own alcohol	90
Do their own laundry	72

Source: Derived from Godlove *et al.* (1980).

more generous view of rules than residents, who may well experience other, unwritten rules and restrictions.

Conclusions on Quality of Institutions

Institutions for the elderly may then be characterised as places where inactivity is the norm, where there is little social interaction, where staff contact mainly relates to physical care, and where dependence is likely to be positively encouraged. Lipman, Slater and Harris (1979) comment that 'relationships are characterised by staff dominance; principally the power to determine, where, when, how and with whom residents eat, sleep, sit, bath and go to the toilet'. Similarly Clough (1981) emphasised the pervasive extent of staff control, in the exercise of coercive sanctions — occasionally extending to physical force; utilitarian rewards and sanctions — the granting or removal of privileges, such as a particular seat, room, food, etc.; and normative rewards and sanctions — the power of statements made by staff about residents, often in the presence of other residents, establishing expectations of behaviour.

Against this almost totally negative view, differences between institutions do emerge, and certain features have been shown to be potentially modifiable with relatively simple interventions (e.g. Jenkins *et al.*, 1977; Davies and Snaith, 1980; McCormack and

Whitehead, 1981).

Effects of the Institution upon Intervention

We have thus far gone into some detail regarding types of institution in order to emphasise that in setting up an individual or group treatment programme in an institutional setting in many respects it is the institution that is being treated. Institutional values, expectations and norms must be taken into account; staff attitudes and reinforcement cannot be neglected. If behaviour is viewed as an interaction between the individual and their environment, then the temptation to attribute deviant behaviour to dementia or depression or whatever can be resisted. The tendency is still however to take too limited a view of 'environment' in a behavioural analysis — perhaps to include staff-behaviour, but not the broader institutional contingencies that influence staff and their attitudes. This is an important aspect of behavioural ecology (see Burton, 1982). The whole institutional context must be understood. Intervention programmes aiming at major changes may require a fundamental restructuring of the institutional setting for success. Less far-reaching schemes may be possible if the conflict with the institution is sufficiently small.

This area is not well documented. Interventions that fail because of institutional problems are seldom written up. Those that succeed skate over this crucial area of how the intervention was introduced, how staff were persuaded to play their part appropriately and consistently and how the intervention was maintained over a period of time.

In a rare example of a study describing changes which were not maintained, Galliard (1978) gives two examples: making afternoon tea more sociable and allowing patients to stay up longer in the evenings. In both cases an initially positive intervention slipped back once the active involvement of the change agent finished; the interventions to *improve* the patients' environment had in fact *reduced* staff reinforcement. Wallis and Cope (1978) report on difficulties in implementing RO in a psychogeriatric hospital. A previous attempt initiated by medical staff had met with opposition from nursing staff, to whom it seemed as yet another imposition, without additional help. Here, however, some additional aid was offered by the research team and so RO sessions began. The programme soon became embroiled in a long-running difficulty in the ward (namely whether it was the day or night staff's responsibility to get patients up in the morning), and commitment to the programme varied considerably among the staff. The apparent reason for the programme being suspended was the increase in agitation of a few patients. The research team felt that other factors included the staff feeling threatened by the research team feeding back observations of the activity of staff and patients on the ward. The staff's general frustration with the hospital administration was also involved. There seemed to be no response to staff requests, which appeared lost in a monolithic bureaucracy.

A report by Davies (1982) commented that, a year after a successful intervention study (Davies and Snaith, 1980) improving the social atmosphere at mealtimes in a geriatric ward, 'only token symbols of the "changes" remained'. Generally changes suggested by the researcher had not been maintained, except where the change had produced an (unanticipated) side-effect that staff found rewarding.

Doubtless there are many other examples of intervention programmes that have, sooner or later, come to grief because of these sorts of institutional and attitudinal problems. It is as if the needs of the institution predominate over those of the patients they are theoretically meant to serve.

Staff attitudes form one aspect of the institutional environment and Woods and Britton (1977) drew attention to their effect on a variety of types of psychological intervention with the elderly. Positive staff attitudes seemed crucial to the success of these programmes, although it is difficult to evaluate whether any of them in themselves succeed in influencing attitudes. Coulshed (1980) shows how RO was successfully introduced into a psychogeriatric ward, using a dual approach, involving both the teaching of RO techniques and the establishment of weekly staff group meetings. In these meetings literature on ageing was read with the aim of increasing awareness of patients' needs. Staff were encouraged to discuss and question traditional practices and attitudes. This attempt at attitudinal change alongside an intervention programme has much to commend it. Coulshed's paper is rare for its explicit analysis of the social systems among the ward staff and of the efforts to change them. It illustrates that awareness of these variables can lead to a worthwhile intervention — institutions may indeed be suitable cases for treatment.

The Ideal Institution

A Contradiction in Terms?

Some would say that the ideal institution cannot be envisaged — ideally they would not exist. Indeed Townsend (1962) recommended a progressive reduction in the number of residential homes in the UK. He commented that even with liberal policies the disadvantages would probably not be overcome, as many were felt to arise from the very nature of a communal home, bringing individuals from diverse backgrounds together to share the events of daily life. 'Institution' has become a word full of negative connotations, associated with deprivation, resignation and apathy (Erber, 1979). However, it is not clear that the institution itself is totally responsible for producing the inactivity and social withdrawal noted earlier. The reasons for the person entering the institution in the first place, and the very acknowledgement by the person that they are going into a residential home may also contribute to institutionalisation (Tobin and Lieberman, 1976). Passivity and dependence may be seen as also arising from the process preceding admission, confirming the person's self-perception as someone having no valid social roles rather than simply resulting from the institutional life-style (Clough, 1981).

Could the provision of domiciliary care in the community overcome these problems? Clough (1981) argues that too often ideal domiciliary care is contrasted with inadequate residential care; community care too has its drawbacks which are seldom pointed out (Hawks, 1975) — often the community may *not* in fact care. Clough sees residential homes as being appropriate for some people in some circumstances, and that for some people it will have advantages over domiciliary care — 24-hour observation and care, ability to deal with fluctuating abilities, support in facing aspects of loss and so on. Many of the inadequancies of institutional care might be viewed, it is suggested, as examples of bad practice, rather than as inevitable consequences of communal living.

Clough argues that the primary function of the old people's home should be 'to provide a living base in which basic physical needs are met in a way which allows the individual the maximum potential for achieving mastery'. He acknowledges the complexity of this task, and the skill needed to accomplish it, but with this positive function in mind he would not see residential care as a last resort, to be avoided by all means possible.

Desirable Features of Institutions

Whether or not one accepts that institutions do have a positive function, they are likely to exist for the foreseeable future, and it is essential to have a clear idea of desirable institutional features in order to set targets for psychological intervention.

Holden and Woods (1982) list basic attitudes which staff must develop in order to maximise the quality of life (Table 9.8); from Pincus's (1968) analysis of the institutional environment described above, we need to add that the physical features of the environment and the rules, regulations and regime of the institution, as well as staff behaviour, need to work in the same direction.

Table 9.8: Basic Attitudes

Staff attitudes must allow the elderly person:
1. Individuality as an adult
2. Dignity
3. Self-respect
4. Choice
5. Independence

Source: Holden and Woods (1982, p. 156).

Clearly these attitudes relate to Clough's 'mastery' concept, which implies choice, individuality and dignity. The only likely point of dispute would be a resident who *chooses* to be dependent; in Clough's scheme such a choice would be honoured — would not this pose a problem for Holden and Woods in the apparent conflict between choice and independence? The important point here is that the institution should *allow* both choice and independence; it should not *compel* people to be independent or whatever. Also, physical dependence, in the ideal institution, would not be accompanied by emotional dependence.

To return to Pincus's environmental dimensions, these considerations imply that the ideal institution would allow residents privacy, which relates to dignity and adulthood, would have a minimum of rules and regulations — which decrease choice, individuality and dignity — and be rich in resources of all kinds — which again increases residents' degree of choice. Ideally it would not be isolated from the outside world; the possibility of contact outside, ease of visiting, going on shopping trips and so on increases the range of choice and independence.

From a consideration of institutionalisation in younger people, King and Raynes (1968) have derived four further factors ideally to be avoided. These are depersonalisation, where privacy is limited, and the resident has few personal possessions; block treatment, where residents are dealt with in batches, e.g. for toileting, bathing or feeding; rigidity of routine, where the routine is the same each day for each resident; and social distance, where staff and residents do not mix, except for specific functional activities, staff live away from residents and do not mix socially with them.

Clough accepts the validity of the concepts of block treatment and depersonalisation in relation to the elderly. He questions rigidity of routine, in relation to the individual resident, arguing that if a resident wants an inflexible routine for themselves this should be allowed.

Social Distance. He also queries the 'social distance' concept for the elderly, suggesting it may be a basic human right, as residents may not want intrusions in their lives. Clough views staff as a background resource, keeping a low profile, much as Lipman and Slater (1977) have advocated. In their design proposals for old people's homes they have tried to separate resident and staff areas as much as possible, arguing that the range of resident staff contacts should be limited, so as to maximise resident initiative. This conception of 'social distance' needs to be seen in a broader context for its usefulness to be clearer. If social distance is too great, then there are implications for the quality of social contact as well as the frequency; interactions will only be those of greatest urgency and importance, and mainly initiated by those of greater status — usually the staff in institutional settings (Davies and Snaith, 1980). What the ideal institution would provide is a setting where residents feel they can approach staff readily, where they will receive an accepting (rather than a rejecting) response. Shepherd and Richardson (1979) showed with younger people that client-centred care (as opposed to institution-orientated care) of this type is associated with a warmer quality of staff−client interaction and a more personal approach to client's problems, and it is this quality of social interaction that is most relevant in considering social distance. An important way of achieving the right social distance is to increase the status of the residents, perhaps by acknowledging the often forgotten fact that the institution exists for their benefit!

Individual-centred. Further confirmation of the need for an individual-centred approach comes from research on 'person–environment fit' (Kahana, Liang and Felton, 1980). The theory is that adjustment reflects the goodness of fit between the person and the properties of their environment; if the person's 'needs' and the environmental 'press' match, then the morale is high; if needs exceed press or vice versa, stress and discomfort may follow. Thus in our ideal institution aiming to allow independence, if the person is given too much help, apathy and dependence will result; if too little help is given, stress and anxiety may ensue. The consequence of negative and positive incongruence may differ; in some instances a positive incongruence, e.g. an over-supply of activity sessions, may have little effect of adjustment, with the under-supply being of much greater significance. Kahana *et al.*'s (1980) study showed the relationship of congruence of fit and morale in a number of areas of functioning, although some areas were identified where the person's characteristics or the environment's properties alone were related to morale, rather than their interaction. The common expectations or norms held by staff and residents may be relevant in contributing to environmental press. Clough (1981, pp. 7 and 182) suggests there is some evidence that satisfaction is highest when the person's resources are matched with the prevailing norms. What is required again is an individual-centred approach, which adjusts expectations to the individual's abilities, rather than hoping that one set of norms, whether it be 'everyone is here to have things done for them' or 'everyone here must keep active', will be applicable. In this context, as in others, it is the resident's perception of the prevailing norms that is important — *not* the institution's stated policy or even what the staff say they expect. Thus Pincus and Wood (1970) showed there was often a marked discrepancy between residents' and staff members' perceptions of aspects of the environment, with residents' perceptions being closely related to their overall level of satisfaction.

Engagement. In specifying our ideal institutional environment it should be noted that we are not following a theme apparent in some mental-handicap research, which has been applied to the elderly (Jenkins *et al.*, 1977), namely that a good quality environment is characterised by a high level of 'engagement', where residents are interacting with people or activity materials. The problem with this concept is that the quality of the interaction or activity is ignored, as is the individual's perception of the activity in which they are engaged. We do not then see activity and liveliness as *necessarily* indicators of a good quality environment; rather, where residents are engaged in activities, they should be those seen as meaningful and relevant to themselves, and where residents are inactive it should be from choice, rather than enforced from lack of opportunity to participate. Residents' perceptions of activities are all-important (Simpson *et al.*, 1981). The 'engagement' concept does not allow for individual differences or for activities like reminiscing that cannot be overtly observed.

Normalisation. A more useful concept from mental handicap that is beginning to be applied to the elderly (e.g. Holden and Woods, 1982, p. 249; Hawley *et al.*, 1983) is 'normalisation' (Wolfensberger, 1977). This involves making available to the residents patterns and conditions of life as close as possible to those normally valued by society. It represents a rejection of the pattern of care that segregates disabled and handicapped people from the rest of the community (as in the large psychiatric asylums built well away from centres of population), a rejection of the devaluation of the disabled person, e.g. by the use of labels ('dement', 'geriatric', 'subnormal', 'gerry', 'wrinkly', 'crumbly', etc.) or more subtly by talking to them in a patronising way, and a rejection of patterns of care that lose sight of the individual's rights and interests.

Involving, as it does, changes in society's attitudes to the handicapped and disabled complete normalisation must be a long-term aim. Some progress can be made immediately, however, even in an institutional environment which for many residents can never be completely 'normal'. By individualising care, as discussed above, and considering the whole person, not simply the disability and its associated problems, devaluation may be reduced, especially if we move towards a point where the resident is allowed to experience mastery in aspects of institutional life. Depersonalisation, as discussed above, is also relevant here. It is normal for people to have their own clothes, their own possessions, to have meals consistent with their personal tastes, to decide when to go to bed, what to wear and so on.

Normalisation has implications for the quality of activity available. Normal elderly people spend a fair amount of time each day in basic domestic activities, particularly around mealtimes —

food preparation, laying the table, clearing up afterwards, washing up, drying up and so on, as well as actually eating the food! Activities such as those typical of group living (see Chapter 8) which focus on such everyday domestic routines may then be seen as more 'normal' than, for instance, basketwork or making collages. The size of the group involved is also of course a closer approximation to normal.

Normalisation is then a fine ideal for our ideal institution. Some thought needs to be given when less transparent issues are tackled as to what constitutes 'normal' for the elderly resident. Should we, as Burton (1982) advocates, be guided by the life-styles of old people who are valued and active members of the community? Or should we emphasise the continuity of personality and life-style found in elderly people? Recognising the huge variability found in normal elderly people, should we seek to identify for each individual what their activities, preferences, and pattern of life would have been, and take this as the norm for that individual? For example, Bingo is an activity enjoyed by many elderly people, but to encourage Mr P. to play it when he was more accustomed to chess would not make sense. Elderly residents in an institution have a lifetime of experiences to draw on in establishing the style of life to suit them, given the disability they now have.

A second problem arises from the use of 'cultural norms' in some definitions of normalisation, to validate behaviours or characteristics as desirable. This is to rely on the values of a society which in fact devalues the disabled (and 'the elderly' as a whole, of course). There is a danger here of giving precedence to particular views of what is or is not valued by society at large — when society speaks with more than one voice, which is to be heeded? Again, for the elderly, a life-span approach is possible for the individual who has followed a unique life path and constructed their own norm.

The final problem relates to activities for those people with a very low level of functioning — often these are characterised as more appropriate for young children (e.g. Burton, 1982). Clearly we must beware of treating elderly people (or for that matter children) in a patronising fashion, but, if we are to enable severely deteriorated people to achieve some sense of success and mastery, extremely simple tasks will be needed that may well be similar to those young children are able to manage. What is 'childish' is a subjective matter — often the patronising, talking down manner in which the materials are used is more at fault than the materials themselves. Burton (1982) makes the useful suggestion that independent elderly people should review proposed activities for the impaired elderly. Certainly an openness to external review, readiness to consider aims and methods and a sensitivity to the individual resident and their reactions to particular situations would be features of the ideal institution.

We are advocating then an individual-centred environment, where the whole person is nurtured and given scope for expression of choices and control regarding privacy, activity and the other aspects of daily living, where the person may remain part of the wider community, and where they may receive the level of support needed given their level of disability and impairment. In the next section we look at how we can move towards this ideal, which in the real world so often looks beyond reach!

Changing The Institution

The General Approach

Where do we start to change the institution? In Chapter 8 we saw, for example, that activity levels and rates of interaction can be increased; how can we ensure these changes are maintained? Burton (1982) advocates a fundamental restructuring of the institutional context for the intervention to be worthwhile, The alternative is seen as being content with more minor changes that are not in conflict with the institutional context. Davies (1982) draws attention to the need for relevant groups within the institution to see a discrepancy between 'the way things are' and 'the way things should be' *and* to think the discrepancy important enough to merit action. In the typical institution there are a number of 'relevant groups' and Davies draws attention to the conflict and the lack of communication both within a particular staff group (e.g. nurses) and between different groups of staff (nurses, occupational therapists and domestic staff, for example). There may be a number of different conceptions of 'care' among the staff so that a consistent approach is difficult to implement. Is the only solution to be found in staff selection and training, or can one work within the institution as it is?

Georgiades and Phillimore (1975) argue strongly that better training is not the best way of bringing about institutional change. The person's attitudes may change during training but the 'hero-innovator' who returns to the ward with bright, fresh ideas will, they suggest, be worn down by the harsh institutional realities, and their attitudes may well revert to their pre-training level; 'hospitals, like dragons, eat hero-innovators for breakfast'. The organisation cannot then be changed simply by changing the individuals of whom it consists; it is in their inter-relationships in the institutional system that change is needed. They further suggest that the institution needs to be seen as the client, and that the time-scale for intervention needs to be lengthy — years rather than months. Quick solutions, like demonstration or experimental wards, seldom last long. A great deal of work needs to be done in preparing the ground for intervention, in what may essentially constitute a hostile environment.

Six guidelines are suggested by Georgiades and Phillimore for the strategy of change, that are worth close attention:

1. Work with the forces in the institution that are supportive of change and improvement; follow the path of least organisational resistance, rather than meeting the resistance in a head-on confrontation. Find those who want your help, rather than trying to persuade those who don't see the need. Be sensitive to the individual and group needs which encourage defensiveness, particularly the feeling that any suggested change represents a criticism of existing practices (Davies, 1982). The 'expert' who comes into the institution and suggests changes or the senior doctor or nurse who seeks to impose changes are particularly likely to run into this problem. The change agent must rather come into the institution and *listen*, not attempt large-scale public relations or training exercises.
2. A 'critical mass' should be developed — a team of workers who support and motivate each other, so that the supportive individuals identified in (1) are not left isolated and potentially vulnerable. Key people in the organisation need to be identified and their support gradually won.
3. Work with the organisationally 'healthy' parts of the system. Don't be tempted by lost causes; the worst ward in the hospital, where all previous interventions have failed, may seem an attractive challenge, a desperate need — but the previous interventions failed for a good reason! Similarly staff may be allocated or may volunteer who are unable to cope with existing stresses and conflicts — they will not be ideal key personnel in

the strenuous process of change.
4. Concentrate efforts on staff who have the most freedom and discretion in deciding their own activities and with most control over resources. You have to influence those who have the power to bring about or allow change. These may not always be those in the designated positions of authority. For example, there is often a natural leader among care-staff without whose support all efforts will be to no avail. Part of the necessary groundwork is to identify these workers with formal or informal power.
5. The *permission*, if not the support and encouragement, of top management, needs to be obtained. Those just below the level of top management may be more enthusiastic, being less associated with the *status quo*. All levels of staff need to be worked with.
6. Change can be stressful, so mutual support and learning need to be encouraged, perhaps through regular group meetings where staff can express their anxieties and doubts (cf. Coulshed, 1980).

The model of institutional change described here involves the psychologist as the agent of change (although other workers could fill this role). Dartington (1983) argues for a 'bottom-up' approach to change, where staff monitor their own behaviour and set their own goals for change, out of their knowledge of what is possible. Savage and Widdowson's (1974) report of how a psychogeriatric ward team looked at their own practices and priorities, and revised their use of nursing resources, is illuminating in this respect. However, this innovation required permission from above, and support and encouragement from people outside the ward. This type of 'bottom-up' change is not incompatible with the model of a change agent treating the institution as client, facilitating and supporting these moves at ward level. What is antithetical is the imposition of change from above, or from without. The change agent may feed ideas in, but in this long-term model the reappearance of the ideas from the care-staff — perhaps some months later — must be awaited before any action is possible. The change then is the care-staff's *not* the psychologist's, and has more hope of maintenance (Davies, 1982). The change agent must be an opportunist. A new ward or home opening, even a new charge nurse or whatever, present possibilities for defining aims, re-setting norms and so on, that will be lost once a routine is established and traditions of 'the way things are done here' begin to be laid down.

Staff Reinforcement

Galliard (1978) pointed out that a behavioural analysis in an institution must include the reinforcement staff receive, and how to structure the environment so that staff find reward in those behaviour patterns that are in turn conducive to a high quality of life for the residents. Godlove *et al.* (1980) showed than many care-attendants prefer to look after dependent residents (47 per cent preferring patients who needed help to walk), partly because some staff found these patients easier to deal with, as their needs were more predictable, e.g. 'they are easier to manage — when they are dressed they stay dressed'; 'because they don't walk around and walk away'; partly because staff felt more able to be helpful, e.g. 'we can see how helpful we are'; 'there's more to do — it keeps you busy'. Many staff receive most reward from physically caring for dependent residents, and this may help explain why, as discussed previously, dependency is so often encouraged. How can staff be encouraged to find their reinforcement from encouraging independence, or from personalising care?

Selecting staff with an interest in elderly people and in the application of a positive approach may help (Davies, 1982), but we have seen the institution is capable of overcoming such interest! Positive attitudes can be fostered through a training programme that emphasises frequent contact and positive experiences with elderly people, as shown by Heller and Walsh's (1976) study where nursing students' attitudes towards the elderly became considerably more positive following a carefully designed course. Smith and Barker (1972) report similar findings following a RO training course. Can these positive attitude changes be maintained in the ward setting? Again one enthusiastic and positive person may make little headway. What is needed is for the staff as a group on the ward or in the home to develop more positive attitudes together, so that institutional systems can be revised and reviewed by the staff (or at least the majority of staff). Coulshed (1980), for example, reports this being achieved through regular staff meetings, where the focus for discussion was initially selected literature on ageing and long-term care, aimed at provoking and stimulating empathy with the elderly and creative thinking about the pattern of care. Through this means staff begin to reinforce each other and them-selves for taking a more individualised approach for care, begin to notice, and find rewarding, individual's small improvements, begin to value human contact with the residents.

A more formal way of reinforcing staff for appropriate behaviour has been tried in institutions for other client groups. For example, Quilitch (1975) showed in a mental handicap institution that neither a memo from the administrator exhorting staff to lead daily recreational activities nor a workshop teaching staff to lead such activities made any difference to the number of residents participating each day. However when specific staff were assigned to lead activities at specific times and a daily feedback poster used, giving the name of the previous day's leader and the number of residents each day, there was a dramatic increase in the amount of activity actually taking place. Although this particular method might not be directly applicable to institutions for the elderly, again we can see the importance of changing the institutional system — not simply training staff, but actually setting the scene for staff to put such training into effect. Senior staff in an institution need systematically to reinforce desirable staff behaviour; of course care will not be individualised if all the staff know that anyone caught talking with a patient by the ward sister will be sent to clean lockers! Senior staff alone cannot make a good institution, but by their example and by their encouragement they can do a great deal to create the atmosphere in the ward or in the home (Davies and Snaith, 1980). Alongside a 'bottom-up' attitude change, a change in managerial expectations and contingencies is required, so that, for example, offering a choice of activities could become part of a care-attendant's job in an old people's home (Godlove *et al.*, 1982), as long as senior staff showed that this was valued, gave it priority, and showed appreciation of staff conscientiously carrying it out. It should be made as easy as possible for the staff to carry out what is required of them; in this instance activity materials should be readily available, and other possible 'emergencies' catered for during the activity session (e.g. another care-attendant to cover toileting, telephone calls or whatever).

Staff training in particular skills and techniques *is* needed, but it will only be of consequence if the institution is structured to encourage the trained skill to be exercised. Training in RO (Holden and Woods, 1982, pp. 217–20) and individual programme planning (Davies and Crisp, 1980) and so on is relatively easy — once the institutional groundwork has been carried out! Training should include modelling of the skills being taught, behavioural rehearsal and feedback on performance, as well as didactic material presented in a manner suitable for the particular group of staff. It needs to be an active process, with feedback extended into the real-life situation, perhaps from on-going supervision of the skills learned. Where possible direct observation can be helpful — Hanley (1980) showed that staff after 24-hour RO training said they were carrying it out, but detailed observation revealed discrepancies between their observed and their reported behaviour. Feedback from video tapes of staff behaviour can be potentially powerful. Video tapes of resident behaviour can be useful to develop observational skills when training staff in individual programme planning (Holden and Woods, 1982, pp. 224–6). A regular session with staff to discuss individual plans can provide a useful forum for teaching input from the psychologist. It can be used to develop staff members' knowledge-base, skills of analysis and empathy. Their presentation of the individual's needs and resources and their plans to meet these needs and to utilise the person's resources can be used as a basis for this teaching.

Staff Support

Working in an institution for the elderly can be extremely stressful. The work is often physically hard, dealing with the most basic needs of people who may well not be grateful, and who almost certainly will not improve. The hours are often long and unsocial, appreciation from senior staff and 'society' often muted. Remuneration reflects the low status of the work. Relatives of the elderly people may also appear ungrateful, perhaps full of complaints. There are never adequate levels of staff. Death is a relatively common occurrence.

Quattrochi-Tubin *et al.* (1982) describe the 'staff burnout syndrome'. Burnout involves physical and emotional exhaustion, negative job attitudes, loss of concern for clients and a poor work-related self-concept. It is thought to result from intensive involvement with clients over long periods of time. Burned out individuals can reduce morale generally, because of their negativity. It is important then to have staff-support networks, and to face the reality that this work is difficult and demanding. Staff-support groups where feelings regarding the job can be expressed and shared may be of value. Kolotkin (1981), writing regarding staff burnout in the field of terminal care, suggests that stress management training may help the person cope with stress, express feelings, and be able to talk with the dying person and their family, rather than taking the apparently easier way out of avoiding the subject of death, which in fact leads to greater stress in the long run.

Issues of death and bereavement need to be faced in institutions for the elderly as well as in terminal care settings. Some staff, for instance, feel shame that they still get upset when a resident dies, as if they should learn to harden themselves to death. If personal relationships are formed then of course mourning the loss is perfectly natural. In some settings residents are not told when a fellow-resident dies — the subject is taboo. How much more normal and natural it is if residents who knew the dead person are quietly individually informed, and, if they are unable to attend the funeral, invited to a service in the Home. Often this is rejected as either residents would get upset (as if this were not a part of normal experience), or would not care (suggesting close relationships are hard to make in this setting). Often when residents are *not* told they pick up the cues regardless; it is interesting that we feel the need to protect those who are much more experienced than ourselves, and who often are much more relaxed about death than younger people!

Sex is the other taboo topic in many institutions for the elderly. Some proudly talk of couples who met and married in the home, but Godlove *et al.* (1980) showed that in 40 per cent of the institutions studied residents were not allowed to see a resident of the opposite sex privately. When sex is discussed it is usually the subject of mirth, the implication that people at that age should be beyond such things. Masturbation, for example, is often seen as a problem behaviour to be eliminated, but as Hussian (1981) points out the problem is typically one of where the behaviour takes place (in public rather than in private), not of the actual occurrence of the behaviour. Staff again need support in discussing this area that many find stressful and embarrassing. Information regarding sexuality in the elderly (e.g. Comfort, 1980; Baikie, 1984) is often helpful, but the emphasis — as with death — must be on resolving our own problems with the topic of sex and ageing, and on developing empathy with elderly people as whole people, with the whole range of human needs and emotions.

Community Integration

Much depends on the local situation regarding the extent to which contact with the community can be developed and maintained. In some settings other community organisations might be able to use the facility as a meeting-place, e.g. one old people's home has a bar, and is used by a local darts team; potentially a great deal of informal contact and interest could arise from such links. Residents might be able to attend clubs, visit shops, pubs or whatever in the vicinity. In any setting there are two groups of people who need considerable encouragement and support — relatives and volunteers.

Relatives have a whole range of feelings regarding the institution. Relief, that their physical burden is over; guilt, that they should have carried on longer; resentment, that the care is not perfect, are typical examples. Relatives' guilt may find expression in anger at care-staff over what the latter see as a trivial issue — an item of clothing mislaid perhaps. The visit itself may be traumatic; what does the elderly person have to talk about? Perhaps they become upset, want to go home with the relative, who, confronted with the elderly person's tears, finds it hard to accept the care-staff's reassurance that the elderly person really is settling in well — 'It's only when you're here.' The relative feels that it would be better not to visit so often, and the visits tail off: 'It's such a depressing place, and she only gets upset when I go.' The care-staff are confirmed in their opinion of relatives as uncaring people who ship their elderly people into care at the first opportunity and then never visit, or, if they do, complain a great deal.

If care-staff can be involved in pre-admission home visits they are often able to achieve more empathy with the relative's viewpoint, and sense the burden of 24-hour care. Relatives' meetings, where relatives can discuss their feelings regarding giving up the caring role, and support each other, can be helpful both for relatives and for staff to see the relatives' side of the picture. Such groups often lead to relatives becoming more involved in the home — perhaps helping to fund-raise or to organise activities, or to assist in the care of their own relative. Obviously this can only be achieved in an institution which is open to such community integration. Where relatives are viewed as a nuisance, with restricted visiting time, collaboration of this type will be very difficult, to the detriment of residents, relatives and staff. Davies (1981) shows in an interesting case-study that relatives can, with help from the staff, find visits more rewarding and less aversive, to the benefit of all concerned.

Similarly volunteers are often viewed negatively — 'they're more trouble than they're worth — by the time you've shown them what to do you might as well have done it yourself', or 'you can't rely on volunteers, they come a few times, and then you never see them again'. It must be recognised that volunteers do take some work — they cannot just be sent into the ward and told to get on with it. They do need support, just as staff do. If carefully selected, they can be of enormous value, but they do need to be given a definite task within the home, and if necessary the appropriate training for the task. For example, chatting to cognitively impaired elderly people can be extraordinarily difficult; a volunteer asked to do this would soon lose heart and drift away, or talk only to the less impaired residents. With some training in reminiscence or RO techniques, however, the volunteer can begin to make meaningful contact, and derive some personal satisfaction from the task. Volunteers then do need some staff input, especially at first, but they are well worth the effort, as again they decrease the institution's isolation from the community, and help to create a more 'normal' atmosphere.

Integration

One of the most contentious issues in residential care is whether 'confused' and 'rational' residents should share the same accommodation, or whether there should be separate facilities for the 'confused' elderly. Those in favour of integration (e.g. Meacher, 1972) argue that it is advantageous for all — confused residents have the assistance and the stimulation of their more able fellows, and rational residents have the opportunity to accept responsibility for the confused and frail. Separatists argue that it is unfair for 'rational' residents to spend their remaining days with confused residents who wander, take other people's handbags, act in a noisy or disinhibited fashion; confused residents suffer by being rejected by their more able fellows, even being pushed out of a chair 'owned' by a 'rational' resident (Lipman, 1968). A point in favour of the separatists' argument is that integration seldom occurs, even when it is meant to happen! Harris, Lipman and Slater (1977) studied eight homes, and found that segregation — whether formal or informal — occurred in each; particular sitting-rooms were used only by rational residents, and rational residents seldom talked to confused residents. Whether the home was intended to be integrated made little difference to the reality.

If integration is seen as a desirable goal, then it is clearly not enough to place confused and rational residents in the same building. Segregation, whether intitiated by staff or residents, will almost certainly occur. In an institution run with a large living group, confused residents are soon placed in an 'out' group, and rational residents do not form the relationships with them that would be required for the supposed benefits to occur. Two approaches to changing this situation look worth developing. The first is to operate a small group-living scheme (Marston and Gupta, 1977). If each small group includes a few confused residents, it is much less likely that they will be rejected, and much more likely that they will be tolerated and assisted in the group's shared tasks. The second is to work with the rational residents to help them understand the problems of their confused fellows, and seek to recruit their help in RO and reminiscence schemes for the confused residents (Hanley, 1980). What is still unknown is what proportion of confused residents such programmes could include. With an ever-growing proportion of institutional elderly being 'confused' it seems inevitable that some facilities will be almost exclusively for them. If staffing levels reflect the amount of care needed, and if care is geared to meeting the particular needs of the individual confused residents, the quality of life need not be lower than in a supposedly integrated institution.

Conclusions

In this chapter we have tried to describe the realities of institutional care, and to point to some practical ways of approaching psychological intervention in institutional settings. Institutions can be improved, the quality of life and functioning of residents can be enhanced. The way forward is not however to lift a treatment package from Chapter 8 off the shelf and expect it to 'work' in your particular facility. The psychologist must analyse the institutional environment — from top to bottom — and in the long term seek to develop positive attitudes and a readiness for change. It may be at some stage a treatment package can be introduced, but the time must be carefully chosen, and efforts made to build the package into the structure of the facility, so that it is maintained and not quietly forgotten.

It can be a hard, at times unrewarding task — change agents can suffer burnout too! The psychologists must not neglect to have their own support system, so that they are not working isolated and unsupported. The reward may come months later, when a suggestion made months ago emerges *de novo* from the charge nurse who initially appeared hostile, or when a healthy part of the institution emerges and their enthusiasm almost has to be held in check!

Summary

1. Most formal studies of psychological intervention with the elderly have been carried out in institutional settings.
2. Institutions vary considerably in physical facilities, size, care provision and environmental setting.
3. The elderly are often placed in an institutional setting inappropriate to their needs or inflexible in its response to them.
4. Models of care for the elderly are being developed, both in their own right and drawing on experience with other deprived, disabled or handicapped groups.
5. Many recent studies have provided welcome evidence on activity levels and on both the quality and quantity of social interactions, in institutional settings.
6. The whole institutional setting — staff, buildings and environment — must be considered in any intervention strategy, but few reported studies give sufficient detail in this respect.
7. The need to change attitudes in staff and fundamental physical features of the environment means that a long-term (often many years) approach may in the end be more productive than instant intervention, quickly eroded and counter-productive.
8. Specific staff training in skills and technique can only *follow* attitude change if it is to be fruitful.
9. Caring institutions for the elderly are a stressful environment for staff — effective support mechanisms are essential to overcome high rates of 'burnout'. Sources of staff reinforcement are an important aspect of behavioural analysis.
10. Community volunteer and relative support and encouragement needs to be fostered. They need support and direction; staff may be initially reluctant to involve them fully.
11. Experience encourages those who want to see advances in institutional care to persevere. Seeds sown and ideas scattered may appear to have little effect at the time. Six months to two years later things begin to happen!

10 INTERVENTION IN THE COMMUNITY

Introduction

We have examined the popular supposition that the majority of the elderly are in institutional care in detail in Chapter 1 and the previous chapter. It would be wise to re-emphasise that in fact only 6 per cent of elderly people over the age of 65 are in institutions of any kind. Even when those suffering from some form of dementia are considered, the majority are to be found in the community — only about one in four are in residential care or hospital (Kay *et al.*, 1964). Surely only the milder cases can survive without skilled care; those in institutions must be the most deteriorated? Surprisingly enough this does not seem to be the case. Elderly people with dementia as severe as that seen in institutions are to be found in the community. Is this simply because not enough places in institutions are available? This may be one factor, but against this is the strong desire of many people, and many relatives also, to avoid institutional care if at all possible. It has been argued more generally that 'community care' may not always be superior to the institutional care that has been so heavily criticised over the years (Hawks, 1975). Can 'the community', which so often seems to have a negative attitude to the elderly, really care for disabled elderly people in its midst? In this chapter we will examine clinical psychology's contribution to facilitating and developing the community's caring resources.

Who actually supports elderly people who are unable to cope independently? A striking feature about community work is the number of people who may be involved. Firstly, there is the person's family network; secondly, an informal social network of neighbours and friends; thirdly, statutory agencies such as social services and community health services; fourthly, voluntary agencies, church groups, etc. Not all these groups will be involved with every elderly person, of course, but it can be seen there is a need for a careful analysis of 'who is doing what' with each elderly patient in order to avoid unnecessary duplication and miscommunication, and to identify possible gaps in the support provided.

The amount of informal social support by neighbours and friends should not be underestimated. Much of this in fact is carried out by fit active elderly people. Many such claim to be busier after retirement than before, as anyone who has tried to arrange a control group of normal old people will confirm! In the luncheon club or day-centre the 75-year-old volunteer says she likes helping the 'old people', many of whom are years younger than herself! The elderly widower does odd jobs for half-a-dozen widows in his street. The retired nurse calls frequently on her increasingly confused neighbour. Another lady bakes delicious apple pies for her neighbour who is looking after his severely demented wife . . . In some instances to characterise the supporting relationship as consisting of one person depending upon another would be quite inaccurate. The helper's needs too may be met — feeling needed and useful, having a meaningful role and so on. For example, the brother-in-law of a widower, who was in hospital with depression for several months, gave considerable help with his financial affairs. When the patient recovered he was able to give his brother-in-law a great deal of help with his garden and his car. Or the couple, one mentally alert but physically frail, the other fit in body but whose memory had gone, filling in for each other's deficits, surviving as a team, neither being able to manage on their own. Interdependency then may be a more appropriate model than supporter and dependant.

Good community care aims to support and mobilise these informal networks, not to take over from them, nor to pressure them into doing more than they feel able; to help them feel valued and needed, not abused and exploited. In order to do this effectively an accurate picture of what is really going on around the individual must be obtained and fitted into an appropriate psychological and caring model. Many of the factors discussed in the previous chapter on institutional care are equally relevant to the elderly in the community.

Family Support

Despite the prevailing impression that families no longer care about their older members, we saw in Chapter 3 that families by and large still do care — greater mobility has not prevented fairly frequent contact, and the family remains the primary support at times of illness. Undoubtedly many elderly people remain in the community because of the support they receive from their families. Isaacs, Livingstone and Neville (1972) examined in detail a consecutive series of 280 geriatric patients. They found that for only a tiny proportion of these was the family refusing to give care where it could have been possible for them to do so. In some cases where 'rejection' seemed to have occurred this could be related to a breakdown in family relationships many years previously. In other cases the family was 'unavoidably preoccupied' with other problems that prevented them giving assistance, e.g. their own health, or caring for another family member. Bergmann, Foster, Justice and Matthews (1978) showed clearly the coping abilities of many families. They followed up a series of first referrals to a day-hospital for dementia, for twelve months. They found that family support — not medical and social measures — related significantly to survival in the community. Younger relatives (mainly daughters) were most effective in aiding survival in the community, followed by elderly relatives (usually spouses). Elderly people living alone in the community were most vulnerable, despite receiving more formal social support than the family-supported patients.

The Cost of Family Care

Care by family members has several advantages over institutional care; the elderly person is more likely to be treated as an individual; their past and background, likes and interests are well known so it is easier to make sense of the elderly person's efforts at communication; the elderly person is more likely to be in familiar surroundings, and perhaps to see friends and other relatives; the relative avoids guilt about 'putting the person away'. However, it has been recognised for some time that there can be a price to pay for these gains. For instance, Grad and Sainsbury (1968) rated over 75 per cent of the families of a large sample of elderly psychiatric patients as facing some burden, with the burden being severe in 40 per cent. The impact of caring may be considerable. In a typical example, with problems in both sets of elderly parents, a caring family has seen the mother's evening job given up; a teenage daughter and son turning against their parents; physical health problems, from keeping three homes in reasonable condition; and marital difficulties. Interestingly, in this case there was little or no outside support from friends or agencies initially and such help enabled the family to cope.

Isaacs *et al.* (1972) defined strain in relatives as 'a state of physical and mental exhaustion of the helper'. It was *not* a measure of how great the burden of care was — different relatives having differing abilities to cope with an identical burden. Over two-thirds of patients in their consecutive sample of admissions to a geriatric unit who were receiving adequate basic care at home had relatives suffering from undue strain. Strain was greater when the patient was very old (and so the spouse or child was also probably correspondingly older) or the relative had a young family of their own. When the patient lived with the supporter, the strain of care was again greater. These relatives received very little support, from, for example, home help or home nursing.

Sources of Strain

The sources of strain were partly related to the patient's physical condition: lifting, putting the person to bed, disturbances at night, incontinence. Most relatives, however, found the strain caused by mental abnormalities to be much greater: the disinhibited disturbed behaviour of dementia, or simply an exacerbation of a difficult personality.

There have been a number of studies more recently detailing the factors that make it difficult for relatives to continue caring. Sanford (1975) looked at 50 'social' admissions to a geriatric unit and interviewed the principal supporter in each case. Problems were categorised as related to the dependant's behaviour patterns, the supporter's own limitations or to environmental and social conditions. Factors that, if alleviated, would restore a tolerable situation at home were identified from these. The major problems identified are shown in Table 10.1.

Sleep disturbance was a particularly common problem, which relatives found difficult to tolerate. This might arise from the patient's need to urinate, from them wandering, or from the patient shouting. Faecal incontinence similarly was found difficult to cope with, although urinary incontinence was reported to be much more tolerable. Immobility was the other relatively frequent but poorly tolerated problem in the dependant's behaviour. Within the supporter's own limitations it should be noted that over half of these key supporting relatives reported feelings of anxiety and/or depression, and that a quarter experienced personality conflicts with the elderly person. Many of these relatives (nearly half) had an extremely restricted social life — a quarter reported that they were

Table 10.1: Major Problems Identified in Interviews with Principal Supporters of 50 'Social' Admissions to a Geriatric Unit

Problems	Frequency (% of cases)	Tolerance (% of supporters able to tolerate problem)
1. In dependant's behaviour patterns:		
sleep disturbance	62	16
inability to get on/off commode unaided	38	21
inability to walk at all	16	13
faecal incontinence	56	43
urinary incontinence	54	81
dangerous irresponsible behaviour	32	38
2. In supporter's own limitations:		
anxiety/depression	52	65
personality conflicts	26	54
insufficient strength for lifting	22	73
3. In environmental and social conditions:		
restriction of social life	42	57
inability to leave dependant for more than one hour	28	71
stairs within accommodation	26	85

Source: Derived from Sanford (1975).

never able to be away from the dependant for even an hour.

In the USA, Zarit, Reever and Bach-Peterson (1980) used a questionnaire to assess the level of burden perceived by the relatives of patients with senile dementia, and related this to a number of other variables. They found no relationship between the level of perceived burden and the duration of the patient's illness, the degree of cognitive impairment, the level of memory and behaviour problems, and self-care ability. There was a significant relationship, however, with the frequency of visits by other family members, so that relatives with least perceived burden received most visits. There were no differences in any of the variables for families where the spouse was the supporter as against where the daughter was the primary supporter. For both groups only the frequency of family visits related to the level of burden. Although the authors acknowledge a possible bias in their sample, in that all had decided to continue at least for the present in caring for the patient at home, the study illustrates the potential importance of both formal and informal support for care-givers in the difficult task which they undertake.

Wives looking after their elderly disabled husbands were the focus of a study by Fengler and Goodrich (1979). On average, women live longer and tend to marry men older than themselves, so they are probably more likely to be called on to act as care-giver than their husbands. They describe these wives as the 'hidden patients'. On average the life-satisfaction scores of both husbands and wives were relatively low, but there was a range of scores, with a clear association between the satisfaction of each partner and their spouse. Factors differentiating high- and low-morale groups were examined. In many ways the groups were remarkably similar — the level of disability, the wife's health and so on. Low-morale wives felt their income was inadequate, and more were employed because of this, perhaps leading to 'role overload'. Other low-morale wives were looking after several relatives. High-morale wives were able to see their husbands as a confidant, whilst low-morale couples seemed to have greater difficulty in shared communiation. The low-morale group also had less support from friends and other relatives, adding support to Zarit *et al.*'s finding mentioned previously.

Gilleard *et al.* (1981c) have looked at measures of mood, degree of burden and estimated ability to cope in a sample of 46 supporters all caring for a dementing relative or dependant attending a psychogeriatric day-hospital. The most frequent problems are listed in Table 10.2. Factor analysis of these data produced five factors (Table 10.2) thought to reflect the multifaceted nature of both the problems and the stresses.

Further analysis indicated that 'demand' problems are mostly responsible for the reported level of strain. These problems were highly related to negative mood states in the supporter. In addition, importantly, it is only these demand problems that predict outcome at twelve months (in terms of whether care in the community is likely to continue). Lack of self-care skills, physical disability and even aggression did not predict outcome; the level of reported attentional and emotional demands did. 'Demand' problems included attention-seeking, disruption of social life, continual questioning, being noisy and creating arguments. It is worth noting that there is some scope for interpretation in many of these behaviours, so that the relatives' expectations of the patient and the meanings they attribute to the patient's behaviour may well be

Table 10.2: Problems Reported by Relatives and Factors Emerging from Factor Analysis

Most frequent problems reported	*Dimensions identified*
Inability of dependant to be left alone	1. Dependency
Inability of dependant to be outside alone	2. Disturbance
Disruption of personal life	3. Disability
Inability to hold sociable conversation	4. Demand
Lack of self-help skills	5. Wandering
Continual questioning	
Incontinence	
Demands for attention	

Source: Derived from Gilleard *et al.* (1981c).

significant. In a later study from the same research team (Gledhill *et al.*, 1982) it emerged that day-hospital staff were able to predict which supporters were under the most strain, but could not identify accurately which problem areas the relatives found most difficult, emphasising the degree of subjective perception involved as to what constitutes 'a problem'. In this study no less than 70 per cent of relatives scored above the threshold for psychiatric disorder on the General Health Questionnaire (Goldberg, 1978), a frequently used screening measure for level of distress. These relatives had received day-relief for 3—6 months, and so were not unsupported!

Greene *et al.* (1982) similarly have studied 38 relatives looking after dementing elderly people attending a Glasgow psychogeriatric day-hospital. They conclude that 'the severity of dementia . . . does not . . . greatly upset relatives'. The behavioural manifestations of dementia, and in particular mood disturbances (especially instability of mood), were the features that again relatives found most difficult to tolerate.

From a much larger-scale survey, Levin (1983) reports increasing stress in supporters who continue to care for the dementing person, as their behaviour worsened. Similar problems to those described above were found to be most distressing. Levin emphasised the ability of relatives to find ways of coping with particular problems, an issue discussed further below.

An in-depth survey of supporters with dementing relatives attending a psychogeriatric day-hospital is reported by Gilhooly (1980). She confirmed that lack of basic self-care skills does not seem to increase the burden on the supporter — in fact, if anything, the supporters' morale was higher the worse the patient's self-help ability! There was also a tendency for relatives who had been coping longer to have higher morale, and these two factors could, of course, be related. She was unable to confirm the effects of frequency of contact with relatives on the supporter's morale; often when one person had taken on formal responsibility the remaining family stopped helping at all. Supporters often used 'emotional blackmail' to obtain help from relatives, and it was evident that some estimate of the *quality* of support from other relatives is needed in addition to the measures of frequency.

Gilhooly (1984) has also commented on the relevance of the strength of relationship before commencement of the intense caring process. She related this to willingness to consider institutional care, finding an association between this and the quality of the relationship previously. Those with the closest relationships also experienced most distress.

Coping with the Strain

It is also interesting to see from this study how supporters cope with the burdens of care (Table 10.3).

Table 10.3: Coping Mechanisms Used by Supporters (N = 16; some supporters use several mechanisms)

	Number using	Average morale score (Max. 7)
Behavioural	5	5.3
Psychological (cognitive)		
Making positive comparisons	2	2
Selective ignoring	1	4.5
Re-ordering of life priorities	3	6
Converting hardship into a virtue	6	2.5
None identified	5	0.6

Source: Derived from Gilhooly (1980).

A high-morale group used behavioural coping responses — finding out and utilising all available services, mobilising friends and relatives to help. Other relatives, and some of the first group also, made use of cognitive psychological coping responses 'attempting to modify or control the meaning of the stressful experience'. These include making positive comparisons (e.g. count your blessings); selective ignoring — ignoring the negative aspects whilst emphasising the positive attributes of the situation (e.g. at least she's in her own home); re-ordering of life priorities (shrinking the significance of the problem), and converting hardship into virtue (e.g. take the bad with the good). Supporters having none of these mechanisms tended to have very low morale scores. Gilhooly also comments that several supporters coped with repetition and continual demands by leaving the situation, going for a walk and so on, to cope with the stress induced.

Relationship factors

The effects of the quality of the relationship between patient and supporter have been further investigated by Bergmann, Manchee and Woods (1983). Their sample was drawn from relatives of patients assessed at a psychogeriatric assessment unit and day-hospital. A number of variables were related to outcome three months following admission. Behavioural disability, level of cognitive impairment, age or sex did not differentiate good and poor outcome groups. In the relationship area, neither the level of dependence nor the extent of the patient being dominant in the relationship was related to outcome. Only the degree of positive communication in the relationship differentiated the outcome groups significantly. Where the relationship had been characterised by one or other partner using coercion or withdrawal to attain satisfaction, outcome tended to be poor; where the partners had sought to reward each other, outcome tended to be good. This pattern was evident both in the overall sample and in those suffering from functional psychiatric disorder.

In cases where dementia was present, other relationship factors apart from the degree of positive communication were also important. Here, poor outcome was associated with a lower level of dependence, and with the patient being more dominant. This might reflect the greater 'manageability' of a submissive, highly dependent patient. Immobility might entail a greater physical burden, but at least the relative knows the patient will still be in the same place when they return, that they will not be followed around the house, or need to fear that they will get lost outside the house! One is again reminded that it is mental disturbance and not physical disability that relatives find most difficult.

Bergmann (1979) describes particular patterns of relationship difficulty which may be encountered where negative communication occurs. The 'mother–daughter' syndrome is where a child remains dependent, emotionally at least, on the parent, perhaps not moving very far away or remaining in the parental home. The parent's influence then remains powerful, but, as they lose physical power through ill health and infirmity, the child receives less support, and in fact is expected to meet more and more of the parent's needs. The child in this situation finds it difficult to resist the parent's control, which may be exerted through emotional blackmail and other coercive means. The child becomes enmeshed in the care of the patient, denied any separate existence or contact. Both parent and child may complain of depression and anxiety. A converse situation (power reversal) is where the lifelong passive dependent elderly person, conforming, obedient and unassertive, but useful within the household, experiences what the family see as a life-threatening illness. The family respond by meeting the person's every need and showing loving concern. This new position of power may then be maintained, once the initial crisis has passed, by demanding or hypochondrial behaviour. Finally the 'fallen tyrant' is described, where a dominant, harsh and (physically) powerful family member reacts strongly to loss of physical power and financial dominance (say, after a stroke), and resorts to manipulative behaviour to retain control, where once a strong tongue and physical aggression had sufficed. Other patterns almost certainly arise; they all have in common the use of a negative communication system in adapting to a change in the perhaps previously stable family equilibrium.

Conclusions on Family Support

These studies and the variety of their conclusions suggest that there is a great deal more work to be carried out on how families cope with the care of an elderly person. The present studies are generally small-scale, and often draw their samples from a particular service provision, potentially biasing the results obtained. Families in the community *not* receiving any help or services also need to be included in this sort of research, which would be improved by a longitudinal component, so that *changes* in relationship patterns, morale and strain could be observed.

We have seen, however, that many relatives are experiencing considerable strain, that being disturbed at night and being further worn down by demands for attention or continual repetition increases the burden considerably in a way that the physical burden does not. Cognitive stress seems more likely to cause problems than behavioural stress. Perhaps behavioural coping is easier, being more dependent on the adaptation of well-established skills in the relative. Cognitive coping mechanisms may be, in comparison, poorly developed, and a fruitful area for intervention (see Williams, 1984).

Support from other relatives may be helpful — depending on the quality of the relationships in the broader family. The quality of the relationship between supporter and patient has been implicated in several studies; exactly how it is associated with the desire to continue caring is still unclear. This may be because the wish to continue caring probably has several components; positively wanting to continue caring; feeling guilty about any alternative care; wanting to avoid the stigma of the institution; or possibly having a poor relationship, but feeling emotionally blackmailed into continuing. The association between desire to continue caring and quality of relationship could not then be expected to be direct. 'Quality of relationship' is itself probably a multi-dimensional concept, to complicate the association further.

Although there has been much publicity in recent years concerning 'Granny battering' (e.g. Johnson, 1979; Eastman, 1982), it is important not to jump to the conclusion that relatives are being cruel and heartless to frail old people. Old-age abuse is a significant problem, but it also includes the abuse of relatives *by* old people, perhaps using emotional blackmail and sometimes physical agression effectively to keep the relative under control. Indeed we have come across probably more instances of the caring relative being attacked by the patient than vice versa (see Matthews and Woods, 1980). It is inevitable that relatives will lose their tempers and become angry in situations where too little support is provided, or when what support there is proves to be inappropriate. It reflects the great strain that relatives experience in looking after an impaired elderly person, and their depth of feeling for them, as they continue to care in the most difficult circumstances. The priority for those working with the elderly is not to set up elaborate procedures for recording bruises, but to recognise the harmful nature for all parties of both physical and emotional abuse. The focus of attention should be the reduction of strain, by the early identification of problems, and by the development of services that are perceived as useful and supportive by those involved.

Work with Families — Supporting the Supporters

There is a growing interest in working with families to assist in reducing the strain felt by relatives, to provide them with support in the task of caring (e.g. Sheldon, 1982). The implicit aim would appear to be to enable them to continue caring for longer, avoiding the increase of stress to a point where rejection is inevitable (Bergmann, 1979). The wide variety of potential sources of strain indicated in the previous section suggests that a wide range of interventions may be be helpful.

Information and Practical Support

At a very basic level Gilhooly (1980) has shown that relatives may be unaware of even the most basic facts concerning the problems being experienced by the client. Simple information on the nature and extent of illness and the likely prognosis may well lead to considerable attitude change.

Practical help is often particularly relevant, especially where some relief from the burden of caring can be offered. A special laundry service for incontinent elderly, adaptations to the home to relieve some of the physical strain, a home help to help with domestic tasks are examples of this.

Relief for a period of time — even in some cases as little as an hour or so — can be immensely valuable to the hard-pressed relative. Day-centres are one way of offering this relief; an alternative is someone going in to sit with the elderly person, if they are perhaps unable or unwilling to attend day-care. Regular holiday relief admissions to hospital or other residential settings or to a foster family can provide a longer recuperative break.

None of these interventions are in a strict sense psychological, but the psychological aspects of each are ignored at some peril. What is the most helpful way, for instance, of presenting information regarding, say, senile dementia? Too much emphasis on the negative prognosis and inevitable deterioration may lead to self-fulfilling expectations in the relative. If the information is grossly different from the relative's previous conception, their coping mechanisms may inadvertently be undermined. Practical aids may lie unused, the relative may spend hours cleaning up before the home help arrives — to use their services might be perceived as a blow to the relative's pride. The relative may accept 'relief' for a brief period, but spend the time thinking about the elderly person, wondering if they are all right, or on a longer relief stay may visit every day instead of going away on holiday. Alternatively, the relief may be so enjoyable, they refuse to take the elderly person back from the 'holiday' admission!

It is not being argued that practical interventions are doomed to failure; in many cases they are beneficial for all concerned. To separate them, however, from intervention at a psychological level is misguided. Their success depends on how they are perceived by the carer, and by the carer's perception of the caring task.

Relatives' Support

Psychological intervention can be at a number of levels. The most basic is the provision of emotional support, allowing the person to share the emotional burden of caring, to discuss the irritations and frustrations, the joys and the heartaches. More complex is the endeavour to teach the relative skills, say for changing or managing particular aspects of the elderly person's behaviour, in order to reduce the stress on the relative. Often, both levels are attempted in a group setting, and there are now several published accounts of relative support groups, although as yet empirical data on their effects are lacking. An additional and potentially important factor in these groups is the sharing of group experiences, the realisation that they are not alone in their caring task, that others have experienced similar problems to themselves.

Hausman (1979) describes her experience of 5 eight-week 'short-term counselling groups' for people with elderly parents. Some of the parents lived with their children, others lived separately, some close by, others further away, and some were in nursing homes. Hausman states the goals of the groups as helping members to deal with their parents in a mature way, and finding a balance between responsibilities to oneself, one's spouse and children, and one's parents. Common issues in the groups included being unprepared for the burden of care, it often coming at a time of life when freedom from child-care and financial worries had been anticipated.

Members often expressed fears of their own ageing, wondering whether they would become disabled and dependent in the way that their parents had. The elderly parents were often described as self-centred, selfish, demanding and inconsiderate; often a brother or sister of the carer who visited rarely would be constantly praised, whilst the carer would bear the brunt of the parent's anger and criticism, despite the time and attention they were giving. Problems of communication with both their parents and the professionals involved was a common theme also. Relatives found most helpful the opportunity to share with others having similar problems, and to discuss and modify their own attitudes and beliefs.

Fuller, Ward, Evans, Massam and Gardner (1979) describe their experiences with groups initially for the relatives of elderly patients with dementia, based in a psychogeriatric day-hospital. The group had to be opened to relatives of the depressed patients as well, because of the demand from them also. A common theme from these groups was a desire for identification of similarities between group members' relatives in the problems they caused and the behaviours they showed. There was also a tendency to search for a cause, some explanation for the dementia occurring, often linked to the presumably false hope that the relative would get better. Relatives found it particularly difficult to cope when they were no longer recognised by the patient, and clearly experienced a great deal of anger and resentment, feeling often that the patient was being difficult deliberately.

Our own experience of supportive groups for relatives echoes many of these themes. Often emotional blackmail is described, where the elderly person puts pressure on the carer in a variety of ways to remain and meet their needs. The carer may feel guilty about leaving the elderly person because she cries when she mentions going out, or seems about to have one of her 'turns'. The carer may be compared unfavourably with other relatives who in reality hardly visit at all. In this type of negative communication system both carer and elderly person may present as depressed. Carers often describe their elderly relatives as 'selfish', 'self-centred' and so on, for example recounting how they remain impervious to other people's major illnesses, while continuing to complain of their own chronic conditions.

Some carers express feelings of guilt regarding their negative feelings toward the elderly person: 'She is my mother, I should love her, but now I hate her.' They continue to 'care' as a duty, but appear to derive no pleasure from the relationship. Some carers describe becoming very angry with the elderly person, sometimes verbally, occasionally physically. Support groups can be very helpful in giving a 'safe' place where such taboo topics can be discussed. Often the 'confession' of one member will lead to others expressing similar feelings and actions.

Another common theme is the lack of appropriate help from the services available. Often less help seems to be given simply because a relative is present, and services often seem to be directed more towards elderly people on their own — a policy which Bergmann *et al.* (1978) have suggested is mistaken, at least for the demented elderly. Even where support is given to the supporters, so often it does not meet needs which the carer is often able to define precisely. For example, an 89-year-old member of a support group looking after his 68-year-old wife suffering from multiple sclerosis needed help getting her up and dressed in the morning and back to bed in the evening. A home nursing service was offered, but the timing of visits was, to say the least, unpredictable. The wife didn't want to stay in bed till 11.00 a.m. and go to bed at 6.00 p.m. to fit in with the nurse's other duties! Or the day-care that is provided as a much needed relief for a hard-pressed daughter, where the transport is so unreliable that the promised relief becomes more of a burden, as the daughter is left disappointed so often.

Controlled evaluations of relatives' support groups are only just beginning to be reported. Hausman (1979) used an evaluation questionnaire at the conclusion of her group. Results from this suggested relatives had found the groups extremely helpful.

Issues in Establishing Relatives' Support Groups

Before a sensible evaluation can be carried out, however, some work is needed to identify the important components of a relatives' support group and a number of issues arise over, for instance, the setting for the group, the style of the leadership and the length of the group.

The first issue is recruitment of relatives; being based in a particular facility — a nursing home, day-hospital, etc. — is clearly one way of being able to contact a discrete group of relatives. Making contact with the much larger population of relatives not in touch already with a supportive facility is much more difficult. It has been our experience that, despite letters to general practitioners, social service agencies, newspaper and local radio coverage, recruitment from the community at large can be extremely slow. Broadhurst (1981) reports similar difficulties and analyses some possible reasons for this apparent reluctance.

1. Lack of time: there will already be many demands on the carer's time. Often there are already potentially conflicting demands, e.g. a young family, a busy job, so fitting in an extra commitment can be difficult. However, when evening groups are offered for the convenience of those who are working, there has been a lower take-up than for day-time groups — it seems that

those working either are too busy caring in the evening or find in their work an outlet or some relief and so feel less the need for other support.

2. Health: often the carer may be elderly themselves, and have poor health making attendance at a group difficult.

3. Carers may not see anything in their situation that could change: for instance, they may view caring for their parents as a natural, inevitable part of life — perhaps to be endured — but not one for which any outside help could influence the course of events.

4. The relative may have suffered previous disappointments in seeking support, perhaps receiving tranquillizers from her general practitioner, or being told 'It's old age, there's nothing that can be done!'

5. The relative may be embarrassed about their distress, anger or guilt: they may feel it is something that any *normal* person *ought* to be able to cope with, or they may feel too proud to seek help.

6. The relative may be so enmeshed in the day-to-day caring that they may be quite literally cut off and isolated from channels where they might hear about the existence of such groups.

7. Some relatives may be suffering distress but may be unwilling to make the changes in their relationship with the elderly person that they realise might be necessary to improve their situation, e.g. by being firmer, fearing the effects on the elderly person.

It is possible through consistent continued publicity, personal contact and reminders to social services and hospital staff, through voluntary agencies and so on to overcome some of these difficulties. Unfortunately, the day when somebody beginning to undertake the care of an elderly person automatically seeks support and help is a long way off — considerable changes in attitudes to old age, dementia and family relationships would be needed for this to happen in the way it might, say, for the parents of a mentally handicapped child.

Whatever else is important about the actual group, in order to increase the likelihood of relatives continuing to attend the following points need to be considered. There do need to be a variety of meeting times to suit the personal commitments of members. Transport may need to be provided, particularly for carers who are elderly themselves. Some will require somebody to sit with the elderly person while they are at the group. Above all the group needs to be cohesive (Hausman, 1979) — which is facilitated by a social atmosphere, by members being encouraged to talk and share with each other and not simply to talk to the leader, by the members being encouraged to support each other outside the group, perhaps exchanging phone numbers, etc., and by the group being kept to a maximum size of about twelve members, so that discussion does not split into several sub-groups.

Should the group be for a fixed time, e.g. eight or ten sessions? Should it be a closed group or should new members be introduced at any time? Ideally a fixed time does tend to concentrate attention and encourage review of goals, and a closed group does encourage cohesiveness. Members needing long-term support can always join subsequent groups. However in some settings, particularly where new relatives are continually seeking immediate help, it may be more appropriate to have open groups without a time-limit imposed.

A common problem surrounds the style of leadership. A key issue is the extent to which the leader actively offers suggestions directly changing the interactions between carer and elderly person. Thus several types of groups could be envisaged.

First could be supportive groups where members could be encouraged to share their difficulties, suggest useful practical tips to each other and generally provide encouragement in the difficult task they undertake.

The second type of group could be supportive and informative — as above, but including a series of topics, perhaps introduced by guest speakers (e.g. Church and Linge, 1982) (see Table 10.4 for sample programme).

Third, there could be a training group. This could emphasise changing the carer, e.g. by teaching relaxation as a way of managing the tension felt from time to time, or in developing a psychological coping strategy (cf. Gilhooly, 1980); instead of thinking 'the situation is awful' to think 'the situation is pretty difficult, but I've coped for some time, and I can probably manage another two weeks until I get my holiday'. Some relatives, whilst being relieved physically of the burden of care by, say, a holiday admission, maintain the emotional burden, worrying about the elderly person continually; they can benefit from training in reducing the frequency of these negative thoughts, releasing them to enjoy their relief. At a different level, the training could teach the carer ways of coping with the elderly person — perhaps encouraging and reinforcing less dependent behaviour, using

Table 10.4: Sample Programme for a Support Group for Relatives Caring for Elderly People at Home

1. Introduction	
2. Psychology of ageing	— Clinical Psychologist
3. 'Confusion' and dementia	— Psychiatrist
4. Social services help available	— Social Worker
5. Nursing the elderly person at home	— Nursing Officer
6. Depression and bereavement	— Clinical Psychologist
7. Financial help available	— Welfare rights worker
8. Voluntary help available	— Organiser of 'Age Concern'
9. Coping with confusion (RO, reminiscence etc.)	— Clinical Psychologist
10. Helping each other	— Arranging further self-help meetings, etc.

straightforward behavioural techniques to maintain the elderly person's adaptive skills, using RO and reminiscence to facilitate communication (e.g. Davies, 1981, describes teaching a relative to use reminiscence to facilitate conversation with her disabled husband).

Holden and Woods (1982) caution that RO and other techniques need to be taught in the context of appropriate attitudes — the point of crisis is not the best time for such training! Our experience is that self-help, support and information are more likely to be acceptable to relatives in a group setting, although the information needs to be directly related to the person's own particular situation. Training is often better accomplished on an individual basis. Often there is considerable resistance to trying different strategies, perhaps because usually the person has been caring for some time and has developed their own ways of managing the person, which — however ineffectual — are better to hold on to than the uncertainty of trying a new approach with the risk of the problems becoming even worse. Thus there is a particular need for tailoring the approach to the individual situation.

Research on Relatives' Support

Fortunately, some investigation has been made of the issues regarding relatives' support (Collins, 1983). Eighty carers took part in a study comparing help given either individually, or in a group, or in writing. Two types of help were offered: support, mainly providing information about help available, the nature of the problems, etc.; and training, where behavioural techniques for changing the behaviour of both carer and dependants were taught to the carer. Individual sessions proved to be the most effective means of providing help, with group meetings being effective to a lesser extent. Training did not emerge as more beneficial than the supportive help. The relative lack of success of the training materials may be partly attributed to the brevity of training given (eight weeks), giving insufficient time for carers to assimilate several techniques and apply them satisfactorily. Collins reports that carers preferred topics related to information regarding actual physical and financial help, and seemed particularly uninterested in any form of self-help. Church and Linge (1982) similarly found that their carers' group found the information provided most helpful, with sharing problems with other relatives being rated as much less help. Meeting others with similar problems was seen as useful, however; many relatives are quite surprised to find they are not alone! The groups initiated both by Collins and by Church and Linge were quite structured and time-limited, with an emphasis on information giving. It may be that a group having the aim of facilitating mutual support, and using appropriate group-work methods to achieve this, would have a different impact on the carers involved.

Alternatives to Groups

The use of written materials is increasingly popular as a supplement to other methods — several books are available for relatives advising on the care of elderly people (e.g. Gray and Isaacs, 1979; Dartington, 1980; Gray and McKenzie, 1980; Gilleard and Watt, 1983; the Alzheimer's Disease Society publishes its own guide for carers and reading lists for both relatives and professionals). Groups should certainly not be viewed as the only way of working with relatives. Particularly in situations where relationships are difficult and there is a great deal of negative communication, individual sessions will be needed if any positive change is to occur.

The Elderly Person Alone in the Community

The elderly person alone in the community, with few friends or acquaintances, let alone relatives, poses significant problems. Yet this person is as likely as anyone else to suffer from the range of physical and mental-health problems. Effective care is much more difficult, for example the elderly dementing person living alone is unlikely to survive long in the community (Bergmann *et al.*, 1978). Yet it is relevant to consider whether the techniques of psychological management outlined in Chapter 8 are of potential value to this group.

Reality Orientation

Obviously 24-hour RO is inappropriate, but aspects of the communication approach can be useful for home helps, volunteers, neighbours and other visitors, seeking to have meaningful interaction with the elderly person. Memory aids can be encouraged, particularly building on those the person has habitually used. For example, Mrs P. had a large diary, by which she kept the daily paper, crossing out each day as it passed; visitors were encouraged to record their visits in the diary, which also served to remind her of which days she visited the day-centre, and when she should expect meals-on-wheels. Other patients have found signs and reminder notices helpful and useful. Important items should be kept in a particular place and this taught to the patient, e.g. placing the purse by the door. At day-centres RO sessions can be carried out — Greene *et al.* (1983) showed these to be effective on a twice-a-week basis in increasing verbal orientation.

Behavioural Approach

Here a careful analysis is needed of what problems the elderly person is having (or causing for others) and which of their needs they are not capable of meeting. The problem list must then be divided into those where change in the patient's behaviour might be possible, and those where a practical solution is needed (and of course those where perhaps more tolerance by the community might be possible). For instance, a problem of leaving a gas cooker on unlit might be modifiable by special training for a mildly demented person, or it might require replacement by an electric cooker, or in some circumstances neighbours might need to be informed that the patient was not in fact a particular risk.

Often practical solutions are conceivable, but the appropriate services are not available. For instance, say a patient can no longer cook for themselves, meals-on-wheels seven days a week may seem a realistic solution — but in may places simply are not available so often. Services are often provided that do not directly meet the need — seldom are services tailored to meet the individual problems. A major new development in community care for the elderly has been the demonstration that services can be made to fit the situation instead of vice versa (Challis and Davies, 1981).

Community care-workers are given a budget per client (initially two-thirds of the cost of a place in a residential home) to spend on reinforcing gaps in the informal and formal support network, identified through a problem-orientated assessment system. Rather than simply plugging-in the readily available services — which may be the quickest and easiest course of action in the first instance — professional time is spent carefully analysing the exact nature of the needs and setting up or encouraging ways of meeting those needs using a flexible combination of the established services, relatives and volunteers/neighbours (who can be paid a nominal sum for their services). In the long run it may be cheaper to pay the neighbour three doors down the street to provide a meal at weekends or to shop twice a week than to provide the statutory services, as well as perhaps more effectively meeting the need (Challis, Luckett and Chessum, 1983). In the project, care has been taken to reinforce the new way of working, to use experienced social workers — who are more confident in taking the risks such an approach does involve — and to give the elderly more priority in terms of skilled social work input. This has been assisted by peer review, careful documentation and manageable case-loads.

Results from a controlled evaluation are still emerging but are encouraging. For example, experimental cases were more likely to remain in their own homes and less likely to go into residential care, and had a lower death rate. Experimental cases reported higher morale, less loneliness and boredom, more social contact and more control over their lives and importantly a much increased perceived capacity to cope. In addition the cost per case for the experimental group was on average lower than for the control group, many more of whom entered residential care.

Clearly replications of this work in other settings are needed, but it does seem that some conclusions about the way in which elderly people at home alone should be helped are possible. Firstly services should be geared to the actual problems experienced; secondly informal resources should be used wherever possible — and recognised as important — not having their function removed by the 'professionals'; thirdly, the management of these cases is a skilled task, which can have far-reaching effects on the lives of the elderly people involved. Such approaches seem relevant to a situation in which full-time professional help may not be available as costs increase, with professionals being involved as catalysts of other resources.

Working with Voluntary Agencies

There are of course many agencies working with the elderly and their families. In the UK at least, health services and social services tend to be seen as responding to crises; is there any way of working with elderly people in the community before crisis point is reached? One possibility is to work alongside a voluntary agency, having contact with the whole range of elderly people, not just those who are experiencing particular problems in health or in coping. It is difficult to make generalisations here as in the UK the major voluntary agency, 'Age Concern', although having a central resource body, is basically organised at a local level and so huge differences exist in the way in which it operates. The experience of one of the authors with two different local Age Concerns may help illustrate how the practice of community psychology may be approached with elderly clients.

Project A

This Age Concern had a large city centre headquarters with a day-centre for frail elderly and a Pop-In centre for their fitter counterparts who did not require transport. In addition, other staff worked in various areas of the city facilitating the operation of luncheon clubs, day-centres, over-sixties clubs, volunteer visiting schemes, and so on. All the facilities were largely run by volunteers, with the paid staff often spending a fair amount of time supporting and co-ordinating the volunteers. Some day-centre staff were teenagers employed under various government schemes to provide work experience.

Involvement of the clinical psychologist with this work began in 1977; a weekly group session for elderly people with adjustment difficulties, in retirement, bereavement or relationships, was commenced in response to a need perceived by the Age Concern staff, who were encountering elderly people with such difficulties in the various Age Concern facilities. At the same time a monthly meeting for staff with the psychologist was set up, with the general aim to use it as a means of development and training. The adjustment group met for about three months with five or six members, dealing with problems of adjustment to physical disability and housing as well as the retirement, family and bereavement issues that had been anticipated. A staff member from Age Concern participated in the group in addition to the psychologist. The role of the group leader was to facilitate openness in sharing of problems, and to encourage mutual support and problem solving. One member, suffering from multiple physical illnesses, wrote after the group finished that the group's meetings 'gave me the courage to persevere . . .' Staff members began to discuss their clients with the psychologist, particularly where they were concerned how to counsel them. Some referred clients on to the psychologist for individual counselling sessions — the broad categories of presenting problems included lack of confidence in going out and marital difficulties, in addition to the problems mentioned above in relation to the group. One client had been referred from the local police and victim support scheme; she had been convicted of shoplifting, and had a number of family problems, as well as having a minor stroke. A few clients expressed ideas of being persecuted; here the person's anxiety and fear were dealt with rather than the ideas which seemed likely to be delusional. The psychologist's psychiatric colleagues had offered to assist in such cases, although in fact this never arose. Some of the clients were in fact volunteer helpers (usually elderly) with bereavement or other problems.

Staff training also developed; specific sessions on work with the elderly were held with the teenage workers mentioned above — in particular their response to elderly people was discussed, and the difficulties that some found initially in their interactions with them were explored. Sessions with the whole staff group also continued, including a session on 'positive approaches to mental health' on a pre-retirement course for the staff.

Involvement was extended to work with families caring for elderly relatives; counselling was provided on an individual basis for families, many of whom were known to Age Concern through their various day-centres. A ten-session 'course for carers' was set up with the aim of providing support for relatives on a group basis.

Another aspect of the work that should be mentioned is that the psychologist acted as a contact point between Age Concern and the psychogeriatric service, with some useful interchanges occurring in both directions, of clients and of information. Finally a number of discussions were held with staff on psychological issues relating to the operation of day-centres, lunch clubs and so on.

After this involvement had gone on for about 2½ years staff were invited to complete anonymously a questionnaire, asking them to rank various aspects of the work in order of importance and to indicate which areas needed more (or less) input, before making free comments about the service provided. There was considerable variation in opinion among the staff, the consensus order of priority is shown in Table 10.5.

Table 10.5: Order of Priority for Psychologist's Involvement as Perceived by Age Concern Staff

1. Individual counselling of elderly clients
2. Discussion of clients seen by Age Concern staff
3. Training and support of volunteers
4. Work with families
5. Training and support of Age Concern staff
6. Discussion of psychological issues relating to the running of day-centres and lunch clubs
7. Group work with elderly clients
8. Liaison with psychogeriatric unit

Regarding the amount of input provided, almost without exception more input was requested in each category! Several staff commented similarly that the amount of time available (1–3 hours per week) needed to be increased. This project demonstrated the variety of roles for a clinical psychologist in a voluntary agency — and the positive reception often to be found outside institutional settings. In view of the limited time available it is regrettable that individual counselling was seen as so important — a more efficient use of resources would of course emphasise even more the training and support of staff in their own counselling skills.

Project B

The second Age Concern where one of the authors came to be involved is again in a city area, but with a much less centralised basis for its operations. In this area day-centre facilities are provided by the local authority, so this Age Concern has concentrated more on co-ordinating a number of projects, some providing practical support for elderly people at home, Pop Ins, a club for elderly people who have suffered strokes, and so on. Fortuitously at the time the Age Concern was approached regarding a possible input of a clinical psychology service it was beginning to plan a mental-health project, partly funded by a local mental-health voluntary body. The psychologist was thus able to join the project at the planning stage. One of the most exciting features of the project was the collaboration between health and social services and the voluntary agency; with the project being under the auspices of the voluntary agency, much of the usual bureaucracy could be circumvented, and in a relatively short space of time the project got off the ground.

The project is based in a converted shop-front, formerly used as a doctor's surgery, in a busy street, well situated for public transport. The centre consists of an office, a small Pop-In lounge and a meeting room. The Pop-In lounge is manned by volunteers and is open to any elderly person to drop in for a cup of tea and a chat. The two workers at the centre take referrals from a variety of sources including self-referral of clients with mental-health difficulties. This broad remit covers elderly people who feel lonely and isolated, bereaved elderly people, elderly people who have been mugged or robbed, families caring for an elderly person, etc. The workers visit clients at home, and often encourage and/or enable them (by providing transport) to visit the centre where they can mix with the 'normal' elderly people who drop in and with others with similar problems. Relatives' support groups are held regularly, with a choice of times to accommodate relatives who have a job.

Self-help is a key feature of the centre's approach. For example, a group has developed its own small 'granny sitting' service, where retired nurses sit with the elderly person to allow the relatives some relief. Another illustration is provided by Mr F., aged 71, who began attending a relatives' support group; he was referred by the psychiatric hospital where his wife, severely cognitively impaired following several strokes, was a day patient, with fairly frequent admissions to give Mr F. relief. The major difficulties he experienced at home related to her repeatedly calling his name, despite him being with her, or repeating herself time after time, and also nocturnal disturbance, so that he rarely got a good night's rest. The group was a great help to him — he had looked after his wife for many years, giving up his job to do so, and was becoming less fit himself.

At the end of one group session he commented that 'it helps just to talk it over with people who understand because they're going through it themselves'. A few months later his wife died in hospital, but Mr F. continued attending the group and discussed his loss there. He offered his services as a volunteer at the centre, as a volunteer driver initially and later on as a visitor to some of the lonely or bereaved clients. He continues to attend the relatives' support group, now more as a counsellor, and has been able to offer valuable support particularly to husbands caring for wives with dementia. He has commented that the centre has been a life-line for him since his bereavement — without it his life would have been almost completely empty as he had devoted more and more time over the years to the care of his wife, losing friends and interests and social life as he did so. The centre he feels gives him a great deal of social contact and most importantly a feeling of worth and purpose, of being needed and useful. Some of the other volunteers have a history of depression; to them too the centre provides a role they can feel is meaningful — many describe it as their 'job'. It is not then only among those designated as 'clients' that such a centre can operate.

Support for the workers is provided by local authority and hospital social workers and by a clinical psychologist; there is regular opportunity for discussion of clients, aims and difficulties. The psychologist led the relatives' support groups jointly with one of the social workers, until the Age Concern workers acquired the necessary skills and confidence to allow the psychologist to take on a consultative role with respect to the groups.

The centre also acts as a mental-health resource for the remainder of the local Age Concern organisation, which can seek advice and information and pass on clients. In addition regular training sessions on mental health of the elderly are held at the centre for all the Age Concern staff — covering topics such as dementia, bereavement and depression. These are led by the clinical psychologist and a hospital social worker, and emphasise the application of any information given to the particular elderly people with whom each member of staff has experience.

Neither of these two projects is intended as a model for clinical psychology practice with the elderly in the community. They do illustrate however how some of the features of community psychology as highlighted by Bender (1976) can be applied to the elderly.

1. Serving the interests of the client/consumer rather than those of the profession or its employees.

Both projects have sought to be flexible, both in identifying needs and in meeting them — an exercise often more fruitful outside the bureaucracy of health and social services. In the sense that the agencies have been the consumer of the service again there have been regular reviews of the most useful way of operating.

2. Mental illness not regarded in isolation from its familial and social nexus; more involvement of relatives in treatment.

The emphasis on work with families has been evident in both centres and, although there was some emphasis on individual counselling in project A, the focus was much more on interpersonal relationships even then than on seeking to treat mental disorder as if it were simply within the person in isolation from their social context.

3. Facilities should be near the client's home and geared towards local needs.

Both projects were clearly sited in the community from where the clients were drawn, and were thus more likely to detect and respond to the needs of that community.

4. Preventative services should be provided.

Both projects were offering help to clients at an earlier stage than traditional services — thus elderly people could come and talk over their bereavement long before the grief would have been regarded as pathologically abnormal and so within the psychiatric domain. The local police referred an elderly lady who had been mugged to project B. She was then visited within a day of the incident. A few days later she was still terrified to venture out alone and had stopped attending her local over 60s club. The worker encouraged her to regain the confidence to go out again alone before a week had elapsed. Possibly if help had not been available at such an early stage a more serious psychiatric disorder might have emerged some months later. Of course without proper empirical evaluation of a kind that would be quite difficult to undertake in practice, it cannot be claimed that these projects are necessarily preventative. Undoubtedly they certainly do offer help at a less severe level of distress than traditional services.

5. Psychological methods applied to a far greater variety of clients/consumers than previously.

Both projects were of course much more accessible to the elderly than conventional services, and there is no doubt that a a greater variety of clients were thus able to take advantage of them.

6. Involvement in planning and policy formation.

The psychologist was involved in the planning of project B and was able to be part of the policy-making group for that specific project, and indeed also sat on the management committee for the whole of the particular Age Concern organisation.

7. Development of consultant and skills-transmitter roles.

In both projects a major component was staff training, and discussion with Age Concern workers on particular clients on a consultant basis, both having the aim of improving the worker's own skill by imparting the psychologist's skills, approach and techniques. The psychologist is not then to have the monopoly of psychological skills.

8. Train non-professionals and traditional recipients of help.

The work with volunteers and the self-help nature of project B in particular illustrate this point. Mr F. provided a dramatic instance of an elderly 'client' becoming an effective and valuable counsellor.

9. Role of the psychologist becomes more diffuse.

The diffusion of role becomes apparent from the number of different roles adopted!

It is argued then, that community psychology with the elderly is attainable — in these instances through working alongside a voluntary agency. Other voluntary agencies may also be appropriate settings for such collaboration, e.g. Alzheimer's Disease Society groups.

Similar opportunities may be possible in primary care, particularly in practices where health visitors and district nurses attached to a group of general practitioners are involved with many elderly people. We know of at least one feasibility study of clinical psychological involvement in a general practitioner practice focusing on the elderly (Stirling, 1980) where individual counselling, work with relatives and consultancy with health visitors and district nurses proved possible.

These projects are of course as yet unevaluated, although it can be seen that there are strong indications that such approaches are an efficient way of spreading clinical psychology resources outside the traditional hospital settings. It should be added that there certainly are rewards in such projects for the psychologist; above all they have regular exposure to 'normal' elderly people and so gain a better view of the range of functioning and of resourcefulness of elderly people. Carrying out such work it is easier to internalise the knowledge that most elderly people do not become demented, that many continue to be fit and active and make a positive contribution to society in a wide variety of ways. Such projects provide excellent experience for the clinical psychologist in training as a counter to the back-wards full of demented elderly people that so often form the stereotype of work with the elderly.

Summary

1. A substantial proportion of the elderly needing care continue to live in the community. They may be supported by a complex informal network involving family and voluntary help from a variety of sources.

2. Families often do care and often do support their elder members. The task of all agencies is to attempt to support these supporters, who often experience considerable strain. This arises as much from the emotional demands of caring as the physical burden.

3. Coping requires attention to both the behavioural skills (what to *do* about it) and the cognitive skills (what to *think* about it) of the supporters.

4. Relatives should be given a clear basic description of the problems of the patient, what is wrong and its likely implications, in simple straightforward language.

5. Relatives' support groups can provide a focus for communication, and sharing of problems and support, both practical and emotional.

6. The elderly person living alone, with few or no relatives, poses considerable problems; innovative patterns of community care may be needed to avoid premature hospitalisation. Services need to be geared to the specific needs and risk factors of the particular patient's situation.

7. Voluntary agencies are a primary target for the spreading of the concepts of good psychological care for the community elderly. They are invaluable in helping the psychologist maintain a perspective of 'normal ageing'.

11 CONCLUSIONS

Clinical Psychology with the Elderly

We have attempted in this book to make the reader more aware of the potential application of psychology to improving the quality of life of the increasing number of elderly people in our society. In discussing the topics raised under various chapter headings there is an inevitable tendency to fragmentation — to lose the feeling of the integrated approach of a profession to a client group. In this chapter we will overview some of the ways in which a clinical psychological approach to the elderly might be structured. Some reference will be made to the personal and ethical issues which arise and we will conclude with some remarks on future developments.

Even at the risk of accusations of repetition it is worth reminding readers of the extent of the problems outlined in Chapter 1. The elderly form an ever-increasing proportion of our population. There will be a particular increase in the proportion of the very old (80 +) in the remaining years of this century. In the UK and other countries there is a growing recognition of the demands these increases will place on national resources, ranging from pensions to health care. In the UK guidelines for planning of services in the National Health Service emphasise the elderly as a priority client group. Massive expansion of services is needed to keep pace with the numbers of elderly people involved. It must be realised that provision of even the most basic care for the elderly is currently absent in a significant proportion of the comparatively well-developed United Kingdom. Adequate basic physical care is not available in many places, let alone effective attempts to improve, rather than just to maintain the quality of life.

In such a context many of the studies in earlier chapters reflect the questioning, attitudes and developments in good practice which are possible in the more developed services. We would, however, argue strongly against those who would see an emphasis in the less well-developed locations on the establishment of purely physical resources for the care of the physical needs of the elderly. This book contains powerful evidence that effective care of the whole person is possible, incorporating psychological care into every phase of interaction with the client. The planning and development of new services provide exciting opportunities to avoid the worst mistakes of existing services, both in institutions and in the community.

Models of Psychological Practice

At this juncture it is interesting to examine what psychologists actually do when working with the elderly. It is apparent from comparisons of reports such as that of Gottesman (1977) and Mumford and Carpenter (1979) that roughly similar developments have occurred in the USA and UK despite vastly different patterns of social and health care. More recent publications (Jeffery and Saxby, 1984; Larner and Leeming, 1984), reflect an increasing maturity of development.

Clinical psychologists have constant problems with role models. One can view extremes from the 'applied experimental scientist' to the 'informed practitioner' models. In the former case the psychologist is seen as the interface between rapidly expanding psychological knowledge and the client's needs. The psychologist will evaluate the problem, apply psychology and monitor outcome. Once a technique or model is established it will be 'sold' to those most capable of intelligent exploitation of its potential — care agent, nurse, psychiatrist. The psychologist moves on to the next problem. In contrast, the 'informed practitioner' will see continued 'hands-on' involvement with the client group as essential to effective professional work. Development of technique, research, evaluation are, perhaps, played down. Somewhere between these models lies an optimal role: the informed, aware, questioning practitioner.

Gottesman (1977) outlines a role model in work with the elderly in the USA:

1. Construction and administration of facts — particularly with regard to competence in daily living.
2. Therapy and Counselling
3. Development of treatment programmes — and taking on a major role in the team in their administration and management.
4. Working with community services in encouraging co-operation,

new approaches and in monitoring cost effectiveness.

5. Acting in relation to administrators as an interpreter of research findings, an advocate of the needs of individual clients and an agent of change in patterns of care.

In a recent paper Larner and Leeming (1984) describe the clinical work of a psychologist with the elderly in a geriatric setting in the UK using the following categories:

1. Cognitive assessment.
2. Behavioural assessment.
3. Disruptive 'problem' behaviours.
4. Lethargy and 'confusion'.
5. Training in the activities of daily living.
6. Personal distress and behavioural psychotherapy.
7. Advice on overall management strategies.

Leng (1982b) describes similar categories in relation to the role of a clinical psychologist in a psychogeriatric setting: psychological assessments, behavioural modification, behavioural psychotherapy, and management, rehabilitation and training.

There are a number of common elements in these role models which may be extracted and used as a basis for discussion. One of the consequences of the pressure to develop services for the elderly is the increasing number of administrators defining roles for professions of which they have little knowledge, or even psychologists from other areas of activity looking for advice on the best method of work in relation to a client group of which they may have little awareness.

What considerations should apply to those evolving a role? We have listed some areas of activity which should of course be considered and which have been discussed in detail in previous chapters. However, any psychologist contemplating involvement with the elderly should, in addition, be actively encouraged to stand back from and evaluate patterns of interaction in other clinical areas. In many countries a good example is in work with the mentally handicapped. The impact of more powerful evaluation and intervention techniques and the concepts of normalisation have led to substantial role changes in relation to that client group. There is an increasing international emphasis on effective community care and an emphasis on professional interaction as members of a resource team. In this way it is possible to catalyse and co-ordinate, initiate and monitor. A wide range of resources, individual, family, voluntary and professional agencies, can be mobilised and their effectiveness evaluated. Perhaps, similar models are more appropriate to work with the elderly than purely one-to-one or small group work with time-intensive contact by the psychologist.

In defining the role of clinical psychology with the elderly it is important then not just to consider particular activities such as assessment and treatment, but also to consider the various settings in which the work may take place, and the level at which the work is carried out. Of the examples given above, Gottesman (1977) comes closest to addressing these issues.

A complete psychological service to the elderly must operate in a number of settings at a variety of levels. For example, Twining and Chapman (1983) describe their input to a geriatric medicine department, including acute in-patient care, day-hospital and community work, rehabilitation units and long-term care. A similar range of settings is available in the psychogeriatric sector. Then there are Social Services facilities — residential, day-care, domiciliary, before considering the voluntary sector. The problem seems at times not so much what to do, but where to begin!

In the USA and elsewhere different patterns of service provision apply. The important principle is that elderly people seldom fit neatly into whatever administrative boundaries are drawn, and so psychological services need to be developed that are not confined by the artificial barriers between care agencies of various types. Often, in fact, the psychologist can assist in liaison between different agencies, and help dispel the fears and fantasies that each may develop about the other. In the UK it is relatively easy for an NHS clinical psychologist to undertake work outside the hospital setting — in social services, primary health care or with a voluntary agency. In some areas, posts have been jointly funded by the NHS and Social Services, which greatly facilitates this flexibility. In the USA there are major difficulties in funding posts that are so wide-ranging, with community mental health centres reducing services to the elderly and psychologists being ineligible for direct reimbursement under Medicare for the provision of treatment to the elderly (Roybal, 1984).

An implication of the range of possible settings where clinical psychology might be applied to the problems of the elderly is that work with individual elderly clients should be seen as a limited part of the psychologist's role (Jeffery and Saxby, 1984). We feel it is worth maintaining some individual contact; apart from any benefit to the clients concerned, it helps the psychologist retain credibility, provides refreshment and encourages humility, in their attempts to work at other levels. Group-work, with relatives or a group of elderly people lacking confidence, say, may be time-saving over individual treatment, and may also benefit clients by their receiving peer support.

The second level of work is carried out through others, the psychologist acting in a consultative capacity, as an adviser to the team. This does not only apply to treatment programmes, but also to advising other staff on the psychological assessment they carry out, to advising on research, acting as an 'information resource in gerontology' and emphasising the environmental contribution to behaviour (Garland, 1983).

The third level overlaps with the second, and involves teaching and training. Informal teaching is often an important component of the consultative role. Many more formal teaching opportunities arise or can be developed, again across a range of settings and a range of disciplines. To spread their sphere of influence, psychologists must be prepared to pass on, in a relevant manner, psychological skills, approaches and techniques appropriate for particular staff to use in their work with the elderly.

The final level seems the furthest removed from direct contact with clients. Psychologists need to become involved in the planning, monitoring and development of services for the elderly. Psychological care needs to be an integral part of service provision, not tagged on as an afterthought. Psychologists have a particular responsibility to argue for services that are geared to individual's assessed needs, and that are satisfactorily evaluated to ensure they do serve the purpose intended. In these days of scarce resources it is essential that they are used rationally and effectively.

At each level of operation, opportunities for the application of the psychologist's research skills will be manifold. There are so many unanswered questions in this field, it is difficult to avoid promising lines of enquiry of a theoretical or a more applied nature.

In any individual case the role adopted will depend on the interaction of the work environment and the individual's experience. Whilst the overall needs of the client group may demand a multi-level input to many settings, it may be a disaster for an inexperienced psychologist to overstretch their potential in responding initially to the total demand of the setting. As in most psychological work, a clear evaluation of the problem with defined and attainable goals should help to avoid unrealistic expectancies and frustration. It is regrettable that too often in the UK freshly qualified clinical psychologists are expected to provide a service for the elderly single-handed. This can only too easily lead to individual assessment and treatment becoming a major part of the role, as the more wide-ranging levels of work described above often require a greater degree of experience and expertise. Of course, once a role expectation has been created it can be very difficult to abandon!

The formation in many countries of 'special interest groups' of those interested in the application of psychology to the elderly has been extremely helpful. Such groups, often involving many varied professions as well as psychologists, provide a useful forum for the exchange of information of many kinds. The Psychologist's Interest Group in the Elderly (PSIGE) of the British Psychological Society Division of Clinical Psychology is a good example of such a group. This exchange can range from the more academic/scientific presentation to the subtle assistance of a supportive nature which can be given to the individual attempting to apply psychological principles in an uncaring, unconvinced or possibly even hostile environment. In an area where the applications of psychological concepts are new and untried, it can be well to guard against the problems of overenthusiasm and overoptimism. Much can be and has been achieved, but the psychologist must apply psychology to the whole situation in order to provide an effective resource for the client.

We then would see the psychologist working with the elderly carefully evolving a cost-effective role. This should aim to apply the whole range of psychological findings to the client group, never losing the questioning and evaluative approach. It should include a contribution to the assessment of the client in their context in the broadest sense; application of intervention procedures to client and care situations; a consultative and teaching role; involvement in development and planning of services and experimental evaluation of their effectiveness. The psychologist is often well placed to work across traditional professional and agency boundaries but is well advised to avoid the perils of battles which cannot be won with a weak resource base. A good rule of thumb is to begin by working with the organisationally healthy parts of the system, to develop alliances with others with a similar point of view, and to resist attempts for the new psychologist to take on the most difficult ward in the hospital!

Finally we cannot emphasise too much the multi-disciplinary nature of work with the elderly (Eisdorfer, 1983; Twining and Chapman, 1983). Team-work is paramount.

Personal and Ethical Issues

Any form of work in the caring professions can be personally demanding. In this respect work with elderly clients is not unique in the problems that may be caused for the individual. The so-called 'culture-shock' phenomenon is occasionally encountered in the individual who suddenly meets the reality of a group of 'demented-incontinent-smelly' elderly in some ill-organised back-ward of the local hospital. An even greater shock may come from the realisation that the staff involved cannot or do not want to do anything to change the system.

These personal and ethical issues cannot be ignored. The personal problems must be dealt with by supervisors and colleagues. Unfortunately, even now, specific experience with elderly clients is not an essential component of training for clinical psychologists. Our experience is that many trainees can and do avoid all but casual contacts within their formal training. The increasing importance of work with the elderly makes this situation highly unsatisfactory. All clinical psychology training courses should and must in the near future include credible academic and practical components on work with the elderly. This could well avoid the traumatic experiences of some who first approach the client group at a later stage in professional development.

There is a role in personal support for the 'special interest groups' mentioned in an earlier section. Whether the problem is with client, the family or the system, the burden on the individual is better handled by sharing it with other peers in the profession. Often a post in work with the elderly can be a very lonely one with no immediate colleagues from one's own profession to call upon for advice. It is also valuable to develop contact with 'normal', coping elderly people in the community, to maintain a perspective of what old age can be like, outside the hospital or old people's home.

Ethical issues arise in work with the elderly in much the same way as with other client groups. The broader aspects of ethics are well covered in professional publications such as those of the British Psychological Society and American Psychological Association (Stolz, 1978). Typical of statements made are the 'why should we bother — they will die anyway' — 'let her die in peace' variety. A recent question to one of the authors — 'how would you define quality of life for a demented person' — raises a different level of argument, but one equally surrounded by ethical issues.

Answers to these questions are not easy to provide or to communicate to the questioner. In an atmosphere where for many years the main aim has been 'caring' and a physical emphasis has predominated, it is undoubtedly difficult to change ingrained attitudes of care-givers. The attitudes of society to their elderly have been referred to in earlier chapters, the myths surrounding ageing abound and it will take a concerted effort to change them.

In this context it is perhaps again appropriate to look at experience with other groups where patterns and emphases of care have changed. The mentally handicapped are an example where many of the battles to change attitudes, which commenced in the 1960s, are being won. Families, care-givers and society seem to be taking, albeit slowly, the themes of normalisation into their day-to-day approaches to their 'clients'. There is much to learn from the experiences of those who have changed attitudes in one care area that we might well apply to our work with the elderly. The questions are very similar: 'Why disturb that multiply handicapped child with a communications programme — they'll never learn', or 'Put the community handicap base anywhere but Acacia Grove — we know these people need care, but not here!' The answers in short-term persuasion and long-term education may be very similar.

Holden and Woods (1982, pp. 248–51) discuss in detail the ethical issues involved in work with dementing patients. This is a complex area, as usually the dementia prevents the person giving 'informed consent'. There is a need for greater advocacy of the rights of dementing people to be treated as *people*, and to be allowed to live as normal a life as possible, to be involved in valued activities and experiences. Psychological intervention with carers and with non-dementing elderly people presents fewer ethical problems. They are able to ask for help (or to refuse it) in order to cope with their particular difficulties.

Developments in the Clinical Psychology of the Elderly

One of the more exciting observations which we can report as we conclude our overview of this area is the upsurge of interest, as evidenced by a rapid increase in the quantity and quality of psychological research. There was a slow start to serious studies in the 1960s and a maintenance of momentum during the 1970s. However, the early 1980s have seen a dramatic increase in both basic and applied research in ageing. To see the formation of new units for research in ageing in the UK and USA in a time of economic difficulty is heartening and their output should have a useful impact on practice in the future.

In previous chapters we have tried to identify and monitor various lines of development and will not attempt to summarise any other than some basic and important trends which we feel are worth observing. The increase in knowledge of the basic age-related changes in the normal individual will have a fundamental effect on clinical practice. To give an example: in the area of cognitive ability the work of Rabbitt promises to get behind the vague generalisations of earlier work on intellectual change to the individual components and control systems of cognitive function, their nature and variability. Such work, if successful, will enable clinicians to be much more precise in assessment and intervention in the individual case.

Work of this nature is also increasing our understanding of the disorders such as dementia where more precise knowledge of psychological factors must assist in effective care. In relation to personality and adjustment, the reformulation of approaches outlined in provocative reviews such as that by Rorer and Wigider (1983) is likely both to assist in the interpretation of work in the past, but also and more usefully to suggest new directions for research which will enable personality theory to have a more powerful impact on care-planning.

Psychological interventions with the elderly will benefit from the above basic research. There is an ever-present need to avoid ossification of ideas and applications. The use of intervention techniques should be a dynamic process monitored by studies of process and cost-effectiveness. There is an ever-present danger of static established techniques emerging with a spurious respectability based on little or no hard evidence. Those working with the elderly must not allow themselves to be divorced from the methods and insights of work in clinical psychology with other client groups.

The growth of interest in *practice*, as well as in research, is also encouraging. A significant proportion of clinical psychologists in the UK (estimated at between 5 and 10 per cent) now show an interest in work with elderly clients. This interest is founded probably not just on a realisation of the growing need, but also on a recognition of the possibilities for innovation and new developments, of a speciality that can encompass the whole field of psychological endeavour from neuropsychology to psychotherapy. The interest and enthusiasm of those working in the field is beginning to have an impact, through their involvement in training and in encouraging the profession as a whole to take the elderly seriously as a client group. The availability of funds in the UK specifically for work with the elderly has also helped!

In the last ten years job opportunities for clinical psychologists working with the elderly have increased dramatically in the UK. What prevents the even greater development of the speciality is a vicious circle involving negative attitudes, training in the elderly not being mandatory, and lack of good training placements. As we saw in Chapter 1, students come on to clinical psychology training courses biased against work with the elderly; because training in work with the elderly is not compulsory, they can avoid direct contact that could well change their attitudes; training in work with the elderly cannot yet be made compulsory as there are insufficient good training placements; there are insufficient good placements because students are not exposed to the elderly during training and so do not consider it as a career choice. Similar training problems arise in the USA (Birren, 1983). Storandt (1983) points out that few clinical or counselling psychology training programmes in the USA include a course on the psychology of ageing, let alone practical experience with the elderly.

In addition to compulsory training with the elderly prior to qualification, there is a great need for continuing education, for those already in the profession, particularly where their work involves some contact with elderly clients. Although we want to see many more specialists working full-time with the elderly — in order to develop the field further, create more training opportunities and so on — in practice many clinical psychologists combine work with the elderly with commitments to other client groups (Garland, 1983; Storandt, 1983). It might be considered ageist to suggest that generic practitioners need additional knowledge or skills to work with the elderly (Lawton and Gottesman, 1974). It will be clear from this book that, whilst we see many areas in common with other client groups, there are sufficient special considerations for clinical psychology with the elderly to be considered a distinct speciality in its own right. It will, however, benefit from the involvement of those working with other client groups, who can help prevent it becoming cut off and isolated from mainstream psychology.

Whilst in the USA there are many employment opportunities for psychologists with the elderly (Chatfez, Ochs, Tate and Niederehe, 1982), major problems exist in finding posts in nursing homes and so on (Salamon, 1983). Roybal (1984) suggests that psychologists need to be able to demonstrate their cost-effectiveness in relation to existing provisions, if they are ultimately to gain reimbursement through Medicare. Storandt (1983) suggests that masters level psychology graduates could play a useful and cost-effective role in direct services for the elderly. A national health insurance programme could overcome some of these funding difficulties (Neugarten, 1983).

In Conclusion

It is the firm belief of the authors that psychology and particularly clinical psychology has much to offer in relation to the effective care of the elderly, in collaboration with other disciplines. The earlier chapters contain clear evidence of a substantial and cost-effective contribution. As psychological knowledge increases, the efficiency and effectiveness of that contribution will grow. A major task of the clinical psychologist working with the elderly must be to communicate the value of the contribution to quality of life which can be made through the application of psychological principles by all concerned with the care of the elderly.

Are there rewards from work with this age group — 'a dead end job with no future' as it was cynically described to one of us? There are indeed rewards that quickly become apparent; sometimes in the obvious appreciation of a job well done, sometimes in a small step forward by a patient or an institution; sometimes in being able to see the resources, as well as the problems, of our elders; sometimes in the sheer variety of the work, with its tremendous scope for innovation. We have a responsibility to the elderly to ensure that their ability to enjoy as normal a life as possible, to the full, is maintained throughout the whole life span.

REFERENCES

Abrams, M. (1978) *Beyond three-score and ten: a first report on a survey of the elderly*, Age Concern Research Unit, Mitcham, Surrey

Abramson, L. Y., Seligman, M. E. P. and Teasdale, J. D. (1978) 'Learned helplessness in humans: critique and reformulation', *Journal of Abnormal Psychology*, **87**, 49–74

Acker, W. (1980) 'In support of microcomputer based automated testing: a description of the Maudsley Automated Psychological Screening Tests (MAPS)', *British Journal on Alcohol and Alcoholism*, **15**, 144–7

Adams, D. L. (1969) 'Analysis of a life satisfaction index', *Journal of Gerontology*, **24**, 470–4

Adams, J., Davies, J. E. and Northwood, J. (1979) 'Ridge Hill — a home, not a ward', *Nursing Times*, **75**, 1659–61, 1725–6, 1769–70

Age Concern (1977) *Profiles of the elderly. Volume 2: Their health and the Health Services*, Age Concern Research Unit, Mitcham, Surrey

Akiskal, H. S. and McKinney, W. T. (1975) 'Overview of recent research in depression', *Archives of General Psychiatry*, **32**, 285–305

Albert, M. L. (1980) 'Language in normal and dementing elderly' in L. K. Obler and M. L. Albert (eds.), *Language and communication in the elderly: clinical, therapeutic and experimental issues*, Lexington Books, Lexington, Mass., pp. 145–50

Albert, M. S. (1981) 'Geriatric neuropsychology', *Journal of Consulting and Clinical Psychology*, **49**, 835–50

———, Butters, N. and Brandt, J. (1981) 'Patterns of remote memory in amnesic and demented patients', *Archives of Neurology*, **38**, 495–500

Ankus, M. and Quarrington, B. (1972) 'Operant behaviour in the memory disordered', *Journal of Gerontology*, **27**, 500–10

Apfeldorf, M. and Hunley, P. J. (1971) 'The adjective check-list approach to older institutionalised men', *Journal of Personality Assessment*, **35**, 457–62

Arenberg, D. (1974) 'A longitudinal study of problem solving in adults', *Journal of Gerontology*, **29**, 650–8

——— (1982) 'Changes with age in problem solving' in F. I. M. Craik and S. Trehub (eds.), *Ageing and cognitive processes*, Plenum Press, New York, pp. 221–36

Arie, T. (ed.) (1981) *Health care of the Elderly*, Croom Helm, London

Atkinson, R. C. and Shiffrin, R. M. (1971) 'The control of short-term memory', *Scientific American*, **225**, 82

Averill, J. R. and Wisocki, P. A. (1981) 'Some observations on behavioural approaches to the treatment of grief among the elderly' in H. J. Sobel (ed.), *Behavior therapy in terminal care: a humanistic approach*, Ballinger, Cambridge, Massachusetts, pp. 125–50

Baddeley, A. (1981) 'The concept of working memory: a view of its current state and probable future development', *Cognition*, **10**, 17–23

———, Sunderland, A. and Harris, J. (1982) 'How well do laboratory-based psychological tests predict patients' performance outside the laboratory?' in S. Corkin, K. L. Davis, J. H. Growdon, E. Usdin and R. J. Wurtman (eds.), *Alzheimer's Disease: a report of progress*, (Ageing, Volume 19), Raven Press, New York, pp. 141–8

Baikie, E. (1984) 'Sexuality and the elderly' in I. Hanley and J. Hodge (eds.),

Psychological Approaches to the Care of the Elderly, Croom Helm, London

Bailey, J. and Coppen, A. (1976) 'A comparison between the Hamilton rating scale and the Beck inventory in the measurement of depression', *British Journal of Psychiatry*, **128**, 486–9

Baltes, M. M. and Barton, C. M. (1977) 'New approaches to ageing: a case for the operant model', *Educational Gerontology*, **2**, 383–405

——, Burgess, R. L. and Stewart, R. B. (1980) 'Independence and dependence in self-care behaviours in nursing home residents: an operant-observational study', *International Journal of Behavioural Development*, **3**, 489–500

——, Honn, S., Barton, E. M., Orzech, M. and Lago, D. (1983) 'On the social ecology of dependence and independence in elderly nursing home residents: a replication and extension', *Journal of Gerontology*, **38**, 556–64

Baltes, P. B. (1968) 'Longitudinal and cross-sectional sequences in the study of age and generational effects', *Human Development*, **11**, 145–71

—— and Schaie, K. W. (1976) 'On the plasticity of intelligence in adulthood and old age: where Horn and Donaldson fail', *American Psychologist*, **31**, 720–5

—— and Willis, S. L. (1979) 'The critical importance of appropriate methodology in the study of ageing: the sample case of psychometric intelligence', in F. Hoffmeister and C. Muller (eds.), *Brain function in old age*, Springer-Verlag, Berlin, pp. 164–87

—— and —— (1982) 'Plasticity and enhancement of intellectual functioning in old age: Penn State's Adult Development and Enrichment Project (ADEPT)' in F. I. M. Craik and S. Trehub (eds.), *Ageing and cognitive processes*, Plenum Press, New York, pp. 353–89

Barraclough, B. M. (1971) 'Suicide in the elderly' in D. W. K. Kay and A. Walk (eds.), *Recent Developments in Psychogeriatrics*, British Journal of Psychiatry, Special Publication No. 6

Barrett, T. R. and Wright, M. (1981) 'Age-related facilitation in recall following semantic processing', *Journal of Gerontology*, **36**, 194–9

Beaumont, J. G. (1981) 'Microcomputer aided assessment using standards psychometric procedures', *Behaviour Research Methods and Instrumentation*, **13**, 430–3

Beck, A. T. (1967) *Depression: Clinical, Experimental and Therapeutic Aspects*, Staple Press, London

—— (1973) *The Diagnosis and Management of Depression*, University of Pennsylvania Press, Philadelphia

Bellak, L. and Bellak, S. S. (1973) *Manual for the Senior Apperception Test (S.A.T.)*, CPS, Larchmont, New York

Bellucci, G. and Hoyer, W. J. (1975) 'Feedback effects on the performance and self reinforcing behaviour of elderly and young adult women', *Journal of Gerontology*, **30**, 456–60

Bender, M. P. (1976) *Community Psychology*, Methuen, London

Bennett-Levy, J. and Powell, G. E. (1980) 'The subjective memory questionnaire (SMQ). An investigation into the self-reporting of 'real life' memory skills', *British Journal of Social and Clinical Psychology*, **19**, 177–88

Benton, A. L., Eslinger, P. J. and Damasio, A. R. (1981) 'Normative observations on neuropsychological test performances in old age', *Journal of Clinical Neuropsychology*, **3**, 33–42

Berger, R. M. and Rose, S. D. (1977) 'Interpersonal skill training with institutionalised elderly patients', *Journal of Gerontology*, **32**, 346–53

Bergmann, K. (1971) 'The neuroses of old age' in D. W. K. Kay and A. Walk (eds.), *Recent Developments in Psychogeriatrics*, British Journal of Psychiatry, Special Publication No. 6

—— (1978) 'Neurosis and personality disorder in old age' in A. D. Isaacs and F. Post (eds.), *Studies in Geriatric Psychiatry*, Wiley, New York, pp. 41–76

——— (1979) 'How to keep the family supportive', *Geriatric Medicine*, pp. 53–57
——— (1982) 'Depression in the elderly' in B. Isaacs (ed.), *Recent Advances in Geriatric Medicine* — 2, Churchill Livingstone, Edinburgh, pp. 159–82
———, Britton, P. G., Hall, E. H. and Blessed, G. (1981) 'The relationship of ageing, physical ill health, brain damage and affective disorder' in W. M. Beattie (ed.), *Ageing: a Challenge to Science and Society 2*, Oxford University Press, Oxford
———, Foster, E. M., Justice, A. W. and Matthews, V. (1978) 'Management of the demented elderly patient in the community', *British Journal of Psychiatry*, **132**, 441–9
———, Kay, D. W. K., Foster, E., McKechnie, A. A. and Roth, M. (1971) 'A follow up study of randomly selected community residents to assess the effects of chronic brain syndrome and cerebrovascular disease', *Proceedings of the Vth World Congress of Psychiatry, Mexico*, Psychiatry (Part II), pp. 856–65
———, Manchee, V. and Woods, R. T. (1983) 'Family bonds — the main visible means of support', Paper presented at Psychiatry Section of Royal Society of Medicine, London
Bigot, A. (1974) 'The relevance of American life-satisfaction indices for research on British subjects before and after retirement', *Age and Ageing*, **3**, 113–21
Birchmore, T. and Clague, S. (1983) 'A behavioural approach to reduce shouting', *Nursing Times*, **79** (20th April), 37–9
Birkhill, W. R. and Schaie, K. W. (1975) 'The effect of differential reinforcement of cautiousness in intellectual performance among the elderly', *Journal of Gerontology*, **30**, 578–83
Birren, J. E. (1964) *The Psychology of Ageing*, Prentice-Hall, Englewood Cliffs, NJ
——— (1983) 'Ageing in America: roles for psychology', *American Psychologist*, **38**, 298–9
——— and Sloane, R. B. (1980) *Handbook of Mental Health and Ageing*, Prentice-Hall, Englewood Cliffs, NJ
———, Woods, A. M. and Williams, M. V. (1979) 'Speed of behaviour as an indicator of age changes and the integrity of the nervous system' in F. Hoffmeister and C. Muller (eds.), *Brain Function in Old Age*, Springer-Verlag, Berlin
Blessed, G., Tomlinson, B. E. and Roth, M. (1968) 'The association between quantitative measures of dementia and of senile change in the cerebral grey matter of elderly subjects', *British Journal of Psychiatry*, **114**, 797–811
Blum, J. E., Fosshage, J. L. and Jarvik, L. F. (1972) 'Intellectual changes and sex differences in octogenarians: a twenty-year longitudinal study of ageing', *Developmental Psychology*, **7**, 178–87
Bolton, N., Britton, P. G. and Savage, R. D. (1966) 'Some normative data on the WAIS and its indices in an aged population', *Journal of Clinical Psychology*, **22**, 184–8
———, Savage, R. D. and Roth, M. (1967) 'The MWLT on an aged psychiatric population', *British Journal of Psychiatry*, **113**, 1139–40
Botwinick, J. (1977) 'Intellectual abilities' in J. E. Birren and K. W. Schaie (eds.), *Handbook of the Psychology of Ageing*, Van Nostrand Reinhold, Cincinnati
——— (1978) *Ageing and Behaviour*, Springer, New York
——— and Birren, J. E. (1963) 'Cognitive processes: mental abilities and psychomotor processes in healthy aged men' in J. E. Birren *et al.* (eds.), *Human Ageing: A Biological and Behavioural Study*, Government Printing Office, Washington DC
——— and Storandt, M. (1974) *Memory, Related Functions and Age*, Charles C. Thomas, Springfield, Illinois
———and ——— (1980) 'Recall and recognition of old information in relation to

age and sex', *Journal of Gerontology*, **35**, 70–6

———, West, R. and Storandt, M. (1978) 'Predicting death from behavioural test performance', *Journal of Gerontology*, **33**, 755–62

Bower, H. M. (1967) 'Sensory stimulation and the treatment of senile dementia', *Medical Journal of Australia*, **1**, 1113–19

Bowles, N. L. and Poon, L. W. (1982) 'An analysis of the effect of ageing on recognition memory', *Journal of Gerontology*, **37**, 212–19

Breitner, J. C. S. and Folstein, M. F. (1984) 'Familial Alzheimer's Dementia: a prevalent disorder with specific clinical features', *Psychological Medicine*, **14**, 63–80

Brewin, C. R. and Shapiro, D. A. (1984) 'Beyond locus of control: attribution of responsibility for positive and negative outcomes', *British Journal of Psychology*, **75**, 43–9

Britton, P. G. (1967) 'An investigation of cognitive and personality functions in a sample of the aged in the community', Unpublished PhD dissertation, University of Newcastle upon Tyne

——— and Savage, R. D. (1966a) 'The MMPI and the aged: some normative data from a community sample', *British Journal of Psychiatry*, **112**, 941–3

——— and ——— (1966b) 'A short form of the WAIS for use with the aged', *British Journal of Psychiatry*, **112**, 417–18

Broadbent, D. E., Cooper, P. F., Fitzgerald, P. and Parkes, K. R. (1982) 'The Cognitive Failures Questionnaire and its correlates', *British Journal of Clinical Psychology*, **21**, 1–16

Broadhurst, A. (1981) 'Working with families of elderly in the community', Paper presented at PSIGE Annual Conference, Leicester

Brody, E. M., Cole, C. and Moss, M. (1973) 'Individualising therapy for the mentally impaired aged', *Social Casework*, pp. 453–61

———, Johnsen, P., Fulcomer, M. C. and Lang, A. M. (1983) 'Women's changing roles and help to elderly parents: attitudes of three generations of women', *Journal of Gerontology*, **38**, 597–607

———, Kleban, M. H., Lawton, M. P. and Moss, M. (1974) 'A longitudinal look at excess disabilities in the mentally impaired aged', *Journal of Gerontology*, **29**, 79–84

———, ———, ——— and Silverman, H. A. (1971) 'Excess disabilities of mentally impaired aged: impact of individualised treatment', *Gerontologist*, **11**, 124–33

Brody, M. B. (1942) 'The Measurement of dementia', *Journal of Mental Science*, **88**, 317–27

Bromley, D. B. (1974) *The Psychology of Human Ageing* (2nd edition), Penguin, London

——— (1978) 'Approaches to the study of personality changes in adult life and old age' in A. D. Isaacs and F. Post (eds.), *Studies in Geriatric Psychiatry*, J. Wiley, Chichester

Brook, P., Degun, G. and Mather, M. (1975) 'Reality orientation, a therapy for psychogeriatric patients: a controlled study', *British Journal of Psychiatry*, **127**, 42–5

Bruce, P. R., Coyne, A. C. and Botwinick, J. (1982) 'Adult age differences in meta memory', *Journal of Gerontology*, **37**, 354–7

Bruckner, R. (1967) 'Longitudinal research on the eye', *Gerontologia Clinica*, **9**, 87–95

Buckholdt, D. R. and Gubrium, J. F. (1983) 'Therapeutic pretense in reality orientation', *International Journal of Ageing and Human Development*, **16**, 167–81

Burnside, I. (1979) 'Biofeedback', Paper presented at Introduction to Neuropsychology Conference, Yorkshire Branch of British Psychological Society, Clinical Division

Burrows, B. A., Jason, L. A., Quattrochi-Tubin, S. and Lavelli, M. (1981) 'Increasing activity of nursing home residents in their lounges using a physical design intervention and a prompting intervention', *Activities. Adaptation and Ageing*, **1**, 25–34

Burton, M. (1980) 'Evaluation and change in a psychogeriatric ward through direct observation and feedback', *British Journal of Psychiatry*, **137**, 566–71

—— (1982) 'Reality orientation for the elderly: a critique', *Journal of Advanced Nursing*, **7**, 427–33

—— and Spall, B. (1981) 'Contributions of the behavioural approach to nursing the elderly', *Nursing Times*, **77**(6), 247–8

Busse, E. W. and Blazer, D. G. (1980) 'The theories and processes of ageing', in E. W. Busse and D. G. Blazer (eds.), *Handbook of Geriatric Psychiatry*, Van Nostrand Reinhold, New York, pp. 3–27

Butler, R. N. (1963) 'The life review: an interpretation of reminiscence in the aged', *Psychiatry*, **26**, 65–76

—— (1975) *Why Survive: Being Old in America*, Harper and Row, New York

—— and Lewis M. I. (1973) *Ageing and Mental Health*, Mosby, St Louis

Butters, N. and Cermak, L. S. (1980) *Alcoholic Korsakoff's Syndrome: an information processing approach to amnesia*, Academic Press, New York

Calden, G. and Hokanson, J. E. (1959) 'The influence of age on MMPI responses', *Journal of Clinical Psychology*, **15**, 194–5

Calne, D. B. (1981) 'Parkinsonism and ageing' in T. Arie (ed.), *Health Care of the Elderly*, Croom Helm, London, pp. 57–70

Cameron, D. E. (1941) 'Studies in senile nocturnal delirium', *Psychiatric Quarterly*, **15**, 47–53

Carp, F. M. and Carp, A. (1983) 'Structural stability of well-being factors across age and gender, and development of scales of well-being unbiased for age and gender', *Journal of Gerontology*, **38**, 572–81

Carr, A. C., Wilson, S. L., Ghosh, A., Ancill, R. J. and Woods, R. T. (1982) 'Automated testing of geriatric patients using a microcomputer based system', *International Journal of Man-Machine Studies*, **17**, 297–300

Carroll, K. and Gray, K. (1981) 'Memory development: an approach to the mentally impaired elderly in the long-term care setting', *International Journal of Ageing and Human Development*, **13**, 15–35

Carstensen, L. L. and Cone, J. D. (1983) 'Social desirability and the measurement of psychological well-being in elderly persons', *Journal of Gerontology*, **38**, 713–15

—— and Fremouw, W. J. (1981) 'The demonstration of a behavioural intervention for late life paranoia', *Gerontologist*, **21**, 329–33

Cattell, R. B. (1963) 'The theory of fluid and crystalline intelligence', *Journal of Educational Psychology*, **54**, 1–22

Cauthen, N. R. (1977) 'Extension of the Wechsler Memory Scale Norms to Older Age Groups', *Journal of Clinical Psychology*, **33**, 208–11

Cerella, J., Poon, L. W. and Fozard, J. L. (1981) 'Mental rotation and age reconsidered', *Journal of Gerontology*, **36**, 620–4

Cermak, L. S. and Ryback, R. S. (1976) 'Recovery of verbal short-term memory in alcoholics', *Journal of Studies on Alcohol*, **37**, 46–52

Chafetz, P. K., Ochs, C. E., Tate, L. A. and Niederehe, G. (1982) 'Employment opportunities for geropsychologists', *American Psychologist*, **37**, 1221–7

Challis, D. J. and Davies, B. J. (1981) 'Community care projects: costs and effectiveness', *INSERM*, **101**, 317–26

——, Luckett, R. and Chessum, R. (1983) 'A new life at home', *Community Care*

(24 March), pp. 21–3

Church, M. (1983) 'Psychological therapy with elderly people', *Bulletin of the British Psychological Society*, **36**, 110–12

—— and Linge, K. (1982) 'Dealing with dementia in the community', *Community Care* (25 November), pp. 20–1

Clark, E. O. (1980) 'Semantic and episodic memory impairment in normal and cognitively imparied elderly adults' in L. K. Obler and M. L. Albert (eds.), *Language and Communication in the Elderly: clinical, therapeutic and experimental issues*, Lexington Books, Lexington, Mass., pp. 47–58

Clough, R. (1981) *Old Age Homes*. Allen and Unwin, London

Cohen, D. and Eisdorfer, C. (1979) 'Cognitive theory and the assessment of change in the elderly' in A. Raskin and L. F. Jarvik (eds.), *Psychiatric Symptoms and Cognitive Loss in the Elderly*, Hemisphere, Washington DC, pp. 273–82

——, Kennedy, G. and Eisdorfer, C. (1984) 'Phases of change in the patient with Alzheimer's dementia', *Journal of American Geriatrics Society*, **32**, 11–15

Collins, P. (1983) *Caring for the Confused Elderly: an Experimental Support Service*', Department of Geriatric Medicine, University of Birmingham

Comfort, A. (1980) 'Sexuality in late life' in J. E. Birren and R. B. Sloane, (eds.), *Handbook of Mental Health and Ageing*, Prentice-Hall, Englewood Cliffs, NJ

Constantinidis, J., Richard, J. and de Ajuriaguerra, J. (1978) 'Dementias with senile plaques and neurofibrillary changes' in A. D. Isaacs and F. Post (eds.), *Studies in Geriatric Psychiatry*, Wiley, Chichester, pp. 119–52

Corby, N. (1975) 'Assertion training with aged populations', *Counselling Psychologist*, **5**,(4), 69–74

—— and Solnick, R. L. (1980) 'Psychosocial and physiological influences on sexuality in the older adult' in J. E. Birren and R. B. Sloane (eds.), *Handbook of Mental Health and Ageing*, Prentice-Hall, Englewood Cliffs, NJ

Corkin, S. (1982) 'Some relationships between global amnesias and the memory impairments in Alzheimer's Disease' in S. Corkin, K. L. Davis, J. H. Growdon, E. Usdin and R. J. Wurtman (eds.), *Alzheimer's Disease: a Report of Progress in Research* (Ageing, Volume 19), Raven Press, New York, pp. 149–64

Cornbleth, T. (1977) 'Effects of a protected hospital ward area on wandering and non-wandering geriatric patients', *Journal of Gerontology*, **32**, 573–7

—— (1978) 'Evaluation of goal attainment in geriatric settings', *Journal of American Geriatrics Society*, **26**, 404–7

Costa, P. T. and McCrae, R. R. (1977–8) 'Age differences in personality structure revisited: studies in validity, stability and change', *International Journal of Ageing and Human Development*, **8**, 261–76

—— and —— (1978) 'Age differences in personality structure revisited', *Ageing and Human Development*, **8**, 131–142

Costello, A. L. (1972) 'Depression: loss of reinforcers or loss of reinforcer effectiveness', *Behaviour Therapy*, **3**, 240–7

Coulshed, V. (1980) 'A unitary approach to the care of the hospitalised elderly mentally ill', *British Journal of Social Work*, **10**, 19–32

Council of Europe (1977) 'Preparation for retirement', Council of Europe

Craik, F. I. M. (1977) 'Age differences in human memory' in J. E. Birren and K. W. Schaie (eds.), *Handbook of the Psychology of Ageing*, Van Nostrand Reinhold, Cincinatti

—— and Byrd, M. (1982) 'Ageing and cognitive deficits: the role of attentional resources' in F. I. M. Craik and S. Trehub (eds.), *Ageing and Cognitive Processes*, Plenum Press, New York, pp. 191–212

—— and Lockhart, R. S. (1972) 'Levels of processing: a framework for memory research', *Journal of Verbal Learning and Verbal Behaviour*, **11**, 671–84

Crapper, D. R., Karlik, S. and De Boni, U. (1978) 'Aluminium and other metals in senile dementia' in R. Kalzman, R. Terry and K. L. Bick (eds.), *Alzheimer's Disease, Senile Dementia and Related Disorders*, Raven Press, New York

Crook, T., Ferris, S. and McCarthy, M. (1979) 'The misplaced-objects task: a brief test for memory dysfunction in the aged', *Journal of American Geriatrics Society*, 27, 284–7

Crookes, T. G. (1974) 'Indices of early dementia on WAIS', *Psychological Reports*, 34, 734

—— and McDonald, K. G. (1972) 'Benton's Visual Retention Test in the differentiation of depression and early dementia', *British Journal of Social and Clinical Psychology*, 11, 66–9

Cumming, E. and Henry, W. (1961) *Growing Old: The Process of Disengagement*, Basic Books, New York

Cutting, J. (1978) 'The relationship between Korsakov's syndrome and "alcoholic dementia"', *British Journal of Psychiatry*, 132, 240–51

Damon, S. G., Lesser, R. and Woods, R. T. (1979) 'Behavioural treatment of social difficulties with an aphasic woman and a dysarthic man', *British Journal of Disorders of Communication*, 14, 31–8

Danford, S. (1982) 'Therapeutic design for the ageing' in A. McN. Horton (ed.), *Mental Health Interventions for the Ageing*, Praeger Publishers, New York, pp. 155–71

Dartington, T. (1980) *Family Care of Older People*, Souvenir Press, London

—— (1983) 'At home in hospital?' in M. J. Denham (ed.), *Care of the Long-stay Elderly Patient*, Croom Helm, London, pp. 90–111

Davies, A. D. M. (1981) 'Neither wife nor widow: an intervention with the wife of a chronically handicapped man during hospital visits', *Behaviour Research and Therapy*, 19, 449–51

—— (1982) 'Research with elderly people in long-term care: some social and organisational factors affecting psychological interventions, *Ageing and Society*, 2, 285–98

—— and Crisp, A. G. (1980) 'Setting performance goals in geriatric nursing', *Journal of Advanced Nursing*, 5, 381–8

—— and Gledhill, K. J. (1983) 'Engagement and depressive symptoms in a community sample of elderly people', *British Journal of Clinical Psychology*, 22, 95–106

—— and Snaith, P. (1980) 'The social behaviour of geriatric patients at mealtimes: an observational and an intervention study', *Age and Ageing*, 9, 93–9

Davies, G., Hamilton, S., Hendrickson, D. E., Levy, R. and Post, F. (1977) 'The effect of cyclandelate in depressed and demented patients: a controlled study in psychogeriatric patients', *Age and Ageing*, 6, 156–62

——, ——, ——, —— and —— (1978) 'Psychological test performance and sedation thresholds of elderly dements, depressives and depressives with incipient brain change', *Psychological Medicine*, 8, 103–9

Davis, P. E. and Mumford, S. J. (1981) 'The nature of the memory impairment in senile dementia: a brief review and an experiment', Paper presented at British Psychological Society Annual Conference, Guildford

—— and —— (1984) 'Cued recall and the nature of the memory disorder in dementia', *British Journal of Psychiatry*, 144, 383–6

Demming, J. A. and Pressey, S. L. (1957) 'Tests "indigenous" to the adult and older years', *Journal of Counselling Psychology*, 4, 144–8

De Renzi, E. and Vignolo, L. A. (1962) 'The token test: a sensitive test to detect receptive disturbances in aphasias', *Brain*, 85, 665–78

Diesfeldt, H. F. A. (1978) 'The distinction between long-term and short-term memory in senile dementia: an analysis of free recall and delayed recognition', *Neuropsychologia*, 16, 115–19

———— and Diesfeldt-Groenendijk, H. (1977) 'Improving cognitive performance in psychogeriatric patients: the influence of physical exercise', *Age and Ageing*, **6**, 58–64

Drachman, D. A. and Leavitt, J. (1972) 'Memory impairment in the aged: storage versus retrieval deficits', *Journal of Experimental Psychology*, **93**, 302–8

Eastman, M. (1982) '"Granny battering", a hidden problem', *Community Care* (27 May), pp. 12–13

Eisdorfer, C. (1983) 'Conceptual models of ageing: the challenge of a new frontier', *American Psychologist*, **38**, 197–202

———— and Wilkie, F. (1973) 'Intellectual changes with advancing age' in L. F. Jarvik, C. Eisdorfer and J. E. Blum (eds.), *Intellectual Functioning in Adults*, Springer, New York

Ekerdt, D. J., Bosse, R. and LoCastro, J. S. (1983) 'Claims that retirement improves health', *Journal of Gerontology*, **38**, 231–6

Emery, G. (1981) 'Cognitive therapy with the elderly' in G. Emery, S. D. Hollon and R. C. Bedrosian (eds.), *New Directions in Cognitive Therapy*, Guilford, New York, pp. 84–98

Erber, J. T. (1979) 'The institutionalised geriatric patient considered in a framework of developmental deprivation', *Human Development*, **22**, 165–79

Erikson, E. H. (1963) *Childhood and Society*, Norton, New York

Erikson, R. C., Poon, L. W. and Walsh-Sweeney, L. (1980) 'Clinical memory testing of the elderly' in L. W. Poon, J. L. Fozard, L. S. Cermak, D. Arenberg and L. W. Thompson (eds.), *New Directions in Memory and Ageing*, Lawrence Erlbaum, Hillsdale, New Jersey, pp. 379–402

Ernst, P. A. and Badash, D. (1977) 'Psychiatric problems of the aged: a new approach more useful for patient and doctor', *Israel Annuals of Psychiatry and Related Disciplines*, **15**, 12–15

Evans, J. G. (1982) 'The psychiatric aspects of physical disease' in R. Levy and F. Post (eds.), *The Psychiatry of Late Life*, Blackwell, Oxford, pp. 114–42

Eysenck, M. D. (1945) 'A study of certain qualitative aspects of problem solving in senile dementia patients', *Journal of Mental Science*, **91**, 337–45

Fengler, A. P. and Goodrich, N. (1979) 'Wives of elderly disabled men: the hidden patients', *Gerontologist*, **19**, 175–83

Ferm, L. (1974) 'Behavioural activities in demented geriatric patients', *Gerontologia Clinica*, **16**, 185–94

Ferris, S. H., Crook, T., Clark, E., McCarthy, M. and Rae, D. (1980) 'Facial recognition memory deficits in normal ageing and senile dementia', *Journal of Gerontology*, **35**, 707–14

————, ————, Sathananthan, G. and Gershon, S. (1976) 'Reaction time as a diagnostic measure in senility', *Journal of American Geriatrics Society*, **24**, 529–33

Ferster, C. B. (1973) 'A functional analysis of depression', *American Psychologist*, **28**, 857–70

Fillenbaum, G. and Pfeiffer, E. (1976) 'The Mini-mult: a cautionary note', *Journal of Consulting and Clinical Psychology*, **44**, 698–703

Fisher, K. and Findley, L. (1981) 'Intellectual changes in optimally treated patients with Parkinson's Disease' in F. C. Rose and R. Capildeo (eds.), *Research Progress in Parkinson's Disease*, Pitman Medical, Tunbridge Wells, pp. 53–60

Fiske, M. (1980) 'Tasks and crises of the second half of life: the interrelationship of commitment, coping and adaptation' in J. E. Birren and R. B. Sloane (eds.), *Handbook of Mental Health and Ageing*, Prentice-Hall, Englewood Cliffs, NJ, pp. 337–76

Flower, K. (1978) 'Some frequency response characteristics of Parkinsonism in Pursuit Tracking', *Brain*, **101**, 19–34

Folsom, J. C. (1967) 'Intensive hospital therapy of geriatric patients', *Current*

Psychiatric Therapies, **7**, 209–15

Fox, D. (1981) 'Housing and the elderly' in D. Hobman (ed.), *The Impact of Ageing: Strategies for Care*, Croom Helm, London, pp. 86–108

Foxx, R. M. and Azrin, N. H. (1973) *Toilet Training the Retarded*, Research Press, Champaign, Illinois

Fozard, J. L. (1981) 'Speed of mental performance and ageing: costs of age and benefits of wisdom' in F. J. Pirozzolo and G. B. Maletta (eds.), *Behavioural Assessment and Psychopharmacology* (Advances in Neurogerontology, Volume 2), Praeger Publishers, New York, pp. 59–94

Fransella, F. and Bannister, D. (1977) *A Manual for Repertory Grid Technique*, Academic Press, London

Fuller, J., Ward, E., Evans, A., Massam, K. and Gardner, A. (1979) 'Dementia: supportive groups for relatives', *British Medical Journal*, **1**, 1684–5

Furry, C. A. and Baltes, P. B. (1973) 'The effect of age differences in ability extraneous performance variables on the assessment of intelligence in children, adults and the elderly', *Journal of Gerontology*, **28**, 73–80

Gaber, L. (1983) 'Activity/Disengagement revisited: personality types in the aged', *British Journal of Psychiatry*, **143**, 490–7

Gaine, M. (1978) 'Ageing and the spirit' in D. Hobman (ed.), *The Social Challenge of Ageing*, Croom Helm, London, pp. 222–48

Gale, J. and Livesley, B. (1974) 'Attitudes towards geriatrics: a report of the King's survey', *Age and Ageing*, **3**, 49–53

Gallagher, D. E., Breckenridge, J. N., Thompson, L. W. and Peterson, J. A. (1983) 'Effects of bereavement on indicators of mental health in elderly widows and widowers', *Journal of Gerontology*, **38**, 565–71

Gallagher, D., Nies, G. and Thompson, L. (1982) 'Reliability of the Beck Depression Inventory with older adults', *Journal of Consulting and Clinical Psychology*, **50**, 152–3

――― and Thompson, L. W. (1983) 'Effectiveness of psychotherapy for both endogenous and non-endogenous depression in older adult out-patients', *Journal of Gerontology*, **38**, 707–12

Galliard, P. (1978) 'Difficulties encountered in attempting to increase social interaction amongst geriatric psychiatry patients: clean and sitting quietly', Paper presented at British Psychological Society Annual Conference, York

Garland, J. (1983) 'A service for the elderly: what to do and where to start', *Newsletter of Division of Clinical Psychology of British Psychological Society*, No. 42, 24–8

Garraway, W. M., Akhtar, A. J., Hockey, L. and Prescott, R. J. (1980) Management of acute stroke in the elderly: follow-up of a controlled trial', *British Medical Journal*, **281**, 827–9

Garrison, J. E. (1978) 'Stress management training for the elderly: a psychoeducational approach', *Journal of American Geriatrics Society*, **26**, 397–403

――― and Howe, J. (1976) 'Community intervention with the elderly: a social network approach', *Journal of American Geriatrics Society*, **24**, 329–33

Garside, R. F., Kay, D. W. K. and Roth, M. (1965) 'Old age mental disorders in Newcastle upon Tyne: Part III: a factorial study of medical, psychiatric and social characteristics', *British Journal of Psychiatry*, **111**, 939–46

Gauthier, J. and Marshall, W. L. (1977) 'Grief: a cognitive behavioural analysis', *Cognitive Therapy and Research*, **1**, 39–44

Gedye, J. L. and Miller, E. (1970) 'Developments in automated testing systems' in P. Mittler (ed.), *The Psychological Assessment of Mental and Physical Handicap*, Methuen, London, pp. 735–60

Georgiades, N. J. and Phillimore, L. (1975) 'The myth of the hero-innovator and alternative strategies for organisational change' in C. C. Kiernan and F. P.

Woodford (eds.), *Behavioural Modification with the Severely Retarded*, Associated Scientific Publishers, New York, pp. 313–19

Giambra, L. M. and Arenberg, D. (1980) 'Problem solving, concept learning and ageing' in L. W. Poon (ed.), *Ageing in the 1980s: Psychological Issues*, American Psychological Association, Washington, pp. 253–9

Gibson, A. J. (1981) 'A further analysis of memory loss in dementia and depression in the elderly', *British Journal of Clinical Psychology*, **20**, 179–86

——— and Kendrick, D. C. (1979) *The Kendrick Battery for the Detection of Dementia in the Elderly*, NEFR-Nelson, Windsor

———, Moyes, I. C. A. and Kendrick, D. C. (1980) 'Cognitive assessment of the elderly long-stay patient', *British Journal of Psychiatry*, **137**, 551–7

Gilhooly, M. (1980) 'The social dimensions of senile dementia', Paper presented at British Psychological Society Annual Conference, Aberdeen

——— (1984) 'The social dimensions of senile dementia' in I. Hanley and J. Hodge (eds.), *Psychological Approaches to the Care of the Elderly*, Croom Helm, London, pp. 88–135

Gilleard, C. J. (1984a) 'Assessment of cognitive impairment in the elderly' in I. Hanley and J. Hodge (eds.), *Psychological Approaches to the Care of the Elderly*, Croom Helm, London, pp. 1–21

——— (1984b) 'Assessment of behavioural impairment in the elderly: a review' in I. Hanley and J. Hodge (eds.), *Psychological Approaches to the Care of the Elderly*, Croom Helm, London, pp. 41–60

——— and Pattie, A. H. (1980) 'Dimensions of disability in the elderly: construct validity of rating scales for elderly populations', Paper presented at British Psychological Society Annual Conference, Aberdeen

——— and Watt, G. (1983) *Coping with Ageing Parents*. MacDonald, Loanhead, Midlothian

———, Willmott, M. and Vaddadi, K. S. (1981a) 'Self report measures of mood and morale in elderly depressives', *British Journal of Psychiatry*, 138, 230–5

———, Mitchell, R. G. and Riordan, J. (1981b) 'Ward orientation training with psychogeriatric patients', *Journal of Advanced Nursing*, **6**, 95–8

———, Watt, G. and Boyd, W. D. (1981c) 'Problems of caring for the elderly mentally infirm at home', Paper presented at the XIIth International Congress of Gerontology, Hamburg

Gilmore, A. J. J. (1972) 'Personality in the elderly: problems in methodology', *Age and Ageing*, **1**, 227–32

Gledhill, K. J., Mackie, J. E. and Gilleard, C. J. (1982) 'A comparison of problems and coping reported by supporters of elderly day hospital patients with similar ratings provided by nurses', Paper presented at British Psychological Society Annual Conference, York

Godlove, C., Dunn, G. and Wright, H. (1980) 'Caring for old people in New York and London: the "nurses' aide" interviews', *Journal of the Royal Society of Medicine*, **73**, 713–23

———, Richard, L. and Rodwell, G. (1982) 'Time for action: an observation study of elderly people in 4 different care environments', Joint Unit for Social Services Research, University of Sheffield

Goga, J. A. and Hambacher, W. O. (1977) 'Psychologic and behavioural assessment of geriatric patients: a review', *Journal of American Geriatrics Society*, **25**, 232–7

Goldberg, D. (1978) *Manual of the General Health Questionnaire*, NFER, Windsor

Goldstein, A. (1973) *Structured Learning Therapy*, Academic Press, New York

Goodglass, H. (1980) 'Naming disorders in aphasia and ageing' in L. K. Obler and M. L. Albert (eds.), *Language and Communication in the Elderly: Clinical, Therapeutic and Experimental Issues*, D. C. Heath, Lexington, Mass., pp. 37–46

Gottesman, L. E. (1977) 'Clinical psychology and ageing: a role model' in W. D. Gentry (ed.), *Geropsychology: a Model of Training and Clinical Service*, Ballinger, Cambridge, Mass., pp. 1–8

——, Quarterman, C. E. and Cohn, G. M. (1973) 'Psychosocial treatment of the aged' in C. Eisdorfer and M. P. Lawton (eds.), *The Psychology of Adult Development and Ageing*, American Psychological Association, Washington DC, pp. 378–427

Gottsdanker, R. (1982) 'Age and simple reaction time', *Journal of Gerontology*, 37, 342–8

Gowans, F. and Hulbert, C. (1983) 'Self-concept assessment of mentally handicapped adults', *Mental Handicap*, 11, 121–3

Grad, J. and Sainsbury, P. (1968) 'The effects that patients have on their families in a community care and a control psychiatric service — a two year follow-up', *British Journal of Psychiatry*, 114, 265–78

Graney, M. J. (1975) 'Happiness and social participation in ageing', *Journal of Gerontology*, 30, 701–6

Granick, S., Kleben, M. H. and Weiss, A. D. (1976) 'Relationships between hearing loss and cognition in normally hearing aged persons', *Journal of Gerontology*, 31, 434–40

Gray, B. and Isaacs, B. (1979) *Care of the Elderly Mentally Infirm*, Tavistock, London

Gray, J. A. M. and McKenzie, H. (1980) *Take Care of Your Elderly Relative*, George Allen and Unwin, London

Greene, J. G. (1984) 'The evaluation of reality orientation' in I. Hanley and J. Hodge (eds.), *Psychological Approaches to the Care of the Elderly*, Croom Helm, London, pp. 192–212

——, Nicol, R. and Jamieson, H. (1979) 'Reality Orientation with psychogeriatric patients', *Behaviour Research and Therapy*, 17, 615–17

——, Smith, R., Gardiner, M. and Timbury, G. C. (1982) 'Measuring behavioural disturbance of elderly demented patients in the community and its effects on relatives: a factor analytic study', *Age and Ageing*, 11, 121–6

——, Timbury, G. C., Smith, R. and Gardiner, M. (1983) 'Reality orientation with elderly patients in the community: an empirical evaluation', *Age and Ageing*, 12, 38–43

Gubrium, J. F. (1975) 'Being single in old age', *International Journal of Ageing and Human Development*, 6, 29–41

Gurel, L., Linn, M. W. and Linn, B. S. (1972) 'Physical and mental impairment of function evaluation in the aged: the PAMIE scale', *Journal of Gerontology*, 27, 83–90

Gurland, B. J. (1976) 'The comparative frequency of depression in various adult age groups', *Journal of Gerontology*, 31, 283–92

—— (1980) 'The assessment of the mental health status of older adults' in J. E. Birren and R. B. Sloane (eds.), *Handbook of Mental Health and Ageing*, Prentice-Hall, Englewood Cliffs, NJ, pp. 671–700

——, Copeland, J., Kuriansky, J., Kelleher, M., Sharpe, L. and Dean, L. L. (1983) *The Mind and Mood of Ageing*, Croom Helm, London; Haworth, New York

——, Cross, P., DeFiguerido, J., Shannon, M., Mann, A. H., Jenkins, R., Bennett, R., Wilder, D., Wright, H., Killfeffer, E., Godlove, C., Thompson, P., Ross, M. and Deming, W. (1979) 'A cross-national comparison of the institutionalised elderly in the cities of New York and London', *Psychological Medicine*, 9, 781–8

——, Fleiss, J. L., Goldberg, K., Sharpe, L., Copeland, J. R. M., Kelleher, M. J. and Kellett, J. (1976) 'A semi-structured clinical interview for the assessment of

diagnosis and mental state in the elderly: the Geriatric Mental State Scedule: II —
A factor analysis', *Psychological Medicine*, **6**, 451–9

Gustafsson, R. (1976) 'Milieu therapy in a ward for patients with senile dementia',
Scandinavian Journal of Behaviour Therapy, **5**, 27–39

Gutman, G. M. (1966) 'A note on the MPI: Age and sex differences in extraversion and neuroticism in a Canadian sample', *British Journal of Social and
Clinical Psychology*, **5**, 128–9

Halberstam, J. L. and Zaretsky, H. H. (1969) 'Learning capacities of elderly and
brain damaged', *Archives of Physical Medicine*, **50**, 133–9

——, ——, Brucker, B. S. and Gutman, A. R. (1971) 'Avoidance conditioning
of motor responses in elderly brain damaged patients', *Archives of Physical
Medicine and Rehabilitation*, **52**, 318–36

Hall, J. (1980) 'Ward rating scales for long-stay patients: a review', *Psychological Medicine*, **10**, 277–88

Halstead, H. (1943) 'A psychometric study of senility', *Journal of Mental Science*,
89, 863–73

Hamilton, M. (1960) 'A rating scale for depression', *Journal of Neurology, Neurosurgery and Psychiatry*, **23**, 56–62

Hanes, C. R. and Wild, B. S. (1977) 'Locus of control and depression among non-
institutionalised elderly persons', *Psychological Reports*, **41**, 581–2

Hanley, I. G. (1980) 'Optimism or pessimism: an examination of reality orientation
procedures in the management of dementia', Paper presented at the Annual
Conference of British Psychological Society, Aberdeen

—— (1981) 'The use of signposts and active training to modify ward disorientation in elderly patients', *Journal of Behaviour Therapy and Experimental
Psychiatry*, **12**, 241–7

—— (1982) 'A manual for the modification of confused behaviour', Lothian
Regional Council, Dept. of Social Work, Edinburgh

—— (1984) 'Theoretical and practical considerations in Reality Orientation
Therapy with the elderly' in I. Hanley and J. Hodge (eds.), *Psychological
Approaches to the Care of the Elderly*, Croom Helm, London, pp. 164–91

——, McGuire, R. J. and Boyd, W. D. (1981) 'Reality orientation and dementia:
a controlled trial of two approaches', *British Journal of Psychiatry*, **138**, 10–14

Harkins, S. W., Chapman, C. R. and Eisdorfer, C. (1979) 'Memory loss and
response bias in senescence', *Journal of Gerontology*, **34**, 66–72

Harris, F. C. and Lahey, B. B. (1978) 'A method of combining occurrence and
non-occurrence inter-observer agreement scores', *Journal of Applied Behaviour
Analysis*, **11**, 523–7

Harris, H., Lipman, A. and Slater, R. (1977) 'Architectural design: the spatial
location and interactions of old people', *Gerontology*, **23**, 390–400

Hartmann, D. P. (1977) 'Considerations in the choice of inter-observer reliability
estimates', *Journal of Applied Behaviour Analysis*, **10**, 103–16

Hausman, C. P. (1979) 'Short-term counselling groups for people with elderly
parents', *Gerontologist*, **19**, 102–7

Havighurst, R. J. (1968) 'Personality and patterns of ageing', *Gerontologist*, **8**,
20–3

—— (1978) 'Ageing in western society' in D. Hobman (ed.), *The Social Challenge
of Ageing*, Croom Helm, London, pp. 15–44

——, Neugarten, B. L. and Tobin, S. S. (1968) 'Disengagement and patterns of
ageing' in B. L. Neurgarten (ed.), *Middle Age and Ageing*, University of Chicago
Press, Chicago

Hawkes, D. (1975) 'Community care: an analysis of assumptions', *British Journal
of Psychiatry*, **127**, 276–85

Hawley, E. J., Hirschland, J., Williams, T. F. and Vincent, S. (1983) 'Long-stay institutions in the U.S.' in M. J. Denham (ed.), *Care of the Long-stay Elderly Patient*, Croom Helm, London, pp. 217–31

Hayflick, L. (1965) 'The limited in vitro lifetime of human diploid cell strains', *Experimental Cell Research*, **37**, 614–36

——— (1982) 'The strategy of senescence', *Journal of Gerontology*, **14**, 37–45

Heller, B. R. and Walsh, F. J. (1976) 'Changing nursing students' attitudes toward the aged: an experimental study', *Journal of Nursing Education*, **15**, 9–17

Heller, M. (1979) 'A psychometric and experimental investigation of memory functioning in Parkinson's disease', Unpublished MSc dissertation, University of Newcastle upon Tyne, England

Help The Aged, (1981) *Recall — a Handbook*, Help the Aged Education Department, London

Hendrickson, E., Levy, R. and Post, F. (1979) 'Averaged evoked responses in relation to cognitive and affective state of elderly psychiatric patients', *British Journal of Psychiatry*, **134**, 494–501

Hewson, L. (1949) 'The Wechsler-Bellevue scale and the substitution test as aids in psychiatric diagnosis', *Journal of Nervous and Mental Disease*, **109**, 158–83, 246–65

Heyman, D. K. and Gianturco, D. T. (1973) 'Long-term adaptation by the elderly to bereavement', *Journal of Gerontology*, **28**, 359–62

Hibbard, T. R., Migliaccio, J. N., Goldstone, S. and Lhamon, W. T. (1975) 'Temporal information processing by young and senior adults and patients with senile dementia', *Journal of Gerontology*, **30**, 326–30

Hitch, D. and Simpson, A. (1972) 'An attempt to assess a new design in residential homes for the elderly', *British Journal of Social Work*, **2**, 481–501

Hobman, D. (ed.) *The Impact of Ageing*, Croom Helm, London

Hodge, J. (1984) 'Towards a behavioural analysis of dementia' in I. Hanley and J. Hodge (eds.), *Psychological Approaches to the Care of the Elderly*, Croom Helm, London, pp. 61–87

Hodgkinson, P. E. (1982) 'Abnormal grief — the problem of therapy', *British Journal of Medical Psychology*, **55**, 29–34

Hodkinson, H. M. (1972) 'Evaluation of a mental test score for assessment of mental impairment in the elderly', *Age and Ageing*, **1**, 233–8

Hogan, R., De Soto, C. B. and Solano, C. (1977) 'Traits, tests and personality research', *American Psychologist*, **32**, 255–64

Hogstel, M. O. (1979) 'Use of Reality Orientation with ageing confused patients', *Nursing Research*, **28**, 161–5

Holbrook, M. and Skilbeck, C. E. (1983) 'An activities index for use with stroke patients', *Age and Ageing*, **12**, 166–70

Holden, U. P. and Woods, R. T. (1982) *Reality Orientation: Psychological Approaches to the 'Confused' Elderly*, Churchill Livingstone, Edinburgh

Horn, J. L. and Donaldson, G. (1976) 'On the myth of intellectual decline in adulthood', *American Psychologist*, **31**, 701–9

——— and ——— (1977) 'Faith is not enough: a response to the Baltes-Schaie claim that intelligence does not wane', *American Psychologist*, **32**, 369–73

Howard, D. V., McAndrews, M. P. and Lasaga, M. I. (1981) 'Semantic priming of lexical decisions in young and old adults', *Journal of Gerontology*, **36**, 707–14

Hoyer, F. W., Hoyer, W. J., Treat, N. J. and Baltes, P. B. (1978) 'Training response speed in young and elderly women', *International Journal of Ageing and Human Development*, **9**, 247–54

Hoyt, D. R. and Creech, J. C. (1983) 'The life satisfaction index: a methodological and theoretical critique', *Journal of Gerontology*, **38**, 111–16

Hulicka, I. M. (1966) 'Age differences in Wechsler Memory Scale Scores', *Journal of Genetic Psychology*, **109**, 135–44

Hultsch, D. (1975) 'Adult differences in retrieval: trace dependent and cue dependent and cue dependent forgetting', *Developmental Psychology*, **11**, 197–201

Hunt, A. (1978) *The Elderly at Home*, HMSO, London

—— (1979) 'Some aspects of the health of elderly people in England', *Health Trends*, **11**, 21–3

Hussian, R. A. (1980) 'Stimulus control in the modification of problematic behaviour in elderly institutionalised patients', Paper presented at Association for the Advancement of Behaviour Therapy Convention, New York

—— (1981) *Geriatric Psychology: a Behavioural Perspective*, Van Nostrand Reinhold, New York

—— and Hill, S. D. (1980) 'Stereotyped behaviour in elderly patients with chronic organic mental disorder', *Journal of Gerontology*, **35**, 689–91

—— and Lawrence, P. S. (1981) 'Social reinforcement of activity and problem-solving training in the treatment of depressed institutionalised elderly patients', *Cognitive Therapy and Research*, **5**(1), 57–69

Hutchinson, J. M. and Jensen, M. (1980) 'A pragmatic evaluation of discourse communication in normal and senile elderly in a nursing home' in L. K. Obler and M. L. Albert (eds.), *Language and Communication in the Elderly: Clinical, Therapeutic and Experimental Issues*, D. C. Heath, Lexington, Mass., pp. 59–74

Inglis, J. (1957) 'An experimental study of learning and "memory function" in elderly psychiatric patients', *Journal of Mental Science*, **103**, 796–803

—— (1958) 'Psychological investigations of cognitive deficit in elderly psychiatric patients', *Psychological Bulletin*, **54**, 197–214

—— (1962) 'Psychological practice in geriatric problems', *Journal of Mental Science*, **108**, 669–74

—— and Sanderson, R. F. (1961) 'Successive response to simultaneous stimulation in elderly patients with memory disorder', *Journal of Abnormal and Social Psychology*, **62**, 709–12

Irving, G., Robinson, R. A. and McAdam, W. (1970) 'The validity of some cognitive tests in the diagnosis of dementia', *British Journal of Psychiatry*, **117**, 149–56

Isaacs, B. and Akhtar, A. J. (1972) 'The set test: a rapid test of mental function in old people', *Age and Ageing*, **1**, 222–6

——, Livingstone, M. and Neville, Y. (1972) *Survival of the unfittest: a study of geriatric patients in Glasgow*, Routledge and Kegan Paul, London

Jacoby, R. J. and Levy, R. (1980a) 'Computed tomography in the elderly. 2: Senile dementia: diagnosis and functional impairment', *British Journal of Psychiatry*, **136**, 256–9

—— and —— (1980b) 'Computed tomography in the elderly. 3: Affective disorder', *British Journal of Psychiatry*, **136**, 270–75

——, —— and Bird, J. M. (1981) 'Computed tomography and the outcome of affective disorder: a follow-up study of elderly patients', *British Journal of Psychiatry*, **139**, 288–92

James, O. F. W. (1983) 'Alcoholism in the elderly' in N. Krasner, S. Madin and R. Walker (eds.), *Alcohol-related Problems — Room for Manoeuvre*, John Wiley, Chichester

Jarvik, L. F., Kallman, F. J. and Falek, A. (1962) 'Intellectual changes in aged twins', *Journal of Gerontology*, **17**, 289–94

Jeffery, D. and Saxby, P. (1984) 'Effective psychological care for the elderly' in I. Hanley and J. Hodge (eds.), *Psychological Approaches to the Care of the Elderly*, Croom Helm, London, pp. 255–82

Jenkins, J., Felce, D., Lunt, B. and Powell, E. (1977) 'Increasing engagement in activity of residents in old people homes by providing recreational materials', *Behaviour Research and Therapy*, **15**, 429–34

Johnson, C. H., McLaren, S. M. and McPherson, F. M. (1981) 'The comparative effectiveness of three versions of "classroom" reality orientation', *Age and Ageing*, **10**, 33–5

Johnson, D. G. (1979) 'Abuse and neglect — not for children only!' *Journal of Gerontological Nursing*, **4**, 11–13

Johnson, M. (1976) 'That was your life: a biographical approach to later life' in J. M. A. Munnichs and W. J. A. Van den Heuvel (eds.), *Dependency or Interdependency in Old Age*, Martinus Nijhoff, The Hague, pp. 141–161, and in V. Carver and P. Liddiard (eds.) (1978), *An Ageing Population*, Hodder and Stoughton/Open University, Sevenoaks, pp. 99–113

Jolley, D. (1981) 'Dementia: misfits in need of care', in T. Arie (ed.), *Health Care of the Elderly*, Croom Helm, London, pp. 71–88

Kahana, B. (1978) 'The use of projective techniques in personality assessment of the aged' in M. Storandt, I. C. Siegler and M. F. Elias (eds.), *The Clinical Psychology of Ageing*, Plenum, New York, pp. 145–80

Kahana, E., Liang, J. and Felton, B. J. (1980) 'Alternative models of person-environment fit: prediction of morale in three homes for the aged', *Journal of Gerontology*, **35**, 584–95

Kahn, R. L., Zarit, S. H., Hilbert, N. M. and Niederehe, G. (1975) 'Memory complaint and impairment in the aged: the effect of depression and altered brain function', *Archives of General Psychiatry*, **32**, 1569–73

Kaszniak, A. W., Garron, D. C. and Fox, J. (1979) 'Differential effects of age and cerebral atrophy upon span of immediate recall and paired-associated learning in older patients suspected of dementia', *Cortex*, **15**, 285–95

Kay, D. W. K., Beamish, P. and Roth M. (1964) 'Old age mental disorders in Newcastle upon Tyne', *British Journal of Psychiatry*, **110**, 146–58 and 668–82

——— and Bergmann, K. (1980) 'Epidemiology of Mental Disorders among the aged in the Community' in J. E. Birren and R. B. Sloane (eds.), *Handbook of Mental Health and Ageing*, Prentice-Hall, Englewood Cliffs, NJ, pp. 34–56

———, ———, Foster, E. and Garside, R. F. (1966) 'A four-year follow-up of a random sample of old people originally seen in their own homes: a physical, social and psychiatric enquiry', *Proceedings of the 4th World Congress of Psychiatry*, pp. 1668–1670. Excerpta Medica International Congress Series No. 150, Excerpta Medica, Amsterdam

Kazmar, J. V. (1970) 'The development of a usable lexicon of environmental descriptors', *Environment and Behaviour*, **2**, 153–69

Kear Colwell, J. J. (1973) 'The structure of the Wechsler Memory Scale and its relationship to "Brain Damage" ', *British Journal of Social and Clinical Psychology*, **12**, 384–92

Kearns, N. P., Cruickshank, C. A., McGuigan, K. J., Riley, S. A., Shaw, S. P. and Snaith, R. P. (1982) 'A comparison of depression rating scales', *British Journal of Psychiatry*, **141**, 45–9

Keller, J. F., Croake, J. W. and Brooking, J. Y. (1975) 'Effects of a program in rational thinking on anxieties in older persons', *Journal of Counselling Psychology*, **22**, 54–7

Kendrick, D. C. (1965) 'Speed and learning in the diagnosis of diffuse brain damage in elderly subjects: a Bayesian statistical approach', *British Journal of Social and Clinical Psychology*, **4**, 141–8

——— (1972) 'The Kendrick Battery of tests: theoretical assumptions and clinical uses', *British Journal of Social and Clinical Psychology*, **4**, 63–71

——— (1982a) 'Why assess the aged? A clinical psychologist's view', *British Journal of Clinical Psychology*, **21**, 47–54

——— (1982b) 'Psychometrics and neurological models. A reply to Dr. Rabbitt', *British Journal of Clinical Psychology*, **21**, 61–2

———, Gibson, A. J. and Moyes, I. C. A. (1979) 'The Revised Kendrick Battery: clinical studies', *British Journal of Social and Clinical Psychology*, **18**, 329–40

——— and Moyes, I. C. A. (1979) 'Activity, depression, medication and performance on the revised Kendrick Battery', *British Journal of Social and Clinical Psychology*, **18**, 341–50

Kennedy, R. W. and Kennedy, A. B. (1982) 'Absence of purposeful behavior: issues in training the profoundly impaired elderly', in A. McN. Horton (ed.), *Mental Health Interventions for the Ageing*, Praeger, New York

Kiernat, J. M. (1979) 'The use of life review activity with confused nursing home residents', *American Journal of Occupational Therapy*, **33**, 306–10

King, M. R. (1980) 'Treatment of incontinence', *Nursing Times*, **76**, (5 June), 1006–10

King, R. D. and Raynes, N. V. (1968) 'An operational measure of inmate management in residential institutions', *Social Science and Medicine*, **2**, 41–53

Kirshner, H. S., Webb, W. G. and Kelly, M. P. (1984) 'The naming disorder of dementia', *Neuropsychologia*, **22**, 23–30

Kleemeer, R. W. (1961) 'Intellectual changes in the senium or death and the IQ', Presidential address — Division on Maturity and Old Age — American Psychological Association

——— (1962) 'Intellectual changes in the senium', *Proceedings of the Social Statistics Section*, American Statistical Association, 290–5

Klisz, D. (1978) 'Neuropsychological evaluation in older persons' in M. Storandt, I. C. Siegler and M. F. Elias (eds.), *The Clinical Psychology of Ageing*, Plenum Press, New York, pp. 71–96

Klonoff, H. and Kennedy, M. (1966) 'A comparative study of cognitive functioning in old age', *Journal of Gerontology*, **21**, 239–43

Knight, B. (1978–9) 'Psychotherapy and behaviour change with the non-institutionalised aged', *International Journal of Ageing and Human Development*, **9**(3), 221–36

Kogan, N. (1961) 'Attitudes toward old people: the development of a scale and an examination of correlates', *Journal of Abnormal and Social Psychology*, **62**, 44–54

Kolotkin, R. A. (1981) 'Preventing burnout and reducing stress in terminal care: the role of assertive training', in H. J. Sobel (ed.), *Behaviour therapy in terminal care: a humanistic approach*, Ballinger, Cambridge, Mass., pp. 229–52

Konarski, E. A., Johnson, M. R. and Whitman, T. L. (1980) 'A systematic investigation of resident participation in a nursing home activities program', *Journal of Behaviour Therapy and Experimental Psychiatry*, **11**, 249–57

Kramer, N. A. and Jarvik, L. F. (1979) 'Assessment of intellectual changes in the elderly' in A. Raskin and L. F. Jarvik (eds.), *Psychiatric Symptoms and Cognitive Loss in the Elderly*, Hemisphere, Washington DC, pp. 221–72

Kuriansky, J. and Gurland, B. (1976) 'The performance test of activities of daily living', *International Journal of Ageing and Human Development*, **7**, 343–52

———, ——— and Cowan, D. (1976) 'The usefulness of a psychological test battery', *International Journal of Ageing and Human Development*, **7**, 331–42

Kuypers, J. A. (1972) 'Internal-external locus of control, ego functioning and personality characteristics of the old', *Gerontologist*, **12**, 168–73

Labouvie-Vief, G. and Gouda, J. N. (1976) 'Cognitive strategy training and intellectual performance in the elderly', *Journal of Gerontology*, **31**, 327–32

———, Hoyer, W. J., Baltes, M. M. and Baltes, P. B. (1974) 'Operant analysis of intellectual behaviour in old age', *Human Development*, **17**, 259–72

Langer, E. J. and Rodin, J. (1976) 'The effects of choice and enhanced personal responsibility for the aged: a field experiment in an institutional setting', *Journal of Personality and Social Psychology*, **34**, 191–8

Lansing, J., Maraus, R. and Zehner, R. (1970) 'Planned residential environment', Survey Research Centre, Institute for Social Research, University of Michigan

Larner, S. (1977) 'Encoding in senile dementia and elderly depressives: a preliminary study', *British Journal of Social and Clinical Psychology*, **16**, 379–90

—— and Leeming, J. T. (1984) 'The work of a clinical psychologist in the care of the elderly'. *Age and Ageing*, **13**, 29–33

Laurence, M. W. (1967) 'Memory loss with age: a test of two strategies for its retardation', *Psychonomic Science*, **9**, 209–10

Lawson, J. S. and Barker, M. G. (1968) 'The assessment of nominal dysphasia in dementia: the use of reaction time measures', *British Journal of Medical Psychology*, **41**, 411–14

Lawton, M. P. (1971) 'The functional assessment of elderly people', *Journal of American Geriatrics Society*, **19**, 465–81

—— (1975) 'The Philadelphia Geriatric Center Morale Scale: a revision', *Journal of Gerontology*, **30**, 85–9

—— and Brody, E. M. (1969) 'Assessment of older people: self-maintaining and instrumental activities of daily living', *Gerontologist*, **9**, 179–86

—— and Gottesman, L. E. (1974) 'Psychological services to the elderly', *American Psychologist*, **29**, 689–93

——, Whelihan, W. M. and Belsky, J. K. (1980) 'Personality tests and their uses with older adults' in J. Birren and R. B. Sloane (eds.), *Handbook of Mental Health and Ageing*, Prentice-Hall, Englewood Cliffs, NJ

Lazarus, A. A. (1968) 'Learning theory and the treatment of depression', *Behaviour Research and Therapy*, **6**, 83–99

Lazarus, R. S. and DeLongis, A. (1983) 'Psychological stress and coping in ageing', *American Psychologist*, **38**, 245–54

Leech, S. and Witte, K. L. (1971) 'Paired associate learning in elderly adults as related to pacing and incentive conditions', *Developmental Psychology*, **5**, 180

Leng, N. (1982a) 'Behavioural treatment of the elderly', *Age and Ageing*, **11**, 235–43

—— (1982b) 'The role of clinical psychologists in psychogeriatrics', *British Journal of Occupational Therapy*, **45**, 237–8

Lesser, J., Lazarus, L. W., Frankel, R. and Havasy, S. (1981) 'Reminiscence group therapy with psychotic geriatric inpatients', *Gerontologist*, **21**, 291–6

Levin, E. (1983) 'The supporters of confused elderly persons in the community' in *Elderly People in the Community: their Service Needs*, HMSO, London, Chapter 8, pp. 153–4

Levy, R., Little, A., Chuaqui, P. and Reith, M. (1983) 'Early results from double-blind placebo controlled trial of high dose phosphatidyl choline in Alzheimer's Disease', *Lancet* (April), 987–8

—— and Post, F. (1975) 'The use of an interactive computer terminal in the assessment of cognitive function in elderly psychiatric patients', *Age and Ageing*, **4**, 110–15

—— and —— (1982) 'The dementias of old age' in R. Levy and F. Post (eds.), *The Psychiatry of Late Life*, Blackwell, Oxford, pp. 163–75

Lewinsohn, P. M. (1975) 'The behavioural study and treatment of depression' in M. Hersen, R. Eisler and P. Miller (eds.), *Progress in Behavior Modification* Vol. 1., Academic Press, London

—— and Macphillamy, D. J. (1974) 'The relationship between age and engagement in pleasant activities', *Journal of Gerontology*, **29**, 290–4

Lewis, M. I. and Butler, R. N. (1974) 'Life review therapy: putting memories to work in individual and group psychotherapy', *Geriatrics*, **29**, 165–74

Liang, J., Dvorkin, L., Kahana, E. and Mazian, F. (1980) 'Social integration and morale: a re-examination', *Journal of Gerontology*, **35**, 746–57

Liberman, R. P. and Raskin, D. (1971) 'Depression: a behavioural formulation', *Archives of General Psychiatry*, **24**, 515–23

Liddell, A. and Boyle, M. (1980) 'Characteristics of applicants to the MSc in Clinical Psychology at NELP', *Newsletter of the Clinical Division of the British Psychological Society*, **30**, 20–5

Lindsley, O. R. (1964) 'Geriatric behavioural prosthetics' in R. Kastenbaum (ed.), *New Thoughts on Old Age*, Springer, New York, pp. 41–60

Linn. M. W. (1979) 'Assessing community adjustment in the elderly' in A. Raskin and L. Jarvik (eds.), *Psychiatric Symptoms and Cognitive Loss in the Elderly*, Hemisphere, Washington DC, pp. 187–206

Lipman, A. (1968) 'A socio-architectural view of life in 3 homes for old people', *Gerontologia Clinica*, **10**, 88–101

―――― and Slater, R. (1977) 'Homes for old people: toward a positive environment', *Gerontologist*, **17**, 146–56

――――, Slater, R. and Harris, H. (1979) 'The quality of verbal interaction in homes for old people', *Gerontology*, **25**, 275–84

Lopez, M. A., Hoyer, W. J., Goldstein, A. P., Gershaw, N. J. and Sprafkin, R. P. (1980) 'Effects of overlearning and incentive on the acquisition and transfer of interpersonal skills with institutionalised elderly', *Journal of Gerontology*, **35**, 403–8

Loranger, A. W., Goodell, H., McDowell, F. H., Lee, J. E. and Sweet, R. D. (1972) 'Intellectual impairment in Parkinson's syndrome', *Brain*, **95**, 405–12

Lowenthal, M. F. and Boler, D. (1965) 'Voluntary vs. involuntary social withdrawal', *Journal of Gerontology*, **20**, 363–71

―――― and Haven, C. (1968) 'Interaction and adaptation intimacy as a critical variable', *American Sociological Review*, **33**, 20–30

Lubin, B. (1965) 'Adjective check-lists for measurement of depression', *Archives of General Psychiatry*, **12**, 57–62

Lubinski, R. B. (1978–9) 'Why so little interest in whether or not old people talk: a review of recent research on verbal communication among the elderly', *International Journal of Ageing and Human Development*, **9**(3), 237–45

Lyle, R. (1984) 'Evaluation of disability in the elderly' in I. Hanley and J. Hodge (eds.), *Psychological Approaches to the Care of the Elderly*, Croom Helm, London, pp. 22–40

McCormack, D. and Whitehead, A. (1981) 'The effect of providing recreational activities on the engagement level of long-stay geriatric patients', *Age and Ageing*, **10**, 287–91

McDonald, C. (1969) 'Clinical heterogeneity in senile dementia', *British Journal of Psychiatry*, **115**, 267–71

Macdonald, A. J. D. and Dunn, G. (1982) 'Death and the expressed wish to die in the elderly: an outcome study', *Age and Ageing*, **11**, 189–95

Macdonald, M. L. and Settin, J. M. (1978) 'Reality orientation vs. sheltered workshops as treatment for the institutionalised ageing', *Journal of Gerontology*, **33**, 416–21

McFadyen, M. (1984) 'The measurement of engagement in the institutionalised elderly' in I. Hanley and J. Hodge (eds.), *Psychological Approaches to the Care of the Elderly*, Croom Helm, London, pp. 136–63.

――――, Prior, T. and Kindness, K. (1980) 'Engagement: an important variable in institutional care of the elderly', Paper presented at British Psychological Society Annual Conference, Aberdeen

McKenna, P. and Warrington, E. K. (1983) *The Graded Naming Test*, NFER-Nelson, Windsor

Markides, K. S. (1983) 'Ageing, religiosity and adjustment: a longitudinal analysis', *Journal of Gerontology*, **38**, 621–5.

Marsh, G. (1980) 'Perceptual changes with ageing' in E. W. Busse and D. G. Blazer (eds.), *Handbook of Geriatric Psychiatry*, Van Nostrand Rheinhold, New York, pp. 147–68

Marston, N. and Gupta, H. (1977) 'Interesting the old', *Community Care* (16 November), 26–8

Matarazzo, J. D. (1972) *Wechsler's Measurement and Appraisal of Adult Intelligence*, 5th Edition, Williams and Wilkins, Baltimore

Matthews, V. and Woods, R. T. (1980) 'Abuse in families of psychogeriatric patients' in Open University Course P253 *Conflict in the Family Block 3*, O.U. Press, Milton Keynes, pp. 37–48

Mawson, D., Marks, I. M., Ramm, L. and Stern, R. S. (1981) 'Guided mourning for morbid grief: a controlled study', *British Journal of Psychiatry*, **138**, 185–93

Mayes, A. and Meudell, P. (1981) 'How similar is the effect of cueing in amnesics and in normal subjects following forgetting?' *Cortex*, **17**, 113–24

Meacher, M. (1972) *Taken for a Ride: Special Residential Homes for Confused Old People: a Study of Separatism in Social Policy*, Longman, London

Melin, L. and Gotestam, K. G. (1981) 'The effects of rearranging ward routines on communication and eating behaviours of psychogeriatric patients', *Journal of Applied Behavior Analysis*, **14**, 47–51

Merriam, S. (1980) 'The concept and function of reminiscence: a review of the research', *Gerontologist*, **20**, 604–8

Meudell, P. and Mayes, A. (1981) 'A similarity between weak normal memory and amnesia with two and eight choice word recognition: a signal detection analysis', *Cortex*, **17**, 19–30

Miles, W. R. (1931) 'Measures of certain human abilities throughout the life span', *Proceedings of the National Academy of Science*, **17**, 627–33

Millard, P. H. (1983) 'Long-term care in Europe: a review' in M. J. Denham (ed.), *Care of the Long-stay Elderly Patient*, Croom Helm, London, pp. 206–16

Miller, E. (1971) 'On the nature of memory disorder in presenile dementia', *Neuropsychologia*, **9**, 75–8

———— (1972) 'Efficiency of coding and the short-term memory defect in presenile dementia', *Neuropsychologia*, **10**, 133–6

———— (1973) 'Short term and long term memory in presenile dementia', *Psychological Medicine*, **3**, 221–4

———— (1974a) 'Psychomotor performance in senile dementia', *Psychological Medicine*, **4**, 64–8

———— (1974b) 'Dementia as an accelerated ageing of the nervous system: some psychological and methodological considerations', *Age and Ageing*, **3**, 197–202

———— (1975) 'Impaired recall and memory disturbance in presenile dementia', *British Journal of Social and Clinical Psychology*, **14**, 73–9

———— (1977a) *Abnormal Ageing: the Psychology of Senile and Presenile Dementia*, Wiley, Chichester

———— (1977b) 'A note on visual information processing in senile dementia', *British Journal of Social and Clinical Psychology*, **16**, 99–100

———— (1977c) 'The management of dementia: a review of some possibilities', *British Journal of Social and Clinical Psychology*, **16**, 77–83

———— (1978) 'Retrieval from long-term memory in presenile dementia: two tests of an hypothesis', *British Journal of Social and Clinical Psychology*, **17**, 143–8

———— (1980a) 'Cognitive assessment of the older adult' in J. E. Birren and R. B. Sloane (eds.), *Handbook of Mental Health and Ageing*, Prentice-Hall, Englewood Cliffs, NJ, pp. 520–36

———— (1980b) 'Psychological intervention in the management and rehabilitation of neuropsychological impairments', *Behaviour Research and Therapy*, **18**, 527–35

—— (1984) 'Verbal fluency as a function of a measure of verbal intelligence and in relation to different types of cerebral pathology', *British Journal of Clinical Psychology*, **23**, 53–8

—— and Hague, F. (1975) 'Some statistical characteristics of speech in presenile dementia', *Psychological Medicine*, **5**, 255–9

—— and Lewis, P. (1977) 'Recognition memory in elderly patients with depression and dementia: a signal detection analysis', *Journal of Abnormal Psychology*, **86**, 84–6

Mintz, J., Steuer, J. and Jarvik, L. (1981) 'Psychotherapy with depressed elderly patients: research considerations', *Journal of Consulting and Clinical Psychology*, **49**, 542–8

Mischel, W. (1968) *Personality and Assessment*, Wiley, New York

Mishara, B. L. and Kastenbaum, R. (1980) *Alcohol and Old Age*, Grune and Stratton, New York

Montgomery, S. A. and Asberg, M. (1979) 'A new depression scale designed to be sensitive to change', *British Journal of Psychiatry*, **134**, 382–9

Moore, V. and Wyke, M. A. (1984) 'Drawing disability in patients with senile dementia', *Psychological Medicine*, **14**, 97–105

Moos, R. H. and Lemke, S. (1980) 'Assessing the physical and architectural features of sheltered care settings', *Journal of Gerontology*, **35**, 571–83

Morris, J. N., Wolf, R. S. and Klerman, L. V. (1975) 'Common themes among morale and depression scales', *Journal of Gerontology*, **30**, 209–15

Morris, R. G. (1981) 'Memory and information processing dysfunction in dementia', Unpublished MSc thesis, University of Newcastle upon Tyne

—— (1984) 'Dementia and the function of the articulatory loop system', *Cognitive Neuropsychology*, **1**, 143–157

——, Wheatley, J. and Britton, P. (1983) 'Retrieval from long term memory in senile dementia — cued recall revisited', *British Journal of Clinical Psychology*, **22**, 141–2

Moscovitch, M. (1982) 'A neuropsychological approach to perception and memory in normal and pathological ageing' in F. I. M. Craik and S. Trehub (eds.), *Ageing and Cognitive Processes*, Plenum Press, New York, pp. 55–78

Moss, G. and Boren, J. (1972) 'Depression as a model for behavioural psychiatry', *Comprehensive Psychiatry*, **13**, 581–90

Mulhall, D. J. (1976) 'Systematic self-assessment by PQRST (Personal Questionnaire Rapid Scaling Technique)', *Psychological Medicine*, **6**, 591–7

—— (1978) 'Dysphasic stroke patients and the influence of their relatives', *British Journal of Disorders of Communication*, **13**, 127–34

Mulley, G. P. (1981) 'Stroke rehabilitation: what are we all doing?' in T. Arie (ed.), *Health Care of the Elderly*, Croom Helm, London, pp. 23–41

Mumford, S. and Carpenter, G. (1979) 'Psychological services and the elderly', *Bulletin of the British Psychological Society*, **32**, 286–8

Murphy, E. (1982) 'Social origins of depression in old age', *British Journal of Psychiatry*, **141**, 135–42

—— (1983) 'The prognosis of depression in old age', *British Journal of Psychiatry*, **142**, 111–19

Murphy, M. D., Sanders, R. E., Gabriesheski, A. S. and Schmitt, F. A. (1981) 'Metamemory in the aged', *Journal of Gerontology*, **36**, 185–93

Nelson, H. E. (1982) *The National Adult Reading Test*, NFER-Nelson, Windsor

—— and McKenna, P. (1975) 'The use of current reading ability in the assessment of dementia', *British Journal of Social and Clinical Psychology*, **14**, 259–67

Neugarten, B. L. (1977) 'Personality and ageing' in J. E. Birren and K. W. Schaie (eds.), *Handbook of the Psychology of Ageing*, Van Nostrand Reinhold,

Cincinnati
——— (1983) 'Health care, Medicare and health policy for older people: a conversation with Arthur Flemming', *American Psychologist*, **38**, 311–15
———, Havighurst, R. J. and Tobin, S. S. (1968) 'Personality and patterns of ageing' in B. L. Neugarten (ed.), *Middle Age and Ageing*, Chicago University Press, Chicago

Neville, H. J. and Folstein, M. F. (1979) 'Performance on three cognitive tasks by patients with dementia, depression or Korsakov's syndrome', *Gerontology*, **25**, 285–90

Newcomer, R. J. and Bexton, E. F. (1978) 'Ageing and the environment' in D. Hobman (ed.), *The Social Challenge of Ageing*, Croom Helm, London, pp. 73–116

Nihira, K., Foster, R., Shellhaas, M. and Leland, H. (1974) *AAMD Adaptive Behavior Scale*, American Association on Mental Deficiency, Washington

Norris, A. D. and Abu El Eileh, M. T. (1982) 'Reminiscence groups', *Nursing Times*, **78**, 1368–9

North, A. J. and Ulatowska, H. K. (1981) 'Competence in independently living older adults', *Journal of Gerontology*, **36**, 566–82

Nunn, C., Bergmann, K., Britton, P. G., Foster, E. M., Hall, E. H. and Kay, D. W. K. (1974) 'Intelligence and neurosis in old age', *British Journal of Psychiatry*, **124**, 446–52

Oberleder, M. (1962) 'An attitude scale to determine adjustment in institutions for the aged', *Journal of Chronic Diseases*, **15**, 915–23

O'Neill, P. M. and Calhoun, K. S. (1975) 'Sensory deficits and behavioral deterioration in senescence', *Journal of Abnormal Psychology*, **84**, 579–82

Orme, J. E. (1955) 'Intellectual and Rorschach test performance of a group of senile dementia patients and a group of elderly depressives', *Journal of Mental Science*, **101**, 863–70
——— (1957) 'Non-verbal and verbal performance in normal old age, senile dementia and elderly depressives', *Journal of Gerontology*, **12**, 408–13

Osborne, D. and Davis, L. J. (1978) 'Standard scores for Wechsler Memory Scale sub-tests', *Journal of Clinical Psychology*, **34**, 115–17

Overmier, J. B. and Seligman, M. E. P. (1967) 'Effects of inescapable shock upon subsequent escape and avoidance responding', *Journal of Comparative and Physiological Psychology*, **63**, 28–33

Owens, W. A. (1966) 'Age and mental abilities: a second adult follow-up', *Journal of Educational Psychology*, **51**, 311–25

Palmore, E. (1972) 'Compulsory versus flexible retirement: issues and facts', *Gerontologist*, **12**, 343–8
——— (1975) 'Differences in the retirement pattern of men and women', *Gerontologist*, **15**, 4–8
———, Cleveland, W. P., Nowlin, J. B., Ramm, D. and Siegler, I. C. (1979) 'Stress and adaptation in later life', *Journal of Gerontology*, **34**, 841–51
——— and Kivett, V. (1977) 'Change in life satisfaction: a longitudinal study of persons aged 46–70', *Journal of Gerontology*, **32**, 311–16

Parkes, C. M. (1972) *Bereavement: Studies of Grief in Adult Life*, Tavistock, London
——— (1980) 'Bereavement counselling', *British Medical Journal*, **281**, 3–6

Parkinson, S. R., Lindholm, J. M. and Urell, T. (1980) 'Ageing, dichotic memory and digit span', *Journal of Gerontology*, **35**, 87–95

Patterson, R. L. (1982) *Overcoming Deficits of Ageing: a Behavioural Approach*, Plenum, New York.
——— and Jackson, G. M. (1980) 'Behaviour modification with the elderly', *Progress in Behaviour Modification*, **9**, 205–39

Pattie, A. H. (1981) 'A survey version of the Clifton Assessment Procedures for the Elderly (CAPE)', *British Journal of Clinical Psychology*, **20**, 173–8
—— and Gilleard, C. J. (1979) *Manual for the Clifton Assessment Procedures for the Elderly (CAPE)*, Hodder and Stoughton Educational, Sevenoaks
Peace, S. (1983) 'Residential homes: a pleasure to live in?' *Community Care* (24 March), pp. 19–21
Perez, F. I., Hruska, N. A., Stell, R. L. and Rivera, V. M. (1978) 'Computerised assessment of memory performance in dementia', *Canadian Journal of Neurological Sciences*, **5**, 307–12
——, Rivera, V. M., Meyer, J. S., Gay, J. R. A., Taylor, R. L. and Mathew, N. T. (1975) 'Analysis of intellectual and cognitive performance in patients with multi-infarct dementia', *Journal of Neurology, Neurosurgery and Psychiatry*, **38**, 533–40
Perlmutter, M. and Mitchell, D. B. (1982) 'The appearance and disappearance of age differences in adult memory' in F. I. M. Craik and S. Trehub (eds.), *Ageing and Cognitive Processes*, Plenum Press, New York, pp. 127–44
Perrotta, P. and Meacham, J. A. (1981–2) 'Can a reminiscing intervention alter depression and self-esteem?' *International Journal of Ageing and Human Development* , **14**, 223–30
Perry, R. and Perry E. (1982) 'The ageing brain and its pathology' in R. Levy and F. Post (eds.), *The Psychiatry of Late Life*, Blackwell, Oxford, pp. 9–67
Peterson, R. F., Knapp, T. J., Rosen, J. C. and Pither, B. F. (1977) 'The effects of furniture arrangement on the behaviour of geriatric patients', *Behaviour Therapy*, **8**, 464–7
Pfeffer, R. I., Kurosaki, T. T., Harrah, C. H., Chance, J. M., Filos, S. (1982) 'Measurement of functional activities in older adults in the community', *Journal of Gerontology*, **37**, 323–9
Pfeiffer, E. (1975a) 'Sexual behaviour' in J. G. Howells (ed.), *Modern Perspectives in the Psychiatry of Old Age*, Churchill Livingstone, Edinburgh/London, pp. 313–25
—— (1975b) 'A short portable mental status questionnaire for the assessment of organic brain deficit in elderly patients', *Journal of American Geriatrics Society*, **23**, 433–41
—— (1975c) *Multidimensional Functional Assessment: the OARS Methodology*, Duke University Center for the Study of Ageing, Durham, North Carolina
Pincus, A. (1968) 'The definition and measurement of the institutional environment in homes for the aged', *Gerontologist*, **8**, 207–10
—— and Wood, V. (1970) 'Methodological issues in measuring the environment in institutions for the aged and its impact on residents', *Ageing and Human Development*, **1**, 117–26
Pitt, B. (1982) *Psychogeriatrics* (2nd edition), Churchill Livingstone, Edinburgh
Plutchik, R. (1979) 'Conceptual and practical issues in the assessment of the elderly' in A. Raskin and L. F. Jarvik (eds.), *Psychiatric Symptoms and Cognitive Loss in the Elderly*, Hemisphere, Washington
——, Conte, H., Lieberman, M., Bakur, M., Grossman, J. and Lehrman, N. (1970) 'Reliability and validity of a scale for assessing the functioning of geriatric patients', *Journal of American Geriatrics Society*, **18**, 491–500
Pollock, D. P. and Liberman, R. P. (1974) 'Behaviour therapy of incontinence in demented in-patients', *Gerontologist*, **14**, 488–91
Post, F. (1982) 'Functional Disorders' in R. Levy and F. Post (eds.), *The Psychiatry of Late Life*, Blackwell, Oxford, pp. 176–221
Powell, G. E. (1981) *Brain Function Therapy*, Gower, Aldershot
——, Bailey, S. and Clark, E. (1980) 'A very short form of the Minnesota Aphasia Test', *British Journal of Social and Clinical Psychology*, **19**, 189–94

————, Clark, E. and Bailey, S. (1979) 'Categories of aphasia: a cluster-analysis of Schuell test profiles', *British Journal of Disorders of Communication*, **14**, 111–22

Powell-Proctor, L. and Miller, E. (1982) 'Reality orientation: a critical appraisal', *British Journal of Psychiatry*, **140**, 457–63

Power, C. A. and McCarron, L. T. (1975) 'Treatment of depression in persons residing in Homes for the Aged', *Gerontologist*, **15**, 132–5

Prigatano, G. P. (1978) 'Wechsler Memory Scale: a selective review of the literature', *Journal of Clinical Psychology*, **34**, 816–32

Puder, R., Lacks, P., Bertelson, A. D. and Storandt, M. (1983) 'Short-term stimulus control treatment of insomnia in older adults', *Behavior Therapy*, **14**, 424–9

Quattrochi-Tubin, S. and Jason, L. A. (1980) 'Enhancing social interactions and activity among the elderly through stimulus control', *Journal of Applied Behaviour Analysis*, **13**, 159–63

————, Jones, J. W. and Breedlove, V. (1982) 'The burnout syndrome in geriatric counsellors and service workers', *Activities, Adaptation and Ageing*, **3**, 65–76

Quetelet, A. (1842) in J. E. Birren (1961) 'A brief history of the psychology of ageing', *Gerontologist*, **1**(2), 69–77

Quilitch, H. R. (1975) 'A comparison of three staff-management procedures', *Journal of Applied Behavior Analysis*, **8**, 59–66

Rabbitt, P. (1977) 'Changes in problem-solving ability in old age', in J. E. Birren and K. W. Schaie (eds.), *Handbook of the Psychology of Aging*, Van Nostrand Reinhold, Cincinnati, Ohio, pp. 606–25

———— (1980) 'A fresh look at changes in reaction times in old age' in D. Stein (ed.), *The Psychobiology of Ageing: Problems and Perspectives*, Elsevier/North Holland, New York

———— (1981a) 'Talking to the old', *New Society* (22 January), pp. 141–1

———— (1981b) 'Cognitive psychology needs models for change in performance with old age' in J. Long and A. Baddeley (eds.), *Attention and Performance*, IX, Lawrence Erlbaum Associates, Hillsdale, NJ, pp. 555–73

———— (1982a) 'How do old people know what to do next?' in F. I. M. Craik and S. Trehub (eds.), *Ageing and Cognitive Processes*, Plenum Press, New York, pp. 79–98

———— (1982b) 'How to assess the aged? An experimental psychologist's view. Some comments on Dr. Kendrick's paper', *British Journal of Clinical Psychology*, **21**, 55–9

Rabinowitz, J. C. and Ackerman, B. P. (1982) 'General encoding of episodic events by elderly adults' in F. I. M. Craik and S. Trehub (eds.), *Ageing and Cognitive Processes*, Plenum Press, New York, pp. 145–54

Rachman, S. (1980) 'Emotional Processing', *Behaviour Research and Therapy*, **18**, 51–60

Radcliffe, J. A. (1966) 'WAIS factorial structure and factor scores for ages 18–54, *Australian Journal of Psychology*, **18**, 228–38

Ramsay, R. W. (1977) 'Behavioural approaches to bereavement', *Behaviour Research and Therapy*, **15**, 131–5

Rankin, J. L. and Kausler, D. H. (1979) 'Adult age differences in false recognitions', *Journal of Gerontology*, **34**, 58–65

Raphael, B. (1977) 'Preventive intervention with the recently bereaved', *Archives of General Psychiatry*, **34**, 1450–4

Raven, J. C., Court, J. H. and Raven, J. (1976) *Manual for Raven's Progressive Matrices and Vocabulary Scales*, H. K. Lewis & Co., London

Rebok, G. W. and Hoyer, W. J. (1977) 'The functional context of elderly behavior', *Gerontologist*, **17**, 27–34

Rechtschaffen, A. (1959) 'Psychotherapy with geriatric patients: a review of the literature', *Journal of Gerontology*, 14, 73–84

Reichard, S., Livson, F. and Peterson, P. G. (1962) *Ageing and Personality: a Study of Seventy Eight Older Men*, Wiley, New York

Reid, D. W., Haas, G. and Hawkins, D. (1977), 'Locus of desired control and positive self concept of the elderly', *Journal of Gerontology*, 32, 441–50

Reitan, R. M. and Boll, T. J. (1971) 'Intellectual and cognitive functioning in Parkinson's disease', *Journal of Consulting and Clinical Psychology*, 37, 364–9

Rimmer, L. (1982) *Reality Orientation: Principles and Practice*, Winslow Press, Winslow, Bucks

Rinke, C. L., Williams, J. J., Lloyd, K. E. and Smith-Scott, W. (1978) 'The effects of prompting and reinforcement on self-bathing by elderly residents of a nursing home', *Behavior Therapy*, 9, 873–81

Robinson, B. C. (1983) 'Validation of a caregiver strain index', *Journal of Gerontology*, 38, 344–8

Robinson, R. A. (1977) 'Differential diagnosis and assessment in brain failure', *Age and Ageing*, 6, 42–9 (Supplement)

Rochford, G. (1971) 'A study of naming errors in dysphasic and demented patients', *Neuropsychologia*, 9, 437–43

Rodin, J. and Langer, E. J. (1977) 'Long-term effects of a control-relevant intervention with the institutionalised aged', *Journal of Personality and Social Psychology*, 35, 897–902

Rogers, J. C. and Snow, T. (1982) 'An assessment of the feeding behaviours of the institionalised elderly', *American Journal of Occupational Therapy*, 36, 375–80

Ron, M. A. (1977) 'Brain damage in chronic alcoholism: a neuropathological, neuroradiological and psychological review', *Psychological Medicine*, 7, 103–12

——, Toone, B. K., Garralda, M. E. and Lishman, W. A. (1979) 'Diagnostic accuracy in presenile dementia', *British Journal of Psychiatry*, 13, 161–8

Rorer, L. G. and Wigider, T. A. (1983) 'Personality structure and assessment', *Annual Review of Psychology*, 34, 431–63

Rose, A. M. (1968) 'A current theoretical issue in social gerontology' in B. L. Neugarten (ed.), *Middle Age and Ageing*, University of Chicago Press, Chicago

Rosen, W. G. (1980) 'Verbal fluency in ageing and dementia', *Journal of Clinical Neuropsychology*, 2, 135–46

—— and Mohs, R. C. (1982) 'Evolution of cognitive decline in dementia' in S. Corkin, K. L. Davis, J. H. Growdon, E. Usdin and R. J. Wurtman (eds.), *Alzheimer's Disease: a Report of Progress in Research* (Ageing, Volume 19), Raven Press, New York, pp. 183–8

Rosin, A. J. (1982) 'Parkinsonism' in B. Isaacs (ed.), *Recent Advances in Geriatric Medicine 2*, Churchill Livingstone, Edinburgh, pp. 41–70

—— and Glatt, M. M. (1971) 'Alcohol excess in the elderly', *Quarterly Journal of Studies on Alcoholism*, 32, 53–9

Roth, M. (1955) 'The natural history of mental disorder in old age', *Journal of Mental Science*, 102, 281–301

——, Tomlinson, B. E. and Blessed, G. (1967) 'The relationship between quantitative measures of dementia and of degenerative changes in the cerebral grey matter of elderly subjects', *Proceedings of the Royal Society of Medicine*, 60, 254–60

Rothwell, N., Britton, P. G. and Woods, R. T. (1983) 'The effects of group living in a residential home for the elderly', *British Journal of Social Work*, 13, 639–43

Rotter, J. B. (1966) 'Generalised expectancies for internal versus external control of reinforcement', *Psychological Monographs*, 80(1) (Whole No. 609), 1–28

Royal College of Physicians (1981) 'Organic Mental impairment in the elderly',

Journal of the Royal College of Physicians, London, **15**, 141–7

Roybal, E. R. (1984) 'Federal involvement in mental health care for the aged: past and future directions', *American Psychologist*, **39**, 163–6

Russell, E. W. (1975) 'A multiple scoring method for the assessment of complex memory functions', *Journal of Consulting and Clinical Psychology*, **43**, 800–9

Salamon, M. J. (1983) 'Opportunities for geropsychologists?' *American Psychologist*, **38**, 613

Salthouse, T. A. and Somberg, B. L. (1982) 'Isolating the age deficit in speeded performance', *Journal of Gerontology*, **37**, 59–63

Salzman, C., Kochansky, G. E. and Shader, R. I. (1972) 'Rating scales for geriatric psychopharmacology — a review', *Psychopharmacology Bulletin*, **8**(3), 3–50

Sanavio, E. (1981) 'Toilet retraining psychogeriatric residents', *Behaviour Modification*, **5**, 417–27

Sanford, J. R. A. (1975) 'Tolerance of debility in elderly dependents by supporters at home: its significance for hospital practice', *British Medical Journal*, **iii**, 471–3

Savage, B. and Widdowson, T. (1974) 'Revising the use of nursing resources', *Nursing Times*, **70**, 1372–4, 1424–7

Savage, R. D. (1973) 'Old age' in H. J. Eysenck (ed.), *Handbook of Abnormal Psychology* (2nd Edition), Pitman's Medical, London

——— (1981) 'Intellect, personality and adjustment in the aged' in R. Lynn (ed.), *Dimensions of Personality: Papers in Honour of H. J. Eysenck*, Pergamon, Oxford

———, Britton, P. G., Bolton, N. and Hall, E. H. (1973) *Intellectual Functioning in the Aged*, Methuen, London

———, Gaber, L. B., Britton, P. G., Bolton, N. and Cooper, A. (1977) *Personality and Adjustment in the Aged*, Academic Press, London

——— and Hall, E. H. (1973) 'A performance learning measure for the aged', *British Journal of Psychiatry*, **122**, 721–3

Schaie, K. W. (1967) 'Age changes and age differences', *Gerontologist*, **7**, 128–32

——— (1977–8) 'Towards a stage theory of adult cognitive development', *Journal of Ageing and Human Development*, **8**, 129–38

——— and Baltes, P. B. (1977) 'Some faith helps to see the forest: a final comment on the Horn and Donaldson myth of the Baltes–Schaie postition on adult intelligence', *American Psychologist*, **32**, 1118–20

——— and Labouvie-Vief, G. (1974) 'Generational versus ontogenetic components of change in adult cognitive behaviour: a fourteen year cross-sequential study', *Developmental Psychology*, **10**, 305–20

———, ——— and Buech, B. U. (1973) 'Generational and cohort specific differences in adult cognitive functioning: a fourteen-year study of independent samples', *Developmental Psychology*, **9**, 151–66

——— and Parham, I. M. (1976) 'Stability of adult personality traits: fact or fable', *Journal of Personality and Social Psychology*, **34**, 146–58

Schneider, F. W. and Coppinger, N. W. (1971) 'Staff-resident perceptions of the needs and adjustment of nursing home residents', *Ageing and Human Development*, **2**, 59–65

Schulz, R. (1976) 'Effects of control and predictability on the physical and psychological well-being of the institutionalised aged', *Journal of Personality and Social Psychology*, **33**, 563–73

——— (1980) 'Ageing and control' in J. Garber and M. E. P. Seligman (eds.), *Human Helplessness: Theory and Applications*, Academic Press, New York, pp. 261–77

——— and Brenner, G. (1977) 'Relocation of the aged: a review and theoretical analysis', *Journal of Gerontology*, **32**, 323–33

—— and Hanusa, B. (1978) 'Long term effects of control and predictability-enhancing intervention: findings and ethical issues', *Journal of Personality and Social Psychology*, **36**, 1194–201

Schwab, J. J., Holzer, C. E. and Warheit, G. J. (1973) 'Depressive symptomatology and age', *Psychosomatics*, **14**, 135–41

Schwenk, M. A. (1981) 'Reality orientation for the institutionalised aged: does it help?' *Gerontologist*, **19**, 373–7

Seligman, M. (1975) *Helplessness: On Depression, Development and Death*, W. H. Freeman, San Francisco

Semple, S. A., Smith, C. M. and Swash, M. (1982) 'The Alzheimer Disease Syndrome' in S. Corkin, K. L. Davis, J. H. Growdon, E. Usdin and R. J. Wurtman (eds.), *Alzheimer's Disease: a Report of Progress in Research*, (Ageing, Volume 19), Raven Press, New York, pp. 93–108

Shanas, E. (1979) 'The family as a social support system in old age', *Gerontologist*, **19**, 169–74

Shapiro, M. B. (1961) 'A method of measuring psychological changes specific to the individual psychiatric patient', *British Journal of Medical Psychology*, **34**, 151–5

Sheldon, F. (1982) 'Supporting the supporters: working with the relatives of patients with dementia', *Age and Ageing*, **11**, 184–8

Shepherd, G. and Richardson, A. (1979) 'Organisation and interaction in psychiatric day-centres', *Psychological Medicine*, **9**, 573–9

Siegler, I. C. (1980) 'The psychology of adult development and ageing' in E. W. Busse and D. G. Blazer (eds.), *Handbook of Geriatric Psychiatry*, Van Nostrand Reinhold, New York, pp. 169–221

—— and Botwinick, J. (1979) 'A long term longitudinal study of the intellectual ability of older adults — the matter of selective subject attrition', *Journal of Gerontology*, **34**, 242–8

Simpson, S. (1979) 'Depression and engagement in a residential home for the elderly', Unpublished MSc dissertation, University of Newcastle upon Tyne, England

——, Woods, R. T. and Britton, P. G. (1981) 'Depression and engagement in a residential home for the elderly', *Behaviour Research and Therapy*, **19**, 435–8

Skilbeck, C. E. and Woods, R. T. (1980) 'The factorial structure of the Wechsler Memory Scale: samples of neurological and psychogeriatric patients', *Journal of Clinical Neuropsychology*, **2**, 293–300

Slater, P. E. and Scarr, M. A. (1964) 'Personality in Old Age', *Genetic Psychology Monographs*, **70**, 229–69

Smith, B. J. and Barker, H. R. (1972) 'Influence of a reality orientation training programme on the attitudes of trainees towards the elderly', *Gerontologist*, **12**, 262–4

Smith, J. M. (1979) 'Nurse and psychiatric aide rating scales for assessing psychopathology in the elderly: a critical review' in A. Raskin and L. Jarvik (eds.), *Psychiatric Symptoms and Cognitive Loss in the Elderly*, Hemisphere, Washington DC, pp. 169–86

——, Bright, B. and McCloskey, J. (1977) 'Factor analytic composition of the geriatric rating scale (GRS)', *Journal of Gerontology*, **32**, 58–62

Snow, D. L. and Gordon, J. B. (1980) 'Social network analysis and intervention with the elderly', *Gerontologist*, **20**, 463–7

Snyder, L. H., Rupprecht, P., Pyrek, J., Brekhus, S. and Moss, T. (1978) 'Wandering', *Gerontologist*, **18**, 272–80

Solyom, L. and Barik, H. C. (1965) 'Conditioning in senescence and senility', *Journal of Gerontology*, **20**, 483–8

Sommer, R. and Ross, H. (1958) 'Social interaction on a geriatric ward', *International Journal of Social Psychiatry*, **4**, 128–33

Sparacino, J. (1978–9) 'Individual psychotherapy with the aged: a selective review', *International Journal of Ageing and Human Development*, **9**(3), 197–217

Sperling, G. (1960) The information available in brief visual presentations, *Psychological Monographs: General and Applied*, **74**, 1–28

Squire, L. R. (1980) 'Specifying the defect in human amnesia: storage, retrieval and semantics', *Neuropsychologia*, **18**, 368–72

Stern, L. D. (1981) 'A review of theories of human amnesia', *Memory and Cognition*, **9**, 247–62

Steuer, J., Bank, L., Olsen, E. J. and Jarvik, L. F. (1980) 'Depression, physical health and somatic complaints in the elderly: a study of the Zung self-rating depression scale', *Journal of Gerontology*, **35**, 683–8

—— and Hammen, C. L. (1983) 'Cognitive-behavioural group therapy for the depressed elderly: issues and adaptations', *Cognitive Therapy and Research*, **7**, 285–96

Stevenson, O. (1981) 'Caring and Dependency' in D. Hobman (ed.), *The Impact of Ageing*, Croom Helm, London, pp. 128–42

Stirling, E. (1980) 'Support of the elderly in a general practice', Paper presented at British Psychological Society, London Conference

Stock, W. A. and Okun, M. A. (1982) 'The construct validity of life satisfaction among the elderly', *Journal of Gerontology*, **37**, 625–7

Stolz, S. B. (1978) *Ethical Issues in Behaviour Modification*, Jossey-Bass, New York

Storandt, M. (1983) 'Psychology's response to the graying of America', *American Psychologist*, **38**, 323–6

Strehler, B. L. (1982) 'Ageing: concepts and theories', in A. Viidik (ed.), *Lectures on Gerontology. Vol. 1A: on Biology of Ageing*, Academic Press, London

Suchett-Kaye, A. I., Sarkar, U., Elkan, G. and Waring, M. (1971) 'Physical, mental and social assessment of elderly patients suffering from cerebrovascular accident with special reference to rehabilitation', *Gerontologia Clinica*, **13**, 192–206

Swenson, W. M. (1961) 'Structured personality testing in the aged: an MMPI study of the geriatric population', *Journal of Clinical Psychology*, **17**, 302–4

Tarrier, N. and Larner, S. (1983) 'The effects of manipulation of social reinforcement on toilet requests on a geriatric ward', *Age and Ageing*, **12**, 234–9

Taulbee, L. R. and Folsom, J. C. (1966) 'Reality orientation for geriatric patients', *Hospital and Community Psychiatry*, **17**, 133–5

Teri, L. and Lewinsohn, P. (1982) 'Modification of the Pleasant and Unpleasant Events schedules for use with the elderly', *Journal of Consulting and Clinical Psychology*, **50**, 444–5

Thomae, H. (1970) 'Theory of ageing and cognitive theory of personality', *Human Development*, **13**, 1–16

Thompson, J. A. and Wilson, S. L. (1982) 'Automated psychological testing', *International Journal of Man-Machine Studies*, **17**, 279–89

Thurnher, M. (1973) 'Adaptability of life history interviews to the study of adult development' in L. F. Jarvik, C. Eisdorfer and J. E. Blum (eds.), *Intellectual Functioning in Adults: Psychological and Biological Influences*, Springer, New York, pp. 137–42

Thyer, B. A. (1981) 'Prolonged in-vivo exposure therapy with a 70-year-old woman', *Journal of Behaviour Therapy and Experimental Psychiatry*, **12**, 69–71

Tobin, S. S. and Lieberman, M. A. (1976) *Last Home for the Aged*, Jossey-Bass, San Franscico

Tomlinson, B. E., Blessed, G. and Roth, M. (1968) 'Observations on the brains of non-demented old people', *Journal of the Neurological Sciences*, **7**, 331–56

Townsend, P. (1962) *The Last Refuge*, Routledge and Kegan Paul, London

Tulving, E. (1972) 'Episodic and semantic memory' in E. Tulving and W. Donaldson (eds.), *Organisation of Memory*, Academic Press, New York, pp. 382–403

Turner, R. K. (1980) 'A behavioural approach to the management of incontinence in the elderly' in D. Mandelstam (ed.), *Incontinence and its Management*, Croom Helm, London

Twining, C. and Chapman, J. (1983) 'The clinical psychologist's input to the geriatric team', *Geriatric Medicine* (January), 41–6

UN (1979) *World Population Trends and Prospects*, United Nations, New York

Verwoerdt, A. (1981) 'Psychotherapy for the elderly' in T. Arie (ed.), *Health Care of the Elderly*, Croom Helm, London, pp. 118–42

Vezina, J. and Bourque, P. (1984) 'The relationship between cognitive structure and symptoms of depression in the elderly', *Cognitive Therapy and Research*, **8**, 29–36

Volans, P. J. and Levy, R. (1982) 'A re-evaluation of an automated tailored test of concept learning with elderly psychiatric patients', *British Journal of Clinical Psychology*, **21**, 93–101

—— and Woods, R. T. (1983) 'Why do we assess the aged?' *British Journal of Clinical Psychology*, **22**, 213–14

Wade, D. T., Skilbeck, C. E., Wood, V. A. and Hewer, R. L. (1984) 'Long-term survival after stroke', *Age and Ageing*, **13**, 76–82

Walker, S. A. (1980) 'Application of a test for aphasia to normal old people', *Journal of Clinical and Experimental Gerontology*, **2**, 185–98

—— (1981) 'Communication as a changing function of age' in *Communication Problems of the Elderly*, College of Speech Therapists (UK)

—— and Williams, B. O. (1980) 'The response of a disabled elderly population to speech therapy', *British Journal of Disorders of Communication*, **15**, 19–29

Wallis, D. and Cope, D. (1978) 'UWIST action research project on the job satisfaction of nursing and ancillary staff. Report on research done in a psychogeriatric unit', Department of Applied Psychology, UWIST, Cardiff

Wallis, G. G., Baldwin, M. and Higginbotham, P. (1983) 'Reality orientation therapy: a controlled trial', *British Journal of Medical Psychology*, **56**, 271–8

Walsh, D. A. (1982) 'The development of visual information processes in adulthood and old age' in F. I. M. Craik and S. Trehub (eds.), *Ageing and Cognitive Processes*, Plenum Press, New York, pp. 99–126

—— and Thompson, L. W. (1978) 'Age differences in visual sensory memory', *Journal of Gerontology*, **33**, 383–7

Walton, D. and Black, D. A. (1957) 'The validity of a psychological test of brain damage', *British Journal of Medical Psychology*, **20**, 270–9

Warrington, E. K. and Sanders, H. I. (1971) 'The fate of old memories', *Quarterly Journal of Experimental Psychology*, **24**, 432–42

—— and Weiskrantz, L. (1970) 'Amnesic syndrome: consolidation or retrieval', *Nature*, **228**, 628–30

—— and —— (1982) 'Amnesia: a disconnection syndrome?', *Neuropsychologia*, **20**, 233–48

Watson, H. W. (1979–80) 'Resistances to naturalistic observation in a geriatric setting', *International Journal of Ageing and Human Development*, **10**, 35–45

Wattis, J. P. (1983) 'Alcohol and old people', *British Journal of Psychiatry*, **143**, 306–7

Waugh, N. C. and Barr, R. A. (1982) 'Encoding deficits in ageing' in F. I. M. Craik and S. Trehub (eds.), *Ageing and Cognitive Processes*, Plenum Press, New York, pp. 183–90

——, Thomas, J. C. and Fozard, J. L. (1978) 'Retrieval time from different memory stores', *Journal of Gerontology*, **3**, 718–24

Wechsler, D. (1945) 'A standardised memory scale for clinical use', *Journal of Psychology*, **19**, 87–95

—— (1955) *Manual for the Wechsler Adult Intelligence Scale*, Psychological Corporation, New York

—— (1958) *The Measurement and Appraisal of Adult Intelligence*, Williams and Wilkins, Baltimore.

Wedgwood, J. (1982) 'The automated pictorial paired and associate learning task', *International Journal of Man-Machine Studies*, **17**, 241–6

Weingartner, H., Kaye, W., Smallberg, S., Cohen, R., Ebert, M. H., Gillin, J. C. and Gold, P. (1982) 'Determinants of memory failures in dementia' in S. Corkin, K. L. Davis, J. H. Growdon, E. Usdin and R. J. Wurtman (eds.), *Alzheimer's Disease: a Report of Progress in Research* (Ageing, Volume 19), Raven Press, New York, pp. 171–6

——, ——, ——, Ebert, M. H., Gillin, J. C. and Sitaram, N. (1981) 'Memory failures in progressive idiopathic dementia', *Journal of Abnormal Psychology*, **90**, 187–96

Welford, A. T. (1958) *Ageing and Human Skill*, Oxford University Press, London

—— (1977) 'Motor performance' in J. E. Birren and K. W. Schaie (eds.), *Handbook of the Psychology of Ageing*, Van Nostrand Reinhold, Cincinnati

White, J. G., Merrick, M. and Harbison, J. J. M. (1969) 'Williams' scale for the measurement of memory: test reliability and validity in a psychiatric population', *British Journal of Social and Clinical Psychology*, **8**, 141–51

Whitehead, A. (1973a) 'The pattern of WAIS performance in elderly psychiatric patients', *British Journal of Social and Clinical Psychology*, **12**, 435–6

—— (1973b) 'Verbal learning and memory in elderly depressives', *British Journal of Psychiatry*, **123**, 203–8

—— (1974) 'Factors in the learning deficit of elderly depressives', *British Journal of Social and Clinical Psychology*, **13**, 201–8

—— (1975) 'Recognition memory in dementia', *British Journal of Social and Clinical Psychology*, **14**, 191–4

—— (1976) 'The prediction of outcome in elderly psychiatric patients', *Psychological Medicine*, **6**, 469–79

—— (1977) 'Changes in cognitive functioning in elderly psychiatric patients', *British Journal of Psychiatry*, **130**, 605–8

Wilensky, H. and Barmack, J. E. (1966) 'Interests of doctoral students in clinical psychology in work with older adults', *Journal of Gerontology*, **21**, 410–14

Wilkie, F. and Eisdorfer, C. (1971) 'Intelligence and blood pressure in the aged', *Science*, **172**, 959–62

Wilkinson, I. M. and Graham-White, J. (1980) 'Psychogeriatric dependency rating scales (PGDRS): a method of assessment for use by nurses', *British Journal of Psychiatry*, **137**, 558–65

Williams, J. M. G. (1984) *The Psychological Treatment of Depression*, Croom Helm, London

Williams, M. (1968) 'The measurement of memory in clinical practice', *British Journal of Social and Clinical Psychology*, **7**, 19–34

Wilson, B. A. and Moffat, N. (eds.) (1984) *Clinical Management of Memory Problems*, Croom Helm, London/Aspen Systems Corporation, Rockville, Maryland

Wilson, D. G. (1955) 'The pathology of senility', *American Journal of Psychiatry*, **3**, 902–6

Wilson, R. S., Bacon, L. D., Kaszniak, A. W. and Fox, J. H. (1982a) 'The episodic-semantic memory distinction and paired-associate learning', *Journal of Consulting and Clinical Psychology*, **50**, 154–5

——, Kaszniak, A. W., Bacon, L. D., Fox, J. H. and Kelly, M. P. (1982b) 'Facial recognition memory in dementia', *Cortex*, **18**, 329–36

——, Bacon, L. D., Fox, J. H. and Kaszniak, A. W. (1983a) 'Primary memory and secondary memory in dementia of the Alzheimer type', *Journal of Clinical Neuropsychology*, 5, 337–44

——, Bacon, L. D., Kramer, R. L., Fox, J. H. and Kaszniak, A. W. (1983b) 'Word frequency effect and recognition memory in dementia of the Alzheimer type', *Journal of Clinical Neuropsychology*, 5, 97–104

——, Kaszniak, A. W. and Fox, J. H. (1981) 'Remote memory in senile dementia', *Cortex*, 17, 41–8

Winocur, G. and Weiskrantz, L. (1976) 'An investigation of paired-associate learning in amnesia patients', *Neuropsychologia*, 14, 97–110

Winograd, C. H. (1984) 'Mental status tests and the capacity for self-care', *Journal of American Geriatrics Society*, 32, 49–55

Wisocki, P. A. and Mosher, P. M. (1980) 'Peer-facilitated sign language training for a geriatric stroke victim with chronic brain damage', *Journal of Geriatric Psychiatry*, 13, 89–102

Wolfensberger, W. (1977) *The Principles of Normalisation in Human Services*, National Institute on Mental Retardation, Toronto

Wolk, R. L. and Wolk, R. B. (1971) *The Gerontological Apperception Test*, Behavioural Publications, New York

Wood, V., Wylie, M. L. and Sheafor, B. (1969) 'An analysis of a short self-report measure of life-satisfaction: correlation with rater judgements', *Journal of Gerontology*, 24, 465–9

Woods, R. T. (1979) 'Reality orientation and staff attention: a controlled study', *British Journal of Psychiatry*, 134, 502–7

—— (1981) 'Continuous reaction time in senile dementia', 12th International Congress of Gerontology, Hamburg

—— (1982) 'The psychology of ageing: assessment of defects and their management' in R. Levy and F. Post (eds.), *The Psychiatry of Late Life*, Blackwell, Oxford, pp. 68–113

—— (1983) 'Specificity of learning in reality orientation sessions: a single case study', *Behaviour Research and Therapy*, 21, 173–5

—— and Britton, P. G. (1977) 'Psychological approaches to the treatment of the elderly', *Age and Ageing*, 6, 104–12

—— and Holden, U. P. (1982) 'Reality Orientation' in B. Isaacs (ed.), *Recent Advances in Geriatric Medicine — 2*, Churchill Livingstone, Edinburgh, pp. 181–200

—— and Piercy, M. (1974) 'A similarity between amnesic memory and normal forgetting', *Neuropsychologia*, 12, 437–45

Wright, R. E. (1981) 'Ageing, divided attention, and processing capacity', *Journal of Gerontology*, 36, 605–14

Zacks, R. T. (1982) 'Encoding strategies used by young and elderly adults in a keeping track task', *Journal of Gerontology*, 37, 203–11

Zarit, S. H., Reever, K. E. and Bach-Peterson, J. (1980) 'Relatives of the impaired elderly: correlates of feelings of burden', *The Gerontologist*, 20(6), 649–55

Zepelin, H., Wolfe, C. S. and Kleinplatz, F. (1981) 'Evaluation of a year long reality orientation program', *Journal of Gerontology*, 36, 70–7

Ziegler, M. and Reid, D. W. (1979) 'Correlates of locus of desired control in two samples of elderly persons: community residents and hospitalised patients', *Journal of Consulting and Clinical Psychology*, 47, 977–9

INDEX

abuse, old age 295
accommodation *see* housing
activity
  scales 174
  theories 63
  see also behaviour therapy,
    dementia, engagement
acute confusional states 21, 22, 127,
  247
adaptation, behavioural assessment
  171–83
adjustment 62–4, 68–9
  assessment 164–71
  environmental influences 69–72
  interpersonal factors 72–8
  theories 68–9
  see also physical health
affective disorders *see* depression,
  treatment
Age Concern 306–13
ageing
  mechanisms 10–13
  theories 11–12
ageism 22, 23, 59, 189
alcohol 122–3
  treatment of problems 211–12
Alzheimer's disease *see* dementia
amnesia 91–5, 105, 109, 122–3
anxiety management 195–8, 247,
  279, 301
aphasia 98, 105, 126, 247
  see also language
Army Apha Test 35
assertion training 204
attitudes to elderly 22, 23, 267,
  269, 277
  assessment 187
attributions 119, 120, 121, 198
automated assessment 154–6

Beck Depression Inventory (BDI)
  116, 167, 168, 200
Beck's cognitive theory 115–16, 121,
  198
behaviour excesses
  treatment 238–40
behaviour modification
  in dementia 235–42

behavioural analysis 243–4
behavioural problems 238–40
behavioural procedures 246
  goal planning 245
  incontinence 237
  increasing activity 236
  self-care 236–7
  in the community 304–5
  used by relatives 301–3
  modular treatment 240–2
behavioural assessment 171–83
  activity scales 174–5
  rating scales 171–4
  developments 175–7
  use by relatives 176–7
  use in practice 177–8
behaviour therapy
  activity programmes 198–201
  anxiety reduction 194–8, 247, 279,
    301
  grief therapy 204–7
  in the community 304–5
  sense of control 202–3
  skills training 203–4
Benton Visual Retention Test 143,
  146
bereavement 69, 75, 76, 119, 191,
  211
  treatment 204–7, 212, 307
Bexley-Maudsley Automated Psychological Screening Tests 154
biological adaption 10
burnout 279, 283
  assessment 187

cerebral trauma 125
cerebrovascular accidents (CVAs) *see*
  strokes
Clifton Assessment Procedures for
  the Elderly (CAPE) 104, 138–9,
  172–4
Clifton Behaviour Rating Scale
  172–4
Clinical Analysis Questionnaire
  (CAQ) 162, 166
cognitive assessment 129–58
  automated 154–6
  brief screening 136–9

descriptive 133–7
developments 151–7
diagnostic 129–32
examples 148–51
intellectual assessment 139–40
language 144
memory and learning 140–3, 153
models 134–7
neuropsychological 145–6, 244
special considerations 146–8
speed of processing 143–4, 153
tests for elderly 138–46
problems with 34, 152
cognitive theories of adjustment
68–9
cognitive therapy 198–200
cohort effect 11, 27
community care 285–6
family support 285–95
living alone 303–6
social networks 285–6
social supporters 295–303
information and practical help
296–7
relatives support groups 281,
297–303
written materials 303
voluntary agencies 285, 306–13
community psychology 306–13
compensatory model 69, 71–2
and intellectual function 45
in dementia 110
conditioning
in dementia 96
in stroke patients 126
continence 237–8, 244, 288
control *see* behaviour therapy, locus
of control
coping skills 69–72, 170–1, 224
of relatives 292–5, 301–2
Crichton Geriatric Rating Scale
172–4
cross-sectional studies 26–8, 32, 34,
60
cross-sequential studies 29, 31–3, 36,
50, 60
crystallised intelligence 44, 82, 135

deafness *see* hearing ability
death 233, 280
delirium *see* acute confusional states
dementia
arteriosclerotic 17, 19, 105
behaviour change 103–4

clinical features 18–19
conditioning in 96
coversational speech 97–8
definition 18
diagnosis 19, 132
engagement 262
family support 285, 287–95
see also community care
information processing 96, 109
intellectual change 81–3
language 97–102
memory deficit 83–96, 109
see also memory
naming difficulties 99, 100
neuropathology/neurochemistry
19, 20
perceptuo-motor ability 102
personality change 103
prevalence 16
psychological models 104–11
accelerated ageing 106–7
arousal 108
developmental reversal 108–9
heterogeneity 105–6
sensory deprivation 107–8
reading 101–2
relatives support group 298
treatment *see* treatment, organic
disorders
verbal fluency 90, 101
dependence
in institutions 264, 269, 277
depression
cognitive changes 111–15
incidence 16, 20–1, 189
psychological function 111–21
psychological models 115–21
Beck's cognitive theory 115–16,
121
behavioural 116–21
learned helplessness 119–21, 202
scales 166–9, 184
deterioration indices 37, 43, 82, 131,
140
dichotic listening memory tasks 53
in dementia 86
Digit Copying Test (DCT) 108, 114,
143, 151
digit span 53, 154
in dementia 85, 86
in depression 112
direct observation 178–83
disengagement theories 33, 62
drawing ability 102, 146

drugs, use of 13
drug effects 108, 114, 127, 137,
    189–90
dysphasia *see* aphasia
dyspraxia 102, 105, 126, 180, 244

ecological validity 38–9, 47, 135–6,
    153
elderly, age definition 2
elderly, age distribution 2, 4
elderly, sex distribution 3, 5
engagement 118, 201, 217–18, 222,
    236, 258–62, 271–2
    assessment 182–4
environmental assessment 184–7
ethical issues 320–1
exercise
    in dementia 217–18
Eysenck Personality Inventory (EPI)
    103, 161–3
Eysenck Personality Questionnaire
    (EPQ) 161–3

facial recognition
    in dementia 93–4
family relationships 287–90, 292–5
family support 9, 72–5, 126, 285–95
    supporting supporters 295–303
fluid intelligence 44, 82, 135
Functional Activities Questionnaire
    175

Geriatric Rating Scale 172, 174
graded exposure 195–6, 198
'Granny battering' 295
grief 75–6
grief therapy 204–7
group living 222–3, 262, 273, 283
group treatment 195, 204, 210–11,
    224, 234–5, 306–7
    for relatives 297–303

Halstead-Reitan Test Battery 122,
    145
Hamilton Depression Rating Scales
    168
hearing ability 14, 22, 40, 146,
    190–1
helplessness 119–21, 202, 231, 264
housing 6–10
    sheltered 9

incontinence
    treatment 237–8, 244

individual programme planning 243
institutions
    acivity levels 258–62
    community integration 280–2
        relatives 281
        volunteers 281–2
    effects on intervention 266–7
    ideals 268–74
    interactions in 262–4
    models of care 255–7
    promoting change 274–82
    quality 257–65
    staff reinforcement 277–9
    staff support 279–80
    types 251
        and dementia 255
        in UK 251–3
        outside UK 253–5
Instrumental Activities of Daily
    Living (IADL) 174–5
intellectual assessment *see* cognitive
    assessment
intellectual change 33–5
    factor analysis 43–4
    health 39–43
    individual differences 38
    models 43–6
    short-term 38
    survival 40–3
    terminal decline 41–3
interpersonal environment 72
    and treatment 194
intervention
    in community *see* community care
    in institutions *see* institutions
isolation 73–5, 208

Kendrick Battery for the Detection
    of Dementia 108, 132
Korsakoff's disorder 95, 121–3

language 57–8
    assessment 144–5
    in dementia 97–102
    in dysphasia 126
    treatment 247
life expectancy 2, 3
life review 69, 119, 193, 201, 233–5,
    242, 302
life satisfaction 63
    assessment 164–6, 168
Life Satisfaction Index (LSI) 103,
    164–6, 184
locus of control 68, 120–1, 169,

184, 202–3
loneliness 73–5, 211–12, 222, 258
longitudinal studies 28–30, 32,
    35–6, 41, 69
loss 191
    treatment 204–7

Maudsley Personality Inventory
    (MPI) 61, 161–3
memory 52–7, 83–96
    assessment 140–3
    episodic 84
        in amnesia 123
        in dementia 89–90
    in dementia 83–96, 109
    metamemory 56, 143
    non-verbal 93, 142–3
    primary 53–4, 84
        in dementia 85–9
        in depression 112
    remote 56, 84
        in dementia 94–5
    secondary 54–6, 84, 143
        cued recall 91–3
        in dementia 88–94
        in depression 112–14
        interference in 92–3
        retrieval deficit 91–2
    semantic 84
        in dementia 89–90
    sensory 52–3
        in dementia 84–5
    working 53–4, 84
        in dementia 87–8
mental health problems
    classification 17
    incidence 15–16
methodology
    age related change 26–33
Mill-Hill Vocabulary Scale 81, 131,
    140
Minnesota Multiphsaic Personality
    Inventory (MMPI) 60–1, 65,
    160, 162–3
models of psychological practice
    315–20
Modified Word Learning Test
    (MWLT) 113, 132, 142
morale
    assessment 164–6, 168–9
multi-disciplinary care-planning
    242–3, 245, 320
Multiphasic Evironmental Assess-
    ment Procedure (MEAP) 185–6

Mutiple Adjective Affect Check List
    (MAACL) 168

naming 57
    in dementia 99–100
National Adult Reading Test 102,
    131, 137, 145
network analysis 75
normalisation 71, 185, 217, 272–3,
    316, 321

Object Learning Test (OLT) 108,
    113, 143, 151
organic disorders *see* acute
    confusional states, dementia,
    strokes

paraphrenia 17, 22, 307
    treatment 209
Parkinson's disease 121, 123–5
Performance Test of Activities of
    Daily Living (PADL) 178–80
Personal Questionnaire 170
personality
    assessment 159–71
        adjective checklists 163–4
        life history 170–1
        objective tests 60–2, 160–4
        projective tests 61, 159–60
    change 60–2
    development 68
    questionnaires 60, 160–3
    structure 64–8
    typology 64–8
Philadelphia Geriatric Centre Scale
    (PGC) 164–6
Physical and Mental Impairment of
    Function Evaluation (PAMIE)
    172–3
physical health 13–14, 127
    and adjustment 63–4, 69, 117,
        167–8, 190–1, 193–4, 211
    and intellectual change 39–43, 137
    and reaction time 48
    and retirement 78
    and sexual function 77
Physical Self-Maintenance Scale
    (PSMS) 172–3
plasticity 38
primary care 312
Primary Mental Abilities Test 32–3,
    36
problem solving 49–52
    training in 51

treatment 200–1
projective tests 61, 159–60
prosthetic environment 220
Psychogeriatric Dependency Rating
    Scales (PDGRS) 172–4
psychotherapy 192–4

quality of life
    in dementia 215–17
    in institutions 257–65, 269, 271,
        282–3

Raven's Progressive Matrices 81,
    131, 140, 154
reaction time 46–9
    in dementia 96–7
reality orientation 223–32, 242,
    266–7, 277
    background 223–5
    community use 304
    research 225–6
    twenty-four-hour RO 226
    use by relatives 302
    verbal orientation training 228, 231
    ward orientation training 227–30
reinforcement
    and depression 116–21
relationship problems
    treatment 207, 211–12
relatives
    and institutional care 281
    effects of RO on mood 231
    strain 287–93
        assessment 186
        support groups 297–303, 307,
            309–10
        recruiting relatives 299–300
        types of groups 301–3
    see also family support
relaxation 195–6
religious belief 76, 78–9
reminiscence 69, 119, 193, 201,
    233–5, 242, 302
    therapy 193, 233–5, 242, 302
Repertory Grid 169–70
Reporter's test 99, 144
residential homes 6, 251–5, 259–65,
    268
    integration 282–3
retirement 2, 63, 69, 78, 117, 119,
    211
Revised Kendrick Battery see
    Kendrick Battery
role of psychologist see models of

psychological practice
Rorschach 159–60

Schuell Minnesota Aphasia Test 57,
    98–9, 144
seating arrangements 218–20, 222
sensory loss 14–15, 107, 146, 190–1
    intellectual change 40, 47
sequential studies 29, 31–3, 36, 50,
    60
sexual function 76–7
    in institutions 280
    physical health 76–7
    treatment 208, 239–40
sheltered workshop 221
Sixteen Personality Factor Question-
    naire (16PF) 61, 65, 103, 161–2
sleep problems
    treatment 208
social interaction 218–22, 241–2,
    262–4
social skills training 203–4, 241–2
speed of information processing
    46–9
    in dementia 96–7, 109
    in depression 114
staff
    support 279–80
    training 278–9, 306–7, 310
strokes 125–6
    treatment 247
suicide 21, 189
supporting supporters 295–303
Synonym Learning Test (SLT) 112,
    132

Tennessee Self Concept Scale (TSCS)
    162
terminal decline 41–3
Thematic Apperception Test (TAT)
    159–60
time-sampling 181, 183, 221, 260
    263
Token test 99, 144
treatment
    affective disorders 189–214
        and cognitive loss 191–2
        practical help 209
        rambling 209
        special considerations 189–92
    crisis intervention 212–13
    organic disorders 215–19
        aims 215–17
        behaviour modification 235–42

environmental modification
218–23
integrative approach 242–7
reality orientation 223–42
reminiscence therapy 233–5
stimulation/activity programmes
217–18
psychotherapy 192–4

verbal fluency 90, 101, 145
visual acuity 14
see also sensory loss
voluntary agencies 306–11
volunteers
bereavement counselling 207
in institutions 281–2

wandering 217–18, 240, 244, 288
Wechsler Adult Intelligence Scale
(WAIS) 34–40, 42, 44, 82, 102,
106, 112, 124, 135–6, 139, 144,
148–51
deterioration index 37, 43, 82,
131, 140
short-form 135, 140
verbal-performance discrepancy
81–2, 130, 140
Wechsler Memory Scale 124, 141–2,
150–1
Wernicke's aphasia 99

Zung Self-Rating Depression Scale
166–8